# THE DEVELOPMENT OF INTERNATIONAL LAW
## BY
# THE INTERNATIONAL COURT

AUSTRALIA
The Law Book Co. of Australasia Pty Ltd.
Sydney : Melbourne : Brisbane

GREAT BRITAIN
Stevens & Sons Ltd.
London

INDIA
N. M. Tripathi Private Ltd.
Bombay

NEW ZEALAND
Sweet and Maxwell (N.Z.) Ltd.
Wellington

PAKISTAN
Pakistan Law House
Karachi

U.S.A. AND CANADA
Frederick A. Praeger, Inc.
New York City

# THE DEVELOPMENT

OF

# INTERNATIONAL LAW

BY

# THE INTERNATIONAL COURT

BEING A REVISED EDITION OF
" THE DEVELOPMENT OF INTERNATIONAL LAW BY
THE PERMANENT COURT OF INTERNATIONAL JUSTICE " (1934)

By

SIR HERSCH LAUTERPACHT
Q.C., LL.D., F.B.A.

*Judge of the International Court of Justice;*
*Bencher of Gray's Inn; Member of the*
*Institute of International Law*

*NEW YORK*
FREDERICK A. PRAEGER

BOOKS THAT MATTER

*Published in the United States
of America in 1958 by
Frederick A. Praeger, Inc.
Publishers of 15 West 47th
Street, New York 36, N.Y.*

*Library of Congress
Catalog Card No. 58-8540*

*Published in Great Britain by
Stevens & Sons Limited
of 119 & 120 Chancery Lane
London — Law Publishers
and printed in Great Britain
by The Eastern Press Ltd.
of London and Reading*

*Stevens & Sons Limited*
*London*
*1958*

# CONTENTS

v

## PART THREE

## JUDICIAL LEGISLATION

## PART FOUR

## THE EFFECTIVENESS OF THE LAW

x Contents

## PART FIVE

## THE COURT AND STATE SOVEREIGNTY

### Section A

### Restraints upon Claims of Sovereignty

*Section B*

*Recognition of Claims of Sovereignty*

# PREFACE

THE purpose of this book is to provide the second edition of an essay composed of five lectures which I delivered in 1933 at the Geneva Graduate Institute of International Studies and which was subsequently published under the title " The Development of International Law by the Permanent Court of International Justice." The essay consisted of just over one hundred pages. The expansion of the size of the book is due largely to the fact that the period now to be covered has grown from ten to over twenty-five years, which include the first nine years of the activity of the International Court of Justice.

Like its predecessor, the present edition is not concerned primarily with giving a complete account of the substantive contribution of the Court to the various branches of international law. Its object is to present an assessment of the work of the Court—the two Courts—in terms of the persistent problems of the judicial function in general and of international tribunals in particular. The titles of the five Chapters of the original essay expressed well that purpose and I have decided for that reason to retain them. Unavoidably, while the present book examines mainly the general tendencies and methods of the Court, it does so by reference to the substantive law as formulated by it. However, primarily it is concerned with the more general aspects of judicial method and function. It is largely in that way that we can hope to appreciate the factors encompassing the contribution of the Court to the development of international law and the problems with which it has been confronted in administering a system of rules and principles which are often less clearly defined than those of the law within the State.

The manuscript of this book was almost complete when, at the end of 1954, I was elected one of the Judges of the Court. I have come to the conclusion that, notwithstanding that event, which imposes a clear obligation of restraint, I ought to proceed with the publication of this edition in compliance with the wish, frequently expressed, that I should prepare a new and enlarged version of the essay which first appeared in 1934. That essay was intended to be mainly descriptive and informative. That feature I have attempted to preserve in the present edition. In any case I have considered it proper not to comment upon or to refer to any of the Judgments or Opinions given by the Court since I became one of its members. Clearly, any views expressed here are liable to change in the light of further study, reflection, or argument. I regret that, owing to circumstances outside my control, the publication of this second edition has been somewhat delayed.

I desire to express my warm thanks to Mrs. E. E. Jansen for her efficient secretarial assistance and her patience in copying the successive versions of the manuscript. I am grateful to Mrs. G. Lyons, B.SC.(ECON.), for the scholarly care which she bestowed upon reading the proof.

I am indebted to Messrs. Stevens & Sons and their printers and compositors for their co-operation.

H. LAUTERPACHT.

CAMBRIDGE,
   *January* 1, 1957.

# TABLE OF CASES

# PART ONE

## THE LAW BEHIND THE CASES

CHAPTER 1

# THE INTERNATIONAL COURT AS AN AGENCY FOR DEVELOPING INTERNATIONAL LAW

## 1. *The Court as an Agency of Pacific Settlement*

It would appear that the primary purpose of the International Court—a term which is here intended to cover both the Permanent Court of International Justice and the International Court of Justice, seeing that, in effect, the latter is a continuation of the former [1]—lies in its function as one of the instruments for securing peace in so far as this aim can be achieved through law. It is beyond the scope of this book to examine in detail how far the Court has fulfilled that purpose. Some of its pronouncements—such as the various Judgments and Opinions relating to the treatment of minorities,[2] the Judgment which finally disposed of the Eastern Greenland [3] dispute between Denmark and Norway, the Advisory Opinions relating to the boundary disputes between Turkey and Iraq [4] or Poland and Czechoslovakia,[5] and the Judgments in the *Fisheries* case between Norway and the United Kingdom [6] and in the *Asylum* case between Colombia and Peru [7]—have contributed to the solution of important or acute controversies.[8] Others have prevented minor disputes from becoming a dangerous source of friction, which they might have become had they been left unsolved or allowed to be settled by the *ipse dixit* of an interested party. The very existence of the Court, in particular when coupled with the substantial measure of obligatory jurisdiction already conferred upon it, must tend to be a factor of importance in maintaining the rule of law. For what matters in this connection is not the number of disputes actually decided by

---

[1] See below, pp. 11 *et seq.*   [2] See below, pp. 257–262.
[3] See below, p. 210.   [4] See below, p. 159.
[5] See below, p. 232.   [6] See below, pp. 190 *et seq.*
[7] See below, pp. 142 *et seq.*
[8] This has been so, occasionally, even in cases in which the Court, because of the exigencies of its Statute or for other reasons, has deemed itself constrained to decline to act in literal compliance with the instrument said to confer jurisdiction upon it. See, for instance, below, p. 213 as to the *Free Zones* case, and p. 222 as to the case of *Société Commerciale de Belgique*.

the Court, but the fact that a contemplated wrong was not proceeded with or that controversies have been settled without its intervention in conformity with justice for the reason that, in the absence of a satisfactory solution, one party was at liberty to bring the dispute before the Court. In some cases the existence of the Court has given the Governments concerned the opportunity of an amicable and authoritative settlement of a dispute which, having regard to public feeling in their countries on the subject, they might have been reluctant to settle through diplomatic negotiations for fear of laying themselves open to factious criticism on the ground that they showed undue readiness to compromise in respect of a weighty national interest.

At the same time it would be an exaggeration to assert that the Court has proved to be a significant instrument for maintaining international peace. The degree of achievement of this end by an international, as indeed by any other, court is dependent upon the state of political integration of the society whose law it administers. But international society has in this respect, in the years following the two World Wars, fallen short of the expectation of those who in the Covenant of the League of Nations and in the Charter of the United Nations intended to create, through them, the basis of the future orderly development of the international community. These constituent instruments themselves did not proceed on the view that there exists an international legal community in the sense that disputes which arise between its members and in which one or both parties rely on a legal right must be subject to the compulsory arbitrament of the law. In the Statute of the Court its jurisdiction was rendered optional, but that option has not been generally exercised. Where Governments have accepted the compulsory jurisdiction of the Court they have done so, in most cases, subject to far-reaching reservations which on occasions have gone to the length of reserving to the Government concerned the right to determine, after the dispute has been brought before the Court, whether it is bound to submit it to the Court—a reservation the legal validity of which, or of the entire jurisdictional instrument in which it is contained, is controversial. It is a truism, repeated with somewhat excessive frequency, that law is not a panacea and that not all causes of international conflict or tension can be settled by law. But it is a fact that, once the parties have submitted a dispute for judicial determination, the principle of the completeness of the legal order fully applies, with the result that all disputes thus submitted are capable of a legal solution.[9] Governments have not availed themselves of these potentialities of international justice. This is the main reason why the Court has not been in the position to make that contribution to peace which would stem from a general conviction of the members of the international community that no State should deny to other States the elementary benefit of a contested legal right being adjudicated by a tribunal administering international law.

## 2. *The Part of International Tribunals as Agencies for the Development of International Law*

What, then, is the explanation of the wide recognition of the achievement of the Court? The explanation is that, debarred from directly acting as an important instrument of peace, the Court has made a tangible contribution to the development and clarification of the rules and principles of international law. In sociology this phenomenon is at times described as " a heterogeny of aims." Institutions set up for the achievement of definite purposes grow to fulfil tasks not wholly identical with those which were in the minds of their authors at the time of their creation. It is useful to assess both the positive contribution of the Court in this respect and the difficulties standing in the way of its fuller accomplishment. The present chapter is concerned with both these aspects of the activity of the Court.

The task of clarifying and developing international law by the highest international tribunal was an object which was present in the minds of those who, at the close of the First World War, urged the establishment of a permanent court of international justice. The study of the plans for the establishment of the Arbitral Court of Justice which the Second Hague Conference sought to set up shows that this purpose loomed large in the minds of the protagonists of a true and permanent international court. The Permanent Court of Arbitration established by the First Hague Conference was not deemed to be adequate. One of the reasons usually given for its inadequacy was that the awards rendered by its tribunals were not

---

[9] This is the only proper meaning of the principle of the completeness of the legal order —a principle whose validity remains unshaken notwithstanding occasional criticism levied against it. See Charles De Visscher, *Théories et réalités en droit international public* (1953), pp. 396 *et seq.*, and throughout the volume.

legal in substance and that they tended to confuse law with a diplomatic solution aiming at pleasing both parties.[10] It may be difficult to substantiate that charge. An analysis of the awards given by tribunals under the aegis of the Permanent Court of Arbitration, before and after the First World War, must reveal that their decisions were legal awards in form and substance. In some cases, like the *North Atlantic Fisheries Arbitration*, the award created with some writers the impression of a compromise on the ground that the tribunal availed itself of the right conferred upon it in the arbitration agreement to propose recommendations of a legislative character for the future regulation of the exercise of the fishery rights by citizens of the United States.[11] In others, like the *Casablanca* case,[12] the somewhat dialectical inconclusiveness of the reasoning (though not of the decision) was due to the difficulties and the complexities of a novel legal situation. In others still— *e.g.*, in the *Venezuelan Preferential Claims* case [13]—writers expressed their disagreement with the law, as laid down by the tribunal, by reliance on the argument, which begged the question, that the decision was not of a legal nature.

However, although there was in fact no sufficient reason to question the determination of the tribunals, chosen from its panel, to administer international law, there is warrant for the view that there was absent in the awards of the tribunals of the Permanent Court of Arbitration the necessary tradition of continuity, with all the advantages of a resulting relative certainty of the law. There was no assurance that the decisions of the arbitrators chosen from the panel of the Court of Arbitration would serve a purpose other than that of disposing of the dispute between the parties. They could not invariably be relied upon to develop and clarify international law. This was one of the principal reasons militating in favour of the establishment of an Arbitral Court of Justice (and, subsequently, of the Permanent Court of International Justice) as distinguished from the Permanent Court of Arbitration.

### 3. *The Part of the International Court*

The development of international law by international tribunals is, in the long run, one of the important conditions of their

---

[10] See, for instance, Wehberg, *The Problem of an International Court of Justice* (English transl., 1918), pp. 12–29.  [11] See below, p. 218, n. 1.

[12] Scott, *Hague Court Reports* (1916), p. 111.  [13] *Ibid.*, pp. 54 *et seq.*

continued successful functioning and of their jurisdiction.   For Governments have often manifested an inclination to make the scope of obligatory jurisdiction conferred upon international tribunals dependent upon the existence of clear rules of international law.   The Committee of Jurists who in 1920 drafted the Statute of the Court, were conscious of that connection, and, in a special Resolution, urged upon the Council of the League of Nations the necessity of taking steps towards the codification of international law.   Yet experience has shown the limitations of that method of developing international law and the corresponding importance of other methods.   Admittedly, the experience of the First Hague Codification Conference of 1930 did not justify the strident and exaggerated proclamations of failure or the pessimism of the Resolution of the Assembly of the League of Nations which, in 1931, in effect abandoned the initiative in the matter of codification so far as the League was concerned.   The Statute of the International Law Commission which was set up in 1948 in pursuance of Article 13 of the Charter leaves room both for a " re-statement " of parts of international law by methods approaching private scientific effort, such as that undertaken by the Harvard Research, and for codification, more properly so called, by means of international conventions concluded by Governments.[14]   The progressive codification of international law by the latter method must be regarded as one of the important conditions of enhancing the authority and the usefulness of the law of nations.   However, as within the League of Nations so also within the United Nations, codification so conceived, being essentially a political and legislative as distinguished from a purely scientific effort, is to a large extent a function of the stability and the growing integration of international society. That condition was not realised after the First World War.   Neither has it come nearer fruition in the period following the Second World War.   While, therefore, the codification of international law under the aegis of the United Nations must continue to be regarded as a rational and practical object of the collective endeavour of Governments,[15] the achievement of part of that object by other means, and in particular through the activity of the International Court itself, acquires special significance.

14 See Art. 20 of the Statute of the Commission.
15 For an assessment of the results of the first phase of codification under the United Nations see Lauterpacht in *American Journal of International Law*, 49 (1955), pp. 16–43.

## 4. *Judicial Precedent in the Statute of the Court*

Although the need for a tribunal ensuring, through its continuity, the development of international law was one of the main reasons for the creation of a permanent court of international justice, it is possible that the lawyers and statesmen who in 1920 drafted the Statute of the Court did not fully appreciate all the possibilities, in this direction, of the activity of the Court about to be established. This may explain the somewhat wide provision of Article 59 of the Statute which lays down that the decisions of the Court have no binding force except between the parties and in respect of a particular case. That provision is at first sight reminiscent of Article 5 of the French *Code Civil*, which forbids judges to lay down general principles in connection with the cases submitted to them— apparently on the theory that the determination of general legal principles going beyond the decision in a particular case is reserved for the sovereign legislature. Is it the object of Article 59 to put beyond doubt that the Signatories of the Statute intended to make impossible the development of law by agencies other than those specially set up for that purpose? It is doubtful whether this is so. It is arguable that that Article of the Statute has reference not to the major question here discussed, but to an altogether minor point relating to intervention—a point connected with Article 63 of the Statute which lays down that if a third State, *i.e.*, a State which is not a party to the dispute, avails itself of the right of intervention the construction given in the Judgment shall be equally binding upon it. Article 59 would thus seem to state directly what Article 63 expresses indirectly. This construction finds support in the final report of the Committee of Jurists of 1920.[16] It has also been suggested, more plausibly, that the limiting terms of Article 59 refer to the actual " decisions " of the Court, *i.e.*, to the operative part as distinguished from the reasoning underlying the decision and containing the legal principles on which it is based.[17] Moreover, the apparent rigour of Article 59 is mitigated by Article 38, which admits judicial decisions —including, it must be assumed, the decisions of the Court itself— as a subsidiary means for determining the rules of law.

---

[16] See *Documents concerning the Action taken by the Council under Article 14 of the Covenant*, p. 50. And see *Procès-Verbaux* of the meetings of the Committee, p. 746.

[17] See Beckett, " Les Questions d'intérêt général au point de vue juridique dans la jurisprudence de la Cour Permanente de Justice Internationale," *Recueil des Cours*, 39 (1932) (I), p. 141.

## 5. *Judicial Precedent in the Practice of the Court*

In fact, the practice of referring to its previous decisions has become one of the most conspicuous features of the Judgments and Opinions of the Court. That practice has assumed various forms. It ranges from mere illustration and " distinguishing " to a form of speech apparently indicating the authoritative character of the pronouncement referred to. On occasions the Court merely says: " As the Court has said in Judgment No. 12," [18] or " As the Court has had occasion to state in its previous judgments and opinions." [19] While that form of reference may be regarded as being in the nature of mere illustration, frequently the manner is much bolder. Thus we find the Court saying: " Nothing has been advanced in the course of the present proceedings calculated to alter the Court's opinion [as expressed in Advisory Opinion No. 6] on this point " [20]; or, simply: " Following the precedent afforded by its Advisory Opinion No. 3. . . ." [21] In the case concerning *United States Nationals in Morocco* the Court referred,[22] as a matter of course, to its Opinion in the *Interpretation of Peace Treaties (Second Phase)* case in support of the statement that " it is a duty of the Court to interpret treaties, not to revise them " [23]; to the *Asylum* case on the requirements of custom [24]; and to the *Free Zones* case on the technical point of the distinction between fiscal duties and customs duties.[25] In its Advisory Opinion on *Awards of the United Nations Administrative Tribunal* the Court took its previous Opinion on *Reparation for Injuries Suffered in the Service of the United Nations* [26] as the starting point for answering one of the crucial issues before it—namely, whether having regard to its objects, the United Nations must be considered to possess an implied power to establish a judicial tribunal to adjudicate upon contracts of service between the United Nations and its employees.[27]

---

[18] *Chorzów Factory* case (Indemnity; Merits), Series A, No. 17 (1928), p. 37. (The references in this book to Series A, B, C and E apply to the various Series of the publications of the Permanent Court of International Justice.)

[19] *Jurisdiction of the European Commission of the Danube*, Series B, No. 14 (1927), p. 36.

[20] *German Interests in Polish Upper Silesia* (Merits), Series A, No. 7 (1926), p. 31.

[21] *Greco-Turkish Agreement of December, 1926*, Series B, No. 16 (1928), p. 15.

[22] *I.C.J. Reports* 1952, at pp. 196, 200 and 206 respectively.

[23] *I.C.J. Reports* 1950, p. 229.

[24] *Ibid.*, p. 276.

[25] Series A/B, No. 46 (1932), p. 172.

[26] *I.C.J. Reports* 1949, p. 182.

[27] *I.C.J. Reports* 1954, p. 56.

On occasions the Court attaches importance to explaining an apparent inconsistency in relation to a previous pronouncement. Thus, when in the Judgment relating to the *Mavrommatis Palestine Concessions* it decided to examine in detail the jurisdictional question as to whether the action could be decided by the application of the clauses of the Palestine Mandate, it hastened to add that this method of proceeding was not inconsistent with its pronouncement in the Advisory Opinion concerning the *Tunis and Morocco Nationality Decrees*, in which it declared that the jurisdiction of the Council of the League of Nations under Article 15 must be presumed to exist on the basis of a provisional decision as to the international character of the grounds advanced by the parties.[28] In the case of the *Serbian Loans* the Court devoted a substantial portion of the Judgment to the consideration of its jurisdiction on the ground that the jurisdiction which the *compromis* conferred upon it, and which it accepted, seemed " at first sight to constitute a departure from the principles which the Court, in previous judgments," had laid down in the matter.[29] The Court subsequently referred the parties " to what the Court has said on several occasions, and in particular in Judgments Nos. 2 and 13," [30] on the nature of claims brought by States on behalf of their nationals, and, by reference to Judgment No. 8 (the *Chorzów Factory* case), it distinguished the case before it from one in which legal remedies within the State had not been exhausted.[31] In a later Opinion—in the case of the *Treatment of Polish Nationals in Danzig*—the Court, on four occasions, either simply referred the parties to a previous pronouncement of its own, or stated that the principle applied by it was in conformity with principles applied in a previous decision, or that it had already expressed a similar view.[32] In the Advisory Opinion relating to the *Interpretation of the Convention of 1919 concerning Employment of Women during the Night* the Court referred to its

---

[28] Series A, No. 2, p. 16. The examples here given are not meant to be exhaustive. For a more detailed survey of the practice of the Court in the matter of following its own decisions see Lauterpacht, " The So-called Anglo-American and Continental Schools of Thought in International Law," in *British Year Book of International Law*, 12 (1931), p. 60; Series E, No. 3, pp. 217, 218; No. 4, pp. 292, 293; No. 6, p. 300; *Annual Digest*, 1925–1926, Case No. 329, and 1927–1928, Case No. 355; Beckett, *op. cit.*, p. 138, n. 1; Hudson, pp. 628–630; Sørensen, *Les sources du droit international* (1946), pp. 166–176.

[29] Series A, No. 20 (1929), p. 16.

[30] *Ibid.*, p. 17.

[31] *Ibid.*, p. 19.

[32] Series A/B, No. 44 (1932), pp. 24, 25, 28, 30.

Advisory Opinions No. 2, 3 and 13 bearing upon the International Labour Organisation. These pronouncements were not *in pari materia*, but, the Court said, " the principles underlying these earlier decisions throw light on the question whether there is any solid foundation for the suggested rule of interpretation." [33]     In the Advisory Opinion on *Minority Schools in Albania*,[34] the Court, in applying the principle that the equality provided for in the Treaty must be one both of fact and of law, lent emphasis to the element of continuity in its jurisprudence by relying not only on what it said on the subject in its Opinion on *Acquisition of Polish Nationality* [35] but also by its reliance, in the latter Opinion, on a previous Opinion which declared as inadmissible an interpretation that would deprive the Minorities Treaties of a great part of their value.[36]

### 6. *Continuity of Precedent in the Permanent Court and in the International Court of Justice*

The continuity of jurisprudence, as outlined above, has been prominent in the way in which the International Court of Justice has relied upon—or indirectly acknowledged the persuasive authority of—the Judgments and Opinions of the Permanent Court of International Justice as well as its own pronouncements. Thus, in giving the Advisory Opinion on the *Interpretation of Peace Treaties with Bulgaria, Hungary and Romania*, the Court, in view of the refusal of these three States to participate in any way in the proceedings before it, attached importance to distinguishing that case from the superficially similar case relating to *Eastern Carelia* [37] and decided, over a quarter of a century before, by the Permanent Court of International Justice. In the latter case, it said, " that Court declined to give an Opinion because it found that the question put to it was directly related to the main point of a dispute actually pending between two States, so that answering the question would be substantially equivalent to deciding the dispute between the parties, and that at the same time it raised a question of fact which could not be elucidated without hearing both parties." [38]     In

---

[33] Series A/B, No. 50 (1932), p. 375.     [34] Series A/B, No. 64 (1935), p. 20.
[35] Series B, No. 7 (1923).     [36] Series B, No. 6 (1923).
[37] Series B, No. 5 (1923).
[38] *I.C.J. Reports* 1950, p. 72. That " famous case of Eastern Carelia " was strongly relied upon by the Dissenting Judges (see p. 89 of the Dissenting Opinion of Judge Winiarski and his intimation that the Permanent Court considered itself bound by its practice, and the Dissenting Opinions of Judges Zoričić (p. 103) and Krylov (p. 106)).

the present case, the sole object of the Opinion was " to enlighten
the General Assembly as to the opportunities which the procedure
contained in the Peace Treaties may afford for putting an end to a
situation which has been presented to it." [39]   The Court as a whole
relied in a previous case on one of the pronouncements of its predecessor [40] in support of the principle of effectiveness—the principle
that in interpreting the Charter of the United Nations there must be
implied in it powers essential for the fulfilment of the duties of the
Organisation.[41]

In the Advisory Opinion concerning *Conditions for Admission of a State to Membership in the United Nations* the Court
found that the natural meaning of the words of Article 4 of the
Charter admitted of no doubt and that " consequently, it does not
feel that it should deviate from the consistent practice of the
Permanent Court of International Justice " in the matter of the use
of preparatory work.[42]   Similarly, in the Advisory Opinion on the
*Competence of the General Assembly for the Admission of a State
to the United Nations* [43] it relied on the principle formulated in the
case concerning the *Polish Postal Service in Danzig* [44] and prescribing the interpretation of words in accordance with " the sense
which they would normally have in their context " as a reason for
excluding, in the case before it, recourse to *travaux préparatoires.*

[39] But see below, p. 353. In a subsequent stage of the same case Judge Read, in a
Dissenting Opinion, invoked a long list of former pronouncements of the Court and of
its predecessor as substantiating the principle of effectiveness, as he conceived it, in the
interpretation of treaties. In so doing he put forward an interesting explanation of the
binding force of the precedents of the Court. He said: " There can be no doubt that
the United Nations intended continuity in jurisprudence, as well as in less important
matters. While this does not make the decisions of the Permanent Court binding, in
the sense in which decisions may be binding in common law countries, it does make
it necessary to treat them with the utmost respect, and to follow them unless there
are compelling reasons for rejecting their authority " (*I.C.J. Reports* 1950, p. 233).
See also, to the same effect, p. 240. And see the Dissenting Opinion of Judge Read in
the *Anglo-Iranian Oil Company* case deprecating reliance on some previous expressions
of the Court on the ground that they were *obiter dicta* (*I.C.J. Reports* 1952, p. 143).

[40] *Advisory Opinion* No. 13 (*Competence of the International Labour Organisation to
Regulate, incidentally, the Personal Work of the Employer*; Series B, No. 13 (1926),
p. 18).

[41] *I.C.J. Reports* 1949, p. 183 (*Reparation for Injuries Suffered in the Service of the United
Nations*). See below, p. 178. In the same case the Court recalled and quoted a
passage from its Judgment in the case concerning the *Factory at Chorzów* (Series A,
No. 9 (1927), p. 21) and relating to the principle that a breach of an engagement
involves an obligation to make reparation in an adequate form.

[42] *I.C.J. Reports* 1947–1948, p. 63. See below, p. 121.

[43] *I.C.J. Reports* 1950, p. 8.

[44] Series B, No. 11 (1925), p. 39.

In rejecting the contention that it was not competent to interpret a provision of the Charter on account of the allegedly political character of the question put to it, the Court simply recalled [45] its ruling on the same issue given in an Opinion which it had previously rendered.   In deciding in the *Ambatielos* case that that case fell within the category of disputes covered by a previous Declaration, the Court attached importance to stating that it was "not departing from the principle, which is well established in international law and accepted by its own jurisprudence as well as that of the Permanent Court of International Justice, to the effect that a State may not be compelled to submit its disputes to arbitration without its consent." [46]   In the *Corfu Channel* (*Merits*) case the Court referred to the decisions of its predecessor in support of the principle securing the effectiveness of undertakings submitting disputes for adjudication by the Court.[47]   In the *Nottebohm* case (*Preliminary Objection*) the Court referred to the jurisprudence of the Permanent Court, in particular in the *Losinger* and *Phosphates in Morocco* cases, as showing that the withdrawal of the Acceptance of the jurisdiction of the Court under Article 36 (2) of its Statute has no effect upon cases already pending before the Court.[48]

## 7. The Significance of International Judicial Precedent

It is not suggested that in pursuing the practice of relying upon and following its previous decisions the Court has adopted the common law doctrine of judicial precedent.  The Court has not committed itself to the view that it is bound to follow its previous decisions even in cases in which it later disagrees with them.  It may be a matter of controversy how far in countries in which courts are bound by judicial precedent they do in fact respect decisions of tribunals of co-ordinate or higher jurisdiction with which they happen to disagree [49]; but there is no doubt here as to the existence of the legal duty obliging them to do so.  No such duty hampers the discretion of the International Court.  However, while not

---

[45] At p. 6.
[46] *I.C.J. Reports* 1953, p. 19.  And see the Dissenting Opinion of Judges McNair, Basdevant, Klaestad and Read for frequent, though not always identifiable, references to previous Judgments and Opinions (pp. 28, 31, 33).
[47] *I.C.J. Reports* 1949, p. 24.
[48] *I.C.J. Reports* 1953, p. 121.
[49] Compare, for instance, the view of Professor Allen, *Law in the Making* (5th ed., 1951), pp. 269 *et seq.*, with that of Professor Goodhart in *Law Quarterly Review*, 50 (1934), p. 59.  And see Beckett in *Recueil des Cours*, 39 (1932) (i), p. 9, n. 2.

fettered by the rigidity of the formal doctrine of precedent, it has, as shown, largely adopted its substance. What are the reasons for that practice?

The Court follows its own decisions for the same reasons for which all courts—whether bound by the doctrine of precedent or not—do so, namely, because such decisions are a repository of legal experience to which it is convenient to adhere; because they embody what the Court has considered in the past to be good law; because respect for decisions given in the past makes for certainty and stability, which are of the essence of the orderly administration of justice; and (a minor and not invariably accurate consideration) because judges are naturally reluctant, in the absence of compelling reasons to the contrary, to admit that they were previously in the wrong. The cumulative effect of these factors is shown clearly by the way in which English Chancellors, administering the originally elastic and flexible rules of equity, by degrees learned to recognise the authority of case law with a rigidity frequently surpassing that of the common law whose conservatism they set themselves to combat. Moreover, the Court relies on its own decisions for the reason which, more than anything else, has caused the establishment of the formal doctrine of precedent in the countries of the common law,[50] as distinguished from the continent of Europe, namely, the absence of a code or of a generally recognised system of law, such as Roman law, which is an ever-present source of judicial inspiration. It is to be expected that in a society of States in which opportunities for authoritative and impartial statements of the law are rare, there should be a tendency to regard judicial determination as evidence or, what is in fact the same, as a source of international law. Above all, for reasons which—once more—are even more compelling in the international sphere than within the State, reliance on precedent is not only in keeping with the ever-present requirement of certainty in the administration of justice, but with the necessity of avoiding the appearance of any excess of judicial discretion. No legal rule or principle can bind the judge to a precedent which, in all the circumstances, he feels bound to disregard. In that case he will contrive to do what he considers to be justice through the elastic process of " distinguishing " and in other ways. But he is not free to disregard judicial precedent altogether.

---

[50] See, as to English law, Goodhart, *op. cit.*, p. 62.

He is bound to adduce reasons for departing from the obligation of consistency and of observance of settled principles. These considerations are of particular urgency in relation to international jurisdiction, which is essentially voluntary in character.

## 8. *International Arbitral Precedent in the Practice of the Court*

For this reason the practice of the Court in the treatment of decisions of international tribunals other than its own calls for explanation. With the exception of the distinguishing reference in *The Lotus* to the case of the *Costa Rica Packet*,[51] in the case of the *Polish Postal Service in Danzig*[52] to the award of the Permanent Court of Arbitration in the case of the *Pious Funds of the Californias*, and, in the *Nottebohm* case,[53] to the *Alabama* arbitration, there seems to be no case on record in which the Court has referred to a decision of an international arbitral tribunal. It has referred occasionally, though not frequently, to arbitral practice generally on a specific issue. Thus in the *Chorzów Factory (Jurisdiction)* case it stated it to be " a principle generally accepted in the jurisprudence of international arbitration, as well as by municipal courts, that one Party cannot avail himself of the fact that the other has not fulfilled some obligation or has not had recourse to some means of redress, if the former Party has, by some illegal act, prevented the latter from fulfilling the obligation in question, or from having recourse to the tribunal which would have been open to him." [54] In another phase of the same case, in considering the principle governing compensation for unlawful dispossession, the Court stated that " this principle, which is accepted in the jurisprudence of arbitral tribunals, has the effect, on the one hand, of excluding from the damage to be estimated, injury resulting for third parties from the unlawful act and, on the other hand, of not excluding from the damage the amount of debts and other obligations for which the injured party is responsible." [55] The Court referred in the same case to " the

---

[51] The Court pointed out that the alleged depredations took place on a vessel which was adrift without flag or crew: Series A, No. 10 (1927), p. 26.

[52] Series B, No. 11 (1925), p. 30.

[53] *I.C.J. Reports* 1953, p. 119.

[54] Series A, No. 9 (1927), p. 31—a principle relied upon by the Court to substantiate its finding that as Polish legislation had prevented the interested party from having recourse to the international tribunal provided for in the Convention the Polish Government could not expect that party to have recourse to tribunals which might be open to it if the Convention had been applied.

[55] *Chorzów Factory (Merits)* case: Series A, No. 17 (1928), p. 31.

essential principle contained in the actual notion of an illegal act—
a principle which seems to be established by international practice
and in particular by the decisions of arbitral tribunals—that reparation must, as far as possible, wipe out all the consequences of the
illegal act and re-establish the situation which would, in all
probability, have existed if that act had not been committed." [56]
Finally, again in the same case, the Court declined to award
damages, in connection with unlawful dispossession resulting from
possible commercial competition, for the reason, *inter alia*, that such
dispossession " would come under the heading of possible but contingent and indeterminate damage which, in accordance with the
jurisprudence of arbitral tribunals, cannot be taken into account."

General references to other international decisions were made in
the *Eastern Greenland* case [57] where the Court stated that " it is
impossible to read the records of the decisions in cases as to territorial sovereignty without observing that in many cases the tribunal
has been satisfied with very little in the way of the actual exercise
of sovereign rights, provided that the other State could not make
out a superior claim."   In the *Anglo-Norwegian Fisheries* case, it
dealt in a similar fashion with the issue of the ten-mile rule for
bays, which it held not to have acquired the authority of a rule of
international law.   This was so because " although the ten-mile rule
has been adopted by certain States . . . and although certain arbitral
decisions have applied it as between these States, other States have
adopted a different limit." [58]   The Court did not attempt a higher
degree of precision on the subject.   In the case of *Reparation for
Injuries to Officials of the United Nations*, in discussing the contingency of the claim of an official being espoused both by his State
and by the United Nations, it stated, without embarking upon
detailed exposition, that " international tribunals are already familiar
with the problem of a claim in which two or more national States
are interested, and they know how to protect the defendant State in
such a case." [59]   The nearest the Court has ever come to particu-
larising what arbitral decisions it had in mind was in the *Peter
Pázmány University* case, where it referred to the consistent practice
of Mixed Arbitral Tribunals [60] to the effect that discrimination was
not a condition laid down in the treaty in question.

---

[56] *Ibid.*, p. 47.                                    [57] Series A/B, No. 53 (1933), p. 46.
[58] *I.C.J. Reports* 1951, p. 131.          [59] *I.C.J. Reports* 1949, p. 186.
[60] Series A/B, No. 61 (1933), p. 243.

The instances here given of recourse to international arbitral precedent call for comment not only by reason of their rarity, but also because of their generality. There is room for the view that in some cases detailed elaboration of the reference to previous arbitral practice may be of use both for the student and for the practitioner. This is so, for instance, in the matter of the measure of damages [61] —a question on which arbitral practice has exhibited a pronounced degree of vacillation and inconclusiveness. The finding of the tribunal in the *Alabama* arbitration to the effect that indirect losses do not constitute a proper foundation for the award of compensation, has not, in general, been followed by later arbitral tribunals. Although they have rejected claims for compensation for loss of merely speculative profits,[62] they have awarded compensation for loss of profits and earnings.[63] These are often necessarily " contingent and indeterminate." But, as pointed out, the Court rejected them in reliance on previous arbitral practice. In the same case the Court held that reparation must, " as far as possible, wipe out all the consequences of the illegal act and re-establish the situation which would, in all probability, have existed if that act had not been committed."

Similar considerations may apply to the general reference, quoted above in the *Eastern Greenland* case, to international arbitral decisions relating to the requirement of effective possession as a condition of acquisition of territorial sovereignty. These decisions have not been numerous. Occasionally, as in the *British Guiana* and *Alaska* arbitrations, they were not accompanied by reasons. The case of *Eastern Greenland* afforded an opportunity for putting within the framework of existing practices the principle, which has met with general approval, adopted by the Court. This and the other cases here surveyed raise the question of the desirability of making full use of the provision of Article 38 of the Statute as to the place of arbitral decisions in the jurisprudence of the Court. It is in the interest of international justice that its continuity should not be confined to the jurisprudence of the Court itself. International arbitral law has produced a body of precedent which is full of

---

[61] See below, p. 315.

[62] See Lauterpacht, *Private Law Sources and Analogies of International Law* (1927), p. 219.

[63] For a balanced survey of the practice of arbitral tribunals on the subject see Cheng, *General Principles of Law as Applied by International Courts and Tribunals* (1953), pp. 233–253. And see, to the same effect, Reitzer, *La réparation comme conséquence de l'acte illicite en droit international* (1938), pp. 175–192.

instruction and authority. Numerous arbitral awards have made a distinct contribution to international law by reason of their scope, their elaboration, and the conscientiousness with which they have examined the issue before them. On the other hand, considerations of economy in the method of the pronouncements of the Court may explain the tendency to avoid a detailed examination of arbitral awards.

### 9. *The Limits of Judicial Precedent*

The Court's practice—not enjoined in any absolute terms by its Statute—of invoking its own decisions is not only an instructive phenomenon in the field of administration of international justice and of jurisprudence generally. It has resulted, over a prolonged period of years, in the formulation—or clarification—of an imposing body of rules of international law. That result represents varying degrees of crystallisation. There are rules and principles which the Court has had occasion to apply repeatedly, with the consequence that there has established itself a kind of fixed " jurisprudence " with regard to matters covered by them. There are, further, rules and principles which the Court has applied without having had, so far, an opportunity of following them by way of precedent. Finally, there are rules and principles which analysis may legitimately deduce from those already applied by the Court in other spheres. The outcome of this general recognition of the persuasive force of judicial precedent has been the development of a comprehensive body of law which, in proportion to its intrinsic merit, can be used not only as direct evidence of specific rules of law as understood by the Court, but also as indicative of the method and the spirit in which the Court may be counted upon to approach similar cases. This applies, in particular, to questions with regard to which the instruction to be derived from the activity of the Court is due not only to uniformity but also to hesitation and a measure of inconsistency—for, perhaps fortunately, these are not absent from its Judgments and Opinions when surveyed in their entirety.

This latter consideration raises the question of the limitations, actual and desirable, of the place of precedent in the jurisprudence of the Court. For the beneficence of adherence to precedent is not unqualified. When the precedents vary—and they have in fact varied on such questions as the admissibility of recourse to preparatory work in the interpretation of treaties [64] or the restrictive interpretation of limitations of State sovereignty [65]—there may be an inclination to rely on one set of precedents and to disregard the others without an attempt being made, in the wording of the decision, to explain the choice thus made. When, for instance, in the *Admission* case,[66] the Court invoked the rule previously enunciated in some decisions that there is no reason to have recourse to preparatory work when the terms of the treaty are clear, it may have created the impression of simplifying a problem which precedents pointing to a different solution made appear less straightforward. This does not necessarily mean that the Court did not in fact consider the implications of its previous practice viewed in its entirety.

Moreover, while the Court may be powerless, without embarking upon the hazardous course of judicial legislation, to effect changes in conventional or customary international law, it is not so hidebound in relation to its own previous Judgments and Opinions. In most countries in which otherwise the doctrine of judicial precedent is supreme, the highest tribunals enjoy a substantial—and formal—degree of latitude in respect of their own decisions. This is so although there is available within the State the machinery of legislation for remedying the rigidity of the existing law, both statutory and that made by judges. In the international sphere, where no such legislative process is normally available, there is no room for rigid veneration of precedent. To that extent the emphatic language of Article 59 of the Statute of the Court which limits the formal authority of the decision to the case actually before the Court is not without usefulness or significance. Subject to the overriding principle of *res judicata*, the Court is free at any time to reconsider the substance of the law as embodied in a previous decision. As has been shown, it will not do so lightly and without good reason. But it may do so, and it has done so. In some cases it accomplished the change through the process of " distinguishing." In others—as in the matter of preparatory work in the interpretation of treaties [67]—it has in fact modified a position which experience has shown to be untenable. The same applies, in fact, to the principle

---

[64] See below, pp. 121 *et seq.*
[65] See below, pp. 300 *et seq.*
[66] See below, p. 121.
[67] See below, pp. 121 *et seq.*

enunciated in the case of *Eastern Carelia* according to which, in relation to its advisory jurisdiction, the consent of the interested State is invariably required as a condition of the jurisdiction of the Court.[68]  For this reason, to give a concrete example, it cannot be asserted with any justifiable assurance that if the issue decided in the *Lotus* case—an issue which was determined by a Court equally divided and whose purport has not met with general approval on the part either of various maritime States or of legal opinion [69]—were to present itself before the Court in any subsequent case, the Court would feel itself precluded from considering it afresh on its merits.

### 10. *Judicial Precedent as a Source of International Law*

In the practice of the Court departures from precedent, necessary as they may be on occasions, constitute an exception to the general rule.  The general rule, as illustrated by the survey undertaken in the preceding Sections, is the constant and normal operation of precedent in the jurisprudence of the Court.  That survey suggests the usefulness of an examination of the part played by the decisions of the Court, and of other international tribunals, as a source of international law.  The authority, in this respect, of decisions of international tribunals is in a different category from that of municipal courts.  The part played by the latter as a source of international law in the international sphere results from the fact that municipal courts are organs of the State.  Their decisions within any particular State, when endowed with sufficient uniformity and authority, may be regarded as expressing the *opinio juris* of that State.  When, further, a point of international law is covered by a series of concordant and authoritative decisions of municipal courts of various States, such decisions may properly be regarded as evidence of international custom.  In that sense, those decisions are not merely a subsidiary means for determining rules of international law in the sense of Article 38 (4), but also " evidence of a general practice accepted as law " in the meaning of Article 38 (2) of the Statute.[70]

Decisions of international courts are not a source of international law in that sense.  They are not direct evidence of the practice of

---

[68] See below, p. 353.

[69] See below, pp. 359 *et seq.*

[70] This view, it must be observed, does not command general agreement.  See the author's article in the *British Year Book of International Law*, 10 (1929), pp. 75–92.

States or of what States conceive to be the law. ⌈International tribunals, when giving a decision on a point of international law, do not necessarily choose between two conflicting views advanced by the parties.[71] They state what the law is. Their decisions are evidence of the existing rule of law. That does not mean that they do not in fact constitute a source of international law. For the distinction between the evidence and the source of many a rule of law is more speculative and less rigid than is commonly supposed.⌉ Witness the animated, but highly unreal, controversy as to whether judges create the law or whether they merely reveal the rule already contained *in gremio legis*. Witness the indifference with which lawyers are prepared to accept the paradoxical assertion that judges are at the same time docile servants of the past and tyrants of the future. The imperceptible process in which the judicial decision ceases to be an application of existing law and becomes a source of law for the future is almost a religious mystery into which it is unseemly to pry. We recall the reply of Dürer to Pirkheimer's remark that the Last Supper cannot be painted: " It should not be *thought*." In fact, the legal profession is not unduly troubled by the phenomenon of the mysterious birth of an authoritative source law out of what is supposed to be no more than evidence of the existing law. It can afford such indifference seeing that the exact definition of the process is of insignificant practical importance.

The position is the same with regard to courts generally, including international tribunals. ⌈It is of little import whether the pronouncements of the Court are in the nature of evidence or of a source of international law so long as it is clear that in so far as they show what are the rules of international law they are largely identical with it. For what are rules of international law for the purpose of judicial settlement? They are rules which, according to legal opinion, based—among other things—on the study of the work of the Court, the latter will apply.⌉ It is to a large extent in this practical aspect of its operation, namely, in the ability of the lawyer to attempt to predict the nature of the decision, that law is a science. This is, of course, not the assertion of the rigid positivist view. For while it must be assumed that the judge will apply existing law, the law thus applied is not the mechanical product of an effortless

---

[71] See below, pp. 206 *et seq*.

interpretation of clear manifestations of the will of States. For the reasons stated, previous decisions of the Court are, as a matter both of legal principle and of actual experience, one of the enduring factors which influence its future decisions. They are evidence of what the Court considers to be the law; they are a reliable indication of the future attitude of the Court; for most practical purposes they show, therefore, what international law is. In fact they are to a substantial degree identical with the sources of law enumerated in the first three paragraphs of Article 38. In form they may be merely a subsidiary means for determining what these sources are. The effect is the same.

Accordingly, the Court was doing no more than expressing the correct legal position when it declared in the Judgment concerning *Certain German Interests in Polish Upper Silesia* that the object of Article 59, which limits the effects of the decisions of the Court to the case actually decided, is " to prevent legal principles accepted by the Court in a particular case from being binding upon other States or in other disputes." [72] They are not binding *upon States*. Neither are they *binding* upon the Court. However, no written provision can prevent them from showing authoritatively what international law is, and no written rule can prevent the Court from regarding them as such. The fact that they have been given expression by the Court itself will certainly not tend to diminish their authority in its eyes. It is in their intrinsic power, and not in the fourth sub-paragraph of Article 38 (1) of the Statute [73]—which by referring to " decisions " might seem to exclude, inadvertently, Advisory Opinions—that lies the source of the authority of the Court's pronouncements [74] and the explanation of their actual influence. The Statute by itself cannot give life to a source of law which circumstances do not permit to become effective.

[72] Series A, No. 7 (1926), p. 19.

[73] " The Court shall apply : . . . Subject to the provisions of Article 59, judicial decisions and the teachings of the most highly qualified publicists of the various nations, as subsidiary means for the determination of rules of law."

[74] That Governments normally recognise the authority of international judicial precedent may be seen from the concluding passage of the letter addressed on February 26, 1923, by Mr. Charles E. Hughes, United States Secretary of State, to the Norwegian Minister at Washington. In that letter, referring to the award given in the *Norwegian Shipowners* case, the United States Government, having regard to certain alleged short-comings of the award, declared that the award cannot be deemed by that Government " to possess an authoritative character as a precedent ": Scott, *The Hague Court Reports*, Second Series (1932), p. 82.

## 11. *The " Teachings of Publicists " as a Source of Judicial Decision*

That this is so is shown by the manner in which the Court has applied the other subsidiary source enumerated in Article 38 of its Statute. On no occasion has the Court, as distinguished from dissenting or separate Opinions of individual Judges, found it necessary to refer to the writings of a single author as representing the " teachings of the most highly qualified publicists of the various nations." [75] In the *Lotus* case the Court inquired in some detail into the accuracy of the French contention that according to the teachings of publicists (this being the English translation of " *la doctrine* " in the authoritative French text of the Judgment) the State of the flag of the ship had exclusive jurisdiction with respect to offences committed thereon. " Apart from the question as to what their value may be from the point of view of establishing the existence of a rule of customary law," the Court found that writers did not fully or invariably support the French view. The Court did not refer specifically to any individual author. It acted in the same way in some other cases. In the case concerning *Certain German Interests in Polish Upper Silesia* it referred to the " much disputed question in the ' teachings of legal authorities ' (dans la doctrine des auteurs) and in the jurisprudence of the principal writers " [76] as to the standing of the doctrine of *litispendence* as between courts of various countries; it did not consider it necessary to discuss the matter in detail for it found that there were not present in the case before it the essential elements of *litispendence*. Similarly, in the Advisory Opinion on the *Austro-German Customs Union* it did not feel called upon, in the circumstances of the case, to discuss the definition of the independence of States " which may be given by

[75] In their Dissenting or Separate Opinions Judges of the Court have frequently referred to the writings of publicists. See Series A, No. 1 (1923), p. 47 (*The Wimbledon*). See also the references to writings of authors in the Dissenting Opinion of Judge Hudson in the case concerning the *Diversion of Water from the Meuse* (Series A/B, No. 70 (1937), pp. 76, 77) and of Judge McNair in the case of the *International Status of South-West Africa (I.C.J. Reports* 1950, pp. 146 *et seq.*). In particular, see the Joint Dissenting Opinion in the case concerning *Reservations to the Convention on the Prevention and Punishment of the Crime of Genocide, I.C.J. Reports* 1951, pp. 32 *et seq.*, and the passage in which the dissenting Judges stated that they were unable to discover " any trace of any authority in any decision of this Court or the Permanent Court of International Justice or any other international tribunal, or in any textbook " in support of the rule laid down by the majority of the Court (pp. 42, 43). And see the Dissenting Opinions of Judge Read in the case of the *Interpretation of Peace Treaties with Bulgaria, Hungary and Romania (Second Phase), I.C.J. Reports* 1950, p. 235, and Judge Azevedo in the *Asylum* case between Colombia and Peru, *I.C.J. Reports* 1950, pp. 332 *et seq.*

[76] Series A, No. 6 (1925), p. 20.

legal doctrine or may be adopted in particular instances by the practice of States." [77] In the *Jaworzina* case the authoritative French text refers to the "*doctrine constante*" according to which it is an established principle that the right to give an authoritative interpretation of a legal rule belongs solely to the person or body who has the power to modify or rescind it [78]; in the English text the expression "suivant une doctrine constante" appears as "according to an established principle." It is possible—and perhaps probable—that when in other cases, as in *The Wimbledon* [79] or the case of *German Settlers in Poland*,[80] the Court referred to the "general opinion," what it actually had in mind was opinions of writers. However, as stated, the Court has never found it necessary to refer to or to consider the work of any particular writer.

Different views may be held as to the desirability of generalising that practice of refraining from seeking assistance, in a manner apparent from the text of the decision, in the writings of authors. There is no doubt that the availability of official records of the practice of States and of collections of treaties has substantially reduced the necessity for recourse to writings of publicists as evidence of custom. Moreover, the divergence of view among writers on many subjects as well as apparent national bias may often render citations from them unhelpful. On the other hand, in cases —admittedly rare—in which it is possible to establish the existence of a unanimous or practically unanimous interpretation, on the part of writers, of governmental or judicial practice, reliance on such evidence may add to the weight of the Judgments and Opinions of the Court.

The same applies to cases in which, apart from any uniformity of doctrinal views, the recognised competence, impartiality and authority of any particular writer render proper and legitimate express reliance upon or examination of his work. Article 38 is explicit on that subject; it is mandatory in its reference to the "teachings of publicists" as a subsidiary source of the law to be

---

[77] Series A/B, No. 41 (1931), p. 45.

[78] Series B, No. 8 (1923), p. 37.

[79] Series A, No. 1 (1923), p. 28, where the Court relied on "the general opinion according to which when an artificial waterway connecting two open seas has been permanently dedicated to the use of the whole world, such waterway is assimilated to natural straits. . . ."

[80] Series B, No. 6 (1923), p. 36—where the Court pointed out that the contention that private rights acquired by the former sovereign are extinguished "is based on no principle and would be contrary to an almost universal opinion and practice."

applied by the Court.  A study of the deliberations of the Committee of Jurists who drafted the Statute of the Court does not bear out any suggestion that the authority thus conferred upon the Court ought to remain nominal.[81]  In no case has the Court committed itself to any such view.  Undoubtedly, the prolific and occasionally indiscriminate citation of authors in the written and oral pleadings of the parties may create a problem,[82] but it is not certain whether that problem can always be solved by ignoring altogether the views of writers.  This, in most countries, has not been the practice of the highest municipal tribunals—especially in the field of international law.[83]  While the availability of other sources of information may have altered the nature of the function of " publicists " as recorders of the practice of States,[84] their part as its qualified interpreters cannot always be disregarded.

---

[81] See Sørensen, *op. cit.*, pp. 177–180, for an analysis of the deliberations of the Committee from this point of view and, generally, for an illuminating discussion of the subject.

[82] This problem arises in particular in connection with the habit, which is objectionable and a potential source both of abuse and embarrassment, of referring—with some hopeful emphasis—to previous expressions of opinions by adjudicating Judges themselves.  For these may, without any legitimate imputation of inconsistency, undergo a change in the light of the argument and information supplied by the parties or of the deliberations of the Court.  In *McGrath* v. *Kristensen* (1950) 340 U.S. 162, 176–178, Mr. Justice Jackson, confronted with an opinion previously given by him as Attorney-General, said: " I am entitled to say of that opinion what any discriminating reader must think of it— that it was as foggy as the Statute the Attorney-General was asked to interpret. . . ." He referred to Lord Westbury who, it is said, rebuffed, in the following words, a barrister's reliance upon an earlier opinion of his Lordship: " I can only say that I am amazed that a man of my intelligence should have been guilty of giving such an opinion."

[83] See, *e.g.*, the copious references to writings of authors in the decisions of the highest tribunals in Italy, Germany, some Latin-American countries and, in particular, by the Supreme Court of the United States of America.  In English courts, not usually given to citation of authority—especially of living writers—exceptions are often made in the matter of international law.  And see § 19b of the 8th ed. of vol. I of Oppenheim's *International Law* (1955) for a discussion of the question and references to English and American cases on the subject.

[84] See, by way of contrast with the practice of the Court, the decision given in the case of *Central Railroad Company* v. *United Mexican States* by the Mexican-United States General Claims Commission on March 31, 1926 (*International Arbitral Awards*, IV, p. 24), where the Commission pointed out that if the Mexican negotiators of the Treaty were in doubt as to the views of the Government of the United States in the matter of international jurisdiction over contract claims " nothing would have been more obvious than to consult Charles Cheney Hyde's book of 1922, *International Law chiefly as interpreted and applied by the United States of America.*"

# CHAPTER 2

# THE OCCASIONS FOR AND THE SUBSTANCE OF JUDICIAL PRONOUNCEMENTS

## 12. *The Interpretation of Treaties*

In order to appreciate the extent of the development of international law by the Court we must free ourselves of some preconceptions which may affect our estimate of its achievement in this respect. In particular, there is little substance in the impression that as most of the Judgments and Advisory Opinions of the Court have been primarily concerned with the interpretation of treaties, the jurisprudential significance of the work of the Court is necessarily of limited compass. Undoubtedly, the majority of the cases which have come before the Court have arisen out of a disputed interpretation of a treaty. This has been so even in cases in which the general character of the principal issue decided by the Court has altogether obscured the element of treaty interpretation from which it has arisen. Some representative instances may be mentioned. The first Judgment of the Court, given in the *Wimbledon* case, arose out of the disputed interpretation of Article 380 of the Treaty of Versailles which provided that the Kiel Canal and its approaches shall be maintained free and open to the vessels of commerce and war of all nations at peace with Germany on terms of entire equality. The issue, as stated in the *compromis*, in the *Lotus* case was one of interpretation of the Treaty of Lausanne of July, 1923, namely, whether Turkey, in assuming jurisdiction for an offence committed on the high seas by an alien, acted contrary to Article 15 of the Treaty, which provided that all questions of jurisdiction shall, as between Turkey and the other Contracting Parties, be decided in accordance with the principles of international law. The Orders and the Judgment in the *French-Swiss Free Zones* case were in form concerned with the interpretation of the Treaties of 1815, of Article 435 of the Treaty of Versailles, and—last but not least—of the agreement submitting the case to the Court. In the *Asylum* case between Colombia and Peru the main issue before the Court was the interpretation of the crucial term " urgent cases " in the Havana

Convention on Asylum.[1] Yet, as will be suggested presently, in all those cases the decision of the Court provided a weighty contribution to substantive rules of customary international law.

Similarly, with insignificant exceptions, the Advisory Opinions given by the Court were in the form of answers to questions of treaty interpretation. Thus, for instance, its Advisory Opinion on the *Jurisdiction of the Courts of Danzig*—an Opinion which constituted the first authoritative breach in a hitherto firmly established doctrine inasmuch as the Court rejected, by obvious implication, the view that States only can be the subjects of rights conferred by international law [2]—was concerned with the interpretation of a clause of an Agreement between Danzig and Poland. The Advisory Opinion in the *Injuries* case which was concerned with the right of the United Nations to bring an international claim in respect of injuries done to its officials—an Opinion in which the Court, not indirectly, but explicitly and exhaustively, examined and answered the same question in much broader terms [3]—was based on the interpretation of the relevant Articles of the Charter of the United Nations. The Advisory Opinion on *Reservations to the Genocide Convention*—an Opinion which notwithstanding its unorthodoxy and apparent inconclusiveness constitutes an important contribution to the law of treaties—was technically an Opinion concerned with the interpretation of that Convention.[4] The numerous monographs and articles on the question of reservations seem almost theoretical when compared with the cumulative impact of that Opinion of the Court and the Dissenting and Separate Opinions in that case.

In fact, it would be a mistake to assume that the function of interpretation of treaties, consisting as it does in ascertaining what was the intention of the parties, is a process divorced from the application and development of customary international law. The eliciting of the intention of the parties is not normally a task which can be performed exclusively by means of logical or grammatical interpretation. As a rule, the established canons of construction— which themselves partake of the nature of customary law—must be supplemented by the principle that when the intention of the parties is not clear it must be assumed that they intended a result which is

---

[1] See below, p. 142.
[2] See below, p. 173.
[3] See below, p. 176.
[4] *I.C.J. Reports* 1951, p. 15. And see below, p. 187.

in conformity with general international law. Undoubtedly, conventional international law may derogate from customary international law, but it is no less true that the former must be interpreted by reference to international custom.[5] In many a case of treaty interpretation the effect of the treaty will depend on our view as to the position of customary international law on the question. Whether the effect of an agreement between Poland and Danzig was to confer directly rights upon Danzig railway officials was dependent on whether general international law makes at all possible, even if the parties so wish, the direct acquisition of rights by individuals.[6] The answer, in the *Free Zones* case, to the question whether Switzerland acquired rights under a treaty to which she was not a party had to be determined by the answer to the wider question whether customary international law enables a State which is not a party to a convention to acquire rights under it in cases in which the contracting parties so desired.[7]

The priority as intimated by the apparently hierarchical order laid down in Article 38 of the Statute of the Court—a subject examined elsewhere in this book[8]—of conventional international law over customary international law is therefore of a highly relative nature. This is the reason why the *Lotus* case, formally expressed in terms of a controversy as to the interpretation of an article of the Lausanne Treaty, resulted, in addition to the elaborate treatment of customary law on the question of jurisdiction over foreigners for crimes committed abroad, in a Judgment answering more general questions such as the basis of international law and the relative importance of its various sources. The Judgment in that case— given by an equally divided Court—was not received with universal approval. But there is hardly room for doubt that, when read in conjunction with the numerous Dissenting Opinions, it provides the most instructive treatment of the subject of the jurisdiction of States over aliens for offences committed abroad.

---

[5] For a clear affirmation of this principle see the *Georges Pinson* case, French-Mexican Mixed Claims Commission (Verzijl, President), *Annual Digest*, 1927–1928, Case No. 292, and the decision of the Permanent Court of Arbitration (Borel, Arbitrator) in *The Kronprins Gustav Adolph* and *The Pacific*, *American Journal of International Law*, XXVI (1932), p. 839. And see McNair, *The Law of Treaties* (1938), p. 113, and the Individual Opinion of Judge Schücking in the *Oscar Chinn* case: Series A/B, No. 63 (1934), p. 150.

[6] See below, p. 173.

[7] See below, p. 306.

[8] See below, p. 166.

To a greater or lesser extent the same may be said of most of the Judgments and Advisory Opinions of the Court. In most of them, behind the formal complexion of interpretation, there reveals itself the entire legal background—in fact, we may say without fear of exaggeration the " sociological background " [9]—of the issue in a manner which makes international law and the study of the hidden springs of its development a reality in comparison with which doctrinal disquisitions as to whether international law is law or not appear to be academic. The Advisory Opinion on *Reparation for Injuries Suffered in the Service of the United Nations*—an Opinion which is concerned with the interpretation of the Charter but which is of a quasi-legislative character on the question of subjects of international law [10]—provides at the same time the most significant contribution made by the Court to the question of the nature, growth and functions of international law.

The *French-Swiss Free Zones* case—a case of treaty interpretation —brought an important contribution to such questions as the relevance of *travaux préparatoires*, the effect of treaties on third parties, the doctrine *rebus sic stantibus*, abrogation of treaties by subsequent treaties, abuse of rights, the limits of the competence of the Court to decide *ex aequo et bono*, the binding force of declarations made in the course of proceedings before the Court, and the admissibility of judgment by consent. The Judgment in the *Wimbledon* case, while answering the specific question as to the meaning of Article 380 of the Treaty of Versailles, is now an authority on the status of artificial waterways of an international character, on some aspects of neutrality, on restrictive interpretation of treaties—not to mention such matters as the measure of damages and award of interest. In the case concerning *Access of Polish War Vessels to the Port of Danzig*, Counsel for Danzig in opening his argument stated, with some emphasis, that the case before the Court raised no general question of international law and that the task of the Court was confined to giving an interpretation of documents.[11] But before he had proceeded very far he submitted that " . . . there is perhaps one general consideration which I know the Court will bear in mind,

---

[9] Consider, for instance, the implications of what is essentially the main issue in the Opinion on the *Reservations to the Genocide Convention*, namely, the relative value of universality and effectiveness in multilateral conventions. See below, pp. 186 *et seq.*

[10] See below, p. 176.

[11] Statement by Sir John Fischer Williams, Series C, No. 55, p. 217. See also below, p. 80.

and that is the general presumption which obtains in the whole field of international law against limitation of sovereignty or independence." [12]

The *Asylum* case between Colombia and Peru was, in the main, concerned with the question whether the asylum granted by the Colombian Ambassador in Peru to a Peruvian revolutionary was in accordance with the terms of Article 2 of the Havana Convention of 1928 which provided that " asylum may not be granted except in urgent cases and for the period of time strictly indispensable for the person who has sought asylum to ensure in some other way his safety." The crucial term—" urgent cases " [13]—which the Court was called upon to interpret was not even a term of art in international law, a term the interpretation of which would seem to call for resort to wider principles. Yet the Judgment of the Court is not only a contribution to the question of diplomatic asylum, in particular with regard to the right—which the Court denied—of the State granting asylum conclusively to determine its justification. It refers directly to the question of the meaning of customary international law—by reference to which the Treaty had to be interpreted—inasmuch as it forms part of the law to be applied by the Court under Article 38 of its Statute. Thus, although the Judgment of the Court in the principal *Asylum* case may seem to be of limited compass inasmuch as it appears to bear on a single expression in a treaty, there is probably no single written contribution in international law—no book or article—which illustrates more vividly the problem of diplomatic asylum as a whole than the Judgment of the Court in this case and the various Opinions accompanying it. In a different sphere, the controversy, hitherto largely theoretical, as to the existence of a Latin-American international law acquired, through the Judgment and the Dissenting Opinions in that case, a complexion of reality inasmuch as it raised the issue of the universality of principles of international law and their capacity of adaptation to regional custom.

In one case—that of *Diversion of Water from the Meuse*—the Court was at pains to emphasise that the issues submitted to it by the parties did not entitle it to go outside the field covered by the Treaty and that " the points at issue must all be determined solely

---

[12] Series C, No. 55, p. 219.
[13] *I.C.J. Reports* 1950, pp. 284 *et seq.* See below, p. 142. And see the Opinions of Judges Alvarez, Badawi Pasha and Read, on pp. 302, 304 and 326 respectively.

by the interpretation and application of that Treaty." [14]   Accordingly, a first reading of the Judgment creates the impression that it is devoid of any general interest for international law.   That impression may not be altogether justified—as may be seen from the insistence of the Court that a treaty seeking to reconcile the practical interests of the Parties and to improve an existing situation rather than to settle a legal dispute between them cannot be presumed to place one of the Parties in a position of inequality.[15]

Even when a case is in terms confined to the interpretation of particular provisions of treaties it may provide a contribution to the customary international law on treaty interpretation.   Thus in the case concerning *United States Nationals in Morocco*, in addition to those aspects of the Judgment which shed light on the position of protectorates in international law [16] and on the formation of international custom,[17] the decision made a contribution to the law governing the interpretation of treaties by reference to such questions as the conduct of the parties as an element of interpretation,[18] the relevance of preparatory work,[19] the authority of the preamble,[20] and the interpretation of the most-favoured-nation clause.[21]

## 13. *The Private Origin of Claims*

An attempt has been made in the preceding Section to show that the normal pre-occupation of the Court with the interpretation of treaties is not calculated to impair its more general contribution to the development of international law.   Neither, it is believed, is there substance in the impression that as most of the contentious cases which have come before the Court have arisen out of injuries to rights of private individuals, that is presumably out of matters of

[14] Series A/B, No. 70 (1937), p. 16.
[15] *Ibid.*, p. 20.   And see below, pp. 135, 213, 233, 336.
[16] *I.C.J. Reports* 1952, p. 185.
[17] *Ibid.*, p. 200.   See below, pp. 388 *et seq*.
[18] *Ibid.*, pp. 195, 205, 210.   See below, p. 388.
[19] *Ibid.*, pp. 198, 204.
[20] *Ibid.*, p. 198.
[21] See below, p. 266.   The same applies to the *Esterházy* case (Series A/B, No. 68 (1936)) which was concerned with the question whether, having regard to existing agreements, there lay an appeal from certain judgments rendered by the Hungaro-Yugoslav Mixed Arbitral Tribunal.   In that case, apparently devoid of a general legal interest, there will be found a valuable reference to the question of the authority of the Preamble to a treaty (see pp. 60, 80, 82, 86).   See also p. 62 of the Judgment for the rejection of an interpretation amounting to laying down a condition the fulfilment of which would be dependent upon the will of either of the interested Parties.

minor importance, it is not likely that they would have raised issues of general importance for international law. This is not so. Apart from territorial disputes, the great majority of cases of international judicial and arbitral settlement arise out of actual or alleged infractions of private interests—a not untimely reminder that although international law is a law primarily between States, it regulates and protects the interests of the individual, who is the ultimate unit of the law of nations, as indeed of all law. For this reason the private nature of the claim underlying the dispute is not decisive as to its importance for general international law. Thus the claims put forward by Germany for compensation on account of Polish interference with the *Chorzów Factory* in Upper Silesia [22] gave rise to pronouncements on such points as the conditions of jurisdiction of international tribunals, the question of litispendency, the effect of armistices and of recognition of belligerency upon third parties, State succession, expropriation of alien property, the position of ceded territory in the period between the signature of a treaty and its ratification, the plea of non-discrimination in the treatment of aliens, the competence of the Court to issue declaratory judgments, its right to decide on claims for compensation in the absence of express treaty provisions to this effect, the implications of State control over private claims, measure of damages, counter-claims and set-off.

The various Advisory Opinions connected with the treatment of Minorities had their origin in private interests adversely affected by the action of a State. Yet they resulted in important contributions to international law on such questions as State succession or, as also did the Judgment in the *Oscar Chinn* case,[23] the formulation of the principle of equality of treatment not only in law but also in fact.[24] The numerous cases, such as those of *Phosphates in Morocco*,[25] the *Railway Line Panevezys-Saldutiskis*,[26] the *Electricity Company of Sofia*,[27] the *Ambatielos* case,[28] and the *Anglo-Iranian Oil Company* case,[29] which clarified the meaning of the various clauses of the Optional Clause and other problems of the compulsory jurisdiction

---

[22] *Case Concerning Certain German Interests in Polish Upper Silesia*, Series A, No. 7 (1926).
[23] See below, p. 262.
[24] See below, p. 264.
[25] See below, p. 97.
[26] See below, p. 78.
[27] See below, p. 97.
[28] See below, p. 106.
[29] See below, pp. 344–347.

of the Court, as well as other questions such as exhaustion of legal remedies and nationality of claims, arose out of claims on behalf of private persons. The Advisory Opinion which affirmed the international personality of the United Nations and, in principle and in appropriate cases, of bodies other than sovereign States arose—as its name shows—out of injuries suffered by officials of the United Nations.[30] So did, in effect, the Advisory Opinion of the *Awards of the Administrative Tribunal of the United Nations*—a pronouncement which affirmed the general principle of *res judicata* in relation to the General Assembly itself.[31] The *Fisheries* case between the United Kingdom and Norway—one of the most significant cases of a general character decided by the Court—was on the face of it a claim arising out of interference with the activities of British subjects on the high seas.[32] This enumeration is not intended to be exhaustive.[33] But it is sufficient to dispel the view that the predominance of cases arising out of injuries to private persons can be interpreted as likely to impair the contribution of the Court to the general body of international law. In fact, the contrary is bound to be the case if we consider that disputes of this character are disputes involving the typical aspects of State responsibility.

## 14. *Pre-occupation with Pleas to Jurisdiction*

Similarly, the fact that in the work of the Court there has loomed large the question of jurisdiction[34] may create the impression that a considerable part of its activity has been of a somewhat formal character. This is not so. For questions of jurisdiction have to be decided by reference not only to conventional but also to customary international law and to general principles of law. Of the Judgments of the Court bearing exclusively on the issue of jurisdiction only three have been confined to the interpretation of the technical clauses of the relevant instruments without providing an occasion for a decision on wider issues of international law. They were the case of *Phosphates in Morocco*[35] between France and Italy, where

---

[30] See below, p. 176.
[31] See below, p. 325.
[32] See below, pp. 192 *et seq.*
[33] See, *e.g.*, the case of the *United States Nationals in Morocco* (above, p. 31), the *Peter Pázmány University* case (Series A/B, No. 61 (1933)), the *Lighthouses* case (Series A/B, No. 62 (1934), and the *Pajzs, Csáky, Esterházy* case (Series A/B, No. 68 (1936)).
[34] See below, pp. 91 *et seq.*, 243 *et seq.*, 338 *et seq.*
[35] Series A/B, No. 74 (1938).

the Court was called upon to interpret the so-called reservation of past disputes—a reservation of no mean importance; the *Corfu Channel (Jurisdiction)* case [36]; and, perhaps, the case of *Monetary Gold Removed from Rome*.[37] But, generally, the jurisdictional issue has provided a framework for judgments and opinions of wider import. Thus in the case of the *Panevezys-Saldutiskis Railway* between Estonia and Lithuania [38] the question of jurisdiction was decided largely by reference to the law relating to the nationality of claims and exhaustion of legal remedies. In the case of the *Electricity Company of Sofia* between Belgium and Bulgaria [39] a highly interesting jurisdictional issue—that of the simultaneous operation of two instruments apparently providing for the jurisdiction of the Court (which feature in itself raised a question of general importance for the law of treaties) [40]—was, once more, coupled with the question of exhaustion of legal remedies. The two *Ambatielos* cases,[41] in addition to making a contribution to various aspects of treaty interpretation, elucidated—though in a controversial fashion—weighty questions connected with the procedure of concluding treaties, in particular the question as to the extent to which a Declaration said to have been annexed to a treaty forms part of the treaty. The Judgment in which the Court declared itself incompetent to adjudicate in the *Anglo-Iranian Oil Company* case [42] is one of the more important pronouncements of the Court on various aspects of interpretation of treaties.

In some other cases the decision on the matter of jurisdiction has covered an even wider variety of subjects. Consider, for instance, the vast scope of the Court's pronouncement at the stage of the case of the *Mavrommatis Palestine Concessions* which was concerned solely with the question of jurisdiction.[43] Its Judgment can now be quoted as authority, in addition to purely jurisdictional matters, for such questions as the interpretation of bilingual treaties, the function of negotiations in international relations, the obligations of the successor State in the matter of concessions,

---

[36] *I.C.J. Reports* 1947–1948, p. 15. But see the Joint Separate Opinion of seven Judges on the binding force of recommendations of the Security Council (pp. 31, 32).
[37] *I.C.J. Reports* 1954, p. 19. But see below, p. 342.
[38] Series A/B, No. 76 (1939).
[39] Series A/B, No. 77 (1939).
[40] See below, p. 244.
[41] *I.C.J. Reports* 1952, p. 28; 1953, p. 10.
[42] *I.C.J. Reports* 1952, p. 93.
[43] Series A, No. 2 (1924).

renunciation by a Mandatory Power of its rights under the mandate, the limits of requirements of form in international relations, and the effects of an unratified treaty.

## 15. *Findings on Questions of Fact*

Finally, even in cases in which the Court has been called upon to pronounce primarily upon questions of fact, the opportunity—and the necessity—have arisen for applying and laying down rules of law of a general character. Thus in the Judgment on the merits in the *Corfu Channel* case, the principal question put to the Court and as formulated in the Special Agreement concluded by the Parties was on the face of it of a purely factual character. It was the question whether Albania was responsible under international law for the explosions which occurred in Albanian waters and for the damage and loss of human life which resulted from them and whether there was any duty to pay compensation.[44] But the Judgment of the Court, in addition to eliciting, with the assistance of naval experts specially appointed, the decisive issue of fact, is an authority on weighty questions of general importance such as the nature and degree of the responsibility of a State for damage occurring to foreign States on its territory; the burden of proof to be discharged in this connection; the obligations of the State in respect of the notification of minefields placed in its territorial waters; freedom of navigation in international straits and the limits of such freedom; the meaning of "innocent passage" through international straits; the limits of self-help and intervention in international law; the question whether the competence to pronounce on the question of liability to compensation implies the jurisdiction to assess the amount thereof; and various questions of interpretation of treaties connected with the interpretation, in that respect, of the Special Agreement submitting the dispute to the Court.[45]

[44] *I.C.J. Reports* 1949, p. 12.
[45] See below, p. 247.
   The observations in the text do not, of course, imply that the finding of facts either with the assistance of experts or by the Court itself is not an important part of its work. The subjects entrusted to the compulsory jurisdiction of the Court under Art. 36 (2) of its Statute include "the existence of any fact which, if established, would constitute a breach of an international obligation." The existence of such facts the Court ascertained, with the assistance of experts, in the *Corfu Channel* case (*I.C.J. Reports* 1949, pp. 4 *et seq.*). However, the facts which the Court may have to investigate need not be of that character. They are not necessarily confined to those

The two cases in which the Court was concerned with disputed claims to territorial sovereignty—the case of *Eastern Greenland* [46] and of the *Minquiers and Ecrehos* [47]—turned largely on disputed questions of fact many of which lay in the remote past. However, in addition to the general treatment, in the former case, of the question of the requisite degree of effectiveness as a condition of acquisition of territorial sovereignty, the manner in which the Court decides upon the relevance of the facts relied upon by the parties provides, when adequately generalised,[48] a contribution of considerable value for this branch of international law. The manner in which facts are marshalled in relation to any particular topic may be decisive for the elaboration of the governing legal principles. For this reason the question is raised elsewhere in this book as to the requisite degree of particularity, apparent in the decision itself, in the examination of facts claimed to establish international customary law.[49]

---

which give rise to the responsibility of the State. The Court may have to inquire into facts which exonerate a State from liability as, for instance, with regard to a plea of State necessity or *force majeure*. See, *e.g.*, the Dissenting Opinions of Judges Sir Cecil Hurst and van Eysinga in the *Oscar Chinn* case (Series A/B, No. 63 (1934)) and the case of the *Société Commerciale de Belgique*: Series A/B, No. 78 (1939), pp. 178, 186.

[46] Series A/B, No. 53 (1933), p. 22.

[47] *I.C.J. Reports* 1953, p. 47.

[48] See, for instance, the analysis by Sir Gerald Fitzmaurice of the treatment by the Court in the *Minquiers and Ecrehos* case of the concept of the " critical date " in territorial disputes in *British Year Book of International Law*, 32 (1955–1956), pp. 20–44.

[49] See below, pp. 386 *et seq.*

# CHAPTER 3

# THE REASONS BEHIND THE CASES

## 16. *International Adjudication and Exhaustiveness of Judicial Reasoning*

The instances enumerated in the preceding Sections suggest that we must not permit appearance to discourage us from looking for the law behind the cases decided by the Court. There is meaning in the attempt to discover the rich mine of law beneath the niceties of interpretation of treaties, the limited compass of private interests, the technicality of jurisdictional problems, and the deceptive simplicity of mere issues of fact. At the same time the variety of issues determined by the Court in the cases decided by it raises the question whether the normal—though not invariable—method of elaboration and exhaustiveness of its pronouncements constitutes a necessary or indispensable element in the work of the Court. Does not the Court wander away from the main point of the decision for the sake of what are no more than *obiter dicta*? Does it not indulge in academic disquisitions which might well be avoided? Does it not sacrifice judicial caution for the sake of an appearance of completeness or of flattering the self-esteem of the parties by answering all the contentions advanced by them? These questions —some of which have been asked occasionally [1]—must be answered in the negative. It will be submitted in the course of this chapter that there are compelling considerations of international justice and of development of international law which favour a full measure of exhaustiveness of judicial pronouncements of international tribunals.

When a defendant State puts forward a series of objections— procedural and on the merits—against the claim of the plaintiff Government, the Court must, of course, examine every single objection in all cases in which it finds it necessary to reject all of them. In such cases the decision on every point adduced by the defendant State forms an essential part of the final decision. The result may

---

[1] See, for instance, Fisscher Williams, *Chapters on Current International Law and the League of Nations* (1929), p. 214.

be a Judgment or Opinion of what may appear to be excessive length. It is not easy to see how that result can be avoided.[2] When the issue at stake is important—and the fact that a case has reached the Court shows that it is so—and when the parties, being States, can afford the cost of elaborate preparation of their case and of expert legal advice, then it is not surprising that the arguments are long and the pleas numerous.

However, even in cases in which the defendant State succeeds it is not sufficient for the Court to decide the issue by reference to one point or objection. This is so particularly in cases in which the plaintiff State invokes the jurisdiction of the Court on a number of independent grounds. It must examine them all. It may be instructive to refer here to the award of the Permanent Court of Arbitration in the *Russian Indemnity* case in 1912.[3] In that case the Tribunal rejected the various Turkish objections put forward in opposition to the claim, *e.g.*, that moratory interest had no place in international law, that the award of such interest would be contrary to State sovereignty, that Russia was not entitled to claim interest on the ground that she had made no formal demand for payment, and, finally, that Turkey was prevented by *force majeure* from fulfilling her obligations. In the end the Tribunal found against the Russian claim on the formal ground of presumptive and unrebuttable waiver, *i.e.*, on the ground that the Russian Government did not, subsequent to the Turkish default, reserve its rights to interest on the receipts given to Turkey or in the notes granting extension of payment. Possibly the Tribunal might have drastically shortened the award by rejecting the Russian demand on the last-mentioned formal ground. Yet if it had done so the award would not have ranked as one of the more valuable decisions given by a Tribunal of

---

[2] Similarly, when the plaintiff State invokes the jurisdiction of the Court on a number of independent grounds, the Court must examine all of them. It did so with considerable thoroughness in the case of the *Anglo-Iranian Oil Company*. It examined in detail, and rejected, the contention that the Iranian Declaration extended to treaties concluded by Iran at any time. It then examined, and dismissed, the contention that the various most-favoured-nation treaties concluded by Iran subsequent to her Declaration brought the dispute within the terms of the Declaration. Finally, it declined to accept the view that the " Convention " between Iran and the Anglo-Iranian Oil Company constituted, in the circumstances, a treaty under international law. Moreover, it felt it its duty to answer the contention, put forward in the course of the oral proceedings, that Iran accepted the jurisdiction of the Court by implication as the result of the principle of *forum prorogatum*. It did so, although the Agent for the United Kingdom stated subsequently that he did not wish to press that contention, for the reason that it was not formally withdrawn: *I.C.J. Reports* 1952, p. 114.

[3] Scott, *The Hague Court Reports* (1916), p. 297.

the Permanent Court of Arbitration. The administration of justice within the State can afford to rely on purely formal and procedural grounds. It can also afford to disregard the susceptibilities of either of the parties by ignoring such of its arguments as are not indispensable to the decision. This cannot properly be done in international relations, where the parties are sovereign States, upon whose will the jurisdiction of the Court depends in the long run, and where it is of importance that justice should not only be done but that it should also appear to have been done.

Experience has shown that Governments as a rule reconcile themselves to the fact that their case has not been successful—provided the defeat is accompanied by the conviction that their argument was considered in all its relevant aspects. On the other hand, however fully they may comply with an adverse decision, they do not find it easy to accept it as expressive of justice—or of law—if they feel that their argument was treated summarily, that it was misunderstood, or that dialectics have usurped the place of judicial reasoning. Any such impression, if lasting, is bound to affect adversely the cause of international justice. A tribunal which fails to give full reasons for its decision invites the reproach that it lays down new law. Even the legislator often gives, in the preamble to the statute, a detailed explanation of the action taken. Absence of reasons—or of adequate reasons—unavoidably creates the impression of arbitrariness. It is significant that in various codes of international arbitral procedure the absence of reasons is treated as a reason for the nullity of the award.[4] We recall the vigour of the protest of the United States, in the *Norwegian Shipowners* case, against the alleged failure of the arbitrator to state his reasons for the amount awarded by him.[5] A decision which rests not on the manifest foundation of the law—and this is the case of a decision not accompanied by reasons or adequate reasons—but on the personal authority of the judges who compose the majority or of the tribunal as a whole is particularly open to criticism in cases in which the subject-matter of the controversy is connected with political interests of importance. When a tribunal, by failing to base a decision on articulate grounds, makes it difficult to scrutinise the law

[4] Thus the Draft Convention of Arbitral Procedure submitted in 1954 by the International Law Commission provided, in Art. 30, that the validity of the award may be challenged, *inter alia*, for the reason that " there has been a serious departure from a fundamental rule of procedure, including failure to state the reasons for the award."

[5] See Scott, *The Hague Court Reports*, Second Series (1932), p. 82.

underlying the decision, it leaves the door wide open for imputing motives extraneous to the proper exercise of the judicial function.

If government by men, and not by laws, is resented within the State by individuals, any appearance of it is likely to be viewed with even greater suspicion on the part of sovereign States in relation to judges of foreign nationality. The problem of judicial impartiality, however exaggerated it may be on occasions, is an ever-present problem in relation to international tribunals—in particular those of an institutional character as distinguished from *ad hoc* tribunals.[6] It is bound to arise—whether in fact or in the imagination of writers and disappointed suitors—not only in cases involving directly the State of which a Judge is a national, but also States to which his State is related by political or ideological affinity. It is a problem which cannot be solved by mere devices of machinery. But it can be considerably alleviated by the fullest possible completeness of judicial reasoning which renders it practicable for everyone to know and to assess the value of the grounds of the decisions given by an international tribunal. Even if there existed no other inducement prompting the full elaboration and exhaustiveness of judicial pronouncements, this aspect of the matter must in itself constitute a factor of compelling cogency in discouraging any semblance of deliberate brevity. It is not without significance that in the history of international arbitration allegations of improper exercise of the arbitral function have been mostly made in cases in which the award was not accompanied by reasons.

However, there are other weighty considerations, which have decisively influenced the work of the Court, urging the fullest possible completeness of judicial reasoning. Thus the opportunities of and inducements to exercising judicial latitude are particularly more pressing in international adjudication because of the uncertainties of the customary law and for other reasons.[7] This factor makes it imperative to frame the decisions of international tribunals so as to avoid any suspicion of wide and inarticulate discretion on the part of the tribunal. The same obligation follows from the circumstance that, again for reasons more clearly applicable to disputes between States than elsewhere, there is often only a small margin of decisive merit between competing claims.[8] The legal and

---

[6] See for a full discussion of the problem the present writer's *Function of Law in the International Community* (1933), pp. 218 *et seq*.

[7] See below, pp. 368 *et seq*.                    [8] See below, pp. 396 *et seq*.

moral authority of a judicial pronouncement acquires an important accession of strength if it bears the visible hall-mark of comprehensive effort and of a studious avoidance of short-cuts of reasoning. The case of the successful plaintiff is seldom so strong that it does not stand to gain by the demonstration, evidenced in the contents of the judgment, that the Court rejected, after a conscientious examination, his alternative submissions or that his case finds support in more than one argument.

For the reasons stated, these considerations are even more compelling in international judicial proceedings than in the sphere of private litigation.[9] In the long run the course of international justice would be bound to suffer if the authority of the pronouncements of international tribunals were to be sought not in their intrinsic merit, but in the finality and authority of the tribunal which renders them. Their enforcement, it will be noted, is not automatic. It is not so, as far as the Judgments of the International Court of Justice are concerned, according to the Charter of the United Nations.[10] However competent, however august, however final, and however authoritative a tribunal may be, it cannot, in conditions in which its jurisdiction is in law, and compliance with its decisions is in fact, essentially of a voluntary character, dispense with that powerful appeal to opinion which stems from the reasoned content of its pronouncements. These considerations explain—and justify—the deliberate pursuit, as a normal feature of its practice, of the principle of exhaustiveness of judicial reasoning on the part of the International Court of Justice and its predecessor. As within the State, there may be a danger that the finality, the dignity and the acknowledged authority of a court of ultimate

---

[9] It is also for these reasons that international tribunals may not be at liberty to follow the method of the concise judgments, consisting of a recital of " *considérants*," practised by the courts of some countries. The following example will illustrate the pitfalls of the fascination which brevity occasionally exercises upon commentators: A learned writer (Hamson, *Executive Discretion and Judicial Control* (1954), p. 119), in referring to the clarity and precision of the judgments of the French *Conseil d'Etat*, states that "it is a real intellectual pleasure to come to judgments of this brevity and accuracy after the meanderings of some of the pronouncements of English courts." He then proceeds to qualify his approval as follows: " But it also requires a considerable art intelligently to read these judgments; they are almost a concatenation of formulas." In a footnote he gives expression to yet another doubt: " It would on occasion be virtually impossible to grasp the real point of a decision without collating the Commissaire du Gouvernement's ' conclusions.' "

[10] See Art. 94 of the Charter, which lays down that at the request of the interested party the Security Council " may, if it deems necessary, make recommendations or decide upon measures to be taken to give effect to the judgment."

jurisdiction, may on occasions encourage a method of exposition which is summary in character and therefore not calculated to carry conviction. There may be a disposition to state a legal rule without any intimation of the difficulties and vicissitudes surrounding its evolution. There may be a tendency to lose sight of the fact that the authority of a Court's decisions must be based on a power of persuasion more compelling than their formal finality, and that the learning and the effort which have shaped them ought not merely to be assumed but must also find clear expression in the content of the decision. Any such tendency is probably unwholesome within the State, where the validity and enforceability of decisions of courts are automatic and where their jurisdiction is compulsory. It is particularly open to objection in the international sphere where these conditions do not obtain. The history of the Court's work, viewed in its entirety, is a history of a determination, deliberately pursued— notwithstanding the difficulties involved in the method of collective drafting obtaining within the Court—to avoid these dangers.

In comparison with these considerations the insistence that comprehensiveness of judicial pronouncements is of importance for the development and clarification of international law appears to be of limited significance. This does not mean that it is a factor without importance. For a decision which is not based on adequate reasoning does not constitute a precedent of general application. It does not do so for the simple reason that it has refrained— deliberately or otherwise—from formulating the law which could serve as a precedent. It fails to fulfil one of the essential functions of the Court, namely, to contribute by its decisions to the development of international law. This is a weighty additional consideration why the Court has deemed it desirable that Article 56 of the Statute, which lays down that the judgment shall state the reasons on which it is based, should be adhered to fully and generously.[11] If the part

---

[11] This part of the Statute refers throughout to "judgments," but it ought to be read in the light of the subsequent substantial assimilation of Advisory Opinions to the contentious procedure. The revised Art. 68 of the Statute lays down that "in the exercise of its advisory functions the Court shall further be guided by the provisions of the present Statute which apply in contentious cases to the extent to which it recognises them to be applicable." For a reminder that such assimilation is not complete, see the Advisory Opinion in the matter of the *Interpretation of the Peace Treaties with Bulgaria, Hungary, and Romania*: *I.C.J. Reports* 1950, p. 72, and below, pp. 353 *et seq.* However, any differences between the two aspects of the jurisdiction of the Court have no relevance to the subject discussed in the text above.

which the Court can play directly [12] as a factor in maintaining peace is necessarily limited, that may be an additional reason why it ought to avail itself to the full of the opportunity of fulfilling its secondary purpose, which is the developing of international law through reasoned decisions.   Occasionally a detailed statement of reasons may prove to be of practical usefulness to the parties anxious to avail themselves of the decision of the Court for regulating the details of a dispute which the Judgment or the Opinion have decided only in large outline.   In one case—the Advisory Opinion on the question of the *Greco-Bulgarian Communities*—the absence of detailed reasons for the decision of the Court seemed to have deprived it of some of its possible effectiveness.[13]   On the other hand, the relative frequency of cases in which the Court has been asked to interpret its previous Judgments and Advisory Opinions [14] is probably not relevant to the question here discussed.   While there may be only limited force in the view that elaboration, being in the nature of prolixity, opens the door to questionings and to the necessity for re-interpretation, this may equally be the result of brevity.

## 17. *The Necessity for Cumulation of rationes decidendi*

Some of the cases decided by the Court illustrate this aspect of the international judicial process.   In the *Lotus* case the Court could,

[12] For reasons stated above (p. 3) the indirect contribution of the Court in that sphere is not inconsiderable.

[13] It appears that the brevity of this Opinion, in which the Court, without detailed explanation, laid down a number of definitions, was subjected to some criticism by the Commission for Exchange of Populations on the ground that the absence of reasons considerably impaired the usefulness of the Opinion.   See League of Nations Doc. C 238, M. 1931, 1932 (I) Annex, p. 29, and the authoritative article of André Becker in *Revue de droit international et de la législation comparée*, Series III, vol. XIII (1932), p. 542, who refers, with some disapproval, to the " *sobriété extrème* " of the Judgment of the Court.

An elaboration of reasons, seemingly not essential for the operative part of the pronouncement of the Court, may serve a useful purpose in a different sphere.   Thus in his Dissenting Opinion in the case of the *Membership of the Free City of Danzig in the International Labour Organisation* Judge Huber seems to have suggested that it was within the province of the Court to frame its Opinion so as to " best assist the Parties in finding a solution " by means of purely juridical considerations (Series B, No. 18 (1930), p. 29).

[14] See Judgment No. 4, given by the Chamber of Summary Procedure, concerning the *Interpretation of Judgment No. 3* (Series A, No. 4); Judgment No. 11 interpreting Judgments Nos. 7 and 8 in the *Chorzów Factory* case (Series A, No. 13); Judgment of November 27, 1950, concerning the Interpretation of the Judgment of November 20, 1950, in the *Asylum* case (*I.C.J. Reports* 1950, p. 395); the Judgment of June 13, 1951, in the same case (*I.C.J. Reports* 1951, p. 71) which was substantially in the nature of interpretation—in some respects inconclusive (see below, pp. 143 *et seq.*)—of the previous Judgment in the same case.

if it had so wished, have based its judgment on the sole principle of the locality of the effect of the offence as distinguished from its causation. It could have relied on the theory that the offence was committed not on the high seas but in Turkish territory, *i.e.*, on the Turkish ship where the offence could be deemed to have taken effect. Had it acted in this way, the Court would have been in a position, instead of giving judgment by a nominal majority made possible by the casting vote of the President, to render a decision by a clear majority of at least seven to five in respect of the operative part of the Judgment.[15] It would also have avoided the criticism directed against some of the more general grounds on which it based its Judgment,[16] namely, that international law does not forbid a State to assume jurisdiction over aliens for crimes committed abroad. At the same time, had it acted in that manner, it would have given a decision covering an important issue in the sphere of international law but based on a controversial technicality—a decision which, for that reason, would have been incomplete and unsatisfactory.

The decision in the *Eastern Greenland* case could have been based—according to the Dissenting Opinion of Judge Anzilotti it ought to have been based—on a single point, namely, on what the Court construed to be a promise given by the Norwegian Foreign Minister, in the course of his oral negotiations with the Danish Minister, not to occupy any part of Eastern Greenland.[17] But the Court refused to decide an important case on that single ground as determined by a somewhat drastic departure from the ordinary forms adopted in the international procedure of assuming contractual obligations.[18] It preferred, in addition, to base its decision on the broader ground of the general international law in the matter of acquisition of territorial sovereignty. The Norwegian Foreign Minister's oral undertaking constituted one—but certainly not the most important—of the several reasons underlying the Judgment. From a different point of view, the Court would have been able to decide the issue by reference to its conclusion that during the crucial period between 1921 and 1931 Denmark regarded herself as possessing sovereignty over all Greenland and displayed and exercised her

---

[15] Judge Moore, while disagreeing with the general reasoning of the Court, agreed with it on the decisive point of the application of the principle of the locality of the offence, namely, that it was in fact committed in Turkish territory.

[16] See below, p. 210.

[17] See below, p. 211.

[18] *Ibid.*

rights of sovereignty to an extent sufficient to constitute a valid title.[19] However, it thought it desirable—indeed, imperative—to add weight to its Judgment by a detailed consideration of the question of sovereignty in the centuries preceding that crucial period. In fact, that aspect of the decision constitutes the main contribution which that important Judgment made to international law.

In the Advisory Opinion on *Reparation for Injuries Suffered in the Service of the United Nations* the Court could have based its ruling, *i.e.*, the right of the United Nations to bring an international claim, on the principle, paramount over all, of the effectiveness of the relevant provisions of the Charter.[20] Instead, it deemed it its duty to give its Opinion against the background of the growing attrition of the—for some still venerable—doctrines of the exclusiveness of the State as a subject of international law and of nationality of claims. It reduced both of them to their true proportions. To disregard them altogether and to base the Opinion solely on a view which had not yet acquired a complexion of orthodoxy or on the more general principle of effectiveness in relation to the Charter would have created the justifiable impression of an act of judicial legislation.

The Judgment in the *Anglo-Norwegian Fisheries* case affords yet another example of the same disinclination to base the decision on one single ground. It would have been sufficient for the Court in that case to " avoid trouble " by simply limiting the decision to what may be described as the prescriptive aspect of the controversy, namely, to the finding that whatever may be the position of customary international law with regard to the base line of territorial waters and the ten-mile rule as to bays, Norway had acquired a prescriptive right to the regulation of fisheries in the areas in question as determined by her own system of delimitation and that this was so largely as the result of the implied acquiescence of the United Kingdom in the Norwegian claims. The Court did not do so. The bulk of the Judgment was devoted to a consideration of the customary international law on the subject.[21] Although the decision of the Court could have been given on the sole basis of the historic title of Norway—this, in fact, was the only ground on which Judge Hackworth expressed his concurrence in the operative part of the

[19] Series A/B, No. 53 (1933), p. 63.
[20] See below, p. 177.
[21] See below, pp. 192 *et seq.*, 368 *et seq.*

Judgment of the Court—the Court preferred to complicate, as it were, its task and to base its Judgment, in the first instance, on its interpretation of substantive customary law.[22] This, in the light of general observations as set forth above, was the only course which was open to the Court consistently with a broad and, it is believed, enlightened conception of its function. There are grounds for the view that it would have been inconsistent with the interests of international justice, as here conceived, if a dispute of some magnitude were to be allowed to hinge on the essentially formal issue of acquiescence. For there is only limited persuasive power in the suggestion that such a course might have been preferable to what critics believe to be the controversial manner of the treatment of the main substantive issue.[23] It is only seldom that a particular ground of decision is so obvious and so uncontroversial as to permit a court to rely on it to the total exclusion of alternative grounds supporting the same conclusion. The importance which the Court attaches to exhaustiveness of the reasons of its pronouncements is shown by the occasional express insistence that in performing its duty it is not circumscribed by the assistance received from the parties. Thus in the *Lotus* case the Court observed that " in the fulfilment of its task of itself ascertaining what the international law is, it has not confined itself to a consideration of the arguments put forward, but has included in its researches all precedents, teachings and facts to which it had access and which might possibly have revealed the existence of one of the principles of international law contemplated in the special agreement." [24]

Admittedly not every argument, however strained and far-fetched, put forward by a party requires an answer. Thus, for instance, the Court could safely afford to omit any reference in its Judgment in the *Eastern Greenland* dispute to the Danish argument based on the alleged violation by Norway of Article 10 of the

22 The Court said: " The notoriety of the facts, the general toleration of the international community, Great Britain's position in the North Sea, her own interest in the question, and her prolonged abstention [from protests] would in any case warrant Norway's enforcement of her system [of straight lines] against the United Kingdom " (*I.C.J. Reports* 1951, p. 139).

23 See below, pp. 196, 371. This is also the view of Professor Bourquin who suggests that if the Court had found in favour of Norway by reference to historical title alone " son arrêt aurait été loin d'offrir l'intérêt qu'il revêt effectivement " (*Acta Scandinavica*, 22 (1952), p. 105). It is submitted that the defect of any such limited approach would have been of a seriousness transcending mere absence of general interest.

24 Series A, No. 10 (1927), p. 31.

Covenant of the League of Nations.[25]   In its Judgment on the Preliminary Objection of Albania in the *Corfu Channel* case the Court did not consider it necessary to examine in detail the unorthodox contention advanced on behalf of the United Kingdom that, in the circumstances of the case, a resolution of the Security Council recommending the parties to submit their dispute to the Court was binding upon them [26]—though seven Judges, while concurring with the Judgment of the Court, attached importance to expressing, in a Separate Opinion, their disapproval of the, somewhat strained, British argument.   Similarly, the Court has not considered itself bound to answer questions which have not been put by either party although an answer to them could conceivably have proved useful at a subsequent stage of the controversy.   In the Advisory Opinion concerning Danzig's membership of the International Labour Organisation the Court did not deem it necessary to pronounce on the general question whether membership of the League of Nations was essential for membership of the International Labour Organisation.   The Dissenting Opinion of Judge Anzilotti was largely devoted to a consideration of that question.[27]

## 18. *Elaboration of Reasons in Relation to Assessment of Facts and Contingencies.   The* Customs Union *Case*

The thoroughness of the pronouncements of the Court stands out even more clearly when compared with those cases which cannot be regarded as typical and in which, according to some, it has followed a different method.   Of these cases the Advisory Opinion in the matter of the *Customs Régime between Germany and Austria* offers an instructive example.   One of the features, perhaps unavoidable, of this Opinion is that, except for one consideration of undoubted persuasiveness,[28] it contains only few reasons for the conclusion reached by the majority to the effect that the proposed Customs Union was incompatible with the Protocol of Geneva of 1922 in which Austria undertook not to alienate her independence and to " abstain from any economic or financial

---

[25] See Series C, vol. 63, pp. 968 *et seq.*, 1451 *et seq.*

[26] *I.C.J. Reports* 1948, p. 26.

[27] Series B, No. 18 (1930), pp. 18–21.

[28] See Series A/B, No. 41 (1931), p. 52.   The reason was that the projected union constituted a " special régime " and that it afforded Germany in relation to Austria advantages which were withheld from third Powers.

engagement calculated directly or indirectly to compromise this independence." Criticism of the Opinion of the Court in the *Customs Union* case has been directed mainly not to the nature of the conclusion reached by the Court—nor, even less, because it agreed to give an Opinion on a matter involving the assessment of future political contingencies [29]—but to the absence of a more ʽtangible intimation of the reasons underlying the Opinion.[30]

It may not be easy to answer the question whether the circumstance that in a particular case the reasoning of the Court must consist largely of an assessment of facts or probabilities relevant to the situation affects the obligation to make the decision rest on the broadest possible basis of all requisite detail. A substantial part of the task of judicial tribunals consists in the examination and the weighing of the relevance of facts for the purpose of determining liability and assessing damages. As the *Corfu Channel* case showed, the Court is in the position to perform that task with exacting care.[31] The ascertainment of facts is specifically declared in Article 36 of the Statute to be one of the occasions for the jurisdiction of the Court. At the same time there are a number of factors which may explain the brevity of the Opinion of the Court in the *Customs Union* case. Thus there may be substance in the view that, as the answer to the question put before the Court depended largely upon its opinion as to the political consequences of the proposed Union, it was difficult for it to formulate in detail what was essentially a matter of impression. Although the final view of the Court as to the political consequences of the Union was articulate enough to determine the Opinion, it does not follow that it was sufficiently

[29] For a refutation of the latter criticism see Lauterpacht, *The Function of Law in the International Community* (1933), p. 157.

[30] Professor Brierly in commenting on the brevity of the Opinion suggested that it gave the impression that on account of a clerical error entire pages had been omitted in the crucial part of the Court's pronouncement: *Zeitschrift für ausländisches öffentliches Recht und Völkerrecht*, 3 (1933), p. 71.

[31] In that case the Court devoted three weeks to hearing the evidence of the witnesses and experts called by the Parties in reply to questions put to them in examination and cross-examination on behalf of the Parties and by the President on behalf of the Court or of a Member of the Court. In addition, the Court had before it a lengthy report of experts on a variety of questions formulated by it (Annex 2 to the Judgment: *I.C.J. Reports* 1949, pp. 142–150) as well as a report of experts following upon a decision of the Court ordering an inquiry on the spot (pp. 151–162). And see the Judgment, in the same case, of December 15, 1949, in which the Court, following upon a report of experts appointed by it, assessed the amount of compensation due to the United Kingdom (*ibid.*, pp. 244–251).

articulate to be expressed in the form of reasons underlying the Opinion.[32]

### 19. *" The Natural Meaning of Terms "*

The normal method, pursued by the Court, of treating exhaustively the issues raised by the parties has not been seriously affected by the occasional reliance, to the virtual exclusion of more persuasive means of interpretation, on the " natural meaning of words " in treaties construed by the Court.  That tendency was, for a time, conspicuous in a number of cases in which the Court declined, or professed to decline, an attempt to elicit the intention of the parties by reference to what is usually described as preparatory work in the interpretation of treaties—an attitude which, in effect, the Court subsequently abandoned.  That aspect of the Court's work is discussed elsewhere in this book.[33]  In the present context it may be convenient to refer to one case which illustrates the problems inherent in this method of approach.  In the case of the Advisory Opinion on *Conditions of Admission of a State to Membership in the United Nations (Article 4 of the Charter)* [34] the Court was asked to give an Opinion on the question whether a Member of the United Nations which is called upon, in virtue of Article 4 of the Charter, to pronounce itself on the admission of a State to membership in the United Nations, is juridically entitled to make its consent to admission dependent on conditions not expressly provided in that Article.[35]  The majority of the Court came to the conclusion that having regard to the " natural meaning of the words " used in the Charter the conditions there enumerated constituted an exhaustive enumeration and were not stated merely by way of guidance or example.[36]

The Court did not rule out the possibility of " an interpretation

---

[32] This is so although the oral and written arguments before the Court afforded some material for a statement of reasons in this respect (see, *e.g.,* the *Mémoire* of Czechoslovakia, Series C, No. 53, p. 171).  The Opinion of the Court in the *Interpretation of the Statute of the Memel Territory* (see Series A/B, No. 49 (1932), pp. 325, 326) on the possible repercussions of the steps taken by the President of the Memel Directorate can also be quoted as showing the possibility of formulating reasons of this description.

[33] See below, pp. 124 *et seq.*

[34] *I.C.J. Reports* 1948, p. 57.

[35] Art. 4 of the Charter provides as follows: " Membership in the United Nations is open to all other peace-loving States which accept the obligations contained in the present Charter and, in the judgment of the Organisation, are able and willing to carry out these obligations."

[36] *I.C.J. Reports* 1948, p. 62.

other than that which ensues from the natural meaning of the words," but, it stated, to warrant such an interpretation " a decisive reason would be required which has not been established." [37] Some such decisive reason could come only from a source extraneous to the supposed " natural meaning of words." However, after having conceded the possible admissibility of recourse to some such source, the Court proceeded to deny that reliance on it was admissible in the case before it : " The Court considers that the text is sufficiently clear; consequently, it does not feel that it should deviate from the consistent practice of the Permanent Court of International Justice, according to which there is no occasion to resort to preparatory work if the text of a convention is sufficiently clear in itself." [38] The question of the accurate interpretation of the practice of the Permanent Court of International Justice in the matter of preparatory work is discussed below.[39] In the present context it is sufficient to note that the wording which the majority of the Court regarded as so clear as to rule out any recourse to extrinsic methods of interpretation, was interpreted by six other Judges in an apparently [40] diametrically opposed manner. The Opinion provides an illustration of the inherent limitations of a method of interpretation which

---

[37] *I.C.J. Reports* 1947–1948, p. 63.

[38] *Ibid.*

[39] See pp. 116 *et seq.*

[40] But only " apparently." For an analysis of the conclusions of the majority and of the minority discloses that the difference between them was less substantial than may appear at first sight. While the Opinion of the majority of the Court was that Members of the United Nations acting under Art. 4 of the Charter are not juridically entitled to make their consent to the admission of new Members dependent on conditions not expressly provided in that Article, it was qualified in a manner which rendered the Opinion, in a sense, theoretical. For the majority admitted that Members are entitled to take into account (*i.e.*, in effect, to put) conditions which it is possible reasonably and in good faith to connect with the " very wide and very elastic " conditions laid down in Art. 4; and that no relevant political factor connected with these " very wide and very elastic " conditions need be excluded (p. 63). The Opinion thus qualified was not entirely dissimilar to that handed down by Judge Krylov, according to whom the Members are entitled to take into account: (a) the legal tests laid down in Art. 4 and (b) political considerations consistent with the Purposes and Principles of the United Nations. Similarly, while the four authors of the Joint Dissenting Opinion expressed the view that Members are entitled to make their consent to admission of new Members dependent on any political considerations which seem to them relevant, such freedom of action is legally circumscribed by the " principle of good faith," by the obligation " to give effect to the Purposes and Principles of the United Nations " and by the duty " to act in such a manner as not to involve any breach of the Charter " (p. 92). The circumstance that, in legal effect, the difference between the views of the majority and the minority of Judges was one of emphasis, dependent upon the way in which a Member of the United Nations formulated its reasons for voting on the question of admission—there being, moreover, no duty to formulate any reasons at all—suggests the exceptional difficulty of complying with that particular request for an Advisory Opinion.

is based largely [41] on logical construction and which does not attach decisive importance to exhausting all available guides to the intention of the parties.

The authors of the principal Dissenting Opinion—who admittedly based their Opinion on grounds much wider than a purely logical interpretation [42]—thought it helpful to rely on the rule, frequently applied by the Permanent Court of International Justice, that no restriction upon a principle or rule of law can be presumed unless it is clearly established and that in case of doubt it is that principle or rule which must prevail. [43] In the present case that purported principle or rule was the freedom of decision of members of the Security Council or of the General Assembly in casting their vote in the matter of the admission of a new Member. The alternative method would have been to treat any such principle or rule as the eventual product of interpretation in all its aspects, and as a link, thus firmly forged, in the chain of reasoning. For it is that very question—the unfettered freedom of decision and voting—which was at issue. It is therefore not surprising that, as the result, the majority and the minority relied on the same argument for reaching dissimilar conclusions. If, in the view of the majority, the authors of the Charter had intended to permit the Members to import conditions of admission other than those expressly enumerated in the Charter, they would undoubtedly have said so. [44] If, in the view of the minority, the authors of the Charter had regarded the conditions enumerated in Article 4 as sufficient, they would not have failed to express themselves accordingly. [45] Nevertheless, unlike in the Opinion of the majority of the Court, the logical argument was not the main basis of the Opinion of the minority of the Judges.

Other cases have provided illustrations of the difficulties latent in the reliance upon the " natural " or " plain " or " ordinary " meaning of terms. In the *Anglo-Iranian Oil Company* case Judge Hackworth in his Dissenting Opinion invoked the " plain and

[41] It is not suggested that the Opinion of the majority of the Court was confined to purely logical and verbal reasoning. See, *e.g.*, the insistence of the Court that " the political character of the organ cannot release it from the observance of the treaty provisions established by the Charter when they constitute limitations on its powers or criteria for its judgment " (p. 64).

[42] See below, pp. 121 *et seq.*

[43] *I.C.J. Reports* 1947–1948, p. 86.

[44] *Ibid.*, p. 63.

[45] *Ibid.*, p. 90.

reasonable meaning " [46] of the Iranian acceptance of the Optional Clause; Judge Read invoked the " natural and ordinary meaning " [47] of its terms.    But a large majority of the Court found that the interpretation of the Declaration according to the natural and plain terms yielded opposite results.    In the *Ambatielos Case* (*Merits*) the four Dissenting Judges [48] held that the " natural or ordinary meaning " of the Declaration which the Court was called upon to interpret was not such as to oblige the United Kingdom to submit to arbitration her dispute with Greece.    The Court interpreted it in the opposite sense.    In the section of this book bearing on recourse to preparatory work in the interpretation of treaties, there will be found numerous other examples of reliance on the natural, plain or ordinary meaning of words as a substitute for other methods of eliciting the intention of the parties. [49]

### A Note on the Doctrine of " Plain Meaning "

The doctrine of " plain meaning," or " clear meaning," or " natural meaning " is a rule of interpretation which is relied upon most frequently in diplomatic correspondence and in arbitral and judicial proceedings— both by the parties to the dispute and by the tribunal.    That rule was expounded nearly two hundred years ago by Vattel with a characteristi- cally deceptive lucidity.    He said: " La première maxime générale sur l'interprétation est, qu'il *n'est pas permis d'interpréter ce qui n'a pas besoin d'interprétation.*    Quand un acte est conçu en termes clairs et précis, quand le sens en est manifeste et ne conduit à rien d'absurde, on n'a aucune raison de se refuser au sens que cet acte présente naturelle- ment.    Aller chercher ailleurs des conjectures, pour le restreindre, ou pour l'étendre, c'est vouloir l'éluder." [50]    The rule thus formulated seems to be pre-eminently reasonable.    Its obviousness explains the frequency with which it is invoked.    Its only—but, upon analysis, decisive—drawback is that it often assumes as a fact what has still to be proved and that it proceeds not from the starting point of the inquiry but from what is normally the result of it.    As, in the course of argument generally, the disputants frequently attempt to obtain a tactical advantage over their opponents by describing themselves—or their contentions—as sound and realistic while labelling their adversaries as utopian, so in the matter of interpretation parties incline to characterise the construction which they

[46] *I.C.J. Reports* 1952, p. 140.
[47] *Ibid.*, p. 145.
[48] Sir Arnold McNair, Basdevant, Klaestad and Read: *I.C.J. Reports* 1953, p. 30.
[49] See below, pp. 116 *et seq.*
[50] Book II, ch. XVII, para. 263.

favour as following from the ordinary or natural meaning of terms of the treaty and, accordingly, as self-evident and in no need of corroboration from external sources. If, therefore, the law on the subject had to be deduced from past statements of Governments when parties to a dispute, the search could hardly lead to results which are wholly reliable. For Governments are seldom in the position to lay down principles of interpretation independent of disputes in which they are engaged and therefore partaking of any particular degree of authority. Lord McNair has suggested that if the British Government " were called upon to face squarely the question of ' plain terms ' they would take the view that this so-called rule of interpretation like others is merely a prima facie guide and cannot be allowed to obstruct the essential quest in the interpretation of treaties, namely, to search for the real intention of the contracting parties in using the language employed by them." [51]

This, essentially, is the opinion of other writers of authority who have devoted special study to the practice of international tribunals. In particular, Hyde's weighty chapter on interpretation of treaties, with special reference to the International Court of Justice and the Supreme Court of the United States, has emphasised this crucial aspect of the problem of interpretation. " One must reject," he says, " as an unhelpful and unscientific procedure the endeavour to test the significance of the words employed in a treaty by reference to their so-called ' natural meaning ' or any other linguistic standard, and then to attempt to reconcile therewith the thought or conduct of the contracting parties." [52] Judge Hudson, in referring to the " earlier jurisprudence " of the International Court in making the " natural " meaning the starting point of the inquiry, has pointed to a certain danger inherent in allowing the " natural " meaning to overcome the results of other investigations [53]— though his warning is tempered by the suggestion that to treat the " natural meaning " as a starting point " may be a wise tendency " and that " no objection is to be made to a term which has a soothing effect and which tends to avoid arousals because of its indefinite content." [54] Yet the fact is that, in the view of many, the reliance upon the " natural meaning " may have a soothing effect, in an adverse sense, upon the intensity and the vitality of the interpretative effort of international tribunals—one of the principal, if not *the* principal, tasks which confront them—and that, far from " avoiding arousals " it has given rise to criticism.

[51] *The Law of Treaties* (1938), p. 175.
[52] *International Law. Chiefly as Interpreted and Applied by the United States* (2nd ed., 1945), vol. II, p. 1470. And see, generally, *ibid.*, pp. 1468–1502.
[53] *The Permanent Court of International Justice, 1920–1942* (1943), p. 645.
[54] *Ibid.*

The present attitude of writers, largely critical of the doctrine of " plain meaning," has been determined not so much by individual decisions of international tribunals—for these often tend in the opposite direction—as by the accumulated experience of the lessons of international judicial activity in that sphere. Numerous judgments, opinions and awards seem to favour reliance on " plain meaning "—although more often than not such reliance, far from being the decisive consideration, is due to the desire to make the decision appear more convincing and to give the embellishment of plausibility and apparent soundness to a result reached in other ways. But cases have occurred in which an international tribunal, by invoking the " clarity " of a provision, has contented itself with what must be regarded as a partial and essentially incomplete investigation of the intention of the parties. Frequently, when a Court describes a contested clause as clear and in consequence refuses to have recourse to a source of interpretation other than the assumed textual and grammatical meaning, the only tangible factor is that the provision is far from being clear. The very fact that the clause is so controversial that the parties are willing to go to the expense and the trouble of a litigation or that the request for an Advisory Opinion is preceded by a hotly debated controversy as to the legal merits of the issue shows that the provision or term in question is not " clear." When, in addition, the Tribunal itself is almost equally divided on the subject, for the majority or the minority to assert the " clarity," not requiring or not permitting extraneous evidence, of the controversial clause is to use an argument of doubtful persuasiveness. It may be useful to give some illustrations of the problem involved.

In the Advisory Opinion given in 1948 on the *Conditions of Admission of a State to Membership in the United Nations* (Article 4 of the Charter) the majority of the Court relied almost exclusively on the " natural meaning of the words used " [55] as clearly demonstrating the intention of the authors of the Charter. It did not exclude altogether the possibility of an " interpretation other than that which ensues from the natural meaning of the words." But to do that, it said, " a decisive reason would be required which has not been established." At the same time the Court in effect ruled out, in that case, the main possibility of discovering such a decisive reason which might be found, in particular, in an examination of the relevant preparatory work. It said: " The Court considers that the text is sufficiently clear; consequently, it does not feel that it should deviate from the consistent practice of the Permanent Court of International Justice, according to which there is no occasion to resort to preparatory work if the text of a convention is sufficiently clear in itself.[56]

[55] *I.C.J. Reports* 1947–1948, p. 63.
[56] *Ibid.*

As is pointed out below,[57] the difficulties encompassing recourse to this method of interpretation explain the absence of any pronounced degree of uniformity in the practice of the Court in this matter. However that may be, a method of interpretation which, with reference to an essential aspect of a basic international instrument, confines itself to a deduction from the " natural meaning " of words runs the danger of unduly simplifying the difficult process of interpretation. This is so in particular with regard to a clause the formulation of which, according to common knowledge, had been the product of a prolonged controversy on a fundamental issue. It is not certain that if the Court had considered the clause in question in the light of the circumstances, recorded and otherwise, of its adoption, it would have arrived at a conclusion different from the one which it in fact reached.[58] It would have been a conclusion the persuasive power of which would have been enhanced by the fact of its having taken into account evidence of the intention of the parties more tangible than exclusive reliance on the assumed natural meaning of the clause in question.

When in the *Lotus* case the Court applied, not for the first time, the doctrine of " plain meaning " by stating that " there is no occasion to have recourse to preparatory work when the text of a convention is sufficiently clear in itself," [59] it was apparent that the relevant provision of the treaty was not in fact clear either when standing by itself or even when viewed in the context of the Preamble and other articles of the Treaty of Lausanne. In laying down that questions of jurisdiction shall, as between Turkey and other Contracting Parties, be decided in accordance with the principles of international law, the treaty did not register a clear agreement of the parties on the subject. A study of the records of the Conference pointed conclusively to the different views held by Turkey and France in the matter. The expression " principles of international law " is not one which explains itself with automatic clarity. Neither, as the equal division of the Court showed, was it quite clear what were the principles of international law with regard to the particular problem before the Court. To say, therefore, that in this—and similar— cases the treaty is clear and that therefore no reference to other sources of evidence is required is to use a formula whose artificiality is only

---

[57] See pp. 134 *et seq.*

[58] For it is arguable that although the preparatory work of the San Francisco Conference revealed the disinclination of the majority of the original signatories of the Charter to deprive the Members of the United Nations of a substantial measure of freedom of action in admitting new Members, such freedom of action was quite consistent with the reply given by the majority of the Court to the question put to it: see p. 63 of the Opinion where the Court pointed to " the very wide and very elastic nature of the prescribed conditions " and to the fact that " no relevant political factor—that is to say, none connected with the conditions of admission—is excluded."

[59] Series A, No. 10 (1927), p. 16.

partly reduced by the circumstance that the Court in fact did proceed to examine other evidence of the intention of the parties. When, on the other hand, the formula of " plain meaning " is applied rigidly to the point of excluding evidence extraneous to the text, recourse to such a method is calculated to give rise to criticism.

It is too much to expect that in their legal argument, whether conducted in diplomatic correspondence or before arbitral or judicial tribunals, governments will abandon reliance on a doctrine so plausible —unless it receives at the hands of international tribunals a degree of discouragement which will make resort to it a source of weakness rather than of strength to the party relying upon it. Unlike parties to a controversy, international tribunals are in the position to keep within proper bounds a method which may not be conducive either to the effectiveness or, in the long run, the economy of the task of interpretation. In fact, it would be inaccurate to assume that the practice of international tribunals, taken in its entirety, supports the doctrine of " plain meaning." That doctrine, when fully acted upon, amounts to attaching decisive importance to the literal meaning of words. As such it may occasionally be contrary to the principle of good faith—a principle which is perhaps the only non-controversial canon of interpretation and which, lucidly expressed by Cicero, was fully approved by Grotius: *In fide quid senseris non quid dixeris cogitandum.*[60] International tribunals have often declined to act upon the plain or literal meaning of terms. It is sufficient to refer in this connection to the award in the case of the *Island of Timor,* given in 1913, between the Netherlands and Portugal [61] and other boundary disputes where tribunals refused to attach literal importance to terms and names used in treaties. In the *Chevreau* case, decided in 1930 between Great Britain and France, the arbitrator assumed jurisdiction as to one aspect of the dispute notwithstanding the fact that the plain terms of the *compromis* seemed to exclude it.[62] In the *Sarropoulos* case the Greco-Bulgarian Mixed Arbitral Tribunal held in 1927 that notwithstanding the clear wording of the Treaty of Neuilly it had no jurisdiction except with regard to claims directly connected with the war.[63] In the case of *Polyxene Plessa* v. *Turkish Government,* although Article 58 of the Treaty of Lausanne provided for the renunciation by all contracting Powers, except Greece, of pecuniary claims for loss and damage, the Tribunal held that notwithstanding the very plain wording of the Treaty, the study of the circumstances accompanying the conclusion of the Treaty and the *travaux préparatoires* led to the conclusion that that renunciation

[60] Book II, Chap. XVI, 1.
[61] Scott, *Hague Court Reports* (1916), pp. 355, 382.
[62] See award as printed in *American Journal of International Law,* 27 (1933), p. 176.
[63] *Annual Digest,* 1927–1928, Case No. 291.

applied to Greece also.[64]  In the *Ottoman Debt Arbitration*, with regard to an important aspect of the dispute, the arbitrator preferred what he believed to be the common intention of the parties to a literal interpretation of the Treaty of Lausanne.[65]  In the case of *Lederer* v. *German State* the Anglo-German Mixed Arbitral Tribunal held in 1923, in disregard of the literal and " clear " provision of Article 297 (*h*) of the Treaty of Versailles, that the proceeds of liquidation were not to be credited to the State of which the owner of the claim was a national.[66]

On the other hand, there will be found arbitral decisions which adopt with emphasis the doctrine of " plain meaning "—while at the same time combining it with the enunciation of one or more of the current rules of construction.  Thus in the Opinion of Parker, Umpire, in the *Lusitania* case, Vattel's " first principle "—" it is not allowable to interpret that which has no need of interpretation "—was given decisive weight.  The Umpire held that the " clear and unambiguous " language of the treaty did not authorise the imposition of penalties.  Moreover he insisted, after quoting Vattel, that " if it were competent for us to look to them " all of the other rules of interpretation would lead to the same result.  Of these rules he instanced two: The first was that as the Treaty was framed for the benefit of one party, namely, the United States, it must be " strictly construed against it."  The other was that treaty provisions must be so construed as best to conform to the accepted principles of international law rather than in derogation of them and that as " penal clauses in treaties are odious " they must be construed most strongly against those asserting them.[67]  In the *Georges Pinson* case, decided by the French-Mexican Mixed Claims Commission, a distinguished arbitrator fully committed himself in unequivocal terms to the doctrine of " plain meaning."  He said: " Inasmuch as the text of the Convention is clear in itself, there is no reason to appeal to alleged contrary intentions of its authors unless both parties concerned agree that the text does not cover their common intention." [68]  He amplified that statement by adding that " in so far as the text is not sufficiently clear, it is allowable to have recourse to the intentions of the parties concerned."  He then proceeded to enumerate a number of rules of interpretation.

The preceding considerations, it must be noted, are directed to the exaggerations of and the still widely followed leaning towards exclusive reliance on the doctrine of " plain meaning."  Their object is not to question its general justification and usefulness.  Any criticism of the

---

[64] " The exception in favour of Greece was calculated not so much to regulate legal interests as to take into account certain sentimental considerations." *Annual Digest*, 1927–1928, Case No. 299.

[65] *Ibid.*, 1925–1926, Case No. 270.

[66] *Recueil des Décisions des Tribunaux arbitraux mixtes*, 3 (1928), pp. 762, 769.

[67] *Decisions and Opinions* (1925), p. 31.          [68] *Annual Digest*, 1927–1928, Case No. 292.

tendency to attribute decisive authority to "plain meaning" must be tempered by the following two considerations: In the first instance, it would not be accurate to assert that the doctrine of "plain meaning" has been invariably resorted to as an artificial device for avoiding the more substantial task of eliciting the intention of the parties by means other than a speculative exercise in logical or grammatical interpretation. For the "plain meaning" of a treaty has often been relied upon as a method of defeating appeals to technical rules of interpretation of questionable usefulness and validity. Thus, on a number of occasions, when confronted with the argument that clauses imposing obligations must be interpreted restrictively, the Permanent Court of International Justice, while broadly conceding that principle, denied its applicability to cases in which the treaty is clear or in which its meaning cannot be ascertained by other means of interpretation.[69]

Secondly, in so far as the process of interpretation must start from *somewhere*, it is not unreasonable that it should begin with what appears to be the natural, the common, the "plain" meaning of the terms used. The fact that the plain meaning of a term may appear to one party to be the very opposite of what it appears to the other, warrants no conclusion of relativism in the matter; the same applies to the fact that the plain meaning of a term occasionally leads the majority and the minority of a court to diametrically opposed results. For the purpose of administration of justice words must be deemed—at least as a starting point of the judicial process—to have a meaning of their own. It is therefore legitimate to insist, in the interest of good faith and of a requisite minimum of certainty in legal transactions, that the burden of proof should rest upon the party asserting that the term in question is used not in its ordinary but in an unusual connotation or that the "clear meaning" is not what on the face of it it appears to be.

At the same time that burden of proof must not be so exacting or rendered so onerous by technical rules of construction as to give the complexion of finality to what ought to be no more than a starting point or as to relieve the Court of its own duty of investigating the true intention of the parties. Occasionally, the Permanent Court of International Justice showed an appreciation of the relativity of natural meaning of words. Thus, while in the case concerning the *Legal Status of Greenland* the Court started from the proposition that the expression "Greenland" used by the contracting Parties referred to the geographical meaning of the term as shown in the maps, it added that that fact did not exclude the possibility that that expression was used in some special sense. But, the Court said, the burden of proof that this was so rested

[69] See below, pp. 300 *et seq*.

upon Norway to show that in the treaties in question the term " Greenland " meant only the colonised area.[70]   In its Advisory Opinion on the *Employment of Women during the Night* it found the provisions of the relevant Article of the Convention, in so far as it applied to " women without distinction of age," to be " general in [their] terms and free from ambiguity."   But it did not on that account exclude the possibility that notwithstanding the generality of the terms used the Convention did not apply to some categories of women.   In that case, however, " it is necessary to find some valid ground for interpreting the provision otherwise than in accordance with the natural sense of the words." [71]   In the award of the British-American Claims Arbitral Tribunal in the case of *The David J. Adams* the Tribunal found, not unnaturally, that the provision admitting American fishermen for certain enumerated purposes and " for no other purposes whatever " was " perfectly clear."   But it did not rule out on that account the possibility of " sufficient evidence of contrary intention of the High Contracting Parties . . . to contradict such a clear meaning." [72]   It examined the evidence produced, including that of preparatory work, and found that it did not call for a derogation from the literal meaning of the treaty.

While the apparent degree of clarity must supply the measure of the degree of exactness of the proof required for displacing the initial presumptions of plain meaning, no apparent amount of clarity provides a sufficient justification for ruling out an independent investigation of intention.   Plain meaning may be treated as rebuttable *presumptio juris.* It ought not to be regarded as an irrefutable *presumptio juris et de jure.* External evidence or considerations based on inquiry into the purpose of the treaty may on occasions be more decisively illuminating than processes of logic operating by interpretation through analogy, by textual comparison with other parts of the treaty, or even by means of such apparently unassailable rules as *expressio unius est exclusio alterius.*

At the same time, the doctrine of " plain meaning " properly understood may be of pronounced helpfulness in the matter of interpretation of technical terms.   Treaties are legal documents which as a rule are drawn up by legal experts or by persons availing themselves of legal advice.   In view of this it must be assumed that whenever parties have

---

[70] Series A/B, No. 53 (1933), p. 52.

[71] Series A/B, No. 50 (1932), p. 373.

[72] *American Journal of International Law,* 16 (1922), p. 315.   In *The Francisca* Dr. Lushington expressed himself in the following way: " I apprehend that I must first look to the articles themselves, and if the meaning intended to be expressed is clear, I am not at liberty to go further " (1855) Sp.Pr.Cas. 111, 151.   In *The Ionian Ships* the same Judge said: " . . . terms, however strong and clear in themselves, whatever meaning may be attributed—necessarily attributed—to them standing alone, may be modified by other parts of the same instrument " (*ibid.,* 193, 198).   Both cases are referred to in McNair, *op. cit.,* pp. 184 and 198, respectively.

recourse to terms which in legal terminology have an accepted connotation, they intend to use them in their technical, that is to say, in their ordinary legal meaning. This is a presumption which can be rebutted by cogent considerations as was the case in the Advisory Opinion of the Permanent Court of International Justice in the matter of the *Interpretation of the Greco-Turkish Agreement* where the Court held that the term "arbitration" employed in the Final Protocol was not used in its ordinary technical meaning.[73] However, in the absence of such proof to the contrary, technical terms must be deemed to have been resorted to as such. Thus, for instance, the term "intervention" in Article 2 (7) of the Charter of the United Nations must probably be considered to refer to intervention in its technical sense as distinguished from the popular notion of interference through discussion or other demonstration of interest not accompanied by compulsion or a threat of compulsion or a claim to compliance conceived as a legal duty.[74] Similarly, the term "lease" when used in a treaty is a lease and not a vague expression intended to conceal an outright annexation of territory. So also the terms "mandate" or "trust" are technical terms expressive of the idea of tutelage and delegation of powers incompatible, among others, with the full sovereignty of the mandatory or trustee over the territory concerned. On occasions, as in the latter case, the technical meaning coincides to a large extent with its popular understanding. Failing that, it is the technical connotation of the term which supplies the accurate standard of interpretation. For the lawyer that technical connotation must be identical with the ordinary legal meaning of the term.[75]

---

[73] Series B, No. 16 (1928), p. 22.

[74] See Oppenheim, *International Law*, vol. I (8th ed., 1955), § 168f.

[75] This note is based substantially on one part of a report on the interpretation of treaties submitted by the writer to the Institute of International Law: *Annuaire*, 43 (1950) (i), pp. 377–390. In 1956 the Institute adopted a Resolution which is in accordance with the views put forward in the report and in the present note. The Resolution lays down, in Art. 1, that " as the agreement of the parties is given effect in the text of the treaty, it is necessary to take as the basis of interpretation the natural and ordinary sense of the terms of the text." That general statement is qualified by the principle that " the provisions of the treaty must be interpreted in its entire context, according to good faith and in the light of the principles of international law." There follows the further and decisive qualification: " However, if it is established that the terms used ought to be understood in a different sense, the natural and ordinary sense must be discarded." The second Article proceeds to elaborate that decisive qualification in the following manner:

   " 1. In case of a dispute brought before an international jurisdiction, it is for the tribunal to appreciate, having regard to the provisions of the first article, whether and to what extent recourse is to be had to other means of interpretation.

   2. These legitimate means of interpretation include:

      (a) recourse to preparatory work;

      (b) the practice followed in the actual application of the treaty;

      (c) the consideration of the object of the treaty."

CHAPTER 4

# JUDICIAL TECHNIQUE AND THE DEVELOPMENT
# OF THE LAW

## 20. *The Law behind the Legal Rule*

The instances commented upon in the preceding Sections and pointing to the problems arising out of the reliance upon the natural meaning of words or other factors making for economy of exposition are not typical of the method of the Court. They ought not to be allowed to obscure the significance of its positive contribution to the clarification and the development of international law. In general, the Court has examined, with exacting care, the issues raised by the parties in their pleadings so far as this has been necessary for explaining its decisions. This it has done even if the Judgment or Opinion could be made to rest on a narrower ground than that actually adopted. It is not conducive to clarity to apply to the work of the Court the supposedly rigid delimitation between *obiter dicta* and *ratio decidendi* applicable to a legal system based on the strict doctrine of precedent.[1] We might otherwise find ourselves compelled to maintain that the two Orders in the *Free Zones* case,[2] which decided important points of law, were mere *obiter dicta* in the form of Orders excluding provisionally as evidence a publication filed by the Swiss Government and laying down certain time limits.[3] There are, as we shall see, urgent considerations of judicial caution of which the Court is aware and which have caused it to refrain from indulging in academic disquisitions and redundant expressions of opinion on controversial matters.[4] However, these considerations have not prevented it, in numerous cases, from examining with thoroughness the pleadings of the parties and thus fulfilling at the same time a task of an importance transcending the issue directly before it.

---

[1] See Goodhart, "Determining the *ratio decidendi* of a Case," in *Essays in Jurisprudence and the Common Law* (1931).
[2] Series A, Nos. 22 (1929) and 24 (1930).
[3] See below, p. 236.
[4] See below, pp. 75 *et seq*.

These cases suggest that it is proper to search not only for the law behind the cases decided by the Court, but also for the wider legal principle behind the legal rules authoritatively laid down by it. The actual decision or Opinion of the Court is, obviously, of considerable authority. This is so although according to Article 59 of the Statute the Judgments of the Court are binding only for the case which they decide, although Advisory Opinions are not binding at all, and although the pronouncements of the Court, even if unanimous or approaching unanimity, are a legitimate object of scientific scrutiny.[5] Undoubtedly, so long as the Court itself has not overruled its former pronouncement or so long as States have not, by a treaty of a general character, adopted a different formulation of the law, the ruling formally given by the Court on any question of international law must be considered as having settled, for the time being, the particular question at issue. Yet this result, and the settlement of a particular dispute, are not the only outcome of a decision of the Court. What is almost equally important is that the reasoning of the Court, often as illuminated by the separate —concurring or dissenting—Opinions of individual Judges, sheds an instructive ray of light on the legal problem involved and, often, on some fundamental issues of international law and that it provides the material for a better comprehension of the Judgments and Opinions of the Court.

### 21. *The Method of Judicial Pronouncements*

The two tendencies, analysed in the preceding Sections, in the technique of judicial pronouncements—the tendency to compression and the insistence upon a detailed examination and elaboration of the issue involved—are expressive of the fact that the method of forming and expressing the Judgments and Opinions of the Court is, in turn, in the nature of a compromise between two traditions of the judicial process. According to the method of exposition customary in some

---

[5] From this point of view the authority of a pronouncement of the Court is not necessarily due to any irrefutable excellence of its ruling or its necessary superiority over the view of the minority. Who can maintain, with emphatic assurance, that the legal merits of the views of the majority of the Court in the *Lotus* case, in the *Customs Union* case, and, possibly, in various other cases, are indisputably superior to those of the minority? The presumption—a legitimate and working presumption—is that they are so superior. However, for the purpose of scientific criticism and the development of the law—as distinguished from the legally binding force of these pronouncements—this is only a presumption, and no impropriety attaches to examining its substantive soundness and applicability. See below, pp. 395 *et seq.*

countries, judgments of courts are so phrased that they are intelligible —and, in a distinct sense, instructive and attractive—not only to the expert annotator and practitioner, but also to the layman. In those countries judgments of courts are as a rule not a mere product of formal reasoning from abstract principles or concrete legal rules; they draw freely upon available precedent and other authority in a manner which lifts the administration of the law from the orbit of a technical discipline. This is so in contradistinction to the more formal methods of judicial reasoning adopted, for instance, in France. Reasons have been given in this chapter why, having regard to the conditions in which international justice is administered, the former method is particularly appropriate for the performance of the international judicial function.

Secondly, the practice of the Court—as well as its Statute and Rules—are in the nature of a compromise between the method, followed in some countries, of an anonymous collective pronouncement and that of decisions delivered in a manner clearly revealing the attitude adopted by every individual Judge. With regard to the latter it is only seldom that the insistence on the indication of the attitude of individual Judges assumes the complexion of the requirement that every member of the tribunal is bound to deliver a judgment of his own.[6] As a rule,[7] the attitude of the individual Judges of the International Court is shown—and that is the usual practice—by the express indication, in the published report, of dissent whether accompanied by a Dissenting Opinion or not.

## 22. *Collective Formulation of the Pronouncements of the Court*

It is convenient in this connection to reproduce the Resolution adopted by the Court in 1931 and revised in 1936 concerning its practice on the subject. That Resolution, which reveals the intention to secure meticulous care in the preparation of the Judgments and Opinions of the Court, reads as follows:

" 1. After the termination of the written proceedings and before the beginning of the hearing, the judges meet in private to exchange views with regard to the elements of the written proceedings and to

---

[6] For a survey of the practice of some countries in this respect see McWhinney in *Canadian Bar Review*, No. 6 (1953), pp. 595–620.

[7] This is not the invariable rule. For it is not necessary for a Judge who casts his vote against the Judgment or Opinion to be delivered by the Court, to indicate expressly his dissent in the report as published.

bring out any points in regard to which it may be necessary to call for supplementary verbal explanations.

2. After the hearing, a period of time proportionate to the nature of the case is allowed to judges in order that they may study the oral arguments of the parties.

3. At the expiration of this time, a deliberation is held, under the direction of the President, for the purpose of collectively examining the case as it presents itself after the hearing, bringing out the questions to be solved and discussing them severally. The President ensures that all questions called to notice either by himself or by the judges have been discussed and that each judge has made known his impressions in regard to them.

4. At a suitable interval of time after this deliberation, each judge expresses his personal view in writing in the form of a note, without committing himself to a definite opinion.

5. On the basis of the notes of each judge, the President prepares and submits to the Court for consideration a plan of discussion provisionally determining the order and the terms of the questions on which the Court must give its opinion.

The adoption of this plan affects neither the right of judges, at any stage in the deliberation, to call upon the Court to express its opinion upon any question or in any form which they may consider desirable, nor the freedom of the Court itself subsequently to modify as it may see fit the order of its discussion and the terms of the questions.

6. At a subsequent and final deliberation each question is discussed, put to the vote by the President and decided.

7. On the basis of the votes cast by the majority of judges at the final deliberation, the preparation of a draft decision is entrusted to a committee consisting of the President and of two judges chosen by the Court by secret ballot and by an absolute majority of votes.

8. A preliminary draft of the decision is circulated to the judges, who may submit amendments in writing. When these amendments have been received, the Committee submits a draft decision for discussion by the Court.

Judges who wish to deliver a separate or dissenting opinion shall hand in the text thereof after the adoption of the draft decision in first reading and before the draft of the decision as prepared for second reading has been circulated." [8]

---

[8] The Resolution, which is not formally part of the Rules of the Court, was originally adopted in 1931 and then revised in 1936 (Series D, No. 1 (4th ed.), p. 62). In 1946 it was provisionally adopted by the International Court of Justice: see Series D, No. 1 (May, 1947), where it is annexed, on p. 63, as a footnote to Art. 30 of the Rules. It

The salient feature, in connection with the present discussion, of this procedure is the fact of the collective formulation of the decisions of the Court. That formulation is collective in the sense that the Judgments or Opinions are first drafted by a Committee and that the Judgment or Opinion as eventually formulated is the result of a prolonged collective effort of the Court as a whole. It would thus appear that the Judgments and Opinions of the Court are collective not only in the formal sense that the eventual pronouncement represents the view of the Court as a whole (or of its majority), but also in the manner of its evolution and its final formulation. The process here is different from, for example, the preparation of the judgments of the Supreme Court of the United States, where the decision, although being the decision of the Court delivered on its behalf and although influenced by its internal deliberations and the advice of the members of the Court, is nevertheless the product of the work of one member of the Court—a product which may bear the impress of unity associated with the intellectual effort of a single individual.

The method, adopted by the Permanent Court of International Justice, of collective elaboration and formulation of Judgments and Advisory Opinions has been followed by the International Court of Justice. It does not form part either of the Statute or of the Rules of the Court. As such it partakes of a pronounced degree of flexibility which, in particular cases, may alleviate any shortcomings inherent in the method of collective drafting. These shortcomings cannot be commented upon in the present context. They are, in some measure, counterbalanced by compensatory advantages. Thus the collective method of formulating the pronouncements of the Court provides a means of reconciling legitimate diversities of judicial outlook. In particular, almost up to the final moment in which the views of the Court as a whole and of individual Judges are reduced to print there is, because of collective deliberation, an opportunity of examining and answering the opposing opinions and of modifying, under the impact of argument, the views previously expressed.

was commented upon by A. Hammarskjöld, then Registrar of the Court, in *Michigan Law Review*, 1927 (reprinted in his collected works published in 1938 under the title *La Juridiction Internationale*, pp. 69 *et seq.*); Hudson, *The Permanent Court of International Justice 1920–1942* (1943), pp. 579–582; and Hambro in *Current Legal Problems*, 1954, pp. 218–222.

Inevitably, Judges who subscribe to the pronouncement as a whole cannot always hope to find in the final decision of the Court an exact approximation to all their individual views. These can properly be given expression through Separate Opinions.

### 23. *Individual Opinions. Dissenting and Separate*

The Statute of the Court in making express provision for the right of Judges to append dissenting or separate opinions made, in a variety of ways, a beneficent contribution to the development of international law and the authority of international justice. Experience has shown that so long as it is clear that the decision of the Court is, within its proper limits, binding and authoritative, the individual Opinions of the Judges, far from detracting from the standing of the Judgments or Advisory Opinions, add to their vitality, comprehension and usefulness and greatly facilitate the fulfilment of the indirect purpose of the Court, which is to develop and to clarify international law. It is improbable that such disagreement, expressed in terms of moderation and restraint, impairs the authority of the Court.[9] Undoubtedly, a dissent—whether partial or complete—may, in proportion to its intrinsic merit, impair in some measure the substantive as distinguished from the formal authority of the decision of the Court. But, then, if the dissent is in part expressive of better law or of a better judicial method, no lasting harm need ensue from the fact that the substantive authority of the Court's decision may be to that extent impaired. It would be prejudicial to the cause of international justice to assume that the weight of the Court's decisions is irrefutably entrenched behind its formal authority. From that point of view a judicial dissent is not only an appeal to enlightened and informed legal opinion.[10] It is, indirectly, a powerful stimulus to the maximum

[9] But see the Observations of Judge Hudson in *American Journal of International Law*, 44 (1950), pp. 18–21.

[10] A Chief Justice of the Supreme Court, who was also a member of the International Court, has given clear expression to this purpose of dissenting opinions: " A dissent in a court of last resort is an appeal to the brooding spirit of the law, to the intelligence of a future day, when a later decision may possibly correct the error into which the dissenting judge believes the court to have been betrayed " (Charles Evans Hughes, *The Supreme Court of the United States* (1928), p. 68). Another distinguished member of that Tribunal has said: " Divisions on the Court and the greater clarity of view and candour of expression to which they give rise, are especially productive of insight " (Frankfurther, *The Commerce Clause* (1937), p. 9). For a defence of dissenting opinions by Chief Justice Vinson, see also 69 S.Ct. ix–xi. And see Pritchett, *Civil Liberties and the Vinson Court* (1954), p. 21. See, on the other hand, Jackson, *op. cit.* below (on p. 70), p. 17.

effort of which a tribunal is capable. For no formal authority can in the long run shield a defective decision from the impact, in proportion to its merits, of a dissent. Mere dissent cannot weaken the authority of the decision. The merits of the dissent may have that effect. On the other hand, if the dissent is one-sided or extravagant, it will add emphasis to the balance and the restraint of the decision of the Court.

Admittedly, the right of expressing judicial dissent is not an institution of general application. In some countries, such as Belgium, France and Germany, only one judgment is delivered and there is no indication whether the judgment is given unanimously or by majority.[11] Apparently, although the judgment may at times include the names of the judges composing the tribunal, anonymity is there regarded as a safeguard of the independence of the Judges. However that may be, the Statute of the Court has not adopted that method. The independence of the Judges is safeguarded by other means which may or may not call for expansion.[12] It is arguable that, in some cases, the independence and impartiality of the Judges may be safeguarded by anonymity inasmuch as they may be free to vote without regard to the attitude of the States of which they are nationals. Any such argument, which is of controversial validity,[13] is of limited significance when related to the considerations, outlined above, connected with the necessity of ensuring completeness of the reasoning of the Judgments and Opinions of the Court. Dissenting and Separate Opinions—and the possibility of their being given—act as a stimulus in that direction.

Undoubtedly, the object of preventing anonymity could be achieved by mere indication of dissent not accompanied by a detailed explanation of the dissent. But a bare dissent, unaccompanied by reasons, is of no greater value than a decision without

[11] Occasionally anonymity is capable of a different explanation, as in the case of the Judgments—Opinions—of the British Judicial Committee of the Privy Council which, formally, are in the nature of advice tendered to the Crown. In Switzerland the vote is taken in public. See, for a useful survey and discussion of the question, Hambro in *Zeitschrift für ausländisches und öffentliches Recht und Völkerrecht*, 17 (1956), pp. 229–248.

[12] Art. 18 of the Statute provides that a member of the Court may be deprived of his office only by an unanimous vote of the other Judges if he has ceased to fulfil the required conditions. The Institute of International Law has suggested, in a Resolution adopted in 1954, that, with the view to obviating the necessity of re-election and to increasing the independence of Judges, they should be elected for a period of fifteen years (*Annuaire*, 45 (ii) (1954), p. 297).

[13] For it may be contended that anonymity would enable a Judge to vote invariably in support of the cause of his State without incurring the odium of partisanship.

reasons; it presumes to substitute the authority of the individual Judge for the strength of the argument underlying the dissent. The very appearance of any such claim is open to objection. This was probably one of the reasons why the Informal Inter-Allied Committee which in 1944 prepared a Report on the Future of the Permanent Court of International Justice proposed a change in the Statute of the Court in the sense that " it should be obligatory on any Judge who dissents from the majority to state his reasons for so doing." [14]   To have limited the right of expressing dissent to a mere indication of dissent would, in effect, have frustrated the right of dissent.   Such limitation would hardly meet what is an ever present need in the administration of justice generally and international justice in particular—the need to develop the law and to give a picture of any cleavage of opinion on basic issues.   These considerations explain the growing recognition of the justification of Dissenting and Separate Opinions.[15]   Recurrent suggestions for limiting or abolishing that right have been decisively—and, it appears, unanimously—rejected.

In addition, apart from factors connected with the development of international law, a system which makes it possible for members of the Court to indicate their dissent from the decisions as a whole or some of its aspects and to give reasons for their dissent, has come to be regarded as a safeguard of the individual responsibility of the Judges as well as of the integrity of the Court as an institution.   In a

---

[14] *A.J.*, 38 (1954), Suppl., p. 26; Misc. No. 2 (1944), Cmd. 6531, p. 24.

[15] The following passage from the Report of the Informal Inter-Allied Committee (see the text above, p. 68) may be quoted: " From the point of view of the development of international law, dissenting judgments are also of value.   They act as a useful commentary on the decisions of the Court itself, the precise point and bearing of which is often brought out more strongly in the light of the dissenting judgments.   In addition, the latter often clarify subsidiary points of interest and importance which are not dealt with in the judgment of the Court because not directly necessary for the purpose of its findings " (*loc. cit.*).   When in 1929 the League of Nations Committee for the Revision of the Statute of the Court discussed the question of dissenting opinions, M. Politis stated that although at the time of the drafting of the Statute he had hesitation about accepting the Anglo-Saxon system of permitting dissenting opinions, he had since changed his views in the light of actual experience—" so much so that if, by chance, representatives of the Anglo-Saxon countries were to ask for their suppression, he would feel obliged to oppose the suggestion, because, in his view, those opinions were of immense advantage to international law " (*Minutes of the Committee*, League Doc. C.166.M.66.1929.V., p. 51).   There certainly was no disposition on the part of the Anglo-Saxon countries to propose the abandonment of the system.   Sir Cecil Hurst described a proposal to that effect, made by M. Fromageot, as calculated " to destroy the Court " (at p. 50).   Mr. Elihu Root expressed the view that the suppression of the existing system would be " disastrous " (p. 51).   M. Fromageot then withdrew his proposal.

tribunal which, by reason of the circumstances encompassing its activity, is exposed to imputations of influence of extraneous considerations, a system such as that actually adopted in the Statute of the Court in the matter of Dissenting Opinions and fully operative in the practice of the Court, constitutes a powerful safeguard. It precludes any charge of reliance on mere alignment of voting and lifts the pronouncements of the Court to the level of the inherent power of legal reason and reasoning.[16]

Similar considerations apply to concurring or separate Opinions, which amplify the Judgment or Opinion of the Court, which dissent from some of its reasoning, or which choose a different path for arriving at the same conclusion. The Statute of the Court attaches importance to the requirement that in the Court as a whole " the representation of the main forms of civilisation and of the principal legal systems of the world should be assured." [17] One of the purposes of that provision would be frustrated if that diversity of approach could find expression only in the deliberations of the Court or in the common denominator of the collective decision. From this point of view it may be difficult to name a case in which an individual Opinion has not been of some interest and which, at least indirectly, has not assisted towards a better understanding of the decision of the Court.[18]

The important part played by dissenting and separate Opinions in the activity of the Court is not impaired by the fact that, like any other contrivance of human institutions, they may raise issues of some difficulty. This might happen, for instance, if they were to impair the effort, which ought to be sustained and deliberate, to arrive at a common view of the Court. There is an element of ostensible exaggeration in the suggestion that a separate or dissenting Opinion is no more than a confession of a failure to convince the

---

[16] Dr. Max Huber, a former President of the Court, writing in 1956 says: " I would have hardly decided to accept office as Judge if the Statute had not taken over the Anglo-Saxon system of dissenting opinions . . ." (from an article entitled " Koexistenz und Gemeinschaft " in *Züricher Student*, 1956, No. 3). Speaking in 1929 before the League of Nations Committee on the Revision of the Statute, he said that " the possibility of publication [of dissenting opinions] was a guarantee against any subconscious intrusion of political considerations, and that judgments were more likely to be given in accordance with the real force of the arguments submitted." He added that " it was essential to retain the right of individual Judges to publish their views " and that " this right was an essential condition for the exercise of their [the Judges'] liberty of conscience and their impartiality " (*loc. cit.*, p. 52).          [17] Art. 10.

[18] See the observations of Sir Gerald Fitzmaurice in *British Year Book of International Law*, 27 (1950), pp. 1, 2.

majority of the Court.[19]  Yet it is an aspect of the problem which must be borne in mind.  There is force in the view that there ought to be exhausted the reasonable possibilities of bringing about a collective expression of the views of the Court as an institution instead of allowing its activity to assume the complexion of a series of essays by individual Judges.  However, once these possibilities have been exhausted, there must be admitted the necessity and the justification of individual expressions of view whenever members of the Court deem it their duty to make a contribution of this kind.  The degree of their intrinsic merit will determine in every case the permanence of their place in the development of international law and in the comprehension of the decisions of the Court.

### 24. *The Law behind the Cases and the Place of the Court in International Society*

The problem of judicial technique in the activity of the Court is of sufficient importance to justify the amount of space which has been devoted to it in this chapter.  The potency of ideas is in direct proportion to the efficacy of the means employed in their realisation.  The contribution of the Court to the development of international law and its ultimate effectiveness as an instrument of peace depend to a substantial extent upon the technique of its pronouncements.  This includes the question of the method calculated to secure the requisite degree of completeness of exposition in its Judgments and Opinions.

Any criticism of this aspect of the work of the Court may, if attempted in isolation, obscure and distort the picture of its positive contribution.  For the comprehensiveness and elaboration of many of its decisions have—independently of the fulfilment of its primary object of deciding disputes on the basis of law—proved a notable factor in developing international law.  In an international society in which the jurisdiction of " the principal judicial organ " of the United Nations is of a voluntary character, the opportunities for exercising the jurisdiction of the Court are limited in number.  In cases in which such jurisdiction is exercised the importance of the subject-matter of the Judgment or of the Opinion of the Court is often of a distinctly limited character from the point of view of the

---

[19] See, *e.g.*, Jackson, *The Supreme Court in the American System of Government* (1955), p. 19. Yet Mr. Justice Jackson was a frequent and powerful dissenter of considerable pungency of expression.

political or economic interests involved. Such lasting value as the activity of the Court may have in such cases lies in the potential importance of its contribution to international law; it lies in the law behind the cases. It is in that contribution that the significance of the Court rises sovereign over any disillusionment on account of its lacking power as an agency in securing the rule of law in matters that matter. That contribution can be—and has been—presented systematically.[20] It has now grown in volume to such an extent as to enable us to deduce from it lessons throwing light on some central problems of the international judicial process. These problems it is proposed to examine in the succeeding chapters. In particular, in the next chapter we shall inquire to what extent judicial caution, which is an enduring and legitimate characteristic of the judicial process, has prevented—or ought to prevent—the Court from playing an even more conscious and creative part in the development of international law.

---

[20] See, in particular, the penetrating articles by Fitzmaurice in *British Year Book of International Law* for 1950 and the following years. See also, for a systematic digest of the decisions of the Court, Hambro, *The Case Law of the International Court* (1952). And see the first edition of the present book under the title *The Development of International Law by the Permanent Court of International Justice* (1934); Becket in *Hague Recueil*, 39 (1932) (i), pp. 135–269 and 50 (1934) (iv), pp. 193–305; Salvioli, *ibid.* (1926) (ii), pp. 1–114; Bastid, *ibid.*, 78 (1951) (i), pp. 571–681; Sørensen, *op. cit.*, pp. 153–190; Watrin in *Revue de droit international* (Paris), 8 (1931), pp. 161–219; Dehousse, *ibid.*, 17 (1936), pp. 85–117; and the extensive literature on the subject cited in Oppenheim's *International Law*, vol. II (7th ed., 1952), p. 70, n. 2. See also the successive editions of Dr. Schwarzenberger's *International Law*: vol. I, *International Law as Applied by International Courts and Tribunals* (first published in 1945), in which the contribution made by the International Court to the development of international law is treated in much detail and against the background of awards of international arbitral tribunals.

PART TWO

JUDICIAL CAUTION

# Chapter 5

# MANIFESTATIONS OF JUDICIAL CAUTION

## 25. *Reasons for Caution*

Judicial caution is an attitude of mind resulting, in addition to ordinary counsels of prudence, from the fact that courts have to *apply* the law and that they have to apply the *law in force*. They have to apply—and no more than that—the law. It is not within their province to speculate on the law or to explore the possibilities of its development. This does not mean that their judgments must be limited to the barest minimum which is required for the decision. Reasons have been given in the preceding chapter why it is essential for the proper fulfilment of the judicial function, and of the international judicial function in particular, that the decisions of courts should give a full account of the law which they apply as well as of the grounds on which they are based, and that they should examine in all requisite detail the contentions put forward by the parties— even though, in some cases, such examination is not essential to the operative part of the pronouncement. Neither can the avoidance of mere speculation supply a legitimate reason for disdaining any desirable exposition of legal principle. However, once that admittedly comprehensive duty has been fulfilled, there is room for following the precepts of judicial caution.

Secondly, courts have to apply the law in force. It is not their function deliberately to change the law so as to make it conform with their own views of justice and expediency. This does not mean that they do not in fact shape or even alter the law. But they do it without admitting it; they do it while guided at the same time by existing law; they do it while remembering that stability and uncertainty are no less of the essence of the law than justice; they do it, in a word, with caution. The same considerations apply to the administration of international justice. Moreover, there exist in this sphere additional reasons for the exercise of restraint. These include, in the first instance, the importance of the subject-matter on which courts have to decide. They cannot experiment or innovate as easily in matters in which States have an interest as in those in which private individuals are concerned. If Governments are not prepared to entrust with legislative functions bodies composed of their authorised representatives, they will not be prepared to allow or tolerate the exercise of such activity by a tribunal enjoined by its Statute to apply the existing law.

With this is connected a further reason for restraint and caution in the international sphere, namely, the fact of the voluntary nature of the jurisdiction of international tribunals. An international court which yields conspicuously to the urge to modify the existing law —even if such action can be brought within the four corners of a major legal principle—may bring about a drastic curtailment of its activity. Governments may refuse to submit disputes to it or to renew obligations of compulsory judicial settlement already in existence.

There is, finally, to be considered the fact that in the international sphere there is no certainty of compulsory execution of the judgments rendered by an international court [1]—a circumstance which imposes a duty of particular restraint in order to remove any justification of the plausible, although rightly discredited, allegation that there has taken place an excess of jurisdiction and a usurpation of powers.[2]

---

[1] It will be noted that in this respect the provisions of Art. 94 of the Charter of the United Nations are even more restrained than the corresponding Art. 12 of the Covenant of the League. See above, p. 41.

[2] In the only recorded case of a failure of a State to comply with a Judgment of the Court—in the *Corfu Channel* case—the attitude of the Government concerned, in so far as it was based on legal grounds at all, seems to have been due to the allegation that the Court exceeded the jurisdiction conferred upon it in the *compromis* (see below, p. 247).

There is one aspect, of minor importance and lying within the domain of form rather than of substance, of the activity of international tribunals which calls for a higher degree of caution than one expects from municipal tribunals. In municipal law judges are as a rule protected from legal proceedings in respect of anything said by them during the trial. They need not consider the dignity and susceptibilities of the parties. On the other hand, circumstances impose upon an international judge a large measure of punctilious restraint. The award of the Arbitrator in the *Norwegian Shipowners Claims* case between Norway and the United States (see above, p. 39) exposed him to criticism on the ground that he ventured to question as arbitrary and unwarranted some actions of the United States authorities. The award of the Arbitrator in the *Naulilaa* case between Portugal and Germany was liable to criticism on account of the finding that the Portuguese troops withdrew before the German detachment which invaded the Portuguese colony as a measure of reprisals, " although there was no pressure on the part of the German troops " (*Annual Digest*, 1927–1928, Case No. 179). It will be noted that the Arbitrator disclaimed any intention to criticise the decision of the Portuguese commander from the military point of view. With this we may compare the studious courtesy of the report of the Dogger Bank Commission of Inquiry of 1904 which, after having found in fact that the action of the Russian admiral in command of the fleet was a strategic blunder and disregarded the rules of

At the same time, the necessity for bold judicial action is particularly great in the international sphere, *i.e.,* in a system of law in which legislative opportunities for modifying rigid, unjust and obsolete rules are somewhat nominal. The result of the clash of these conflicting tendencies is not without interest. It shows itself in both the tendency to caution and the apparent desire to create the appearance of caution. The latter has manifested itself even in those cases in which the Court has in fact shown a clear departure from the orthodox view—such as in its Opinion on the question of the unanimity rule in the Covenant of the League of Nations [3] or on the capacity of individuals to derive rights from a treaty.[4] In fact, in some of these cases it is the Court's cautious manner rather than the boldness of its practice that has, at first sight, impressed the reader of its pronouncements.

## 26. *Judicial Limitation of the Scope of the Decision*

The tendency to caution in the work of the Court has expressed itself, in the first instance, in the disinclination to make pronouncements on questions not essential to an exhaustive examination of the contentions of the parties [5] and, generally, in avoiding so far as possible a dogmatic manner in the statement of the law. Where but little practical advantage can be derived from deciding a controversial and somewhat academic point, the Court has been careful not to commit itself to a definite opinion. Thus, in the *Wimbledon* case it steered clear of the question of international servitudes. It said: " The Court is not called upon to take a definite attitude with regard to the question, which is moreover of a very controversial nature, whether in the domain of international law there really exist servitudes analogous to servitudes in private law." [6] The argument, urged by Germany, of restrictive interpretation in case of doubt could, in the view of the Court, be conceded—if it could be

---

humanity, added a rider to the effect that the report cast no aspersion on the military ability or the humanity of the commanding admiral. In holding, in the *Asylum* case, that the grant of asylum by the Colombian Ambassador to a Peruvian revolutionary was not warranted by the terms of the relevant Treaty (see below, p. 142), the Court gave detailed reasons why its finding implied " no criticism of the Ambassador of Colombia " (*I.C.J. Reports* 1950, p. 287). And see below, pp. 374–377.

[3] See below, p. 199.
[4] See below, p. 173.
[5] See below, p. 79.
[6] Series A, No. 1 (1923), p. 24.

conceded at all [7]—on other, more general, grounds.  In the case of
the *Chorzów Factory* it declined to express a view as to how far a
particular kind of injunction proper in relation to individuals and
requested by Germany could be issued at all against a Government.[8]
In the case concerning *Railway Traffic between Lithuania and
Poland* it refused to pronounce on the effect of Article 23 (*e*) of the
Covenant of the League of Nations [9] in regard to a State refusing
to establish any communication with another State even if it had not
signed any convention prescribing freedom of communications and
transit.[10]  The Court was careful " to emphasise that the present
Opinion is not to be construed as giving any view in regard to the
opinion expressed on behalf of the Advisory and Technical Committee to the effect that, by the terms of Article 23 (*e*), ' the Members
of the League have certainly the right to request any Members at
least to refrain from acting in opposition to the objects of this
article.' " [11]   In the *Lighthouses* case between France and Greece
the parties argued at length whether according to general rules of
international law the territorial sovereign is entitled to grant in
occupied territory concessions legally enforceable against the State
which subsequently acquires the territories occupied by it.   The
Court considered it unnecessary to answer that point.  It found that
the relevant provisions of the Treaty of Lausanne contained a clear
—and affirmative—answer to the question whether the successor
State (in this case, Greece) was subrogated to its predecessor as
regards a concessionary contract entered into with the Ottoman
Government prior to 1914.[12]

In the case concerning *Polish Agrarian Reform and the German
Minority* the Court, after having held in its Order that the application for provisional measures of protection could not be granted
for the reason that if granted it would result in a general suspen-
sion of the agrarian reform in so far as Polish nationals were

[7] See below, p. 303.

[8] Series A, No. 17 (1928), p. 59.

[9] Which provided that Members of the League " will make provision to secure and
maintain freedom of communications and of transit and equitable treatment for the
commerce of all Members of the League."

[10] Series A/B, No. 42 (1931), p. 119.

[11] *Ibid*.  See also Series A, No. 2 (1924) (*Mavrommatis Palestine Concessions*), p. 33, for a
refusal to pronounce on a hypothetical contingency.  And see Series B, No. 4 (1923)
(*Tunis and Morocco Nationality Decrees*), p. 22, and Series B, No. 13 (1926) (*Competence of the International Labour Organisation*), p. 12.

[12] Series A/B, No. 62 (1934), p. 25.

concerned,[13] found it unnecessary to consider the two wider questions which arose in this connection. The first was whether a member of the Council of the League of Nations who has recourse to the Court in the exercise of his right of protection by virtue of the Minorities Treaty, is entitled to apply for provisional measures.[14] The second was the extent to which the Court is entitled to indicate measures of protection *proprio motu*. In the case of *United States Nationals in Morocco* the Court arrived at the conclusion that it must reject the French submission relating to discrimination in favour of imports from France and alleged to be justified by considerations relating to exchange control. In view of this it held it "unnecessary to consider whether this submission might be rejected also for other reasons invoked by the Government of the United States."[15] In the Advisory Opinion on *Reservations to the Genocide Convention* the Court, while considering that signature constitutes a first step to participation in the Convention and entails some legal consequences in favour of the signatory States, declined to express a view on "the question of the legal effect of signing an international convention."[16]

There are numerous instances of the Court refusing to answer purely hypothetical points [17] or merely abstract formulations of the subject-matter of the dispute. In the *Fisheries* case between the United Kingdom and Norway the Court was confronted with British submissions containing propositions which, as the Court put it, "in the form of definitions, principles or rules, purport to justify certain contentions and do not constitute a precise and direct statement of a claim." The Court declined to decide the issue before it in that way. It pointed out that such definitions, principles and rules "are elements which might furnish reasons in support of the Judgment, but cannot constitute the decision." And it added: ". . . even understood in this way, these elements may be taken into account only in so far as they would appear to be relevant for deciding the sole question in dispute, namely, the validity or otherwise under

---

[13] Series A/B, No. 58 (1933), p. 178.
[14] The same question arose in the case of the *Prince of Pless* (Series A/B, No. 54 (1933)). It proved unnecessary to answer it as Poland subsequently suspended the measures complained of.
[15] *I.C.J. Reports* 1952, p. 186.
[16] *I.C.J. Reports* 1951, p. 28.
[17] See Series B, No. 9 (1924) (*Monastery of Saint-Naoum*), p. 21; Series B, No. 11 (1925) (*Polish Postal Service in Danzig*), p. 32; Series B, No. 14 (1927) (*European Commission of the Danube*), p. 37.

international law of the lines of delimitation laid down by the 1935 Decree." [18]  It is therefore not necessarily typical of the method of the Court that in the *Anglo-Iranian Oil Company* case it examined the submission of the United Kingdom that Iran by her conduct accepted the jurisdiction of the Court—an acceptance by virtue of the principle of *forum prorogatum* [19]—although the agent for the United Kingdom had expressly declared that he did not wish " to press his contention on this point." The Court did so on the ground that the submission had not been expressly withdrawn.[20]

The same tendency to caution has shown itself in the reluctance of the Court to express an opinion on the political and moral obligations of Governments as distinguished from their legal duties —although on occasions its deliberate and somewhat pointed abstention from making some such pronouncements may not be wholly without effect. The reasons for that attitude, and its limitations, are commented upon in another chapter of this book.[21]

At times the Court guards itself by insisting that the interpretation adopted by it applies only to the " present case." This the Court does even in cases in which there is little likelihood of its being confronted in the future with a similar situation. In the case of *Access of Polish War Vessels to the Port of Danzig* the Court, " without wishing to express any opinion on the meaning of the word ' attributions ' in general," was prepared to admit " for the purposes of the present case the interpretation placed on the word by the representatives of the Governments concerned." [22]  In other instances the attitude of caution assumes the form of limiting the scope of its pronouncement by confining it to cases of doubt. While refusing to recognise that Poland acquired any rights under the Armistice Convention and the Spa Protocol, to which she was not a party, on the ground that a treaty creates rights only as between States which are parties to it and that no rights can be deduced from it in favour of third States, the Court qualified the latter statement by the words " in case of doubt." [23]  This was a measure of foresight which, several years later, made it less difficult for the Court

18 *I.C.J. Reports* 1951, p. 126. And see below, p. 102, as to the *Interpretation of the Statute of the Memel Territory.*
19 See below, p. 106.
20 *I.C.J. Reports* 1952, p. 114.
21 See below, p. 219.
22 Series A/B, No. 43 (1931), p. 140. See also Series B, No. 4 (1923) (*Tunis and Morocco Nationality Decrees*), p. 24.
23 Series A, No. 7 (1926) (*German Interests in Polish Upper Silesia*), p. 29.

to pronounce in favour of the possibility of *pacta in favorem tertii* without exposing itself to a charge of inconsistency.[24]

That there may be good reasons for such exercise of caution may also be seen from the dispute which formed the subject-matter of the Judgment concerning the *Interpretation of Judgments Nos. 7 and 8*. That dispute arose out of the fact that Poland proceeded to adopt certain measures in reliance upon a sentence in the latter Judgment which the Court itself described as " rather to be regarded as containing an additional argument, drawn from generally accepted international law." [25] When in the case of the *Panevezys-Saldutiskis Railway Line* the Court affirmed the general rule of nationality of claims with respect to the right of diplomatic protection, a right which " is necessarily limited to intervention on behalf of its own nationals because, *in the absence of a special agreement*, it is the bond of nationality between the State and the individual which alone confers upon the State the right of diplomatic protection " [26]—the qualification as here italicised was of some usefulness when subsequently, in the *Reparation for Injuries* case, the Court relied on the fact that the established rule of diplomatic protection admits of a number of exceptions.[27]

On those infrequent occasions on which the Court has seemed to adopt an apparently dogmatic interpretation of the law— such as describing the opposing view as " inconceivable " [28]—it has mitigated the rigidity of the statement by a prefatory qualification: " In principle " [29] it was inconceivable that the Havana Convention should have contemplated the grant of asylum in urgent cases to include asylum from ordinary prosecution for revolutionary activities. Similarly, it is only seldom that the Court, in order to underline a point, creates the appearance of disregarding the restraints of caution by relying on argument which savours of polemics. Such impression may not always be justified. A judicial pronouncement which studiously avoids any semblance of emphasis may lack persuasive power. Similarly, there may be an excess of precision in the occasional criticism of the unqualified use by the

---

[24] See below, p. 306.
[25] Series A, No. 13 (1927), p. 10.
[26] Series A/B, No. 76 (1939), p. 16.
[27] See below, p. 352.
[28] It is possible, however, that in most of these cases the word " inconceivable " is no more than an inaccurate translation of the French " on ne conçoit pas "—as, for instance, in the case of *Reservations to the Genocide Convention, I.C.J. Reports* 1951, p. 24.
[29] *I.C.J. Reports* 1950, p. 284.

Court of technical terms.   In its Judgment in the *Asylum* case the
Court, in seeking support for the restrictive interpretation of the
Havana Convention, urged that the grant of asylum was, prima
facie, in the nature of intervention in the domestic affairs of the
territorial State and that any extension of the right of asylum was
particularly objectionable to the traditional attitude of the Latin-
American States opposed to political intervention.[30]   That argument,
it might be said, amounted to a departure from the accepted
definition of intervention as dictatorial interference in the internal
affairs of a State.   There is little, if anything, of such interference
in the grant of asylum—an institution freely accepted and widely
practised especially in Latin-American countries.   Yet it is arguable,
in turn, that a definition which limits intervention to dictatorial
interference is in itself open to question.

The degree of restraint in stating an apparently non-controversial
proposition is shown in a passage in the Advisory Opinion on the
*Interpretation of Peace Treaties* (*First Phase*) relating to the argument that the Court could not give an Opinion bearing upon an
alleged violation of human rights and fundamental freedoms
guaranteed by these treaties on the ground that to do so would be to
intervene in matters within the domestic jurisdiction of a State.
The Court said: " The interpretation of the terms of a treaty *for
this purpose*[31] could not be considered as a question essentially
within the domestic jurisdiction.   It is a question of international
law which, by its very nature, lies within the competence of the
Court." [32]   A less cautious tribunal might have had less hesitation
in expressing the view that a matter arising out of the interpretation
of a treaty binding upon a State is not a matter which is essentially
within its domestic jurisdiction.   The Court did not wish to go so
far.   It stressed the fact that the subject-matter of the interpretation
with which the Opinion was concerned was not a question of substance but one of the applicability of the procedure of settlement of
disputes by the Commissions provided for in the Treaties.

It is in relation to the problem of judicial caution that the Court
has been constantly confronted with the question whether in
deciding the issue before it the Court must not only act on legal

---

[30] *I.C.J. Reports* 1950, p. 285.   See also *ibid.*, p. 286.   And see below, pp. 142 *et seq.*
and 374 *et seq.*

[31] Italics are the writer's.

[32] *I.C.J. Reports* 1950, p. 70.

principle but also state that principle; whether it ought to state not only the legal rule which it applies but also the wider legal principle underlying the rule; and whether in stating that principle it must limit itself to the exigencies of the case before it or state the principle in all its generality, and by reference to all qualifying exceptions, against the background of relevant international doctrine and practice. It is possible to hold that in its capacity as an organ which may be expected to develop international law, in addition to deciding cases before it, and to secure the requisite degree of certainty in the administration of justice, the Court ought to give a wider interpretation of the scope of its task. On the other hand, there is room for the view, frequently acted upon by the Court, that the systematic generalisation of the rules applied by it or of its decisions not accompanied by a statement of the underlying rules is the function of writers—a function which has occasionally been fulfilled with signal success and authority.[33] Reasons have been given in the first chapter of this book for the hope that the conflict between the two views is not irreconcilable.

As with regard to other aspects of the activity of the Court, the attitude of caution is only one of the tendencies which determine the character of its method. Some of its possible disadvantages—as revealed in the occasional disinclination to examine in full the contentions of the parties and the essential points of law invoked by them—are discussed elsewhere in this book. However, caution is not the only—or the principal—trend in the method of the Court. It is counter-balanced, in numerous cases, by the exhaustiveness of judicial reasoning, by the boldness of what is, in effect, judicial legislation and by the determination of the Court to secure the effectiveness of the obligations undertaken by the parties—aspects of its activity which are discussed in the two following chapters of this book. In this as in other matters the international judicial

[33] See, for instance, the remarkable series of articles by Sir Gerald Fitzmaurice in the issues of the *British Year Book of International Law*, beginning in 1950, entitled "The Law and Procedure of the International Court of Justice." See, for example, the statement of the law of State responsibility as applied in the *Corfu Channel* case, 27 (1950), pp. 19–22, and of the nature and conditions of innocent passage of ships through straits, *ibid.*, pp. 28–31; of the principles of interpretation of treaties as applied by the Court, 28 (1951), pp. 9–24; of the so-called doctrine of inter-temporal law, 30 (1953), pp. 5–8 —a doctrine which the Court applied in fact in the case of the *Rights of United States Nationals in Morocco (I.C.J. Reports* 1952, p. 189) and in the *Minquiers* case (*ibid.*, 1953, p. 56); of the principles of maritime law applied in the *Fisheries* case, *B.Y.*, 31 (1954), pp. 371–428; of the doctrine of prescription as applied in the same case, 30 (1953), pp. 27–42; and, indeed, of the jurisprudence of the Court as a whole.

process does not follow a uniform pattern which makes it possible to predict in advance, with any assurance, the substance of the decision in any particular case. Rather is it in the nature of a hesitating and alternating choice, in the unremitting quest for legal justice, between differing and often conflicting methods and tendencies. A greater measure of certainty in this respect is no doubt desirable. Yet it is doubtful whether, in the absence of more frequent recourse to the Court and a resulting greater accumulation of precedent, a notable improvement in this respect can be expected.

### 27. *Combination of Restraint with Positive Contribution. Formulation of the Doctrine* rebus sic stantibus

Moreover, the activity of the Court has shown that a distinct measure of caution is not incompatible with a positive contribution to the development of the law. This may be seen, for instance, in regard to the doctrine *rebus sic stantibus.* An international court which could define with an authority commanding general respect the legal limits and possibilities of that doctrine would render to international law a service of undoubted magnitude. It would remove from it a cause of weakness and make effective the operation of a general and beneficent principle of law. The difficulties and implications of any such judicial undertaking are such that it is not surprising that the Court has approached it with caution. In the *French-Swiss Zones* case France invoked the doctrine *eo nomine.* It was submitted by France that since the conclusion of the Treaties of 1815 establishing the régime of Free Zones there had taken place a change of circumstances so decisive as to justify the Court in holding that the Treaties had lapsed.[34] A more daring tribunal would have seized this opportunity in order to pronounce on the doctrine in all its aspects, for instance, in the words of the Court, " the extent to which the theory can be regarded as constituting a rule of international law, the occasions on which and the method by which effect can be given to the theory if recognised, and the question whether it would apply to treaties establishing rights such as that which Switzerland derived " [35] from the Treaties in question (for it was maintained by Switzerland that these rights, being in the nature of so-called international servitudes, could not in any case be affected by the doctrine). A timid tribunal might conceivably have

[34] Series A/B, No. 46 (1932), pp. 155, 156.                    [35] *Ibid.,* p. 158.

found a pretext for disregarding altogether this aspect of the question. This was in fact what Switzerland asked the Court to do, for the reason that the French Government put forward this part of the argument at an advanced stage of the proceedings. The Court refused to do it on the ground that " the decision of an international dispute of the present order should not mainly depend on a point of procedure." [36]

It chose the middle way of making a useful contribution to the subject without embarking upon a dogmatic statement of the law. It examined in detail the French contention that in 1815 the Canton of Geneva was to all intents and purposes a free trade area, that as the result of the withdrawal of the French customs in 1815 Geneva and the zones were constituted as one economic unit, and that the institution of the Swiss Federal Customs in 1849, by destroying this economic unit, put an end to the conditions underlying the Treaty of 1815. The Court inquired whether in fact it was owing to the absence of customs duties at Geneva that the Powers decided in 1815 to create the régime of the Free Zones. It found (with the help, it may be added, of an examination of the preparatory work of the Treaty of 1815 [37]) that this was not so. The Court also admitted that there had taken place important changes since 1815 such as changes in connection with the requirements of the food supply of Geneva, with the development of communications, and with technical progress. But these, the Court held, had no bearing upon the circumstances, essentially of a geographical character, which were present in the minds of the contracting parties in 1815. The decision thus formulated is a significant—though perhaps not fully satisfying—contribution to the doctrine *rebus sic stantibus*. It is clear that the Court was prepared to recognise the principle, although it refused to say to what extent, that a change of conditions may have an effect on the continuation of treaty obligations. It would not otherwise have considered whether they have in fact changed in a material aspect. Moreover, the rule may legitimately be deduced from the reasoning of the Court that a change of conditions, however important, will not affect the duration of a treaty if it has no reference to conditions which were present in the minds of the contracting parties and which determined the conclusion of the treaty.

[36] Series A/B, No. 46 (1932), p. 155.
[37] See below, pp. 116 *et seq*.

Admittedly, the above formulation by the Court of the conditions of the applicability of the doctrine *rebus sic stantibus* may appear to some to be somewhat narrow. For, it may be urged, the relevant factor is not a change in the circumstances which were present to the minds of the parties when they signed the treaty, but —rather—a change in respect of matters to which, at that time, they attached no importance and which they did not take into consideration. On the other hand, it must be borne in mind that the operation of the doctrine *rebus sic stantibus* as a legal doctrine is necessarily limited. It is not a talisman for revising treaties. Many a treaty can and ought to be revised, but this cannot be done by resorting to the doctrine *rebus sic stantibus*. However, in so far as the doctrine is applicable, it is important that it should be freed of its connection with extreme assertions of State sovereignty according to which it is for the interested State that invokes the doctrine to determine whether it is applicable in any particular case. The Judgment of the Court in the *Free Zones* case is, notwithstanding its deliberate restraint, a significant contribution to this end.[38]

A similar attitude of caution, in a more limited sphere, was exhibited by the Court in the case of the *Société Commerciale de Belgique* between Belgium and Greece.[39] Here the Court was confronted—or nearly confronted (for the case was marked by a substantial degree of indecision in the submissions of the parties)— with an issue akin to that of the *clausula rebus sic stantibus*. If the Court had actually assumed jurisdiction on the substance of the matter it would have had to answer the question whether having regard to the alleged radically changed circumstances of the financial position of Greece that country was bound to give full and immediate effect to an award given by an arbitral commission and arising out of a contract between the Greek Government and the Société Commerciale de Belgique. However, as both parties agreed that the award was final and binding, the Court did not consider itself entitled either to oblige the Belgian Government to enter into negotiations for a friendly arrangement as to the execution of the award or to indicate the basis of some such arrangement. Similarly, the Court refused to make a declaration that the Greek Government

---

[38] For an interesting suggestion as to the possible wider powers of the Court in this sphere see Jessup, *The Modern Law of Nations* (1948), pp. 150, 151.
[39] Series A/B, No. 78 (1939).

was justified, owing to *force majeure*, in not executing the arbitral award. Such a declaration, the Court held, would have been possible only after it had satisfied itself of the actual financial position of Greece and of the effects which the execution of the award would have had on Greek finances. However, as is pointed out elsewhere in this book, the attitude of the Court was not wholly unhelpful or negative with regard to that aspect of the case.[40] Similarly, in the case of the *Brazilian Loans*—a case of a contract between a State and a private lender—the Court found that the economic dislocation caused by the First World War had not, as a matter of legal principle, released the Yugoslav Government from its obligations and that the alleged impossibility of performance on account of the inability to obtain gold coins was only apparent seeing that the equivalent of gold value was obtainable.[41] This was also the view of the Court in the similar case of the *Serbian Loans* where it held, in addition, that the economic dislocation caused by the war did not release the debtor State " although they may present questions which doubtless will receive appropriate consideration " in any subsequent negotiations and arbitral proceedings provided for by the Agreement.[42]

## 28. *The Formulation of the Law of State Responsibility*

The Judgment of the Court in the *Corfu Channel* case, in so far as it concerns the question of the responsibility of a State for damage caused in its territory to other States, provides another instructive example of the way in which a guarded and qualified exposition of the legal rule can be combined with a useful contribution to international law. This is so although the Court did not choose to relate its decision on the subject to the wider background of international practice and doctrine. The Court regarded it as clear that the mere fact that a minefield in Albanian territorial waters caused explosions of which British warships were the victims could not result in the imputation to the Albanian Government of the knowledge of the fact that mines were being laid. The Court agreed that " a State on whose territory or in whose waters an act contrary to international law has occurred, may be called upon to give an explanation " and that " that State cannot evade such a

[40] See below, p. 222.
[41] Series A, No. 21 (1929), p. 120.
[42] Series A, No. 20 (1929), p. 40. See below, p. 221.

request by limiting itself to a reply that it is ignorant of the circumstances of the act and its authors." [43]    The Court admitted that the
State in question may, "up to a certain point," be under an
obligation "to supply particulars of the use made by it of the means
of information and inquiry at its disposal."    After defining the
obligations of the State the Court proceeded to dissociate its finding
from any implications of the doctrine of absolute liability: "But it
cannot be concluded from the mere fact of control exercised by a
State over its territory and waters that the State necessarily knew, or
ought to have known, of any unlawful act perpetrated therein, nor
yet that it necessarily knew, or should have known, the authors.
This fact, by itself and apart from other circumstances, neither
involves *prima facie* responsibility nor shifts the burden of proof." [44]
Having thus qualified the responsibility of the territorial State by a
rejection of the theory of absolute responsibility, the Court went on
to qualify the qualification.    Although the injurious act neither
involved *prima facie* the liability of the State nor shifted the burden
of proof, the fact of the exclusive control of the State over its
territory and the resulting frequent inability of the injured State to
furnish direct proof, had a bearing upon the *methods* of proof.    The
injured State "should be allowed a more liberal recourse to
inferences of fact and circumstantial evidence."    Such indirect
evidence, the Court said, was admitted in all systems of law and its
use was recognised by international decisions.

While there may be room for the view that a measure of
elaboration, by specific reference to international judicial precedent
and perhaps of doctrinal discussion of the subject in the literature
of international law, might have enhanced the usefulness of this
aspect of the Judgment,[45] it must—notwithstanding, or perhaps
because of, its caution—be regarded as an important judicial
contribution to what is the crucial problem of the law of State
responsibility.    Absolute liability, by making the requirement of fault
irrelevant, divorces liability from its moral basis.    If admitted as
the normal standard for gauging the international obligations of the
State, it may in the long run reduce the level of international
conduct.    The Judgment in the *Corfu* case goes a long way towards
avoiding that result.    At the same time, the concession which it

[43] *I.C.J. Reports* 1949, p. 18.
[44] *Ibid.*
[45] See above, p. 17.

makes to the doctrine of absolute responsibility by sanctioning some differentiation in the method of proof is neither nominal nor inconsistent with justice.

## 29. *Judicial Caution and Economy of Expression*

The case of the *Corfu Channel* provides an interesting example of judicial restraint and economy of expression—especially with regard to the main legal issue before the Court, namely, the question of the responsibility of a State for damage done in its territory to the interests of foreign States. The relevant crucial passage of the Judgment contains a series of rules expressing what the Court conceived to be the law on the subject. Except for a general reference to an " international practice " the Court refrained from explaining these rules in detail. This was so although the question of the nature of the responsibility of States for acts occurring in their territory and affecting other States is one of the most persistent problems of the law of State responsibility and although it has been illustrated by an abundant, though not uniform, arbitral and diplomatic practice which has given rise to an acute doctrinal divergence of views as expressed in the dichotomy of the doctrines of absolute responsibility and of responsibility as based on fault. Thus viewed, the passages in question—bearing upon a crucial aspect of the case before the Court—may create, with some, the impression that the Court was laying down new rules of law.

Yet there are reasons for tempering any excessive tendency to criticism of that Judgment on account of the apparent failure to seize the opportunity of making its contribution to international law on the subject more articulate. For the view underlying that attitude of restraint is closely connected with the considerations, adduced at the beginning of this chapter, prompting a persistent attitude of judicial caution. According to these considerations it is for writers, and not for the Judge, to place against the background of previous practice and doctrine the rules of law as laid down by the Court. Any such view may not commend itself to everyone. But it is a weighty factor in the situation. Moreover, it must be borne in mind that a great deal of the effort of the Court in that case was directed to the elucidation of disputed and complicated questions of fact.[46] Also, the passages of the Judgment which qualify

---

[46] See above, p. 35.

the rejection of the absolute liability of the territorial State by imposing upon it the duty to abide by the results of indirect evidence contain a useful explanation of the rule laid down by the Court. Similarly, there was instructive judicial reasoning, as distinguished from a bare statement of the legal rule, in those parts of the Judgment which were concerned with the passage of warships through straits and with the emphatic [47] rejection, possibly controversial in its comprehensiveness, of the right of intervention.

The Judgment afforded an opportunity of clarifying the difference, if any, between passage through territorial waters and passage through straits, as well as the distinction between regulation and previous authorisation of passage. The Court found the former, but not the latter, to be permissible. It did not consider the possibility that regulation may involve an interference with the right of passage much more serious than previous authorisation. It is arguable that any elaboration of this aspect of the question would have been in the nature of an *obiter dictum* not directly relevant to the decision.

[47] After holding that it regarded " the alleged right of intervention as the manifestation of a policy of force, such as has, in the past, given rise to most serious abuses and such as cannot, whatever be the present defects in international organisation, find a place in international law," the Court proceeded to state that " intervention is perhaps admissible in the particular form it would take here." *I.C.J. Reports* 1949, p. 35. There is room for the, possibly pedantic, question : If intervention can find no place in international law at all, can it be said that it is " perhaps " less admissible in some cases than in others?

# CHAPTER 6

## JUDICIAL RESTRAINT
## THE JURISDICTION OF THE COURT

### 30. *Jurisdictional Issues before the Court*

The temper of caution exhibited by the Court in its formulation and exposition of the law manifests itself with some persistence in its attitude of restraint in relation to the question of its own jurisdiction. A very substantial number of the decisions of the Court have been concerned with that question. When appearing before the Court as defendants under a clause giving it obligatory jurisdiction, Governments show no reluctance to plead that they have not in fact conferred upon it jurisdiction in regard to the matter in dispute. The Court has examined such pleas with meticulous care. It has emphasised repeatedly the necessity for extreme caution in assuming jurisdiction, which must be proved up to the hilt. Numerous Judgments show the Court as " bearing in mind the fact that its jurisdiction is limited, that it is invariably based on the consent of the respondent and only exists in so far as this consent has been given." [1] Nothing should be done which creates the impression that the Court, in an excess of zeal, has assumed jurisdiction where none has been conferred upon it. The rule *boni judicis est ampliare jurisdictionem* applies, so far as the Court is concerned, only subject to that fundamental limitation.

This fact explains the protracted history of many a case brought before the Court. Consider, for instance, the case concerning *Certain German Interests in Polish Upper Silesia*—a case turning upon the interpretation of the Geneva Convention of May 1922 between Poland and Germany and arising out of the liquidation of certain German property in Poland. The Geneva Convention conferred upon the Court jurisdiction in regard to differences of opinion respecting the construction and application of some of its Articles. When the case first came before the Court, Poland questioned the jurisdiction of the Court on a number of grounds. She contended

---

[1] Series A, No. 2 (1924) (*Mavrommatis Palestine Concessions* case), p. 16.

that the Court had no jurisdiction, for the reason, *inter alia*, that the Polish Law complained of did not fall within the scope of the Geneva Convention; that as there had been only a notice of expropriation but no actual expropriation there was no dispute as to the *application* of the Convention, but only as to its construction, whereas the Court had jurisdiction only if there was a dispute as to both the construction *and* the application of the Convention; that the dispute involved the interpretation of a provision of the Treaty of Versailles in respect of which the Court had no jurisdiction; and that an action relating to the same matter had already been brought before the relevant Mixed Arbitral Tribunal.[2]   In its Judgment given in August 1925, the Court dismissed these objections.   It then proceeded, in May 1926, to give judgment on the merits.   Even at that stage Poland put forward pleas to the jurisdiction on the ground, *inter alia*, that Germany in fact asked for a declaratory judgment which, it was urged, the Court was prevented from giving by virtue of Article 59.[3]   The Court dismissed that objection.   It then found, on the merits, that the measures taken by Poland were contrary to her international obligations.   That Judgment did not signify the end of the matter.   As, subsequent to the Judgment, Germany and Poland were unable to reach an agreement on the question of compensation, Germany brought a fresh action asking the Court to fix the amount of the indemnity and the method and time of payment.   Poland maintained that the Court had no power to act in that capacity seeing that the clause conferring upon it jurisdiction in regard to the interpretation and application of the Convention did not contemplate jurisdiction with respect to reparation claimed for the violation of the Convention.   The Court, in reliance upon the principle of effectiveness of treaty obligations,[4] overruled this objection to its jurisdiction in a Judgment given in July 1927.[5]   In the meantime, Poland, relying on some passages in the Judgments given in May 1926 and July 1927, proceeded to take further action against the German company in question.   Thereupon Germany brought a further action asking the Court to interpret, in accordance with Article 60 of the Statute, the disputed passages in the two

---

[2] See Series A, No. 6 (1925), *passim*.
[3] Series A, No. 7 (1926), p. 18.  See above, p. 19.
[4] See below, p. 246.
[5] Series A, No. 11 (1927).

Judgments referred to above. Poland contended that the Court had no jurisdiction to comply with the German request on the grounds that, as no negotiations had taken place between the parties, there was no " dispute " between them; that the German application did not in fact bear on the interpretation of the " meaning " and the scope of the Judgment; and, finally, that it did not refer to the operative part of the Judgment. The Court, in a Judgment given in December 1927, dismissed these objections and found that the Polish interpretation could not be sustained.[6] In September 1928 the Court—not without having to decide once more some subtle points of jurisdiction—gave judgment on the principles governing the payment of the indemnity, while reserving for a future judgment the fixing of the actual amount of the indemnity after receiving the report of experts to be appointed by it.[7] After all this it is almost a disappointment to find that Germany and Poland agreed to settle the matter out of Court.[8] But the history of the case shows the caution and the care with which the Court scrutinises its jurisdictional powers.

The *Mavrommatis Palestine Concessions* case offers another instance of the conscientiousness with which the Court interprets its powers. When, in August 1924, Greece invoked the jurisdiction of the Court on account of the alleged violation by the British authorities in Palestine of concessions granted to a Greek subject by Turkey, Great Britain put forward an impressive array of reasons in support of the contention that the Court was not competent in the matter notwithstanding the clause of Article 26 of the Palestine Mandate conferring upon it jurisdiction in regard to disputes relating to the interpretation or the application of the Mandate if such disputes cannot be settled by negotiation. Great Britain contended that the Court had no jurisdiction on the grounds that no negotiations between the two Governments had taken place; that the deposit of ratifications as provided in the Treaty of Lausanne (upon the effects of which the jurisdiction of the Court largely rested) had not yet taken place, or, alternatively, that if the Lausanne Protocol could be invoked it did not provide for the jurisdiction of the Court; that the alleged breach of the Mandatory's obligations had taken place before the Palestine Mandate, assuming that it

[6] Series A, No. 13 (1927).
[7] Series A, No. 17 (1928).
[8] Series A, No. 19 (1929).

conferred jurisdiction upon the Court, entered into force; and that the grant of concessions to Mr. Rutenberg did not constitute a measure of " public control " in the meaning of Article II of the Palestine Mandate whose application gave rise to the Greek action.[9] The Court dismissed these objections. (It declined jurisdiction in regard to the Jaffa concessions for other reasons.) In a subsequent Judgment it found that the Jerusalem concessions were valid and that M. Mavrommatis was entitled to their readaptation.[10] But when M. Mavrommatis, in a subsequent action brought by the Greek Government in 1927, asked for compensation on the ground that the hostile attitude of the British and Palestine authorities during the negotiations for the readaptation of the concession caused him irreparable injury, the Court declared that it had no jurisdiction on the ground, *inter alia*, that the failure of the Palestine authorities to approve the plans submitted by him within a certain time did not constitute a case of the exercise of the full power to provide for " public control " in the meaning of Article II of the Palestine Mandate.[11]

The prominence of the jurisdictional issues before the Court is illustrated by the fact that, with few exceptions,[12] in all cases in which a defendant State has been brought before the Court by unilateral application it has pleaded to the jurisdiction of the Court. In the *Monetary Gold* case that issue was raised, at a subsequent stage of the proceedings, by the very State which brought the application in the first instance. Moreover, it was raised not by the State said to be directly interested—that State ignored the proceedings—but, as mentioned, by the original applicant who, in the words of the Court " after having taken the initial step, felt some doubt as to whether the subject-matter of the dispute was such that the Court could deal with it." [13] Italy, acting upon an offer extended by her in an Agreement concluded between the United States of America, the United Kingdom and France, had brought before the Court a case the decision of which, as the Court found,

[9] Series A, No. 2 (1924), *passim*.

[10] Series A, No. 5 (1925).

[11] Series A, No. 2 (1924), pp. 18 *et seq*.

[12] Such as the case of *Diversion of Waters from the Meuse* between Belgium and Holland and the *Eastern Greenland* case. In the case of *United States Nationals in Morocco* the United States subsequently withdrew its plea to the jurisdiction—without admitting that the Court had jurisdiction under the instrument invoked by the applicant State: see *Pleadings*, vol. I, p. 262.

[13] *I.C.J. Reports* 1954, p. 29.

involved a finding as to whether Albania, who was not a party to the proceedings, had committed a wrong against Italy; whether she was bound to pay compensation; and what was to be the amount of the compensation due. The Court, in a decision approaching unanimity and of which an account is given elsewhere in this book,[14] declined to assume jurisdiction. Both the decision and the size of the majority are expressive of the degree of caution with which the Court approaches the issue of jurisdiction. For it appeared that, regardless of the outcome of the case, there was in any event no question of the actual object of the dispute—the gold—passing to Albania. The Court was not called upon to adjudicate upon that aspect of the question. However, it considered that the established principle of international law in the matter of jurisdiction was sufficiently involved by the fact that, regardless of the practical consequences of its decision in relation to Albania, that decision involved a determination of the international responsibility of that State. It may be noted in this connection that in the Advisory Opinion on the *Interpretation of the Peace Treaties with Bulgaria, Hungary and Romania* the Court had no hesitation in finding itself competent to render an Advisory Opinion—notwithstanding the refusal of these States to take part in the proceedings —an Opinion in which it expressed the view that the refusal of those States to appoint a commissioner to the body provided for in these treaties amounted to a clear breach of their international obligation.[15]

## 31. *Past Disputes*

The examples referred to above need not be interpreted as meaning that the Court will give way whenever its competence is challenged. Far from it. They show only that it will examine in exacting detail the objections put forward against its jurisdiction. But its attitude of caution does not go further than that. As will be seen in the Chapter on " Effectiveness of the Law," the manner in which the Court, by reference to the principle of effectiveness of treaty obligations, has disposed of some pleas to the jurisdiction is such as almost to invite the suggestion that it has constituted judicial legislation. In fact, in perhaps no other sphere of its activity has the unavoidable conflict between judicial restraint and

---

[14] See below, pp. 342 *et seq.*
[15] *I.C.J. Reports* 1950, pp. 77 and 228. See below, pp. 353 *et seq.*

the task of imparting a maximum of reality to the intention of the parties been more conspicuous and more interesting to observe than in the matter of the Court's own jurisdiction.

Undoubtedly, when the obstacles to its jurisdiction are compelling, the Court will not be a party to transforming the original declaration of the parties into something which, on the face of it, they did not intend. This has been shown in particular in cases in which the Court has been confronted with a plea to its jurisdiction on account of the reservation of " past disputes." Thus in the case of *Phosphates in Morocco* between France and Italy it declined, with practical unanimity, to give a limited interpretation to the terms of that particular reservation to the French declaration of acceptance of the jurisdiction of the Court which limited it to situations or facts subsequent to the ratification of the declaration. " In these circumstances," the Court said, " there is no occasion to resort to restrictive interpretation that, in case of doubt, might be advisable in regard to a clause which must on no account be interpreted in such a way as to exceed the intention of the State that subscribed to it." [16] It emphasised that the French acceptance of the compulsory jurisdiction of the Court was a unilateral act and that that jurisdiction existed only within the limits within which it had been accepted. The limiting terms of the declaration *ratione temporis* were, in the view of the Court, " perfectly clear " and so was the intention which inspired it. The Court was so anxious to substantiate the clear import of that reservation that it came near to giving it the hall-mark of its approval. The reservation of " past disputes and situations," it said, was inserted " with the object of depriving the acceptance of the compulsory jurisdiction of any retroactive effects, in order both to avoid, in general, a revival of old disputes and to preclude the possibility of the submission to the Court by means of an application of situations or facts dating from a period when the State whose action was impugned was not in the position to foresee the legal proceedings to which these facts and situations might give rise." [17] It was probably not within the province of the Court to draw attention to the desirability of its judicial qualification so as to exclude from its purview situations the continuance of which does not merely amount to allowing the original alleged illegality to subsist but which in themselves constitute a renewed and repeated

[16] Series A/B, No. 74 (1938), p. 23.
[17] Series A/B, No. 74 (1938), p. 24.

breach of international law. Judicial caution might have counselled some such qualification [18]; on the other hand, judicial caution could just as well have urged—as in fact it did—a measure of reticence on a matter not necessary for the decision.

At the same time, while rejecting the attempt to limit somewhat artificially the consequences of a reservation confining the acceptance of the jurisdiction of the Court to disputes arising out of facts and situations subsequent to the acceptance, the Court nevertheless set a limit to that reservation. It held, on the one hand, that the factors which are merely in the nature of a confirmation or development of situations or facts constituting the real cause of the dispute are not identical with the facts or situations covered by the reservation; it is only the latter, which are the true source of international responsibility, that are relevant for determining the jurisdiction of the Court.[19] This meant that as the French declaration of acceptance was deposited in 1931 and as the original French-Moroccan legislation which was the source of the alleged injury to Italian subjects was enacted in 1920, it was irrelevant that the régime established by that legislation continued after 1931. The legislation of 1920 was " a fact or situation " prior to the acceptance of the jurisdiction of the Court and therefore the Court had no jurisdiction. On the other hand, the Court—in carefully chosen language—was at pains to set a limit to the reservation in question. Thus the circumstance that some subsequent factors presume the existence of earlier situations or facts constituting the real causes of the dispute, does not bring these subsequent factors within the jurisdiction of the Court.[20] It is that very temper of hesitation which constitutes that decision an important contribution to a difficult aspect of the jurisdiction of the Court.

In a subsequent case—that of the *Electricity Company of Sofia* [21] —the Court further clarified the issue by holding that, although the dispute may presuppose the existence of some prior situation or fact, it does not follow that the dispute arises in regard to that situation or fact and that therefore, by virtue of the reservation of past disputes, it is outside the jurisdiction of the Court. In this case the date of the effective establishment of the jurisdiction of the Court was

[18] For an approach to some such qualification see Series A/B, No. 74 (1938), pp. 26–28.
[19] *Ibid.*, p. 24.
[20] *Ibid.*, pp. 24–26.
[21] Series A/B, No. 77 (1939), p. 82.

1926. In 1923 and 1925 the Belgo-Bulgarian Mixed Arbitral Tribunal rendered awards in a dispute between the Electricity Company of Sofia (a Belgian company) and the State of Bulgaria and the Municipality of Sofia. After 1926 (*i.e.*, after the effective date of the acceptance of the jurisdiction of the Court) Bulgarian authorities took action, in alleged pursuance of the award, which the company and the Belgian Government considered to be contrary to the award. Before the Court Bulgaria maintained that it had no jurisdiction for the reason that the date of the material " facts and situations "—namely, of the awards rendered in 1923 and 1925—was prior to 1926. The Court rejected that contention. It said: " The only situations or facts which must be taken into account from the standpoint of the compulsory jurisdiction accepted in the terms of the Belgian declaration [on which Bulgaria relied by virtue of the principle of reciprocity] are those which must be considered as being the source of the dispute. No such relation exists between the present dispute and the awards of the Mixed Arbitral Tribunal. The latter constitute the source of the rights claimed by the Belgian company, but they did not give rise to the dispute, since the Parties agree as to their binding character and that their application gave no rise to difficulty until the acts complained of . . . It is true that a dispute may presuppose the existence of some prior situation or fact, but it does not follow that the dispute arises in regard to that situation or fact." [22] The Court did not elaborate the meaning of the crucial term " source of the dispute." It may be inferred from its Judgment that the " source of the dispute " is the fact or situation of which the plaintiff Government complains as constituting a breach of an international obligation.

It was also in relation to the reservation of past disputes that, in the *Anglo-Iranian Oil Company* case, the issue of jurisdiction revealed with special emphasis the motives of judicial caution. Such commitments of obligatory jurisdiction as are undertaken by Governments are undertaken by them voluntarily. They are, within very wide limits—through reservations and otherwise—the masters of the extent of their obligation. There would accordingly seem to be good reason for acting on the principle that if they wish to limit the scope of their undertaking they ought to do it in express terms

[22] Series A/B, No. 77 (1939).

and that they must take the risk of any uncertainty resulting from their failure to circumscribe explicitly the major commitment thus undertaken. On the other hand, the Court has acted on the principle, which is of cogent application, that, its jurisdiction being grounded in the will of the parties, it must be strictly proved. The conflict between these two sets of considerations is real and cannot be solved or attenuated by a legal formula. The solution must depend on the strength of these considerations as determined by the circumstances of each case. In the *Anglo-Iranian Oil Company* case judicial restraint solved the difficulty, largely in the light of the historic antecedents of the Iranian declaration of acceptance, in favour of the defendant State.

In its declaration the Government of Iran accepted the jurisdiction of the Court " in any disputes arising after the ratification of the present declaration with regard to situations or facts relating directly or indirectly to the application of treaties or conventions accepted by Persia and subsequent to the ratification of this declaration." Iran contended that as the words " and subsequent to the ratification of this declaration " followed immediately upon the expression " treaties and conventions accepted by Persia " the jurisdiction of the Court was limited to the application of treaties accepted by Iran after the ratification of the declaration. The United Kingdom maintained that the words " and subsequent to the ratification of this declaration " referred to the expression " with regard to situations or facts " with the result that the Court had jurisdiction as to the application of treaties even if concluded prior to the ratification of the Persian declaration. The Court found that the contention of Iran was in accordance with a " natural and reasonable " reading of the text. It did not apparently consider its reliance on the " natural and reasonable " reading of the text to be decisive. For it proceeded to find confirmation of its manner of reading the text in the desire of Persia, subsequent to her termination of the capitulatory régime, to exclude from the jurisdiction of the Court the interpretation and application of the various Persian treaties on the subject. It held that the redundancy of certain expressions—a redundancy which the United Kingdom adduced in favour of its interpretation of the text —was due to the Persian desire to exclude, *ex abundante cautela*, the application of the treaties in question from the jurisdiction of the Court. That caution on the part of Persia had, in effect, the opposite

result of introducing into the declaration an element of doubt—
a doubt which the Court resolved in favour of Persia on the ground
that the acceptance of the jurisdiction of the Court does not partake
of the nature of a treaty negotiated by the parties—with the result
that the declaration was not governed by the principle, which the
Court admitted to be generally applicable to the interpretation of
treaties, that a legal text shall be interpreted in such a way that a
reason and a meaning can be attributed to every word in the text.[23]
The Court went to the length of admitting as a relevant factor in
the interpretation of the declaration certain passages in the Iranian
Law approving the declaration and published in the Persian
language.

The decision of the Court must be regarded, notwithstanding
the substantial majority by which it was rendered, as being a
decision in a marginal case. It illustrates the extent to which the
Court may feel bound, in matters of its own jurisdiction, to
proceed in a temper of caution. At the same time it brings into
prominence the fact that on occasions caution may be pursued only
at the expense of the legitimate expectations of one of the parties.
Such disappointments may, in turn, be unavoidable, having regard
to the essentially voluntary character of international jurisdiction
and to the peculiar nature of the undoubted contractual nexus as
constituted by the disjointed multiplicity of the declarations under
Article 36 of the Statute. In fact, as the normal contractual element
—the meeting of wills—inherent in the successive declarations of
acceptance of the compulsory jurisdiction of the Court is to a large
extent fictitious, the contingency of legitimate expectations being
disappointed is correspondingly small.

## 32. *Exhaustion of Legal Remedies*

The attitude of caution on the part of the Court in the matter
of its jurisdiction has been vividly illustrated with regard to the
exception of exhaustion of local remedies. Thus in the *Panevezys-
Saldutiskis Railway* case between Lithuania and Estonia it upheld,
against the strong dissent of three Judges, the objection to its jurisdiction on the ground that Estonia had not exhausted the local
remedies afforded by Lithuanian municipal law.[24] So exacting was

[23] *I.C.J. Reports* 1952, p. 105.
[24] Series A/B, No. 76 (1939). And see below, p. 350.

the Court in interpreting the local remedies rule—and the consequent limits of its own competence—that it based its judgment on the proposition that the question whether or not the Lithuanian courts have jurisdiction "is one on which the Lithuanian courts alone can pronounce a final decision." [25] The alternative view, which has found support in international jurisprudence on the subject, is that there is no necessity to have recourse to national tribunals if, having regard to national law, *as seen by the international tribunal*, the national court has no jurisdiction. This means that it may not be essential, in order to comply with the local remedies rule, to show that the national tribunals have actually declined jurisdiction. In fact, in a sentence almost immediately preceding the passage cited above, the Court said: "There can be no need to resort to the municipal courts if these courts have no jurisdiction to effect relief; nor is it necessary again to resort to these courts if the result must be a repetition of a decision already given." [26] Moreover, the Court itself stated in a subsequent passage that "until it has been clearly shown that the Lithuanian Courts have no jurisdiction" [27] it could not accept the submission that the rule as to local remedies has been complied with. It would thus appear that in the view of the Court itself something less than an actual final judgment of a national court declining jurisdiction might be sufficient. If, in addition, we consider the weighty qualifications of the local remedies rule adduced by the dissenting Judges, we may feel justified in regarding the Judgment of the Court in this case as a conspicuous example of judicial caution in the matter of jurisdiction.[28] It was probably open to the Court to hold that its refusal to assume jurisdiction was only provisional in the sense that an application by virtue of the Optional Clause could effectively be lodged again as soon as local remedies had been exhausted.[29] However that may be, the Court was equally emphatic

---

[25] Series A/B, No. 76 (1939), p. 19.

[26] *Ibid.*, p. 18.

[27] *Ibid.*, p. 19.

[28] See also below, p. 350. On the other hand, the Court declined to entertain the preliminary objection to its jurisdiction by reference to the rule as to nationality of claims. The Court did so on the ground that, in its view, the issue was too closely connected with the merits of the dispute.

[29] In that case an interesting question would arise if in the meantime the validity of the acceptance of the Optional Clause were to lapse because of failure on the part of the defendant—or the plaintiff—State to renew it. Would the jurisdiction of the Court be determined by the date of the original application?

—in a less controversial field—in its affirmation of the rule of local remedies in its Judgment in the case of the *Electricity Company of Sofia and Bulgaria* (*Preliminary Objection*). It held there that that rule " implies the exhaustion of all appeals, including appeals to the Court of Cassation, a decision by which alone renders the judgment final either by annulling the judgment of the Court of Appeal and sending the case back for retrial, or by rejecting the appeal." [30]

### 33. *Examination of Questions of Jurisdiction* proprio motu

The prominence of the " jurisdictional " argument is well illustrated by the fact that it is put forward not only by Governments themselves. Occasionally the jurisdiction of the Court has been questioned by some of its members in cases in which the Court was asked to act as the result of a voluntary submission of the interested parties themselves. In the cases relating to the *Payment of Loans Contracted in France* both the Yugoslav and Brazilian judges thought it incumbent upon them to question the jurisdiction of the Court although the interested States, of which they were nationals, expressed no doubts on the subject.[31] In the case concerning the *Interpretation of the Statute of the Memel Territory*, Judge Anzilotti was of the opinion that, as the parties asked for a decision on an abstract question of interpretation, the Court ought to have refused to act on the ground that the application did not embody the essential features of a claim for legal redress.[32] Moreover, it appears that the Court, even when acting under a clause conferring upon it compulsory powers and without the defendant State raising the question of jurisdiction, will examine of its own accord whether the assumption of jurisdiction is compatible with the provisions of its Statute. Thus, when seised of the question of an appeal from a judgment of the Hungaro-Czechoslovak Mixed Arbitral Tribunal, the Court inquired whether the dispute was one between States, seeing that the judgment appealed against was given in a case in which one of the parties was a private litigant.[33] And although in the *Monetary Gold* case the Court declined jurisdiction at the instance of one of the parties—the applicant party—it is possible

---

[30] Series A/B, No. 77 (1939), p. 79. The ruling of the Court was based on the apparently—though not actually—exacting formulation of the requirement of exhaustion of local remedies in the Treaty in question.

[31] Series A, Nos. 20 and 21 (1929).

[32] Series A/B, No. 49 (1932), p. 349.

[33] Series A/B, No. 61 (1933), p. 221.

that it would have done so *proprio motu* on the ground that the application asked it to determine the question of the legality of the conduct of a State which was not a party to the dispute.[34] This being so, it is not apparent why the applicant State itself felt called upon to question the jurisdiction which it had invoked. In the chapter on the " Court and State Sovereignty " there will be found, as pointing to restraint in the matter of its jurisdiction, other examples of inquiry *proprio motu* on questions of jurisdiction.[35]

## 34. *The so-called* forum prorogatum

Exercise of jurisdiction by virtue of the principle of *forum prorogatum* takes place whenever, after the initiation of proceedings by joint or unilateral application, jurisdiction is exercised with regard either to the entire dispute or to some aspects of it as the result of an agreement, express or implied, which is given by either or both parties and without which the Court would not be in the position to exercise jurisdiction. The manner in which the Court has combined encouragement of the practice of *forum prorogatum* with a determination to set some ascertainable limits to its operation provides an interesting example of a combination of boldness and caution in relation to a principle of an apparently formal and technical character—though in fact the possibilities inherent in that principle are of more general import. For, in conditions in which the obligatory jurisdiction of the Court operates by way of exception rather than otherwise, the principle of *forum prorogatum* often makes possible the exercise of or submission to the jurisdiction of the Court through a method less formal than express acceptance of it. Moreover, inasmuch as it provides some justification for initiation of proceedings in circumstances in which the initial absence of jurisdiction is apparent—and often admitted— it may, in some cases, pave the way for the acceptance of jurisdiction by the party to which an invitation is made in this way.[36] Of some of these possibilities of the principle of *forum prorogatum* the *Corfu Channel* (*Merits*) case provides an informative example.

In that case, after the United Kingdom had brought the case before the Court by unilateral application, Albania addressed to the Security Council a communication where, in what the Court found

---

[34] See below, pp. 342 *et seq.*
[35] See below, p. 347.
[36] See below, p. 104, n. 41.

to be unmistakable terms, she accepted the jurisdiction of the Court.
But for that communication, it was clear that the Court would not
have assumed jurisdiction.  In particular, contrary to the contention
of the United Kingdom, it would not have done so merely for the
alleged reason that the Security Council had recommended the
parties to accept the jurisdiction of the Court.[37]  The acceptance of
the jurisdiction of the Court by Albania was so distinctly devoid of
ambiguity [38] that normally the case would have been of little instruction except as an obvious instance of *forum prorogatum*.  However,
the Court, following largely the practice of its predecessor, used
the contentions of Albania as an opportunity for expressly rejecting
the view that according to its Statute [39] initiation of proceedings by
way of unilateral application is only possible when compulsory
jurisdiction is alleged to exist and that in all other cases proceedings
can be instituted only by special agreement.[40]  It pointed to
Article 32 (2) of the Rules of the Court which require the applicant
to state " as far as possible " only the provisions on which the
applicant founds the jurisdiction of the Court.[40]  This left the door
open for future developments in the sphere of *forum prorogatum*.
In fact, when the Rules of the Court were revised in 1936 the
expression " as far as possible " was introduced with the express
intention of rendering possible unilateral applications not based on
any specific text.[41]

The practice of the Permanent Court of International Justice
provided various examples amounting to or approaching the application of the principle of *forum prorogatum*.  Some of these instances

---

[37] See above, p. 47.
[38] The communication ended with the following passage: " The Albanian Government
wishes to emphasise that its acceptance of the Court's jurisdiction for this case cannot
constitute a precedent for the future."
[39] Arts. 36 (1) and 40 (1).                           [40] *I.C.J. Reports* 1947, p. 27.
[41] Series D, No. 2 (Add. 3), pp. 69 *et seq.*, 157.  Reference may be made in this
connection to the practice of some States of filing applications from which it is apparent
that the State against which the application is brought is not bound to agree to the
jurisdiction of the Court.  See, for instance, the case of the *Treatment in Hungary of
Aircraft and Crew of the United States of America*.  In the application of the United
States it was stated that although Hungary had refused to submit to the jurisdiction of
the Court, she was qualified to do so.  On this fact the United States " founded " the
jurisdiction of the Court.  In this (*I.C.J. Reports* 1954, p. 102) and other similar cases
the Court, after receiving the negative reply from the State concerned, removed the
case from the list.  It is possible that applications of this nature may be mere political
devices intended to embarrass the State whom it is being sought to make defendant.
However, they may in some cases provide the State in question with the opportunity of
voluntarily accepting the jurisdiction of the Court—which it might otherwise find
difficult to do for political reasons.

show recourse so pronounced to that principle as to make it almost out of place to consider them in a chapter entitled " Judicial Caution." Thus in the case concerning the *Rights of Minorities in Upper Silesia* (*Minorities Schools*) the Court rejected the plea to its jurisdiction put forward not in the Counter-Case submitted by Poland but in her Rejoinder. It laid down the principle that " the acceptance by a State of the Court's jurisdiction in a particular case is not, under its Statute, subordinated to the acceptance of certain forms, such as, for instance, the previous conclusion of a special agreement." [42] It referred to its Judgment in the case of the *Mavrommatis Jerusalem Concessions* [43] in which it exercised jurisdiction under Protocol XII of the Treaty of Lausanne although originally the dispute had been brought before it under Article 26 of the Palestine Mandate. But, as the Court pointed out in the *Mavrommatis* case, the respondent had given his consent by an express declaration agreeing to the jurisdiction of the Court in relation to Protocol XII. In the case of the *Rights of Minorities in Upper Silesia* the Court derived its jurisdiction from the fact that the respondent in its Counter-Case argued the merits and raised no objection to the jurisdiction; the objection was raised only in the Rejoinder. Such conduct, *i.e.*, argument on the merits without reserving the question of jurisdiction, the Court construed as an acceptance of jurisdiction. " It seems hard to deny that the submission of arguments on the merits, without making reservations on the question of jurisdiction, must be regarded as an unequivocal indication of the desire of a State to obtain a decision on the merits of the suit." [44] The Court amplified the principle of *forum prorogatum* thus applied by stating expressly that such implied consent may be given to cover questions outside the scope of the compulsory jurisdiction clause under which the dispute has been brought before the Court. The *Minorities Schools* case is thus not only a case of *forum prorogatum*; it is a case of *forum prorogatum* by virtue not of express but of implied consent. The Court declined to accept the Polish explanation,[45] which does not seem to be altogether arbitrary,

---

[42] Series A, No. 15 (1928), p. 23.  [43] Series A, No. 5 (1925).
[44] Series A, No. 15 (1928), p. 24.
[45] At p. 21. See also the *Chorzów Factory* (*Merits*) case, Series A, No. 17 (1928), p. 37, where, however, the jurisdiction of the Court was not effectively contested. This was also the position in the case of the *Société Commerciale de Belgique*, Series A/B, No. 78 (1939), p. 174. For a survey of these cases and a discussion of the whole subject see Waldock in *International Law Quarterly*, 2 (1948), pp. 377–391.

negativing implied consent, namely, that it was only as the result of the German Reply to the Polish Counter-Case that the scope of the dispute had assumed a complexion of clarity.

The instances here discussed signify no more than that the Court will not subject acceptance of its jurisdiction to requirements of form likely to deny effect to the consent of the parties, however expressed; it will not permit a party to withdraw consent—which, in good faith, must be assumed to have actually been given—on the ground that it has not been expressed in accordance with alleged stringent requirements of the Statute. There are no such requirements. But the Court has not gone further than that. When it is clear from the outset that a Government is unwilling to submit the disputed issue for adjudication, the Court will not construe its conduct—although possibly lacking in circumspection—as implying consent to jurisdiction. Thus in the case of the *Anglo-Iranian Oil Company* the United Kingdom submitted that the Government of Iran had by its action conferred jurisdiction upon the Court on the basis of the principle of *forum prorogatum*. The submission was supported by the allegation that the Government of Iran had in its Conclusions submitted for decision by the Court several questions which did not amount to objections to jurisdiction but which could be decided only if the Court had jurisdiction. Although the United Kingdom did not press that submission, the Court felt it necessary to examine it in view of the fact that it had not been formally withdrawn. It said: "The principle of *forum prorogatum*, if it could be applied to the present case, would have to be based on some conduct or statement of the Government of Iran which involves an element of consent regarding the jurisdiction of the Court. But that Government has consistently denied the jurisdiction of the Court." [46] It was true that it had also submitted objections other than those relating to the jurisdiction of the Court, but these were intended only for the case of the objection to the jurisdiction having been overruled. " No element of consent can be deduced from such conduct on the part of the Government of Iran." [47]

In this connection reference may be made to the *Ambatielos* case (*Preliminary Objection*), in which the Court declined to act on the Greek submission which referred to an alleged offer by the United Kingdom, through its Counsel, agreeing that the Court should

[46] *I.C.J. Reports* 1952, p. 114.
[47] *Ibid.*

undertake the function of arbitration in the case before it. The Court examined in some detail the circumstances of that offer; it came to the conclusion that they did not disclose an unequivocal agreement to submit the matter for substantive adjudication by the Court.[48]

## 35. *Jurisdiction in the Matter of Advisory Opinions*

In the matter of Advisory Opinions the Court has shown a similar disposition to scrutinise carefully the basis of its jurisdiction. As a general rule it has regarded its advisory function as subject to the principle, which it has repeatedly affirmed in its Judgments, that it is not entitled to exercise jurisdiction in relation to a State except with its consent. In the case of *Eastern Carelia* it refused to give an Advisory Opinion in what was in effect a dispute between Russia and Finland on the ground that Russia declined to recognise the competence both of the Council of the League of Nations and of the Court in the matter.[49] In the case concerning the *German Settlers in Poland* the Court expressed the view that if, as claimed by Poland, the subject-matter of the controversy were not within the competence of the League of Nations, the Court would not be justified in giving an Advisory Opinion.[50]

[48] *I.C.J. Reports* 1952, pp. 38, 39.

[49] Series B, No. 5 (1923).

[50] Series B, No. 6 (1923), p. 19. See, on the other hand, the Advisory Opinion on the *Interpretation of the Greco-Bulgarian Agreement of December 1927*, in which the Court declined to give an Opinion on a question submitted to it not by the Council but by the parties in the course of the proceedings (Series A/B, No. 45 (1932), p. 87). See also the Advisory Opinion on the *Interpretation of the Greco-Turkish Agreement of December 1926*, Series B, No. 16 (1928), p. 16.

On occasions Judges, in their Dissenting Opinions, have questioned the propriety of the Court rendering an Advisory Opinion in a particular case. The Dissenting Opinions of Judge Anzilotti are instructive in this connection. He considered, for instance, that the Court ought to have refused to give an Advisory Opinion on the question whether the special legal status of the Free City of Danzig was such as to enable it to become a Member of the International Labour Organisation. He was of the view that as it was impossible for a State to be a Member of the latter without being a Member of the League of Nations and that as membership of the League was within the exclusive competence of the Assembly, the Assembly alone was entitled to ask the Court for an Advisory Opinion (Series B, No. 18 (1930), pp. 18, 19). In connection with the Advisory Opinion on the *Consistency of Danzig Legislative Decrees with the Constitution of the Free City* (Series A/B, No. 65 (1935))—an Opinion of great significance inasmuch as it constituted the first instance of international judicial review of a national enactment in the sphere of fundamental human rights—he opposed the assumption of jurisdiction by the Court mainly on the debatable ground that the Court was entitled to decide as to the meaning and scope of municipal law only when this was necessary for ascertaining its consistency with international law (*ibid.*, p. 63), and that in the case before it the Court was not called upon to give its approval to the laws or Constitution of Danzig

While, in the matter of jurisdiction, the general temper of caution which characterises the attitude of the Court in regard to its contentious procedure obtains also, as shown in the case of *Eastern Carelia*, in the matter of its Advisory Opinions, it is subject in this respect to a certain elasticity determined largely by the changed character of its advisory jurisdiction. This was shown in connection with the Advisory Opinion concerning the *Interpretation of Peace Treaties with Belgium, Hungary and Romania*.[51] That case, which is examined in more detail in another part of this book,[52] arose out of the refusal of these countries to admit that the procedure contemplated in the Peace Treaties of 1947 for the solution of disputes between the Parties applied to certain complaints, raised by some Allied and Associated Powers, of violations of the clauses of these Treaties relating to the observance of human rights and fundamental freedom. Bulgaria, Hungary and Romania, while rejecting those charges, maintained that there did not exist a dispute in the meaning of these Treaties and that they were not therefore under an obligation to appoint representatives to the Commission provided for by the Treaties for the settlement of disputes between the Parties. That contention formed the subject-matter of a request by the General Assembly for an Advisory Opinion of the Court. The Court considered the argument that, having regard to the opposition of those countries to the advisory procedure, it could not, consistently with its attitude in the *Eastern Carelia* case, give an Advisory Opinion without violating the principle of international law according to which no judicial proceedings relating to a legal question can take place without the consent of the interested State. That argument, the Court said, disregarded the difference between the contentious and the advisory procedure. In the latter, it urged, the pronouncement, being of an advisory character, has no binding force; it is not given to States but to an organ of the United Nations of which, in turn, the Court is the principal judicial organ. Nevertheless, it is possible—we cannot put it higher than that—that the Court would have been

---

from that point of view. However, probably this was exactly the case before the Court. As the Constitution of Danzig was the subject of an international guarantee, it was assimilated to an international obligation and any relevant facts, in the form of laws or otherwise, were properly within the province of the advisory jurisdiction of the Court.

[51] *I.C.J. Reports* 1950, p. 65.

[52] See below, p. 249.

prepared to follow the precedent of the *Eastern Carelia* case if the Opinion asked of it had reference, as in the latter case, to the merits of the controversy. However, as the object of the request of the General Assembly was merely to enlighten it on the question of opportunities for using the procedure afforded by the Peace Treaties, the Court saw " no reason why it should abstain from replying to the Request." [53]

The position as left by the answer of the Court is perhaps not entirely free from ambiguity: If the decisive factor is that the Opinion is merely advisory, then it may be of little importance whether the subject-matter of the request is one of substance or procedure. The answer to a question of procedure may be of no less importance than the reply to a question of substance. However, it is probably correct to say that the tendency to caution in matters of jurisdiction is—and ought to be—mitigated in the case of Advisory Opinions by the specific character of that particular function of the Court, namely, that it is essentially advisory in nature. In addition, in relation to the International Court of Justice—as distinguished from the Permanent Court of International Justice—there is the further consideration that the Court is expressly described as the judicial organ of the United Nations and that its resulting obligations and powers must—in relation to States which are Members of the United Nations or which have voluntarily conferred certain functions upon the United Nations—be deemed to modify to some extent the previous position on the subject. [54]

Similar considerations have found expression in the emphatic rejection of the argument, put forward in connection with the Advisory Opinion on *Conditions of Admission of a State to Membership in the United Nations (Article 4 of the Charter),* [55] that the question asked of it was a " political one " and that for that reason it fell outside the jurisdiction of the Court. The question, it said, although framed in abstract terms, was one of the interpretation of a treaty; the view that the Court was without jurisdiction to answer an abstract question was " a mere affirmation devoid of any justification." [56] The Court brushed aside the suggestion, in itself

---

[53] *I.C.J. Reports* 1950, p. 72.
[54] See below, Chap. 5, pp. 352 *et seq.*, for a more detailed examination of this aspect of the situation.
[55] *I.C.J. Reports* 1947–1948, p. 61.
[56] *Ibid.*

probably contradictory, that it was not within its province to answer a " political " question which—or because it—involved the interpretation of the Charter: " Nowhere is any provision to be found forbidding the Court, the principal judicial organ of the United Nations, to exercise in regard to Article 4 of the Charter, a multilateral treaty, an interpretative function which falls within the normal exercise of its judicial powers." [57] That view of the Court was reiterated, with equal emphasis, in the Advisory Opinion on the *Competence of the General Assembly for the Admission of a State to the United Nations.*[58]

### 36. *Jurisdiction and Indication of Interim Measures of Protection*

The tendency of the Court, in the matter of its jurisdiction, to combine an attitude of caution with the determination not to allow a stultification of its activity as laid down in its Statute [59] is illustrated by its practice with regard to provisional measures of protection. In Article 41 of its Statute the Court is given the power " to indicate any provisional measures which ought to be taken to preserve the respective rights of either party." The " indication," the binding force of which is controversial,[60] of interim measures of protection raises no serious difficulty in cases in which the jurisdiction of the Court is not disputed. However, when the defendant State declines to recognise the competence of the Court on the ground that the dispute is not covered by the terms of its submission to the Court's jurisdiction, a dilemma arises which, on the face of it, is not easy of solution. From the defendant State's point of view it seems improper that the Court should indicate interim measures of protection so long as it has not ascertained that it possesses jurisdiction. For compliance with the Order may prevent the defendant State—conceivably for a prolonged period— from exercising its legitimate rights in a matter with regard to which the Court may eventually find that it has no jurisdiction. On the other hand, from the point of view of the plaintiff State, an Order " indicating " interim measures may be of such urgency that to postpone it until the Court has finally decided, in proceedings

---

[57] *Ibid.*
[58] *I.C.J. Reports* 1950, p. 6.
[59] See below, pp. 243 *et seq.*, for a discussion of this question from the point of view of the application of the principle of effectiveness in the practice of the Court.
[60] See below, p. 112.

which may take a long time, upon the question of its jurisdiction on the merits may well render the remedy illusory as the
result of the destruction of the object of the dispute or for other
reasons.

The Court has treated that second consideration as decisive. It
has repeatedly acted on the view that the issue of an Order indicating
interim measures of protection is independent of a previous affirmative determination of its jurisdiction on the merits.[61] It has not
accepted the view that its jurisdiction on the merits must be *probable*
before it indicates provisional measures. It could not do so on the
basis of what can be no more than a summary examination of the
question of its jurisdiction.[62] Neither could it do so without committing itself to some extent. For it may be difficult for the Court
to find that it has no jurisdiction after it has acted on the view that
it probably has jurisdiction. At the same time, the Court has not
acted on the view that it can indicate interim measures of protection
in all cases in which its jurisdiction on the merits is merely possible.
To do so would be to open the door to abuse by enabling States
with no more than a flimsy claim to the jurisdiction of the Court
to obtain an interim Order limiting severely and for a relatively
prolonged period the freedom of action of the State concerned.
This is so although, in strict law, there is no obligation to comply
with the provisional Order. For a Government sensitive to the
reaction of public opinion and mindful of its own reputation will
not lightly disregard an Order of the highest judicial organ of the
United Nations—although, it may be added, it was so disregarded
in the case of the *Anglo-Iranian Oil Company*, the principal case in
which this provision of the Statute was applied.[63]

The more accurate construction of the practice actually followed

---

[61] It did so in the case between Belgium and China in connection with the denunciation by
the latter State of a treaty relating to rights of extra-territoriality (Series A, No. 8 (1927),
p. 7); in the case of the *Polish Agrarian Reform and the German Minority* (Series A/B,
No. 58 (1933)); in the case of the *Electricity Company of Sofia* (Series A/B, No. 79
(1939)); and, in particular, in the case of the *Anglo-Iranian Oil Company* (*I.C.J. Reports*
1951, p. 89; see below, pp. 252 *et seq*). This is also the view which has found
general support among writers: see Hudson, *Permanent Court of International Justice*
(2nd ed., 1943, p. 425, n. 12); Dumbauld, *Interim Measures of Protection* (1932), p. 144;
Niemeyer, *Einstweilige Verfügungen des Weltgerichtshofs* (1932), p. 70; Hammerskjöld
in *Zeitschrift für ausländisches öffentliches Recht und Völkerrecht*, 5 (1935), p. 19. See
also the argument of Sir Frank Soskice, the Attorney-General of England, in the
*Anglo-Iranian Oil Company* case for numerous references, to the same effect, to the
jurisdiction of the various Mixed Arbitral Tribunals: *Pleadings, etc.*, pp. 408–413.
[62] See below, p. 255.
[63] See below, p. 347.

by the Court is probably that in cases in which its jurisdiction is challenged or doubtful the Court will, without committing itself in any way, make an Order for interim protection provided that there is in existence an instrument, such as a Declaration of Acceptance of the Optional Clause, made by both Parties to the dispute, which prima facie confers jurisdiction upon the Court and provided that there are no reservations attached to that instrument which clearly exclude the jurisdiction of the Court.[64] While adhering to that practice, the Court has been careful to emphasise that the indication of provisional measures of protection in no way prejudges its ultimate decision on the question of jurisdiction.[65] In the case of the *Anglo-Iranian Oil Company* such note of caution was sounded not only in the Order indicating interim measures but also in an Order fixing the time limits in the written proceedings [66]—a caution which in that case was not misplaced seeing that the Court eventually found that it had no jurisdiction on the merits.[67]

The jurisdiction of the Court in the matter of provisional measures of protection—a jurisdiction which is here discussed as an example of judicial caution—figures also with some prominence in the chapter of this book which surveys the practice of the Court from the point of view of the " Effectiveness of the Law." [68] This circumstance illustrates to some extent the difficulty and the degree of artificiality surrounding the subject of provisional measures— drawbacks which stem from the fact that according to the wording and, perhaps, the intention of the Statute no legally binding force attaches to Orders issued under Article 41 of the Statute. The latter statement is controversial.[69] However, that very fact may suggest the necessity of amending the Statute with the view to removing what is either an ambiguity or, on the assumption that

---

[64] This is probably the reason why it may have been difficult to accept the interpretation which, in the *Anglo-Iranian Oil Company* case, Judges Winiarski and Badawi Pasha put on the Order of the Court as meaning that " if prima facie the total lack of the jurisdiction of the Court is not patent, that is, if there is a possibility, however remote, that the Court may be competent, then it may indicate interim measures of protection " (*I.C.J. Reports* 1951, p. 97). And see below, p. 255, n. 41.

[65] See the case referred to above, p. 111. See also the case concerning the *Administration of the Prince of Pless* (Series A/B, No. 54 (1933), p. 153).

[66] See Order of July 5, 1951 (*I.C.J. Reports* 1951, p. 101).

[67] See below, p. 346.

[68] See below, p. 252.

[69] See, *e.g.*, Hudson, *Permanent Court of International Justice, 1920–1942* (1943), p. 425. And see below, p. 253.

Orders under that Article lack legal force, a provision inappropriate to a legal instrument.

### 37. *Joinder of Jurisdictional Objections to the Procedure on the Merits*

An instructive example of the attitude of caution in the matter of jurisdiction is provided by the frequency of the joinder of jurisdictional objections to the procedure on the merits. It often happens that an objection to the jurisdiction is closely connected with a question relating to the very merits of the dispute and linked with other questions bearing upon the substance of the dispute. If the Court answers these questions in the Judgment relating to the jurisdiction it may be compelled to do so as the result of an examination which, having regard to the character of the procedure relating to preliminary objections, may be cursory and far from exhaustive. Accordingly, if in such cases the Court declines jurisdiction there is the danger that it may have done so by reference to pleadings which lack completeness. If it declares itself competent it may do so in reliance upon a reasoning which prejudges some of the aspects of the case on the merits. For this reason the Court has in some cases in which it accepted jurisdiction expressly reserved its freedom of action with regard to the merits of the dispute. Thus in the case concerning *Certain German Interests in Polish Upper Silesia* the Court, while deciding to proceed with an investigation of certain aspects of the case touching upon issues belonging to the merits, stated as follows: " It is, however, clearly understood that nothing which the Court says in the present Judgment can be regarded as restricting its entire freedom to estimate the value of any arguments advanced by either side on the same subjects during the proceedings on the merits." [70]

In a number of other cases the Court deemed it safer to avail itself of the provision of Article 63 of its Rules which lays down that " after hearing the parties the Court shall give its decision on the [preliminary] objection or shall join the objection to the merits." [71] Thus in the *Pajzs, Csáky, Esterházy* case the Court found, after public hearings, that the preliminary objections of Yugoslavia and the Hungarian submissions on the merits " are too

---

[70] Series A, No. 6 (1925), pp. 15, 16.

[71] Art. 63 (5). For the history of that provision see Series E, No. 3, p. 199; Series D, No. 2, Add., pp. 78 *et seq.*

intimately related and too closely interconnected for the Court to be able to adjudicate upon the former without prejudging the latter " and that proceedings on the merits would enable the Court to obtain " a clear understanding " of some aspects of the preliminary objections and a " full knowledge of the facts " relating thereto.[72] In view of this the Court, by an Order, decided to join the objections to the merits.[73]  Similarly, in the *Losinger* case the Court was of the opinion that the arguments contained in the Yugoslav preliminary objections must be regarded, from some points of view, " as a part of the defence on the merits, or at any rate as being founded on arguments which might be employed for the purpose of that defence." [74]  Accordingly, as " in those circumstances, the Court might be in danger, were it to adjudicate now upon the plea to the jurisdiction, of passing upon questions which appertain to the merits of the case, or of prejudicing their solution " it decided that the objection to the jurisdiction should be joined to the merits.[75]  For similar reasons, and using similar language, the Court joined the preliminary objections to the merits in the case of the *Panevezys-Saldutiskis Railway Line*.  It felt itself entitled to do so " whenever the interests of the good administration of justice require it." [76] Previously, in the case concerning the *Administration of the Prince of Pless* the Court adopted the same procedure for the reason, *inter alia*, that the jurisdictional question at issue " appears to be inextricably bound up with the facts adduced by the Applicant and can only be decided on the basis of a full knowledge of these facts, such as can only be obtained from the proceedings on the merits." [77]

On the other hand, the reasons of caution which counsel the occasional joinder of preliminary objections to the merits may, in turn, be mitigated by other considerations.  A defendant Government which pleads to the jurisdiction of the Court ought not, without good reason and without its consent, to be expected to submit to the effort, expense and uncertainty of engaging in proceedings

---

[72] Order of May 23, 1936: Series A/B, No. 66 (1936), p. 9.                [73] *Ibid*.

[74] Series A/B, No. 67 (1936), p. 23.

[75] *Ibid*., p. 24.  The Court declined, for this purpose, to distinguish between the plea to the jurisdiction and objections relating to the admissibility of the suit.  It did so for the reason that in the written and oral proceedings " the facts and arguments adduced for and against the two objections are largely interconnected and even, in some respects, indistinguishable ": *ibid*.

[76] Series A/B, No. 75 (1938), p. 56.  It is not necessary here to consider the question as to the power of the Court to join the proceedings at the request of both parties.

[77] Series A, No. 52 (1933), p. 14.

on the merits. The same applies, for that matter, to the applicant Government. In the *Anglo-Iranian Oil Company* case the United Kingdom asked the Court to declare that it had jurisdiction or, alternatively, to join the question of jurisdiction to the merits.[78] The Court, without referring to that alternative submission, held that it had no jurisdiction.[79]

---

[78] *Observations and Submissions of the United Kingdom : Pleadings, etc.*, 1952, p. 370.
[79] *I.C.J. Reports* 1952, p. 115. But see the observations on the subject in the Dissenting Opinion of Judge Read at p. 149.

# CHAPTER 7

# JUDICIAL HESITATION. PREPARATORY WORK IN THE INTERPRETATION OF TREATIES

### 38. *The Practice of the Permanent Court of International Justice*

With the attitude of judicial caution, which is a characteristic feature of the work of the Court, there is closely connected what may be described as judicial hesitation. In no aspect of the work of the Court has that approach manifested itself more conspicuously than with regard to the question of preparatory work in the interpretation of treaties. In numerous Judgments and Opinions the Court has had to consider how far—if at all—negotiations and the proceedings of conferences and their commissions preceding the conclusion of a treaty can be invoked for the purpose of interpreting controversial treaty provisions. The question is of obvious practical importance in international judicial and arbitral settlement. Most of the work of international tribunals, including that of the International Court itself,[1] consists in interpreting treaties. Most cases of interpretation of treaties involve the question of the relevance and the authority of *travaux préparatoires* as an element of interpretation. Perhaps unavoidably, those who expected from the Court a clear lead in the matter have been disappointed. This is so although the Court—the International Court of Justice and its predecessor—has repeatedly expressed the view that there is no occasion to have recourse to preparatory work when the text of the treaty is clear. It is convenient to survey separately the practice of the two Courts.

As a matter of practice, the Permanent Court of International Justice in most cases in which it committed itself to that negative statement of the applicable principle examined in some detail the preparatory work adduced by one of the parties. An example will illustrate the position. In the Advisory Opinion on the *Interpretation of the Convention of 1919 concerning the Employment of Women during the Night*[2] the Court held that the expression

---

[1] See above, p. 26.
[2] Series A/B, No. 50 (1932).

116

" women " in Article 3 of the Convention applied also to women who hold positions of supervision or management and who are not ordinarily engaged in manual work. This, the Court held, was the natural meaning of the term used in the Convention. But while stating expressly that it did not " intend to derogate in any way from the rule which it has laid down on previous occasions that there is no occasion to have regard to preparatory work if the text of the convention is sufficiently clear in itself," [3] the Court proceeded to analyse in detail the preparatory work of the Convention in order to refute the view that its provisions applied only to women engaged in manual work. It surveyed the work of the Committee appointed by the First Labour Conference to deal with the subject of the employment of women. It examined the report of that Committee and found, *inter alia*, that the French text of the report supported clearly the view adopted by the Court. It also attached importance to the fact that the *rapporteur* of the Committee, who was of British nationality, used her own language. The Court then reviewed the work of the Drafting Committee of the Conference in order to show that, contrary to the original intention, importance was attached to framing the Convention on the same lines as other conventions drafted at that time and applying uniformly to women without regard to the character of their employment.[4]

In the *Lotus* case the Court, after recalling " what it has said in some of its preceding judgments and opinions, namely, that there is no occasion to have regard to preparatory work if the text of a convention is sufficiently clear," [5] regarded the rule thus enunciated as helpful for the interpretation of the disputed term " principles of international law " according to which, by virtue of Article 16 of the Convention of Lausanne, questions of jurisdiction shall be decided between the parties. These principles, it held, " can only mean international law as it is applied between all nations belonging to the community of States." [6] Nevertheless, the Court acceded in fact to the French contention that the meaning of that term must be sought in the light of the evolution of the Convention. France supported her principal thesis by reference to the fact that

[3] At p. 378.
[4] *Ibid.*, pp. 378–380.
[5] Series A, No. 10 (1927), p. 16.
[6] *Ibid.*

a Turkish draft which, in certain cases, claimed for Turkey jurisdiction over offences committed outside Turkish territory was
rejected by the Conference. The Court found that, with one
exception, no reasons were given for the rejection of the Turkish
draft and that, therefore, from the mere circumstance of its rejection
no conclusion could be drawn that such jurisdiction was contrary to
principles of international law as referred to in the Convention.
Moreover, an examination of the preparatory work showed that
another draft expressly limiting the jurisdiction of the Parties to
offences committed in their territory was equally rejected. A
similar thorough examination of preparatory work, after an initial
deprecatory observation on the legitimacy of its use, was undertaken
by the Court in the Advisory Opinion on the *Jurisdiction of the
European Danube Commission.*[7] In its Judgment on the *Interpretation of the Statute of the Memel Territory* the Court, after
recalling its previous practice according to which preparatory work
cannot be adduced to interpret a text which is in itself sufficiently
clear, recorded its view that the history of the relevant Article
" provides no material which conflicts with the interpretation of the
terms of the Article standing by themselves." [8] It is clear that the
Court could not have arrived at that opinion without a previous
examination of the Article in question.

In some cases the Permanent Court of International Justice went
into the details of preparatory work without any preliminary expression of warning or hesitation. In the Advisory Opinion on the
*Treatment of Polish Nationals in Danzig* [9] the Court seems to have
gone a step further than the examination of the preparatory work
for the purpose of corroborating a conclusion arrived at in another
way. In the first instance, in the recital of the facts the Court gave
a detailed history of the evolution of the text of the relevant paragraph of Article 33 of the Treaty of Paris between Poland and
Danzig.[10] Secondly, it admitted—an admission which is not very
frequent in the Court's pronouncements—that the text was not
" absolutely clear " and that therefore " it may be useful, in order
to ascertain its precise meaning, to recall somewhat in detail the
various drafts which existed prior to the adoption of the text in

---

[7] Series B, No. 14 (1927), p. 31.
[8] Series A/B, No. 47 (1932), p. 249.
[9] Series A/B, No. 44 (1932).
[10] *Ibid.*, pp. 12–18.

force." [11] The Court then examined the various drafts leading up to the controversial provision as finally adopted: the substitution, *inter alia*, in the final text of the term " similar " for the word " identical "; the communication of the Conference of Ambassadors to the Danzig Delegation, to which the Court attached decisive importance; and the letters of the Danzig Delegation to the Conference of Ambassadors. The Court rejected one of the principal Polish contentions on the ground that it would " constitute a fundamental change contrary to the expressed intentions of the Conference of Ambassadors." [12]

The Opinion, in the same case, of Judge Sir Cecil Hurst is not without interest especially having regard to the view, which has found some currency, that recourse to preparatory work is contrary to the practice of English and American courts. In his Separate Opinion he held that the text to be interpreted was so clear that a reference to the " *travaux préparatoires* " of the Convention seemed " scarcely justifiable." However, in the course of the Opinion he expressed the view that the history of the Article was " interesting," and he proceeded to draw attention to one episode of the preparatory work, not mentioned in the Opinion of the Court, which he regarded as being of " considerable importance." [13] He pointed out that in the course of the negotiations Poland proposed the omission, in the relevant passage, of the words " *à l'effet de* "; that the suppression of these words converted the concluding part of the paragraph into a substantive engagement instead of a mere explanation of the first part; and that " the effect of the change is that Poland is entitled to claim as against Danzig under Article 33 all the rights assured to her by Article 104 (5) of the Treaty of Versailles." We see thus that the usual attitude of caution in regard to *travaux préparatoires* can be combined with regarding them not only as interesting and of considerable importance but also as being one of the decisive elements in the process of interpretation.

In the case concerning *Polish War Vessels in the Port of Danzig* the Court refused to give an extensive interpretation to the general provisions of the Treaty of Versailles relating to the access of Poland to the sea. It was prepared to take note " as a matter of history " of the promise given to Poland at the time of the peace

[11] Series A/B, No. 44 (1932), p. 33.
[12] *Ibid.*, p. 37.
[13] *Ibid.*, p. 58.

settlement in respect of a free and secure access to the sea. But, as
the Court put it, " no materials and no reasons have been submitted
to it for assuming " [14] that the relevant provisions of the Treaty and
of the Convention concluded in pursuance thereof did not constitute
a complete fulfilment of the promise. It would thus appear that if
" materials "—which, in substance, means to some extent " preparatory work "—had been submitted to it, the Court would have been
prepared to consider them with the view to ascertaining " the
proclaimed intentions of the authors of the Treaty . . . for which no
provision is made in the text itself." [15] In the Advisory Opinion
concerning the *Interpretation of the Treaty of Lausanne* (*Iraq
Boundary*) the Court held that the relevant provision of the Treaty
was sufficiently clear and that therefore " the question does not
arise whether consideration of the work done in the preparation of
the Treaty of Versailles (*les travaux préparatoires*) would also lead
to the conclusion set out above." [16] The Court continued as
follows: " Nevertheless, it may be well also to consider Article 3
and the construction which the Court has placed upon it, in the
light of the negotiations at Lausanne, for the Turkish Government
has cited certain facts connected with the regulations in support of
its adverse opinion." These regulations, and the circumstances
surrounding them, the Court then proceeded to examine in detail.

The Advisory Opinion on the *Minority Schools in Albania*
provides another instructive example of recourse to the various
stages of the drafting of a disputed provision—the successive
Albanian proposals—for the purpose of " confirmation " of a result
reached by resort to other methods of interpretation. [17] Judge Sir
Cecil Hurst's Dissenting Opinion in that case was based not only
on what he considered to be the " natural sense of the words "—
eight Judges out of eleven attached a contrary meaning to the
provision in question—but also, perhaps predominantly, on the
" events leading up to the preparation of the text of the Albanian "
declaration in the matter of minorities. [18]

In its Judgment in the *Lighthouses* case between France and
Greece the Court, after admitting that the reference in the Treaty
to contracts " duly entered into " invariably possessed the same

14 Series A/B, No. 43 (1931), p. 144.
15 *Ibid.*
16 Series B, No. 12 (1925), p. 22.
17 Series A/B, No. 64 (1935), pp. 16, 21 *et seq.* And see below, pp. 259 *et seq.*
18 *Ibid.*, pp. 28 *et seq.*, 32.

signification and that therefore the import of the question put to it was not clear,[19] proceeded to inquire in detail into the history and the successive drafts of the Special Agreement. It said: "Where the context does not suffice to show the precise sense in which the Parties to the dispute have employed these words in their Special Agreement, the Court, in accordance with its practice, has to consult the documents preparatory to the Special Agreement, in order to satisfy itself as to the true intention of the Parties.[20]

### 39. *The Practice of the International Court of Justice. The First Phase*

While in the work of the Permanent Court of International Justice the phrase that it is not permissible to have recourse to *travaux préparatoires* when the provision of the Treaty is clear was often no more than a form of words actually concealing a contrary practice, the International Court of Justice, apparently considering itself in danger of being overwhelmed by the mass of preparatory work preceding the adoption of the Charter of the United Nations, for a time acted more literally upon the formula favoured by its predecessor. As already mentioned, in the Advisory Opinion on *Conditions of Admission of a State to Membership in the United Nations (Article 4 of the Charter)*[21] it considered that it should not "deviate from the consistent practice of the Permanent Court of International Justice, according to which there is no occasion to resort to preparatory work if the text of a convention is sufficiently clear in itself." The Court—by a majority of nine Judges—considered as "sufficiently clear" the "natural meaning of words," to the point of divesting the Court of the right (or of absolving it of the duty) to consider preparatory work, a provision which six other Judges interpreted in the contrary sense. The latter—or at least four of them [22]—"without wishing to embark upon a general examination and assessment of the value of resorting to *travaux préparatoires* in the interpretation of treaties," admitted that "if ever there is a

---

[19] Series A/B, No. 62 (1934), pp. 14–20.

[20] At p. 13. See also the Separate Opinion of Judge Anzilotti, p. 33. In his Individual Opinion in the case of *Oscar Chinn* Judge van Eysinga expressed regret that "the Court should frequently be called to give decisions in regard to collective conventions concluded after the Great War, without having at its disposal the records of the meetings at which these conventions were elaborated, these records being kept secret (Series A/B, No. 63 (1934), p. 136).

[21] *I.C.J. Reports* 1947–1948, p. 63.

[22] Judges Basdevant, Sir Arnold McNair, Read and Winiarski.

case in which this practice is justified it is when those who negotiated the treaty embodied in an interpretative resolution or some similar provision their precise intentions regarding the meaning attached by them to a particular article of the treaty." [23] Actually, the preparatory work relied upon by them was not in the form of an "interpretative resolution" but of "some similar provision," to wit, reports of committees and observations of rapporteurs. None of these can properly be regarded as an indication of the "precise intentions" of the parties. Moreover, it is not certain whether the "preparatory work" relied upon actually substantiated the contention of the Dissenting Judges. It is more probable that what it showed was not that the organs of the United Nations are free to attach conditions of membership other than those enumerated in the Charter, but that they had full discretion in considering and assessing those conditions which were laid down therein.[24] It is thus possible that the Court would have found in the preparatory work no less comfort than did the Dissenting Judges. However that may be—and here lies such instruction as can be derived from this case—the proper and, it is believed, more satisfying and fruitful method is not to discard preparatory work on account of the purported clarity of the "natural meaning" of terms, but to carry the contest into the opposing camp and to show, if possible, that the preparatory work does not in fact prove what it is alleged to prove.

In a subsequent case—in the Advisory Opinion on the *Competence of the General Assembly for the Admission of a State to the United Nations* [25]—a practically unanimous Court followed the

---

[23] At p. 87.

[24] Perhaps the more convincing aspect of the Joint Dissenting Opinion lay in the considerations showing the reasons for which the authors of the Charter declined to adopt the principle of universality, *i.e.*, of automatic membership of the United Nations, and for which they "were wise *in their generation* in taking the view . . . that it was impossible to do more than to prescribe certain preliminary and essential qualifications of membership and to leave the question of admission to the good faith and the good sense of the Security Council and the General Assembly . . ." (p. 91) (the italicised words do not appear in the French version of the Opinion). However, it is possible that there exists a half-way house between the rejection of universality and a purely political conception of the process of admission. Such a half-way house may consist in a legally qualified duty to admit States in accordance with the conditions, admittedly elastic, enumerated in the Charter.

[25] *I.C.J. Reports* 1950, p. 8. The question asked of the Court was as follows: "Can the admission of a State to membership in the United Nations, pursuant to Art. 4, para. 2, of the Charter, be effected by a decision of the General Assembly when the Security Council has made no recommendation for admission by reason of the candidate failing to obtain the requisite majority or of the negative vote of a permanent Member upon a resolution so to recommend?"

same line: " The Court considers it necessary to say that the first duty of a tribunal which is called upon to interpret and to apply the provisions of a treaty, is to endeavour to give effect to them in their natural and ordinary meaning in the text in which they occur. If the relevant words in their natural and ordinary meaning make sense in their context, that is the end of the matter." [26] Having regard to these considerations the Court was of the opinion that " it is not permissible, *in this case,*[27] to resort to *travaux prépara-toires.*" The main portion of the brief Opinion of the Court was devoted to a general consideration of the part played by the Security Council under the Charter—an indication that, possibly, there may have been limits to the reliance on the " natural and ordinary meaning " of words in their context. Reasons are given elsewhere in this book [28] why the general practice of the Court affords no support for the view that exclusive reliance on the " natural and ordinary meaning of words " provides a sound standard of interpretation—except as a starting point. It is possible that certain, somewhat strained, aspects of the argument advanced before the Court made it impatient of embarking upon what might well be considered as a work of supererogation. That argument included the submission that the absence of recommendation to admit a new Member was equivalent to an " unfavourable recom-mendation " upon which the General Assembly could base a decision to admit a State to membership. It is of some interest to note that the Court pointed to the fact that a reference had been made, in one of the Statements submitted to it, to a document of the San Francisco conference as showing the possibility of an unfavourable recommendation being voted by the Council. The Court, instead of rejecting that document as falling within the category of the inadmissible *travaux préparatoires,* merely stated that such a recommendation had never been made in practice. Differing views may be held on the question whether the Opinion of the Court would have gained in persuasiveness if it had not discarded the consideration of the preparatory work underlying the provisions in question.

Even more conspicuous are the cases decided in that period in which the Court, without making even a negative reference to

[26] *I.C.J. Reports* 1950, p. 8.
[27] The italics are the writer's.
[28] See above, pp. 52 *et seq.*

preparatory work, dispensed with it altogether. This applied particularly to the Advisory Opinions on the *International Status of South-West Africa* and the *Interpretation of Peace Treaties with Bulgaria, Hungary and Romania*. In the first of these cases [29] the crucial question as to the obligations of South Africa as they resulted from the dissolution of the League of Nations and the provisions of the Charter of the United Nations in the matter of trusteeship was answered, with some brevity, by means of doctrinal and logical argument. The Court did not elucidate their content by reference to the proceedings of the San Francisco Conference which adopted them. It was subsequently maintained by South Africa, with some assurance, that if certain phases of these proceedings had been considered by the Court its Opinion would have been altogether different. Similarly, in the Opinion on the *Interpretation of Peace Treaties (Second Phase)* [30] the Court did not find it necessary to substantiate its reasoning by reference to the proceedings of the Conference which adopted the Treaties in question. Instead it relied on the " natural and ordinary meaning " of the terms of the Treaties; on the view that " by [their] very nature " the clauses before it " must be strictly construed "; and on the assumption that their ineffectiveness was in the circumstances in accordance with the letter and the spirit of the Treaties.

It thus appeared that the attitude of hesitation which inspired the Permanent Court of International Justice in this matter tended, in that phase of the work of the International Court of Justice, to assume a complexion of some rigidity in the direction of excluding altogether recourse to preparatory work. It is true that the Court still left open the possibility of recourse to it in cases in which the treaty is not clear, but what is predominant in that period was the readiness to assume that the treaty is clear.

### 40. *The Practice of the International Court of Justice. The Second Phase*

However, the cases surveyed above are not expressive of the definitive attitude of the Court in the matter of preparatory work. It cannot be said that its practice has now definitely crystallised so as to exclude resort to it unless it has found that the disputed

---

[29] *I.C.J. Reports* 1950, at pp. 132–134.

[30] *Ibid.*, pp. 226–230. And see below, p. 131, n. 56, on the failure of the Court to examine preparatory work in the *Reparation for Injuries* case.

provision is "not clear." On the contrary, a number of cases subsequently decided indicate, once more, a change of the previous practice. Preparatory work is henceforth used apparently without qualifications and almost as a matter of course. The Advisory Opinion on the question of *Reservations to the Convention on the Prevention and Punishment of the Crime of Genocide* shows the inaccuracy of the assumption that the Court is in any way committed to a negative attitude in the matter of justification of recourse to *travaux préparatoires*. The majority of the Court, without considering it necessary to explain the apparent change in its attitude, examined the debates in the Sixth Committee of the General Assembly which adopted the Genocide Convention as well as other preparatory work. It did so for the reason that "although it was decided during the preparatory work not to insert a special article on reservations, it is more or less true that the faculty for States to make reservations was contemplated at successive stages of the drafting of the Convention." [31] It also considered that the preparatory work of the Convention contained "nothing to justify the statement that the contracting States implicitly had any practice in mind" in the matter of reservations.[32] The four Judges who joined in a Dissenting Opinion prefaced their detailed examination of the work of the "*ad hoc* Committee on Genocide," of its sub-committee, and of the Committee of the General Assembly, by the simple sentence: "Let us now see how the question of reservations was dealt with during the preparation of the Genocide Convention." [33] Judge Alvarez was the only member of the Court who, in a passage of lofty eloquence and in reliance on an interesting conception of the new international law in the matter of multilateral conventions, maintained his opposition, previously expressed, to the use of preparatory work.[34]

In the case concerning *Rights of Nationals of the United States of America in Morocco* the Court resorted to preparatory work without considering it necessary to give a justifying explanation. In rejecting the submission that the Act of Algeciras established consular jurisdiction or confirmed the existing rights and privileges of the régime of capitulations the Court stated, without giving any details, that "neither the preparatory work nor the Preambles give

[31] *I.C.J. Reports* 1951, p. 22.   [32] *Ibid.*, p. 25.
[33] *Ibid.*, p. 40.
[34] *Ibid.*, p. 53. And see below, p. 134, n. 50.

the least indication of any such intention." [35]   Subsequently, in
connection with the interpretation of the crucial Article 95 of the
Act of Algeciras the Court examined in detail the preparatory work
of the Conference, including the successive drafts of that Article.[36]
Neither were the four dissenting Judges deterred by their understanding of the " natural sense " of that Article from seeking confirmation of their views, " assuming that the text is ambiguous," [37]
in the examination of the *travaux préparatoires*.

In the *Ambatielos* case the Court examined, by reference to the
preparatory work of the Declaration of 1926, the contention of the
United Kingdom that that Declaration only covered claims formulated under the Treaty of 1886 before the Declaration of 1926 had
been signed.   It found that the records of the negotiations did not
support that contention.   They showed that although the Greek
Government originally suggested a draft of the Declaration
referring to anterior claims deriving from the Treaty of 1886, that
draft was not accepted, and that both parties eventually adopted a
draft which omitted the word " anterior."   In the Dissenting
Opinion of Judge Sir Arnold McNair there will be found an
explanation of the circumstances which prompted the text as finally
adopted.[38]   The Court then added, after having in fact examined
the preparatory work, the saving phrase: " In any case where, as
here, the text to be interpreted is clear, there is no occasion to resort
to preparatory work " [39]—an occurrence which may properly be
attributed to the occasional necessity for qualification inherent in the
method of collective drafting.[40]

In the Advisory Opinion on *Effect of Awards of the United
Nations Administrative Tribunal* the Court examined in some detail
the legislative history of the Statutes of the Administrative Tribunals
of both the League of Nations and the United Nations.[41]

The conclusion which may be drawn from the cases surveyed
in this and the preceding sections is that a proper formulation of
the practice of the International Court of Justice—and of its predecessor—is that recourse to *travaux préparatoires* is admissible
except when the meaning of the disputed term or provision is so

---

[35] *I.C.J. Reports* 1952, p. 198.               [36] At pp. 209, 210.
[37] At p. 229.                                    [38] At p. 63.
[39] *I.C.J. Reports* 1952, p. 45.
[40] See above, p. 65.
[41] *I.C.J. Reports* 1954, pp. 54, 55. See also a detailed examination of the *travaux
préparatoires* of the San Francisco Conference by Judge Hackworth (at pp. 78, 79).

abundantly clear as to render resort to *travaux préparatoires* patently redundant or abusive. The Permanent Court of International Justice showed little inclination to act rigidly on the assumption that the Treaty in any particular case is so clear as to render recourse to or study of *travaux préparatoires* inadmissible or otiose. The International Court of Justice in the first phase of its activity— as evidenced in the Advisory Opinion of 1948 on *Conditions of Admission to Membership in the United Nations* and in the Advisory Opinion of 1950 on the *Competence of the General Assembly for the Admission of a State to the United Nations*—was content to assume that the plain and natural meaning of the relevant clauses precluded recourse to *travaux préparatoires*. It may be noted that in the latter case there were unusually strong grounds for a conclusion of that nature. In the former case, a weighty Dissenting Opinion effectively cast doubt on the ruling of the Court that the text of the Treaty was so clear that there was no occasion to have recourse to preparatory work.[42] Cases decided subsequently suggest a modification of that attitude in as much as the Court, in actually examining the preparatory work leading to the conclusion of the texts before it, has tended to adhere to the true substance of the practice of the Permanent Court of International Justice and to what is believed to be a sound principle of interpretation of treaties.[43]

41. *The Reasons for Judicial Hesitation in the Matter of* Travaux Préparatoires : (a) *The " Continental" and the " Anglo-American" Schools of Thought*

There have been three main reasons for the hesitation and the inconclusiveness of the practice of the Court in the matter of *travaux préparatoires*. The first, which is of diminishing importance, is the view that recourse to preparatory work, while congenial to the so-called " Continental School of Thought," is contrary to Anglo-American practice.[44] As with regard to many other current phrases

---

[42] In that case, on the same page in which it enumerated the rule in question, the Court said : " To warrant an interpretation other than that which ensues from the natural meaning of words, a decisive reason would be required which has not been established " (*I.C.J. Reports* 1948, p. 63). It may be suggested that the exclusion of preparatory work may make it impossible to adduce some such decisive reason displacing " the natural meaning of the words."

[43] For an illuminating critical analysis, from a different—and differing—point of view, of this aspect of the work of the Court see Fitzmaurice in *B.Y.*, 28 (1951), pp. 1–9.

[44] See, *e.g.*, Fachiri in *American Journal of International Law*, 23 (1929), p. 752.

on the difference between the Anglo-American and Continental schools of thought in the sphere of international law,[45] there is no substance in that view. The courts of the United States, including the Supreme Court, exhibit no hesitation in having recourse to preparatory work for the purpose of interpreting treaties. They not only have had recourse to preparatory work as a matter of continuous practice; they have expressly affirmed it as a legal rule.[46] A survey of English cases, which has been attempted in detail elsewhere,[47] shows that the position in England is on the whole the same. Undoubtedly, there exists in England a clear rule of evidence to the effect that the parliamentary history of a statute is not admissible for the purpose of interpretation. But it must be borne in mind that treaties are not statutes; that the English rule is confined to England; that it owes its validity there mainly to the theory that an Act of Parliament, being the expression of the will of the three Estates of the realm, cannot be interpreted by reference to the intention of one of them [48]; and, once more, that even English courts do not apply it to the interpretation of treaties. Sir Arnold McNair (as he then was), in an exhaustive examination of the British practice in the matter of interpretation of treaties, came to the conclusion that although English courts in general exclude successive stages of drafting and parliamentary debates in connection with the interpretation of statutes, " there is ample evidence that in the interpretation of treaties a different practice is sanctioned both by governmental opinion and judicial decision." [49] Although

---

[45] See Lauterpacht in *British Year Book of International Law*, 12 (1931), pp. 31–62. In general the past work of the Court has not revealed any such divergences. On no occasion has there taken place an alignment of the Anglo-American element on the bench against the Judges trained in the Continental tradition. The pronouncements of the Court or of individual Judges do not refer, even indirectly, to the " two schools of thought." And—it is almost needless to say—there are numerous cases on record in which the English, American and Canadian Judges represented opposing views. Compare, for instance, in Series A, No. 24 (1930) (*Free Zones* case; Second Order), the Dissenting Opinion (including Judge Hurst) with the Observations of Judge Kellogg. See also the Advisory Opinion on *Reparation for Injuries Suffered in the Service of the United Nations*, *I.C.J. Reports* 1949, p. 196; the *Asylum* case, *I.C.J. Reports* 1950, p. 316; the *Fisheries* case, *I.C.J. Reports* 1951, pp. 158, 186; and many others.

[46] For instances of cases decided by the Supreme Court see: *Factor* v. *Laubenheimer*, *American Journal of International Law*, XXVIII (1934), p. 149; *United States* v. *Texas*, 162 U.S. 1, 23; *Terrace* v. *Thompson*, 263 U.S. 197, 223; *Nielsen* v. *Johnson*, 279 U.S. 47, 52.

[47] See Lauterpacht, *Les travaux préparatoires et l'interprétation des traités*, in *Hague Recueil des Cours*, 48 (1934) (ii), pp. 713–815, and the *Harvard Law Review*, 48 (1935), pp. 549–591.

[48] See Willes J. in *Millar* v. *Taylor* (1769) 4 Burr. 2303.

[49] *The Law of Treaties* (1938), p. 262.

before international tribunals British representatives have at times objected to the use of *travaux préparatoires*, on other occasions they have relied on them. There are cases on record in which after objecting as a matter of principle to the use of preparatory work they found it useful—by way of alternative submissions or otherwise —to invoke it in support of some aspects of their thesis.[50] As shown, Judges of British nationality on the International Court have often relied on preparatory work either in individual opinions or in joint pronouncements to which they have subscribed.[51]

The alleged divergence between the Anglo-American and Continental principles and approach in the field of international law has been exaggerated out of all proportion to its true significance. Probably, it is non-existent.[52] This applies in particular to the question of *travaux préparatoires*. Undoubtedly, the reference to " the divergence of two schools of thought " is an argument of a high degree of attractiveness, and this fact explains to a large extent the caution of the pronouncements of international tribunals, in particular of the Permanent Court of International Justice, on the matter. An international tribunal which considers itself bound to apply principles of international law as generally accepted and general principles of law is reluctant to give its imprimatur to a practice said to be contrary to an important system of law. A catchword asserting a difference on any point between the Continental and Anglo-American schools of thought is an impressive summons to caution inasmuch as it raises the question of the prestige of a great system of law and makes the majority of the Judges of the Court feel that they ought not to use their numerical preponderance to secure a victory for their own " school of thought." Nevertheless, whatever may have been the influence of that particular consideration as a reason discouraging the examination of preparatory work, its importance has tended to diminish and to give way to other factors working in the same direction. These factors will now be considered.

[50] See the statement of Sir Hartley Shawcross, the Attorney-General, in the *Corfu Channel* case (First Part): *I.C.J., Pleadings, Oral Arguments, Documents*, 1950, vol. 3, pp. 73–75, 78–80, 151–153, and the statement of Sir Eric Beckett, *ibid.*, pp. 107, 109–114, 120–125.

[51] See above, pp. 119, 128.

[52] See the writer's " The So-called Anglo-American and Continental Schools of Thought in International Law " in *British Year Book of International Law*, 12 (1931), pp. 31–62. And see, in connection with evidence and proof before the International Court, Lalive in *Annuaire Suisse de droit international*, 7 (1950), p. 102.

## 42. *The Same.* (*b*) *Considerations of Economy in the Work of the Court*

The second reason which has often been adduced in opposition to the use of preparatory work and which may have weighed with the Court in its hesitating attitude in the matter is that preparatory work is frequently so unwieldy, confusing and inconclusive as to render its examination an arduous task likely to complicate the work of the Court to a degree out of proportion to the true usefulness of that method of interpretation. It is difficult to deny the force of that reasoning. Preparatory work is often lengthy, repetitive and contradictory. In relation to multilateral treaties it frequently reveals the views of the more articulate rather than the more important, the better instructed and the more influential participants. The record of preparatory work is on occasions incomplete and faulty. Much depends in this connection on the adequacy of the secretarial arrangements of the Conference. It frequently happens that in the heat or enthusiasm of the debate views are advanced or expressions used which it is subsequently deemed wiser to modify or to qualify in the written record—and yet it is the spoken word which provokes the answers and supplies the substance of the debate. Moreover, in the course of negotiations the participating States change their views as expressed on previous occasions, and the examination of any particular stage of the preparatory work, to the exclusion of others, is therefore liable to be incomplete and misleading.[53] There are other reasons why, unless care is taken to examine preparatory work in its entirety, it may lead to conclusions which are inaccurate and one-sided.[54] Similarly, it is only the examination of the preparatory work as a whole which can

---

[53] Sir Gerald Fitzmaurice in *B.Y.*, 28 (1951), pp. 14–17, and in the *Annuaire* of the Institute of International Law, 44 (ii) (1952), pp. 370–373, has given a detailed and illuminating picture of the difficulties and dangers encompassing the use of preparatory work. However, it is probable that the difficulties and dangers militate not against the use of preparatory work but as a summons to its exacting examination with the view to avoiding an interpretation which is based on isolated phases and incidents torn out of the context of the deliberations taken in their entirety. Professor Guggenheim in *Lehrbuch des Völkerrechts*, I (1947), p. 126, in questioning the applicability of preparatory work to multilateral treaties, attaches importance to the fact that it passes through various stages. Yet it is the business of the interpreting agency to survey and correlate the various phases of the preparatory work. See, however, for a modification of this view, the revised edition in French translation, *Traité de droit international public*, I (1953), p. 136, where the author states that if a decision were to disregard preparatory work containing the declarations of the parties, "l'autorité de la décision intervenue par la suite en serait certainement affaiblie."

[54] See, *e.g.*, below, p. 386, as to the *Lotus* case.

reveal whether there is room for the application of the doctrine of " merger " according to which the conflicting manifestations of intention are merged in and absorbed by the Treaty as finally concluded or whether the divergent expressions of intention can legitimately be permitted to play an independent part in the process of interpretation.

Such thorough examination of the bulky record of preparatory work imposes a considerable strain upon international tribunals. Yet, frequently, there may be no effective alternative to the laborious unravelling of the sequence and the inconsistencies of preparatory work whenever such is available. It is not suggested that preparatory work is the only method—or that it ought to be the regular method—of discovering the intention of the parties. Logic, context, grammar, " natural meaning," presumptions, the principle of effectiveness, the historical circumstances and presumed object of treaty (in the discovery of which preparatory work is not an unimportant element), action taken subsequent to its adoption [55] —they all have an important and legitimate place in the task of disclosing the intention of the parties. But if a tribunal confronted with a controversial provision of an important multilateral treaty were to confine itself to the text before it and to disregard the written record showing what the parties actually said or solemnly declared, its decision might leave an impression of incompleteness. There is all the difference—in so far as the authority and the persuasive force of the judgment are concerned—between disregarding preparatory work altogether and examining it and finding that because of its incompleteness or contradictions it offers no clue to the intention of the parties or that it does not in fact support the contention of the party which invokes it as against what appears prima facie to be the natural meaning of the terms of the treaty.[56]

[55] See below, pp. 170 *et seq.*

[56] Thus the question arises whether the persuasiveness of the unanimous Advisory Opinion of the International Court of Justice in the matter of *Reparation for Injuries Suffered in the Service of the United Nations* would have been enhanced by a decision of the Court to consider or to refer to the relevant preparatory work of the San Francisco Conference. Part of that work—but only part of it—seems to point to the view that the authors of the Charter deliberately refrained from attributing international personality to the United Nations. In fact they rejected the Belgian proposal to recognise expressly that it possesses international status and the corresponding rights (Doc.524.IV/2/26). This was also the understanding of the Secretary of State of the United States in his report to the President (*The Charter of the United Nations, Hearings before the Senate Committee on Foreign Relations*, 1945, p. 135). He explained the omission of an express

The dangers resulting from most of these difficulties encompassing recourse to preparatory work can be overcome by means of a careful examination, on the part of the Tribunal, of the argument put forward by the party invoking that means of interpretation as well as by the party against which a particular contention, based on _travaux préparatoires_, is put forward. Undoubtedly, that very necessity of a meticulous and critical examination of the preparatory work on the part of the Court may be regarded—and has been regarded by some—as providing a powerful argument against the admissibility of preparatory work. How can the Court be expected to engage in detailed research covering, on occasions, bulky volumes containing records of proceedings of the Conference and of its numerous committees and sub-committees? The answer to that objection is, in the first instance, that in any such prolonged research the Court will be naturally aided by the diligence of the parties, in particular that against which the preparatory work in question is relied upon. In fact, a survey of the cases in which the Court examined preparatory work suggests that the task is much less formidable than is occasionally apprehended. However, even if that were not so, an international tribunal may not feel at liberty to avoid, by limiting itself to textual and logical interpretation, the laborious task of unravelling the true intention of the parties. There may or may not be decisive arguments of a different kind against the use of preparatory work. But, as the practice of the Court has shown, the physical difficulty and inconvenience of undertaking that task cannot, consistently with the authority of international justice, be considered as providing a reason for discarding an instrument likely to assist in revealing the intention of the parties. Should the business of the Court expand in a conspicuous fashion as the result

attribution of international personality to the United Nations on the ground that the Committee which discussed the matter " was anxious to avoid any implication that the United Nations will be in any sense a ' super-State ' " (_ibid_.). If no other part of the preparatory work were available, the Opinion of the Court would be less acceptable than it is. However, it appears from the Report of the _Rapporteur_ of the relevant Committee (IV/2) that the fact of the non-acceptance of the Belgian proposal could not properly be regarded as a rejection of the view which prompted it. The Report described such express attribution of international personality as " superfluous " and added that such personality " will, in effect, be determined by implication by reference to the entirety of the provisions of the Charter " (_Report of the Committee_, IV, 2, A., Doc. 803). That is what the Court did in effect. It acted upon the intention of the parties, as in fact shown in the preparatory work, to leave to future developments the exact determination of the juridical status of the United Nations.

of any increased willingness of States to submit disputes to adjudication, the question would arise as to the necessity of changes in the methods of the work of the Court and its organisation, including the necessity of creating subordinate or regional bodies. However, difficulties of that nature cannot be solved by abandoning or discouraging otherwise useful—provided they are in fact useful—means of ascertaining the intention of the parties.

There would seem in any case no justification for ignoring preparatory work in cases in which it is unambiguous and to the point. It may be unprofitable to speculate whether an uncontradicted report of the *Rapporteur* of a Commission approximates in authority to a provision of a treaty. But it is equally idle to deny its probative value, in varying degrees, for the elucidation of the intention of the parties. The same applies, even more cogently, to express and solemn declarations made by a Commission as a whole or by individual members of it. As in the matter of withdrawal from membership of the United Nations, there may be reasons which prompt the parties to refrain from inserting a formal article in the treaty and to be satisfied with what appears to them to be a less formal but adequate expression of their will.[57] The procedure adopted may be open to criticism, but such criticism is irrelevant to the question of discovering and acting upon a clearly revealed intention of the parties. There is no escape from the fact that, unlike in the case of most private contracts, the preparatory work leading to the conclusion of treaties—especially those of a multilateral character—partakes of a deliberation and a degree of authentication commensurate with the importance of their subject-matter. This is one of the main explanations of the ease and alacrity with which the parties appeal to it—including, frequently, the party which at the opening stage of the pleadings denies the probative value of preparatory work, but which in fact relies on it in considerable detail in case the Court should consider recourse to it to be admissible. This is also the reason why such appeal has become prominent in modern times when the negotiations and the conferences preceding the conclusion of treaties, general or particular, are as a rule public and recorded—often with an almost

---

[57] The Charter does not expressly refer to the right of withdrawal from the United Nations. The Committee concerned put on record the view, acquiesced in by the participating States, that nothing in the Charter should deprive Members of the right to withdraw from the Organisation.

embarrassing abundance of documentation. The question of preparatory work may be, in a sense, a technical problem of evidence. In essence it is a fundamental, and perhaps the most important, aspect of interpretation of treaties. This applies, in particular, to the interpretation of general international instruments such as the Charter of the United Nations. To attempt an interpretation of the Charter without reference to the vast resources of preparatory work which preceded its adoption is to adopt the method of " jurisprudence of concepts " in its most questionable connotation. It is significant that practically every commentary relating either to the Charter in its entirety or to any of its aspects is based predominantly or exclusively on what may be described generally as *travaux préparatoires*.[58]

### 43. *The Same. (c) Question of Relevance of the Intention of the Parties*

The objections, discussed so far, to the use of preparatory work seem to spring from the conviction that the intention of the parties is the decisive consideration and that recourse to *travaux préparatoires* is likely to render more difficult—if not to frustrate—the task of discovering the true intention of the parties. However, opposition to resort to that instrument of interpretation has also been prompted by considerations of a diametrically opposite character. For there are some who believe that recourse to *travaux préparatoires* is inadmissible and irrelevant for the precise reason that the common intention of the authors of the treaty does not matter or, even more emphatically, that there is no such thing as the common intention of the parties.[59]

---

[58] Reference may be made in particular to Goodrich and Hambro, *Charter of the United Nations* (2nd ed., revised, 1949); Kopelmanas, *L'Organisation des Nations Unies*, vol. I (1947) (a work of great merit); Dr. Kaeckenbeeck's commentary on the Charter in *Recueil des Cours* of the Hague Academy of International Law, vol. 70 (1947) (i); and the comprehensive work of Professor Kelsen, *The Law of the United Nations* (1950).

[59] This view that, once adopted, the treaty possesses a life of its own independent of the common intention, if any, of its authors was given clear expression by Judge Alvarez in his Dissenting Opinion in the Advisory Opinion on the *Competence of the General Assembly for Admission of a State to the United Nations* (*I.C.J. Reports* 1950, p. 18) and, in particular, in his Dissenting Opinion in the case of the *Genocide Convention* (*I.C.J. Reports* 1951, p. 53). He said, with regard to multilateral conventions of a legislative character: " . . . the said conventions must not be interpreted with reference to the preparatory work which preceded them; they are distinct from that work and have acquired a life of their own; they can be compared to ships which leave the yards in which they have been built, and sail away independently, no longer attached to the

It is submitted that in so far as the objection to the use of preparatory work is based on the view that, at least in relation to treaties, there exists no common intention of the contracting parties or that such intention is not relevant [60] or not ascertainable, that view—though interesting—is jurisprudentially unsound and contradicted by the language and the substance of almost every pronouncement of the International Court of Justice,[61] of its predecessor, and, indeed, of international tribunals generally. This is so although in some cases—which are not typical of situations confronting international tribunals—it is possible to speak of the

---

dockyard. These conventions must be interpreted without regard to the past, and only with regard to the future." The learned Judge suggested there that "it will be necessary in future—unless in exceptional cases—when interpreting treaties, *even those which are obscure* and especially those relating to international organisations, to exclude the consideration of the *travaux préparatoires, which was formerly usual*" (the italics are the author's). The reasons given were: (a) that in the course of the preparatory work Governments often change their view; (b) that when signing a treaty they are not acquainted with the preparatory work; and, above all, (c) that a treaty once signed acquires a "life of its own" and that therefore, in accordance with the "increasing dynamics of international relations," it must be interpreted in accordance with the exigencies of contemporary life rather than the intentions of its authors.

[60] See the observations of Sir Eric Beckett on the "complete unreality" of the reference to the common intention of the parties in the matter of interpretation of treaties (*Annuaire*, 43 (1950) (i), p. 438). See also Fitzmaurice, *ibid.*, 44 (ii) (1952), pp. 369–374, and in B.Y., 28 (1951), pp. 12–17. And see Corry in *Canadian Bar Review*, 1954, July, for an exposition of what he considers to be the almost insurmountable difficulties in finding the "legislative intent." However, the final conclusion of the learned writer is not in the nature of a denial of the propriety of resort to that source of interpretation in relation to the acts of the legislature.

[61] "The Court will seek these replies [to the question of reservations to the Genocide Convention] in the rules of law relating to the effect to be given to the intention of the parties to multilateral treaties" (*I.C.J. Reports* 1951, p. 20). See *ibid.*, p. 24, on "the purposes which the General Assembly and the contracting parties had in mind." And see *ibid.*, p. 43, for the statement, in the Joint Dissenting Opinion, that "if, therefore, such a rule [as laid down by the Court] is to apply to the Genocide Convention, it would have to be deduced from the intentions of the parties." It would be easy to adduce similar passages in practically every pronouncement of the International Court of Justice and its predecessor. However, to do that would probably amount to labouring the obvious. See also the *Pajzs, Csáky, Esterházy* case, *P.C.I.J.*, Series A/B, No. 68 (1936), p. 60, where the Court attached decisive importance to the "intentions of the negotiators of the Paris Agreements" as expressed in the words of their Preamble, which words "clearly express a conviction on the part of the signatories" to settle finally questions connected with agrarian expropriations. And see the case of *Diversion of Waters of the Meuse*—Series A/B, No. 70 (1937), p. 23—for a rejection by the Court of an interpretation the result of which would have been that "the intentions of the Treaty would be entirely frustrated"; the *Ambatielos* case, *I.C.J. Reports* 1952, p. 42 (on "cogent evidence" of the intention of the Parties as shown by the instruments of ratification exchanged between them); the Advisory Opinion on the *Effect of Awards of the United Nations Administrative Tribunal* with respect to the intentions of the General Assembly in establishing the Administrative Tribunal: *I.C.J. Reports* 1954, p. 61.

intention of the parties only by way of a figure of speech.[62] The scope of this chapter does not permit a more detailed elaboration of this aspect of the subject. The problem is to a large extent identical with the question whether the purpose of interpretation is to discover the intention of the parties or the meaning of the words which they used. It is possible to maintain that the intention of the parties is relevant only in so far as it supplies a clue to the true meaning of a disputed term or provision. The alternative and, probably, the correct view is that the discovery of the meaning of the words used in a treaty is only a means for ascertaining the intention of the parties.

### 44. *Preparatory Work in relation to Non-Signatory States*

In this connection reference may be made to the specific limitation put by the Permanent Court of International Justice on the use of preparatory work in cases in which some of the parties to the dispute had not taken part in the preparatory work of the clause forming the subject-matter of the controversy. In the case concerning the *Jurisdiction of the International Commission of the Oder* the Court issued in 1929 an Order laying down that as three of the parties concerned in the case before it did not take part in the Conference which preceded the Treaty of Versailles, " the record of this work cannot be used to determine, in so far as they are concerned, the import of the Treaty." [63] The Court then proceeded to make its ruling more specific—and, possibly, controversial —by laying down that it applied with equal force to passages of the record which had been previously published and to those which were produced for the first time in the written proceedings before the Court. It is not certain that the ruling when thus explained—*i.e.*, when referring to preparatory work previously published—can stand the test either of principle or convenience. When applied, for instance, to the Charter of the United Nations, the effect of the ruling would be that, assuming that resort to preparatory work is admissible in relation to States which participated in the Conference of San Francisco, the interpretation of any

---

[62] For a survey of such contingencies see Lauterpacht in *B.Y.*, 26 (1949), pp. 75–82.

[63] Series A, No. 23 (1929), p. 42. The same view was propounded by Great Britain in the case of the *Tunis and Morocco Nationality Decrees* in relation to the Covenant of the League of Nations: Series C, No. 2, p. 197.

particular provision of the Charter might be the subject of different methods and sources of interpretation with resulting differing or contradictory solutions—the answer in each case being dependent on whether any of the parties to the dispute had an opportunity to participate in the preparatory work. In proportion as the number of States adhering to the Charter increases, the effect of the ruling might be that recourse to preparatory work would be excluded for most practical purposes. It would be sufficient, in order to rule out resort to *travaux préparatoires*, if one of the parties to the disputes was absent from the Conference at San Francisco. Moreover, quite independently of any dispute, any provision of the Charter would be subject to a double standard of interpretation—that in relation to the participants at the Conference of San Francisco *inter se* and that among the Members of the United Nations at large.

But there are reasons even more compelling than the inconvenience of the consequences of the adoption of the principle of the case of the *Jurisdiction of the Commission of the Oder* which render it difficult to accept it without qualification. The very basis of that principle is open to question inasmuch as it assumes the existence of an objective meaning of a term or clause—of a natural, " plain," meaning—divorced from the intention of the parties responsible for it. Apparently, on that view, the States which adhere to a treaty after it has been formulated are bound by an abstraction expressed in words independent of the intent of those who shaped the treaty. However, to assert that once the Treaty has been concluded it has an existence independent of the negotiations which preceded it is to maintain that it has a meaning independent of the intention of the parties who evolved it. There is no more reason why the adhering States should not be bound by the preparatory work than that they should not be bound by the final and unequivocal expression of intention as recorded in the Treaty. For they have no part in either. The only adequate solution seems to be that the adhering States should accept the Treaty as, *to their knowledge*, it was agreed upon—as it was intended—by the original parties. This means that the preparatory work in question must be recorded, public, and accessible. To that extent—but to that extent only—the Order of the Court in the case of the *Jurisdiction of the Commission of the Oder* commends itself as a sound working rule.

## 45. *Conclusions. The Experience of the Two Courts Contrasted*

It may be convenient here to contrast, by way of summary, the practice of the Permanent Court of International Justice and of the International Court of Justice in the matter of recourse to preparatory work. In invoking the rule that it is not permissible to resort to preparatory work when the meaning of the Treaty is clear, the latter has occasionally relied on the authority of the precedent set by its predecessor. Such reliance is not altogether devoid of justification. For pronouncements of some such nature had in fact been made by the Permanent Court of International Justice. The difference between the practice of the two Courts seems to lie in the fact that the Permanent Court of International Justice was less ready to assume, as admitting of no controversy, a natural and ordinary meaning of terms to which effect can be given without difficulty. It did not discard the use of preparatory work on account of an assumed self-sufficiency of the text determined by the apparent clarity of the terms of the Treaty. In addition, notwithstanding its apparently non-committal attitude, that Court, on a number of occasions, made a positive contribution to the question of applicability of preparatory work by laying down the rule that it ought not to be considered at all when an attempt is made to rely on confidential negotiations,[64] or when conclusions are drawn from offers and declarations made in the course of abortive negotiations.[65] In most cases in which the Court declared the admissibility of recourse to preparatory work to be dependent upon the absence of clarity of meaning it actually inquired into the preparatory work either because the treaty was not deemed to be clear or, more often, by way of confirmation of a result reached by other means. In the latter case it is by no means certain that the actual sequence of events was in fact as it appeared in the Judgment or the Opinion of the Court—it is not certain that the clarity of meaning said to have been confirmed by the preparatory work was not actually due to the illumination obtained by the study of the latter. The borderline between confirming a view previously reached by other methods and finding support for it before its actual crystallisation is elastic and indefinite.

Upon analysis, there may be found to be little substance in the

---

[64] Series B, No. 14 (1927) (*European Commission of the Danube*), p. 32.
[65] Series A, No. 17 (1928) (*Chorzów Factory. Indemnity, Merits*), p. 51.

statement that there is no need to have recourse to preparatory work when the meaning of the treaty is " clear." As in other respects, so also here the doctrine of " plain meaning " may result in actual disregard of the true function of interpretation.[66] What is meant by saying that the meaning of the treaty is " clear "? A phrase or word is seldom, if ever, " clear " in itself. A term is clear by reference to the mind of the judge. It is only after weighing the various factors and considerations that the judge arrives at a conclusion as to the meaning of a particular term. It is only then that the term becomes " clear "; the judge has excluded, after weighing them, considerations and factors which militate against a contrary interpretation. Actually he does take these considerations into account. He does not exclude them *a limine*—although examination may reveal that the interpretation suggested by the preparatory work constituted only one phase in the negotiations and proved unacceptable to the parties. But a scrutiny of all evidence—intrinsic and extrinsic—there must be; it must not be hampered by a mere form of words. In most cases the Court has allowed itself to be hampered in theory only. In practice it has examined the preparatory work, although—as some of its pronouncements seem to tell us —only *after* it has arrived at the conclusion that the meaning is clear. But there is no certainty as to the actual sequence of events in the elaborate process in the course of which the Court arrives at its judgment. It is possible that in the process of shaping the judgment preparatory work is considered on the same footing as other available evidence, *i.e.*, before the Court has arrived at the conclusion that the text is " clear."

In adopting, in substance, an affirmative attitude to resort to preparatory work the Court has acted in full conformity with established international practice. The salient fact in the matter is that the recourse to preparatory work is a constant feature of interpretation of treaties by international tribunals.[67] It is not surprising that it should be so. If the task of interpretation is to discover the intention of the parties what better method can there be, in case of

---

[66] See above, pp. 52 *et seq*.

[67] This is the general result of the examination of this question by the author of this book in *Recueil des Cours* of the Hague Academy of International Law, 48 (1934) (ii), pp. 713–815, and in *Harvard Law Review*, 48 (1935), pp. 549–591. This is also the view of practically all writers, including the authors of the Draft on Treaties prepared by the Harvard Research Bureau (1935) (Art. 19, pp. 956–966), who have devoted detailed study to the matter. For a list of these writers see Oppenheim's *International Law* (7th ed., 1948), p. 862.

dispute and in the absence of an overwhelmingly clear expression of purpose, for achieving that object than the examination of the written record of the negotiations leading to the treaty, of the instructions sent to the representatives and of the discussions, of successive drafts, of agreed declarations, and of authorised reports which preceded the adoption of the treaty? This is not the easy method. It is much easier and seemingly more economical to let the sharp knife of logical or grammatical interpretation cut the knot of controversy. Although the International Court of Justice has occasionally given the impression of yielding to some such inarticulate inducement, this has not been its normal attitude. Its practice cannot be regarded as having become crystallised in that sense. The undoubted complexities of the issue fully account for the hesitation of the Court in the matter. For while it is apparently contrary both to principle and practice to exclude preparatory work altogether, the fact remains that the actual text of the treaty and not the contents of the negotiations preceding it express the will of the parties. The nature of the treaty-making process necessitates, in the matter of preparatory work, a solution which lies half-way between the finality of the text and the indiscriminate use of preparatory work. The difficulties and drawbacks of such indiscriminate use of that source of interpretation as a normal instrument for elucidating the intention of the parties have been indicated elsewhere in this chapter.[68] They explain—and, in a sense, justify—the hesitation of the Court in this sphere.

At the same time a critical examination of the contribution of the Court—of the two Courts—to this question suggest that the time is ripe for putting beyond doubt the full justification of the use of preparatory work, in its own right and within proper limits, as a legitimate element in the interpretation of treaties. Such clarification of the position would, by discouraging some redundant forensic argument as to the general justification of the use of preparatory work, conduce to economy in the written and oral pleadings. It would also diminish the danger that international tribunals, when confronted with the difficult task of unravelling the complexities of preparatory work, might feel inclined to solve the difficulty in a summary manner hardly calculated to assist the cause of international justice, namely, by disregarding preparatory work

[68] See above, pp. 132 *et seq.*

altogether.   It is the object of the present chapter, in addition to giving an account of this aspect of the work of the Court, to contribute to such study and clarification.   This explains why the subject of preparatory work in the interpretation of treaties by the Court—an instructive instance of judicial hesitation—has been treated here with what may appear to be excessive detail.

# Chapter 8

# APPEARANCE OF JUDICIAL INDECISION

## 46. *Conflict of Legal Rights.   The* Asylum *Case*

It has been shown that while caution, restraint and hesitation
have constituted a characteristic—a necessary and often unavoidable
characteristic—of the work of the Court, they have not impeded
the fulfilment of the main purpose of the judicial function, namely,
the rendering of a definite decision settling the dispute one way
or the other.   This applies also to those isolated instances in which
superficial examination may create the impression of reluctance, on
the part of the Court, to face a clear decision on the issue with
which it was confronted.   Of such instances the Judgments—there
were three of them—of the Court in the *Asylum* case between
Colombia and Peru provide an interesting example.

In the first Judgment given on this issue, on November 20, 1950,
the Court held that while Haya de la Torre, the refugee to whom
the asylum had been granted by the Colombian Embassy in Peru,
was not a person accused of a common criminal offence in the
sense of Article 1 of the Havana Convention of 1928, the asylum
was not properly granted as this was not an " urgent case " in the
meaning of Article 2 of the Convention.[1]   At the same time the
Court decided that Colombia was not entitled to qualify, by a
unilateral decision binding upon Peru, the nature of the offence
alleged to have been committed by the refugee in question.   It
also rejected the submission of Colombia that Peru was bound
to give the necessary guarantees for his free departure from the
country.

In deciding that the grant of asylum in the case before it did
not fall within the category of " urgent cases " as envisaged in the
Havana Convention, the Court acted on the view that regular
prosecution by judicial authorities, even if such prosecution takes
place in respect of revolutionary activities, does not constitute an
" urgent case " for " in principle . . . asylum cannot be opposed to

---

[1] See above, p. 30, and below, p. 383.

the operation of justice." [2] After stating that rule the Court proceeded to qualify it substantially: " An exception to this rule can occur only if, in the guise of justice, arbitrary action is substituted for the rule of law. Such would be the case if the administration of justice were corrupted by measures clearly prompted by political aims. Asylum protects the political offender against any measures of a manifestly extra-legal character which a government might take or attempt to take against its political opponents." [3] The Court did not attach decisive importance to the fact that the proceedings against de la Torre were instituted after a state of siege had been proclaimed; that certain, though not the judicial, constitutional guarantees had been suspended; and that it may not always be easy to place full reliance on the unimpeded and unprejudiced operation of the rule of law administered by judicial tribunals in circumstances of this nature. For this reason the qualification, which it expressed, of the major rule is instructive and, possibly, reveals the source of what may have created the impression of indecision in the Judgments of the Court on the subject.

Largely owing to the somewhat abstract manner in which the parties put the case before the Court, the latter did not deem it necessary to decide what was to happen to a refugee to whom asylum had been improperly granted and whom it found to be accused of a political—not a common—crime and therefore immune from liability to surrender. It was perhaps not surprising that on the same day on which the Judgment was delivered the Colombian Government informed the Court that it wished to ask for an interpretation of the Judgment, in particular, as to the question whether the Government of Peru was entitled to ask for the surrender of de la Torre (whom the Court had declared to be a person accused of a political offence and not a common crime) and whether Colombia was bound to surrender him (seeing that the Court had declared the grant of asylum to him to have been unwarranted by the terms of the Havana Convention). The Court, in a Judgment rendered on November 27, 1950, declined that request for the interpretation of its previous Judgment. It did so on the ground that these questions were outside the original terms of submission; that they were not in fact aimed at the interpretation of the Judgment already given but at rendering a new Judgment;

[2] *I.C.J. Reports* 1950, p. 284.
[3] *Ibid.*

and that, in any case, there was no occasion for any interpretation of the Judgment as provided in Article 60 of the Statute seeing that there was no dispute between the Parties on the question of interpretation—this being according to Article 60 of the Statute a necessary condition of rendering an interpretative judgment. The fact that the request had been made by Colombia on the same day on which the original Judgment was given showed that there was not yet a dispute between the Parties on this question.[4]

In the nature of things, this second Judgment of the Court could mean no more than a postponement of the issue until the Parties had gone through the motions of a " dispute." On December 13, 1950, Colombia, after an Exchange of Notes with Peru had taken place, filed an application asking the Court to determine in what manner its Judgment of November 20 should be given effect and in particular to find that Colombia was not bound to deliver de la Torre to Peru. The Court held, in the first instance, that the Havana Convention provided no answer to the question in what manner an asylum shall be terminated. It then found that having regard both to the letter and the spirit of the Havana Convention and the extra-legal factors in the development of asylum in Latin-America—an interesting example of a judicial tribunal considering extra-legal factors to be legally relevant—as well as to its first Judgment in which it decided that de la Torre was accused of a political offence, there was no obligation to surrender him. At the same time it held that that part of its Judgment of November 20 in which the grant of asylum had been declared to be illegal entailed a duty upon Colombia to terminate the asylum. It took pains to explain that there was no contradiction between the conclusion that asylum must be terminated and the decision that there was no obligation to surrender the refugee " since surrender is not the only way of terminating asylum." Although the Court attached importance to stating that there was no legal inconsistency between these two parts of its finding, it naturally envisaged the probability of a practical difficulty. However, it declared itself " unable to give any practical advice as to the various courses which might be followed with a view to terminating the asylum, since, by doing so, it would depart from its judicial function." [5] Instead it assumed that " the Parties, now that their mutual legal relations have been made clear,

[4] *I.C.J. Reports* 1950, p. 403.
[5] *Haya de la Torre* case, *I.C.J. Reports* 1951, p. 83.

would be able to find a practical and satisfactory solution by seeking guidance from those considerations of courtesy and good-neighbourliness which, in matters of asylum, have always held a prominent place in the relations between the Latin-American republics." [6] It considered itself to have " completed its task " by defining the legal relations between the Parties with regard to the matters referred to it.

It is proper, in a chapter devoted to Judicial Caution, to give an account of the possible criticism of the decision of the Court in the *de la Torre* case on the—apparently plausible—ground that it constitutes an example of judicial indecision. As will be suggested presently, the justification of the criticism, on that score, of the unanimous decision of the Court is open to question. However, it is convenient to state here in some detail the issue involved, seeing that it throws interesting light upon this aspect of the judicial function. The view which envisages this Judgment as an example of judicial indecision may be stated as follows:

The outstanding feature of the Judgment is that the Court limited itself, in effect, to advising the Parties as to one, the penultimate, phase of the legal position. It declined to decide what the Parties ought to *do* as a matter of legal obligation in relation to the subject-matter of the dispute. It found that there was a lacuna—a gap—in the Havana Convention, but it declined to fill it by way of a decision binding upon the Parties. The advice tendered to the Parties, to rely on considerations of courtesy and good neighbourliness, may have been somewhat theoretical, seeing that, if these sentiments had existed in the first instance with regard to the particular issue, the Parties would probably not have found it necessary to have recourse to the Court. There may have been little purpose in laying down the legal duty of Colombia to terminate the asylum—without surrendering the accused—unless a corresponding legal duty were imposed upon the territorial State to make the termination of asylum possible without disregarding that part of the Judgment which prevented the surrender of the accused person. There may be room for the view that the final Judgment of the Court constituted in effect a *non liquet*—a refusal to give a decision by reference to a legal principle overriding apparently conflicting legal rights. The actual issue before the

[6] *I.C.J. Reports* 1951, p. 83.

L. 10

Court was that of the physical custody—the freedom—of Haya
de la Torre. The original submission of the Parties may have
obscured that issue. Their final submissions left no doubt on the
matter.

Undoubtedly the Court was confronted with a delicate juridical
problem of the priority of two legal rights: the right of Peru not
to permit Colombia (and her protégé) to reap the fruits of an act
which the Court had found to be unwarranted by the Convention—
and the right (as well as the duty) of Colombia not to surrender
the accused, which right and duty were coupled with the obligation
to terminate the asylum. It may be argued—and this seems to be
the brunt of the criticism as here summarised—that in case of a
conflict of legal rights the correct jurisprudential principle is to
assign to one of them a priority and to cause it to prevail. The
margin of preference may be small. Yet, however tenuous, that
margin must be decisive. There must be a legal *finis litis*.
Admittedly, if judicial action is to proceed in accordance with the
principle here suggested, it may be indistinguishable, in some
respects, from judicial legislation. It may have to effect a compromise—which is not a diplomatic but a legitimate judicial
compromise—between conflicting principles of law.[7] There is no
decisive reason why the Court should avoid at all cost some such
outcome. It is in accordance with the true function of the Court
that the dispute submitted to it should be determined by its own
decision and not by the contingent operation of an attitude of
accommodation on the part of the disputants. There is an
embarrassing anti-climax, which is not legally irrelevant, in a
situation in which the Court, after prolonged written and oral
pleadings, is impelled to leave the settlement of the actual issue to
the courtesy and neighbourliness of the Parties. The resulting
considerations are, it is urged, of such transcending importance that,
if necessary, they warrant a measure of disregard, on the part of the
Court, of the wording of the terms of submission if these are such
as to attempt to transform the Court into an agency clarifying the
legal position,[8] instead of settling the controversy. On that view, it

---

[7] See below, pp. 398 *et seq.*

[8] In the field of contentious procedure the practice of the Court—as formulated in its
*Judgment No. 11 on the Interpretation of Judgments Nos. 7 and 8* (Series A, No. 13
(1927), pp. 15, 16)—contains authority for the proposition that the Court, for the
purpose of the interpretation of its judgment, does not consider itself as bound simply
to reply " Yes " or " No " to the propositions formulated by the Parties and that " it

is not conducive to the authority of international justice to permit the use of the contentious procedure of the Court for the purpose of obtaining what may be in effect an Advisory Opinion which is not binding.

It is convenient to complete this account of imputation of indecision by reference to the direct factual issue arising out of these Judgments—namely, the fate of the individual concerned. This aspect of the criticism levelled against them can be stated in the following terms: It may be a matter of controversy whether the institution of asylum as related to prosecution for revolutionary activities merits encouragement through judicial decisions or otherwise. It may also be a matter of dispute whether it is within the province of an international tribunal to discourage or to refuse full recognition to a typical regional custom for some such reason as that the institution of asylum results in protecting the actual leaders while exposing the mass of their supporters to all the risks and perils of the revolutionary struggle.[9] There may be substance in the view that the object of asylum is to grant protection from persecution but not from judicial prosecution. Admittedly, revolutions have more often than not served the cause of freedom and democracy as against tyranny and oppression. On the other hand, there have been instances of revolutionary attempts against orderly and democratic Governments (this, it may be noted, was the contention of the Peruvian Government in relation to Haya de la Torre in the *Asylum* case). However—and this seems to be the main burden of the criticism—regardless of the question whether or not the institution of asylum ought to be given a wide interpretation in any particular instance and whether the individual concerned is deserving of sympathy or not, in the *Asylum* case one of the results of the apparent indecision of the Court was that a person was exposed for a prolonged period to a condition of uncertainty and suspense in a manner incompatible with human dignity.

cannot be bound by formulae chosen by the Parties concerned, but must be able to take an unhampered decision." In the Advisory Opinion No. 16 on the *Interpretation of the Greco-Turkish Agreement* the Court held that as the request for its Opinion did not state exactly the question upon which the Opinion was sought, " it is essential that it shall determine what this question is and formulate an exact answer to it " (Series B, No. 16 (1928), p. 14). See also the Advisory Opinions in the *Jaworzina* case (Series B, No. 8 (1923), p. 50); the *Free City of Danzig and the International Labour Organisation* (Series B, No. 18 (1930), p. 9); the *Competence of the International Labour Organisation* (Series B, No. 3 (1922), p. 59).

[9] See below, pp. 379 *et seq.*

The above critical assessment of the Judgments in the *Asylum* case as making caution border on indecision has been stated here in some detail not because it is thought to be justified but because it sheds light, in a drastic fashion, upon the general issue involved. The answer, which may well be decisive, to that criticism is that if the Parties had desired the Court to give a judgment finally and unequivocally adjudicating upon the issue involved, they had it in their power, at any stage of the dispute, to ask the Court to act in that way. This they failed to do. The Court's attitude to questions connected with its jurisdiction forms the subject of an analysis which is attempted in various parts of this book and which shows that it does not consider it consistent with its function to arrogate to itself jurisdictional powers whose exercise is dependent upon the will of the Parties. In view of this, any hardship [10] caused to the individual concerned cannot justifiably form the subject of criticism in relation to the Judgments of the Court in question.

### 47. *The Political Background of the Issue. The Case of* Conditions for Admission of a State to Membership in the United Nations

While in the *Asylum* cases the caution, said to have bordered on indecision, was probably due to the terms of submission, in other cases the allegation of a substantial degree of indecision in some of the pronouncements of the Court may find an explanation in the elasticity and political complexion of the provision which the Court may be called upon to interpret. This probably was the case in the Advisory Opinion on *Conditions of Admission of a State to Membership in the United Nations*. The Opinion given by the Court was, in relation to the terms of the request, clear and unqualified: " A Member of the United Nations which is called upon, in virtue of Article 4 of the Charter, to pronounce itself by its vote, either in the Security Council or in the General Assembly, on the admission of a State to membership in the United Nations, is not juridically entitled to make its consent to the admission dependent on conditions not expressly provided by paragraph 1 of the said Article." [11] However, among the reasons adduced by the Court there occurs a passage which qualifies the main part of the Opinion and renders it less decisive than may appear at first sight. In that passage the

---

[10] Though not, as was subsequently reported with regard to the stay of M. Haya de la Torre in the Colombian Legation, in conditions of acute physical hardship.

[11] *I.C.J. Reports* 1947–1948, p. 65.

Court stated that the Article in question does not forbid " the taking into account of any factor which it is possible reasonably and in good faith to connect with the conditions laid down in that Article." This was so because, in the view of the Court, " the prescribed conditions are very wide and very elastic." Accordingly, " no relevant political factor—that is to say, none connected with the conditions of admission—is excluded." [12]

What is the practical value of the answer of the Court thus formulated? Once it is admitted that the conditions in question, being " very wide and very elastic," permit the taking into account of political factors there is no insurmountable difficulty in arguing, not necessarily in bad faith, that most political factors are relevant. If Soviet Russia had voted against the admission of Italy on the ground that Bulgaria had not been admitted, that clearly political motive might, in some indirect fashion, have been relevant to the question of the ability and willingness of Italy to carry out the obligations of the Charter. It might be argued—not very plausibly, but not necessarily in bad faith—that Italy, if admitted without the concurrent admission of Bulgaria and other States sponsored by Soviet Russia, would become so much dependent upon the States sponsoring her admission that she would no longer be in the position to fulfil her international obligations in conformity with the spirit of the Charter. A strained explanation of this kind might not be inconsistent with the negative answer which the Court gave to the second part of the question put to it by the Assembly, namely, whether—in the matter of admission—a Member of the United Nations while it recognises the conditions set forth in Article 4 of the Charter to be fulfilled by the State asking for admission " subjects its affirmative vote to the additional condition that other States be admitted to membership in the United Nations together with that State." However, apart from that second aspect of the question put to the Court, the existence, at that time, of two " blocs " of States, each accusing the other of a war-like disposition, would probably have made it legally possible to oppose the admission of States whose candidature was supported by one of the blocs on the ground that the applicant—like its sponsor—was not a " peace-loving " State " able and willing " to carry out in full independence the obligations of the Charter. Thus, it might be

[12] *I.C.J. Reports* 1947–1948, p. 63.

thought, the Advisory Opinion instead of invariably supplying a guide to action in conformity with the Charter, might provide a cloak for any kind of action.

The above critical assessment, which does not necessarily represent the view of the present writer, has been stated here in some detail for the reason that it sheds light on an important aspect of the issue here discussed. For, upon closer scrutiny, there is no warrant for attributing the manner of the Court's reasoning in this case to any decisive tendency to evasiveness. It is probable that the nature of the request as put to it and the wording of the Charter made the far-reaching—and almost mutually inconsistent— qualifications inescapable. This is borne out, with some emphasis, by the fact that the Joint Dissenting Opinion of four Judges shows a similar degree of inconclusiveness. They held, on the one hand, that members of the General Assembly or the Security Council, in voting on the question of the admission of new Members, were participating in a political decision and were therefore legally entitled to base their vote on any political considerations foreign to the qualification specified in Article 4 (1) of the Charter. At the same time it was held that in thus participating in a political decision they were " legally bound to have regard to the principle of good faith, to give effect to the Purposes and Principles of the United Nations and to act in such a manner as not to involve any breach of the Charter "; [13] that therefore they did not enjoy unlimited freedom in the choice of the political considerations which they deemed to be relevant; and that in any given case the question whether they fulfilled their legal duty of keeping within the limits of the Charter was properly a question for determination by the Court. It may be difficult to see how the propriety of political considerations can, in juridical logic, be the subject of a legal decision. But once it is postulated that a decision must be reached in good faith in accordance with the Purposes and Principles of the Charter and " in such a manner as not to involve a breach of the Charter," the decision ceases to be a political one and, notwith-standing its political implications or motives, becomes a legal decision. Thus, essentially, the difference between the Opinion of the Court and that of the Dissenting Judges is one of emphasis, not of substance. This was made even clearer by the manner in which

---

[13] *I.C.J. Reports* 1947–1948, p. 92.

the Dissenting Judges declined to answer the concrete question put to the Court—the question whether a Member may subject its vote to the additional condition that other States be admitted to membership of the United Nations together with the particular State applying for admission. This, the Dissenting Judges said in the penultimate paragraph of their Opinion, is " to ask the Court to assess the validity of any particular political consideration upon which a Member relies; that is a political question and must not be answered." [14] And yet the final sentence of the Joint Dissenting Opinion, after stating that a Member of the United Nations must use " this power [of admission] in good faith, in accordance with the Purposes and Principles of the Organisation and in such a manner as not to involve any breach of the Charter," concludes as follows: " But no concrete case has been submitted to the Court which calls into question the fulfilment of the duty to keep within these limits; so the Court need not consider what it would have to do if a concrete case of this kind were submitted to it." That conclusion prompts the comment that it was exactly a concrete case of that nature which was submitted to the Court in the request for an Opinion and that in the penultimate paragraph as quoted the Dissenting Judges apparently committed themselves to the view that the validity of any particular political consideration upon which a Member relies is a political question which " must not be answered."

There is no occasion here for an expression of view as to the merits, respectively, of the Opinion of the Court and of the Joint Dissenting Opinion. This is so, apart from other reasons, for the reason that the substantive difference between the two Opinions is probably but slight.[15] Both Opinions illustrate the possibility of a substantial degree of elasticity—and, to that extent, of uncertainty— due to the nature of the subject-matter of the request for an Advisory Opinion. It may be an excess of criticism to attribute such elasticity and uncertainty to any tendency to indecision or

---

[14] *I.C.J. Reports* 1947–1948, p. 93.

[15] The substantial identity of the solutions adopted is not affected by the interesting divergence of method in interpreting the crucial provision of para. 1 of Art. 4 of the Charter. The majority of the Court was of the view that " if the authors of the Charter had meant to leave Members free to import into the application of this provision considerations extraneous to the conditions laid down therein, they would undoubtedly have adopted a different wording " (at p. 63). The Dissenting Judges held that if the Charter had regarded the conditions laid down in Art. 4 (1) " as sufficient, it would not have failed to say so " seeing that " the point was one of too great importance to be left in obscurity."

evasiveness. On the contrary, the Opinions of both the majority and the minority of the Court in that case reveal a determination to lift the issue from its political background to the level of a pronouncement based on legal principles capable of general application. The result may, in certain respects, appear to be inconclusive. Yet such apparent indecision, which leaves room for discretion on the part of the organ which requested the Opinion, may—both as a matter of development of the law and as a guide to action—be preferable to a deceptive clarity which fails to give an indication of the inherent complexities of the issue.

In so far as the decisions of the Court are an expression of existing international law—whether customary or conventional—they cannot but reflect the occasional obscurity or inconclusiveness of a defective legal system. These considerations must tend to mitigate the tendency to over-emphasis in any criticism of this feature of the work of the Court. At the same time this aspect of its activity brings into prominence the question of judicial legislation as an instrument—both conscious and inarticulate—for developing and improving, within the legitimate limits of the judicial function, the existing rules and principles of international law. That question it is proposed to consider in the next chapter.

# PART THREE

# JUDICIAL LEGISLATION

# INTRODUCTION

### 48. *Occasions for Judicial Legislation in the International Sphere*

Judicial legislation, conceived as a process of changing the existing law, is not a legal term of art. It is a convenient term in legal philosophy and political science. A system of law expressly sanctioning judicial legislation would be a contradiction in terms. At the same time, the fact remains that judicial law-making is a permanent feature of administration of justice in every society. The reconciliation, in this respect, between fact and legal theory is brought about by means of the fiction that the enunciation of the new rule is no more than an application of an existing legal principle or an interpretation of an existing text. In the international sphere the problem is complicated, on the one hand, by the requirement of caution and restraint called for by the sovereignty of States and by the voluntary and, therefore, precarious nature of the jurisdiction of international tribunals. It is intensified, on the other hand, by the strong inducements to supplement and remedy the deficiencies and inconsistencies of an imperfect system of law. The necessity for caution and restraint, and the manner in which the Court has acted upon it, were discussed in the preceding chapter. We can now consider what, for the sake of convenience, may be described as the legislative side of the activity of the Court.

It is natural that members of a legal tribunal should incline to dismiss with some vigour the suggestion that they have indulged in acts of legislation. Thus the Court has affirmed repeatedly that its task is to interpret treaties, not to re-write them.[1] Probably, in many cases, it would have no difficulty in showing that any apparent innovation is the result of nothing more daring than the application of a general principle of law or of a general legal maxim.

---

[1] See, *e.g.*, *Interpretation of Peace Treaties* case (*Second Phase*), *I.C.J. Reports* 1950, p. 229; *Rights of United States Nationals in Morocco* case, *ibid.* 1952, p. 196. The statement, although apparently effective, in a sense begs the question. For the possible argument in support of the interpretation rejected by the Court is that it is that interpretation which in fact properly interprets the treaty and that any other interpretation amounts to re-writing it. In the *Anglo-Iranian Oil Co.* case Judge Read in his dissenting Opinion held, in effect, that the Court's ruling amounts to a "re-writing" of the instrument in question: *I.C.J. Reports* 1952, p. 145.

This would not necessarily refute the fact of the drastic character of the innovation. For there exist rules of international law which cannot normally be reconciled with a general principle of law— rules such as that which disregards the vitiating influence of duress in relation to the validity of treaties or that which denies, in principle, the compulsory jurisdiction of tribunals adjudicating upon the basis of law. To apply, with reference to situations governed by these rules, a general principle of law is, in effect, to introduce a change of a fundamental character. This explains why, while remaining within the orbit of the application of law—of a general principle of law—the Court has on occasions paved the way for the introduction of far-reaching changes. The denial on the part of the Court or of individual Judges of any intention to legislate is legitimate and proper. Any contrary attitude would constitute a usurpation of powers—doubly dangerous in the international sphere. This does not mean that they have been able to avoid decisions of a legislative character. Judicial legislation, so long as it does not assume the form of a deliberate disregard of the existing law, is a phenomenon both healthy and unavoidable. Through it—and through it alone—the compulsory jurisdiction of international tribunals can contrive to meet the challenge that on occasions it may become an instrument of retrogression inimical to peace and justice alike. This challenge the Court must attempt— and has attempted—to meet although, for the very reason that it is a judicial tribunal concerned fundamentally with the application of existing law, it may be able to engage in judicial legislation only within a limited compass. In the activity of the International Court judicial legislation has expressed itself in the following five ways:

In the first instance, as stated, an appearance of legislative novelty has occasionally been created as the result of the application of a general principle of law. Secondly, judicial legislation by the Court has taken the form of reliance on principles which, though of apparent novelty, have done no more than give effect to and draw the consequences from parallel developments in other spheres of international law. Thirdly, the Court has rendered decisions in which, proceeding on the assumption that there was no generally accepted rule of international law on the subject, it laid down principles governing the matter. Fourthly, on a number of occasions it has allowed what it considered to be the flexibility of international law to serve as a basis of decisions of a legislative character. Finally, while adopting a conservative view of its powers to adjudicate *ex aequo et bono* at the request of the parties, it has at times attempted to regulate, in a manner going beyond the interpretation of the existing law, the interests involved in the dispute before it.

These instances of what, by way of generalisation and, possibly, some exaggeration, may be described as judicial legislation on the part of the Court, will now be considered.

CHAPTER 9

# JUDICIAL LEGISLATION THROUGH APPLICATION
# OF GENERAL PRINCIPLES OF LAW

### 49. *The Principle* nemo judex in re sua

International law, being an immature legal system, departs in some ways from principles of law as generally recognised. Thus, as stated, traditional international law—though not, probably, international law of today—disregards the vitiating influence of duress in the conclusion of treaties. When such departures from the normal rule as recognised by civilised States are clear and unambiguous, the judge has no option but to act upon them. However, there are cases in which the application of a general principle of law, though in the nature of an apparent novelty (and therefore seemingly partaking of the character of legislation), is somehow grounded in an existing principle of international law and to that extent contrives to dispel the appearance of drastic judicial legislation. The Twelfth Advisory Opinion, relating to the dispute between Great Britain and Turkey in the matter of the Iraq Boundary and involving an interpretation of the Covenant of the League of Nations, illustrates clearly this aspect of the activity of the Court.

No rule is more firmly embedded in the practice of modern international law than the principle that States are not bound, in the absence of an agreement to the contrary, to submit their disputes with other States to final adjudication by a third party. The Court itself has repeatedly treated this rule as one of unchallenged authority.[1] And yet the question arises, and it was answered by the Court in the Advisory Opinion referred to above, as to how far that principle is compatible with a legal organisation of States established, among others, for the purpose of the pacific settlement of

---

[1] See, for instance, Series B, No. 5 (1923) (*Eastern Carelia* case), p. 27; Series A, No. 2 (1924) (*Mavrommatis Palestine Concessions*), p. 16; and see above, p. 91, and below, pp. 338 *et seq.* And see the *Ambatielos* case, *I.C.J. Reports* 1953, p. 19, for a broad statement of the principle that " a State may not be compelled to submit its disputes to arbitration without its consent."

international disputes. There were, it would seem, embodied in the Covenant of the League of Nations two principles which could not be easily reconciled. One was the abolition, in regard to disputes likely to lead to a breach of the peace, of the principle that every State is judge in its own cause. There was a duty to submit such disputes either to a legal decision or to inquiry and report by the Council or the Assembly. The other, equally general, principle was the overriding requirement of unanimity except in the cases expressly provided for in the Covenant. The two principles were irreconcilable in a number of ways, unless an attempt were made to make a general principle of law bear upon the interpretation of the Covenant. Thus while the Covenant imposed under Articles 10, 11, 13 and 16 certain duties upon the Members of the League in regard to the enforcement of the obligation of pacific settlement, the effective fulfilment of these duties might have become impossible if the rule of unanimity was adhered to. It might have become impossible for the Council to find that there had taken place aggression under Article 10; or, under Article 13, to propose what steps be taken to give effect to an award or decision with which a Member had failed to comply; or, under Article 16, to recommend measures of a military character against the Covenant-breaking State. The provision of Article 11 to the effect that the League "shall take any action that may be deemed wise and effectual to safeguard the peace of the world" might have been rendered impossible of fulfilment if that Article was interpreted so as to make action under it conditional upon absolute unanimity. The question, therefore, was bound to arise whether the rigid provisions of Article 5 of the Covenant relating to the requirement of unanimity ought not, as a matter of law, to be interpreted subject to general legal principles such as the principle that no one may be judge in his own cause.

In its Twelfth Advisory Opinion relating to the *Interpretation of the Treaty of Lausanne* (*Iraq Boundary*) the Court had occasion to pronounce on this matter. It had to answer the question whether the Council of the League of Nations, in deciding a dispute submitted to it by virtue not of Article 15 of the Covenant but of a Treaty concluded between the parties, could take a valid decision by a vote other than the unanimous vote of all the States sitting at the Council table. Could the Council lay down the frontier of Iraq by a vote other than a unanimous vote including that of Great

Britain and Turkey? If the letter of the Covenant was to be adopted as the sole guide, then a negative answer to that question was the only one possible: "Except where otherwise expressly provided in this Covenant . . . decisions at any meeting of the Assembly or of the Council shall require the agreement of all the Members of the League represented at the meeting" (Art. 5). Nothing could be more explicit. The Court, disregarding the letter of the Covenant, held that Article 5 " does not specially contemplate the case of an actual dispute which has been laid before the Council." [2] The letter of Article 5 seemed to cover all contingencies under the Covenant. However, the Court was of the opinion that to the case of an actual dispute brought before the Council there applied by analogy the principle of paragraphs 6 and 7 of Article 15 and paragraph 4 of Article 16, which, while requiring unanimity, excluded from this requirement the votes of the parties to the dispute. This meant in fact the application of analogy to cases in regard to which Article 5 seemed to have excluded resort to this method. The Court effected that bold piece of judicial legislation by reference to the principle that no one can be judge in his own cause.

There was nothing in the Treaty of Lausanne expressly authorising the Court to depart from the letter of the Covenant. The Treaty was silent on the matter except in so far as it entrusted the Council with the task of laying down the frontier, which task the Court conceived as intimating that the Council's decision must be effective and not liable to stultification by the vote of one of the parties.[3] A considerable part of the reasoning of the Court was devoted to showing that the manner in which the Council must decide the dispute was governed entirely by the provisions of the Covenant, including the general requirement of unanimity.[4] But the Court's vindication of the unanimity rule stopped short of disregarding altogether the general principle of law that no one may be judge in his own cause.

The Opinion was of unusual importance. If it was correct—and it is submitted that it was—then, as the result, there was justification for holding, for instance, that the votes of the parties to the dispute need not affect the validity of the resolutions of the Council under

---

[2] Series B, No. 12 (1925), p. 31.
[3] *Ibid.*
[4] See in particular *ibid.*, p. 29.

Article 11 of the Covenant when interpreting the obligations of the Covenant or acting in pursuance of such interpretation adopted by it.[5] This was not the view which the Council of the League adopted in the dispute brought before it in 1931 by China in consequence of the invasion of her territory by Japan. But it was a view which, following the authoritative Opinion of the Court in the *Iraq Boundary* case, it could have adopted had it been intent upon ensuring the effectiveness of the Covenant. For—and here lies the crux of the problem—this apparent example of judicial legislation must be regarded as a determined effort to see the purpose of the Covenant fulfilled. If the Covenant was a legal—rather than a political—document, then it had to be interpreted so as to be effective unless the contrary clearly appeared from its context or from the otherwise ascertained intention of the parties. In many cases judicial legislation amounts, in fact, not to a change of the law, but to the fulfilment of its purpose—a consideration which suggests that the border-line between judicial legislation and the application of the existing law may be less rigid than appears at first sight.

For reasons which are external to the present discussion, that Opinion of the Court failed to secure the attention and recognition to which it was entitled. No attempt was made to generalise its implications. In particular, it was not resorted to—as it well could have been—in the discussions concerning the question, which then gave rise to much controversy, whether a unanimous vote of the Council of the League was required for a request for an Advisory Opinion of the Court or whether, on the analogy of the principle adopted in the Advisory Opinion concerning the *Iraq Boundary*, the vote of the interested parties did not count for the purpose of ascertaining unanimity.[6]

[5] That Article provided as follows: " Any war or threat of war . . . is hereby declared a matter of concern to the whole League, and the League shall take any action that may be deemed wise and effectual to safeguard the peace of nations." There may be noted in this connection the observation of the Court in the case of the *Peter Pázmány University* to the effect that the Report submitted by Sir Austen Chamberlain and aiming at the settlement of a particular dispute under Art. 11 of the Covenant " was not unanimously accepted by the Council, Hungary, which sat on the Council in accordance with Art. 4 of the Covenant, having refused her consent " (Series A/B, No. 61 (1933), p. 243). The observation seems to lend support to the view expressed in the text above to the effect that the limitation of the rule of unanimity by reference to the principle *nemo judex in re sua* could properly apply only in cases in which the Council, acting under Art. 11, was concerned with the interpretation of the obligations of the Covenant or the consequences of such interpretation.

[6] But see the statement of Sir Cecil Hurst at the Conference of States Signatories of the Statute convened in 1929 in connection with the proposed adherence of the United

## 50. *The Doctrine of Abuse of Rights*

Another instance of judicial legislation by way of an application of a general principle of law is the manner in which the Court, in resorting to the doctrine of abuse of rights, lent its authority to the creation of a new source of international responsibility. Prior to its appearance in the Judgments and Opinions of the Court, the substance of the doctrine of abuse of rights had been recognised by a number of writers and in some arbitral decisions.[7] But it could not be said that it had been authoritatively recognised as part of international law. An attempt has been made elsewhere to show [8] that, regardless of terminology, the principle in question figures in the administration of justice of most of the modern systems of law. It is only at a rudimentary stage of legal development that society permits the unchecked use of rights without regard to its social consequences. The determination of the point at which the exercise of a legal right has degenerated into abuse of a right is a question which cannot be decided by an abstract legislative rule, but only by the activity of courts drawing the line in each particular case. The exercise of such activity—which, in relation to any new set of circumstances, may assume the complexion of judicial legislation— is particularly important in the international society in which the legislative process by regular organs is practically non-existent.

It is therefore of particular interest to note that the Court has not hesitated to associate itself—although not conspicuously or directly —with the doctrine of abuse of rights. In the Judgment given in May 1926 concerning *Certain German Interests in Polish Upper Silesia* the Court found that in the period from the coming into force of the Peace Treaty until the transfer of sovereignty over Upper Silesia Germany retained the right to dispose of State property situated there. But the Court added a rider to the effect that " only a misuse of this right could endow any act of alienation

---

States to the Court. In this statement Sir Cecil Hurst claimed—correctly, it is sub-mitted—that the Advisory Opinion in the matter of the Iraq Boundary could be adduced as an authority for the view that the vote of the Council in requesting an Advisory Opinion could not be affected by the dissent of the parties to the dispute (*Minutes*, p. 24).

[7] See Lauterpacht, *The Function of Law in the International Community* (1933), pp. 286–306.

[8] *Ibid.* See also Gutteridge in *Cambridge Law Journal*, V (1933), pp. 22–45, and Cheng, *General Principles of Law as Applied by International Courts and Tribunals* (1953), pp. 121–136.

with the character of a breach " of Germany's international obligations in the matter. " Such misuse," the Court added, " cannot be
presumed, and it rests with the party who states that there has been
such misuse to prove his statement." [9]   The Court then examined
the question whether the Polish contention that there had taken
place an abuse of right was justified.  The Court held that it was
not.  It found that the German acts of alienation did not overstep
the limits of the normal administration of public property, and that
they were not designed to procure for Germany an illicit advantage
and to deprive Poland of a right to which she was entitled.[10]

Four years later, in the *Free Zones* case, the Court was confronted with another aspect of the doctrine of abuse of rights.  In
that case Switzerland contended that the obligation imposed upon
France by the Treaty of 1815 to withdraw her customs frontier
implied not only the prohibition to levy duties on the importation
and exportation of goods, but also the obligation not to levy other
duties and taxes.  The Court did not accept that view.  It pointed
out that French fiscal legislation applied in the territory of the
Free Zones as in any other part of French territory.  But, the
Court added, " a reservation must be made as regards the case of
abuse of a right, an abuse which, however, cannot be presumed by
the Court." [11]   The same form of words was used in the final
Judgment in the same case in June 1932.[12]

There was possibly an implied reference to the principle of abuse
of rights in the Judgment in the *Anglo-Norwegian Fisheries* case,
where the Court in applying the principle of the general direction
of the coast for the purpose of determining the base-line of territorial waters stated that " one cannot confine oneself to examining
one sector of the coast only, except in a case of manifest abuse." [13]
Moreover, it is possible to see an indirect approach to the principle
prohibiting abuse of rights in the frequent affirmation of the duty
of States to act in good faith in the exercise of their rights.  Thus
in the case concerning *Conditions of Admission to Membership in
the United Nations*, after rejecting the view that the conditions laid
down in Article 4 of the Charter represented an indispensable

---

[9] Series A, No. 7 (1926), p. 30.
[10] *Ibid.*, p. 38.
[11] Series A, No. 24 (1930), p. 12.
[12] Series A/B, No. 46 (1932), p. 167.
[13] *I.C.J. Reports* 1951, p. 142.

minimum in the sense that political considerations could be super-
imposed upon them, the Court proceeded to hold that Article 4
does not forbid the taking into account " of any factor which it is
possible reasonably and in good faith to connect with the conditions
laid down in that Article." [14] It is also in this connection that the
doctrine of abuse of rights has been invoked by individual Judges.[15]

These are but modest beginnings of a doctrine which is full of
potentialities and which places a considerable power, not devoid of
a legislative character, in the hands of a judicial tribunal. There is
no legal right, however well established, which could not, in some
circumstances, be refused recognition on the ground that it has been
abused. The doctrine of abuse of rights is therefore an instrument
which, apart from other reasons calling for caution in the
administration of international justice, must be wielded with
studied restraint. This is so although there is no cogent reason for
accepting the view expressed by Judge Anzilotti, in the case of the
*Electricity Company of Sofia*,[16] that the contrary rule *qui jure suo
utitur neminem laedit* is in complete harmony with the spirit of
international law. In that case the suggestion was apparently made
by Belgium that Bulgaria denounced a treaty of compulsory judicial
settlement for the reason that Belgium was about to submit an
application to the Court under that Treaty and that the action
taken by Bulgaria constituted therefore an abuse of the power of
denunciation. The Court did not consider that point. Judge
Anzilotti in his Separate Opinion, after making the general observation referred to above, said: " The theory of abuse of rights is an
extremely delicate one, and I should hesitate long before applying

---

[14] *I.C.J. Reports* 1948, p. 63. See also the Judgment in the case concerning *Rights of Nationals of the United States of America in Morocco*, where the Court, in laying down the principles governing the fixing of valuation of import goods for customs purposes, stated that while the power of making the valuation rested with the customs authorities, " it is a power which must be exercised reasonably and in good faith " (*I.C.J. Reports* 1952, p. 212).

[15] See the Individual Opinion of Judge Azevedo in the matter of *Conditions of Admission of a State to Membership in the United Nations* (*I.C.J. Reports* 1948, pp. 79, 80), and the Dissenting Opinion of Judge Alvarez in the matter of the *Competence of the General Assembly for the Admission of a State to the United Nations* (*I.C.J. Reports* 1950, p. 15). See, in particular, the Joint Dissenting Opinion, in the former case, of four of the Judges who, while holding that legally any relevant political consideration is admissible in giving or refusing consent to the admission of a new Member of the United Nations, added that in the exercise of their discretion in the matter, Members are legally bound to have regard, *inter alia*, to the principles of good faith (at p. 92). And see Fitzmaurice in *B.Y.*, 27 (1950), pp. 12–14.

[16] Series A/B, No. 77 (1939), p. 98.

it to such a question as the compulsory jurisdiction of the Court. . . .
The Bulgarian Government was entitled to denounce the Treaty
and was sole judge of the expediency or necessity of doing so." It
is difficult to dissent from these propositions which, however, hardly
require the support of the broader and more controversial assertion.
The power to apply some such principle as that embodied in the
prohibition of abuse of rights must exist in the background in any
system of administration of justice in which courts are not purely
mechanical agencies.[17]

### 51. *The Completeness of International Law and the Legislative Application of General Principles of Law*

It might be suggested that whenever the Court appears to
approach international legislation by way of applying general
principles of law, it does so in reliance on its Statute which authorises it to do so and that there is therefore in such cases no question
of judicial legislation. The answer to any such suggestion is
probably that Article 38 of the Statute prescribes recourse to general
principles of law only if conventional and customary rules of international law provide no solution. However, it is probable that that
answer unduly simplifies the situation which is of some latent
complexity. Can it be said that if there is no rule of customary or
conventional law bearing expressly on the case international law is
silent on the subject? Or is it not rather the case that in such
contingencies resort must be had to the overriding rule of presumptive freedom of action of States and that there is no room for the
application of a general principle of law restrictive of that freedom
of action? On the other hand, there is force in the view that in
practice the situation is not that of simple absence or simple presence
of rules of customary or conventional international law; that in
practice these rules are often obscure or controversial; that, as the
result, the question is not one of displacing them but of interpreting
them against the background or in the light of general principles of

---

[17] It is clear that organs which, unlike the Court, are charged with the task of both
formulating and developing international law enjoy greater latitude in relying on the
doctrine of abuse of rights. Thus the International Law Commission in adopting in
1953, *de lege ferenda*, an article on Fisheries which provided that States shall be under
a duty to accept regulations prescribed by an international authority as essential for the
purpose of protecting fishing resources against waste or extermination was influenced
by the view that "the prohibition of abuse of rights is supported by judicial and
other authority and is germane to the situation covered by these articles." *Report of
the Commission, Fifth Session*, Doc. A/CN.4/76, p. 51.

law; and that the difference between disregarding a rule of international law in deference to a general principle of law and interpreting it (possibly out of existence) in the light of a general principle of law may be but a play on words. These, inconclusive, considerations may help to draw attention to the vast potentialities of that source of the law which the Court is authorised to apply and the application of which must be tempered by the knowledge that the primary—though not the exclusive—function of the Court is the application of the existing law. On the realisation of that fact depends in the last resort the usefulness and the authority of the Court. For the same reason, although it has been here deemed convenient to discuss the " general principles of law " of Article 38 within the framework of a chapter on judicial legislation, it would be a mistake to assume that this has been their typical application.

These considerations explain also why the sphere of application of Article 38 (3) of the Statute referring to " general principles of law as recognised by civilised States " has in fact been kept within a limited compass in the jurisprudence of the Court. Its importance as a source of international law and as an ultimate safeguard against the possibility of a *non liquet* remains unaffected by the relative infrequency of or lack of articulation in its use. Experience has shown that the main function of " general principles of law " has been that of a safety-valve to be kept in reserve rather than a source of law of frequent application. As a rule, the two primary sources of law enumerated in Article 38—treaty and custom—have provided a sufficient basis for decision. The very comprehensiveness of the power inherent in the authorisation to resort to " general principles of law " has counselled moderation in its use. This is so in particular having regard to the fact that while in the municipal sphere the consequences of having recourse to general principles of law are limited for the reason that, on the whole, the law does not, in that sphere, depart from the general sense of legal propriety,[18] this is not always so in the realm of international law.[19] This is far from signifying that wherever the Court has had recourse to general principles of law its action amounted to judicial legislation. On the contrary, normally it has constituted no more than an interpretation

---

[18] See on this aspect of the question Meier-Hayoz, *Der Richter als Gesetzgeber* (1951), where the author gives an account of the application by Swiss courts of the provision of Art. 1 (2) of the Swiss Code which authorises the judge, in case of a lacuna in the law, to act as if he were the legislator.

[19] See above, p. 155.

of existing conventional and customary law by reference to common sense and the canons of good faith.

## 52. *The Form and Substance of Reliance upon General Principles of Law*

The relative infrequency of express recourse to " general principles of law " as authorised and enjoined by the Statute of the Court has been accentuated by the fact that in those cases in which the Court has actually applied them it has, perhaps not unnaturally, refrained from resorting to them *eo nomine* and by way of express reference to Article 38 (3).[20] Thus in the *Chorzów Factory* case it used the following language: " The Court observes that it is a principle of international law, and even a general conception of law, that any breach of an engagement involves an obligation to make reparation." [21] Elsewhere it refers to " principles generally accepted in regard to litispendence." [22] In another case it based its Opinion on " accepted principles of law " according to which the individual members of an organisation constituted as a corporate body cannot take action of any kind outside the sphere of proceedings within that organisation.[23] In the Order concerning provisional measures in the case of the *Electricity Company of Sofia and Bulgaria* it invoked " the principle universally accepted by international

---

[20] Individual judges have from time to time, largely by reference to Art. 38 of the Statute, invoked general principles of law recognised by civilised States. See, *e.g.*, Judge Hudson in the *Electricity Company* case in support of the view that a subsequent expression of intention prevails over the earlier (Series A/B, No. 77 (1939), p. 125); the same Judge in the *Diversion of Waters* case in reliance on the proposition that equity is part of international law (Series A/B, No. 70 (1937), p. 76); Judge Anzilotti in the same case to the effect that a party which has failed to execute a treaty cannot rely on it (*inadimplenti non est adimplendum*) (*ibid.*, p. 50); Judge McNair in the *Status of South-West Africa* case in the matter of private law analogies generally (*I.C.J. Reports* 1950, p. 148); Judge Read in the same case with regard to the termination of a legal relationship by all those interested in it (*ibid.*, p. 167). In his Dissenting Opinion in the case concerning the *Interpretation of Judgments Nos. 7 and 8* Judge Anzilotti stated expressly that in basing himself on the rule that " under a generally accepted rule which is derived from the very conception of *res judicata*, decisions on incidental or preliminary questions which have been rendered with the sole object of adjudicating upon the Parties' claims (*incidenter tantum*) are not binding in another case," he relied upon principles obtaining in civil procedure (Series A, No. 13 (1927), p. 27). This, he stated, was particularly appropriate seeing that when the Committee of Jurists who drafted the Statute of the Court elaborated the expression " general principles of law as recognised by civilised States " specific reference was made to the principle of "*res judicata*."

[21] Series A, No. 17 (1928) (*Chorzów Factory.* Indemnity; Merits), p. 29.

[22] Series A, No. 6 (1925) (*German Interests in Polish Upper Silesia*), p. 20.

[23] Series B, No. 16 (1928) (*Interpretation of the Greco-Turkish Agreement*), p. 25.

tribunals . . . to the effect that the parties to a case must abstain
from any measure capable of exercising a prejudicial effect in regard
to the execution of the decision to be given." [24]   In the Judgment
concerning *Certain German Interests in Polish Upper Silesia* the
Court stated that nothing, either in the Statute or the Rules which
govern the Court's activities or in the general principles of law,
prevents it from considering certain aspects of a preliminary objection before proceeding with the examination of the case on the
merits.[25]   In the *Corfu Channel* case the Court invoked certain
" general and well-recognised principles " including " elementary
considerations of humanity, even more exacting in peace than in
war " [26] as substantiating the obligation of Albania to give notification of the existence of a minefield in Albanian territorial waters.
In the same case, in allowing indirect and circumstantial evidence in
favour of a State which had been the victim of a breach of international law in the territory of another State, the Court observed that
" this indirect evidence is admitted in all systems of law." [27]   In the
Advisory Opinion in the *Jaworzina* case the Court invoked " the
traditional principle: *ejus est interpretare legem cujus condere* "—
a principle which " must be respected by all "—in support of the
interpretation given by the Conference of Ambassadors in the matter
of the disputed boundary.[28]   In the Advisory Opinion on the *Effect
of Awards of the United Nations Administrative Tribunal* the Court
relied on the " well-established and generally recognised principle of
law " according to which " a judgment rendered by a judicial body
is *res judicata* and has binding force between the parties to the
dispute." [29]   In the case concerning the *Interpretation of the Greco-
Turkish Agreement* the Court rejected as " contrary to an accepted
principle of law " the contention that it is possible to accord to
individual members of a corporate body the right of independent
outside action in matters affecting the organisation.[30]

The Court relied on a number of occasions on the " principle
generally accepted in the jurisprudence of international arbitration,
as well as by municipal courts," to the effect that " one Party cannot

[24] Series A/B, No. 79 (1939), p. 199.
[25] Series A, No. 6 (1925), p. 19.
[26] *I.C.J. Reports* 1949, p. 22.
[27] *Ibid*., p. 18.
[28] Series B, No. 8 (1923), p. 37.
[29] *I.C.J. Reports* 1954, p. 53.
[30] Series B, No. 16 (1928), p. 25.

avail himself of the fact that the other has not fulfilled some obligation, or has not had recourse to some means of redress, if the former
Party has, by some illegal act, prevented the latter from fulfilling
the obligation in question, or from having recourse to the tribunal
which would have been open to him." [31] A State is estopped from
relying on it own non-fulfilment of an international obligation.
This impatience of evasion and the insistence on holding States
to the attitude previously adopted by them show themselves
in the way in which the Court on a number of occasions was prepared to recognise the operation of the principle of estoppel—which,
although it referred to it as a principle known in "Anglo-Saxon
law," it considered apparently to be a general principle of law.
Thus in the *Serbian Loans* case it examined in detail whether as
the result of a clear and unequivocal representation of one party to
the dispute, on which the other party was entitled to rely and
actually relied, the latter's position had undergone a substantial
change.[32] It is possible, having regard to the language used by the
Court, that it applied the same principle in the case of *Eastern
Greenland* where, after pointing out that " Norway reaffirmed that
she recognised the whole of Greenland as Danish," the Court stated
that "thereby she has debarred herself from contesting Danish
sovereignty over the whole of Greenland." [33] In the same case the
Court denied that Denmark was estopped (*empêché*) by her conduct
from claiming that she " possessed an old-established sovereignty
over all Greenland." [34] In the Advisory Opinion on the *Jurisdiction
of the European Commission of the Danube* the Court discussed
the argument which relied on the alleged inconsistency of the Treaty
of Versailles with the provisions of the Definitive Statute of the
Danube. The Court rejected that argument. It said: " As all the
Governments concerned in the present dispute have signed and
ratified both the Treaty of Versailles and the Definitive Statute, they
cannot, as between themselves, contend that some of its provisions
are void as being outside the mandate given to the Danube Conference under Article 349 of the Treaty of Versailles." [35] In the case
of the *Société commerciale de Belgique* the Court stated that as the

[31] Series A, No. 9 (1927) (*Chorzów Factory*. Indemnity; Jurisdiction), p. 31; Series B,
No. 15 (1928) (*Danzig Railway Officials*), p. 27.
[32] Series A, No. 20 (1929), p. 39.
[33] Series A/B, No. 53 (1933), at p. 69.
[34] At p. 53.
[35] Series B, No. 14 (1927), p. 23.

Greek Government expressly recognised the arbitral awards in question as possessing the force of *res judicata* it could not " without contradicting itself " contest the relevant submission of the Belgian Government.[36]

It does not much matter whether, in considering the parties to be bound by their own conduct, the Court resorts to the terminology of the doctrine of estoppel or not. This applies, for instance, to cases in which the Court accepted jurisdiction as the result of the conduct of the parties [37] or when it interpreted a legal text by reference to the declarations of the Government in question. Thus in the Advisory Opinion on the *International Status of South-West Africa* the Court held that certain declarations made by the Government of the Union of South Africa constituted a recognition on its part of its obligation to submit to continued supervision in accordance with the Mandate and not merely an indication of its future conduct. The Court said: " Interpretations placed upon legal instruments by the parties to them, though not conclusive as to their meaning, have considerable probative value when they contain recognition by a party of its own obligations under an instrument." [38] It is a question of emphasis whether reliance on the conduct of the parties to a treaty subsequent to its conclusion is treated from the point of view of the doctrine of estoppel preventing a party from asserting an interpretation inconsistent with its conduct or whether it is considered as a legitimate factor in the process of interpretation in the sense that subsequent conduct throws light upon the intentions of the parties at the time of the conclusion of the Treaty. Both represent, in substance, a general principle of law.[39]

---

[36] Series A/B, No. 78 (1939), p. 176.

[37] See above, p. 103. And see below, pp. 201 *et seq*.

[38] *I.C.J. Reports* 1950, p. 136.

[39] Yet there may be an element of artificiality in both unless care is taken to circumscribe their operation. Clearly, a party cannot improve its position by relying on conduct which is, wittingly or otherwise, in violation of the apparent purpose of the treaty as expressed in its language or, in some cases, as deduced from surrounding circumstances. Neither may it always be accurate to say that when a party seems by its conduct to acknowledge obligations such acknowledgment is conclusive upon it inasmuch as it throws light upon its true intentions at the time of the conclusion of the treaty. For such acknowledgment may be due to a lack of appreciation of its true position under a treaty; or it may be due to an attitude of accommodation going outside the obligations undertaken in the treaty. It would therefore appear that, when considered from the point of view of estoppel, the conduct of one party can be invoked in favour of the other only when, as the result of such conduct, the position of the latter has altered for the worse—a factor which is of the essence of the doctrine of estoppel in its primary connotation. When considered from the point of view of interpretation, conduct by one party may occasionally, but not invariably, throw light upon its intention when concluding

Similarly, in the Advisory Opinion concerning the *Competence of the International Labour Organisation* the Court, in affirming the competence of the latter in that respect, attached importance to the fact that for a period of two years after the signature of the Treaty none of the Contracting Parties raised the question whether agricultural labour fell within the competence of the International Labour Organisation. " All this might suffice to turn the scale in favour of the inclusion of agriculture, if there were any ambiguity." [40]   In the Advisory Opinion on the *Competence of the General Assembly regarding Admission to the United Nations* the Court, in interpreting Article 4 of the Charter, attached importance to the fact that the organs of the United Nations to which the Charter entrusts the judgment of the Organisation had consistently interpreted the text in the way in which the Court interpreted it by reference to the language of the Article in question and other considerations.[41]   It would thus appear that the Court equated with " subsequent conduct " the uniform practice pursued by the organs of the Organisation established by the authors of the Charter and acquiesced in by them.

While it may be difficult to classify these and similar statements as coming within the orbit of some of the technical aspects of the doctrine of estoppel, they seem to correspond to what is its essential

a treaty. On the other hand, there is considerable probative force in the concurrent conduct of *both* parties. In either case, the practice of the Court has tended to attach importance to conduct as a factor ancillary to interpretation reached by other methods. (For a more emphatic statement of the principle of " subsequent conduct " as an element of interpretation see Fitzmaurice in *B.Y.*, 28 (1951), pp. 9, 20–22.) In the Advisory Opinion in the case concerning the *Interpretation of the Treaty of Lausanne* the Court considered as relevant the facts subsequent to the conclusion of the Treaty " in so far as they are calculated to throw light on the intention of the parties at the time of the conclusion of that Treaty." From that point of view the Court attached importance to the fact that both the British and Turkish representatives at the Council of the League voted in support of a Resolution affirming the definitive and binding character of the decision or recommendation to be made by the Council; this showed that " there was no disagreement between the Parties as regards their obligation " under the crucial Article of the Treaty—a result which " may therefore be regarded as confirming the interpretation which, in the Court's opinion, flows from the actual wording of the Article." (Series B, No. 12 (1925), p. 24.) See also, on the relation between acquiescence and estoppel, MacGibbon in *B.Y.*, 31 (1954), pp. 144–152.

[40] Series B, No. 2 (1922), p. 41.

[41] *I.C.J. Reports* 1950, p. 9. See also, for extensive reliance on " subsequent practice," the Separate Opinion of Judge Basdevant in the *Minquiers* case (*I.C.J. Reports* 1953, p. 82). In the case concerning *Rights of the Nationals of the United States in Morocco* the Court, in the circumstances before it, declined to interpret the fact of the continuing exercise of a measure of consular jurisdiction by the United States as showing that the termination, by the Treaty of 1837, of consular jurisdiction in Morocco did not affect the rights of the United States: *I.C.J. Reports* 1952, p. 200.

feature, namely, that a person may—having regard to the obligation to act in good faith and the corresponding right of others to rely on his conduct—be bound by his own act. This may fairly be regarded as a general principle of law which, once more, is merely an affirmation of the moral duty to act in good faith. Like law as a whole, so also " general principles of law " are, in substance, an expression of what has been described as socially realisable morality. In legal history, courts—as distinguished from formal legislation—have been mainly responsible for the infusion of morals into law.[42] While in the international sphere judicial empiricism must—because of the limited and precarious character of international jurisdiction—proceed with greater caution, this aspect of the contribution of the Court provides one of the not least significant features of its activity.

---

[42] See, as to England and the United States of America, Pound, *The Spirit of the Common Law* (1921), p. 184.

# CHAPTER 10

# JUDICIAL LEGISLATION BY REFERENCE TO PARALLEL DEVELOPMENTS IN INTERNATIONAL LAW

53. *The Individual as a Subject of International Law. Rights Conferred by Treaty. The Case of the* Jurisdiction of the Courts of Danzig

Judicial legislation—or apparent judicial legislation—by the International Court has taken place on occasions by way of giving general and articulate formulation to developments implicit, though as yet not clearly accepted, in actual international custom or agreement of States. What the Court does in such cases is to translate in terms of express principle such changes as have in fact been accomplished. The impact of these developments upon traditional notions is not always fully realised by Governments—even if in fact they have accepted them. It is the revelation of the significance and of the full implications of these changes by reference to international law as a whole that creates the appearance of judicial legislation. The pronouncements of the Court on the question of the subjects of international rights and duties—*i.e.*, on the question of the subjects of international law—provide an interesting example of this aspect of judicial legislation. In relation to that question there already existed, at the time the Court was set up in 1920, a distinct degree of tension between doctrine and practice. While the predominant doctrine adhered to the view that States only and exclusively are subjects of international law, actual practice—both within and outside the State—was in many respects at variance with that view.[1]

The first important pronouncement of the Court in the matter is contained in Advisory Opinion No. 15 concerning the *Jurisdiction of the Courts of Danzig* in the matter of pecuniary claims of Danzig railway officials who had passed into the Polish service. The issue was whether treaties can confer rights directly upon individuals, or whether in each case a so-called act of transformation—to use the

---

[1] For a survey of the relevant developments see Lauterpacht, *International Law and Human Rights* (1950), pp. 6–14, and the literature there referred to at p. 6, n. 2.

terminology of the dualistic theory—is necessary. Poland contended that the agreement between herself and Danzig regulating the conditions of service of Danzig railway officials whom she had taken over conferred no right of action upon the officials in question. She maintained that the agreement, being an international treaty and not having been incorporated into Polish municipal law, created rights and obligations only as between the contracting parties, and that her failure, if any, to carry out the obligations of the agreement made her responsible not to the interested private individuals but only to the Danzig Free State. This was a position apparently fully in accordance with orthodox international law. For had not the principle that States only and exclusively are subjects of the law of nations become one of the firmly embedded dogmas of the doctrine of modern international law and one of the acknowledged guarantees of its scientific character? In the eyes of some that view had already at that time become inconsistent with various developments in positive international law, which, on occasions, recognises persons other than States as subjects of international rights and duties and even admits individuals as parties before international tribunals. For some the view that States only are subjects of international law had already then become synonymous with yet another expression for the glorification of the metaphysical entity of the sovereign State, with the resulting divorce of legal from moral responsibility and the indifference to the rights of the individual as the ultimate subject of law. Since then developments have proceeded, as we shall see, at a quicker pace and with greater intensity.

What was the Court's answer to the Polish contention in the case of the *Jurisdiction of Danzig Courts*? It rejected it in what was in effect a revolutionary pronouncement. It began by paying lip service to the established doctrine; it receded *pour mieux sauter*. It was ready to admit that " according to a well-established principle of international law, the *Beamtenabkommen*, being an international agreement, cannot, as such, create direct rights and obligations for private individuals." [2] But, having said that, it insisted that the actual answer must depend on the intention of the contracting parties. The Court said: " It cannot be disputed that the very object of an international agreement, according to the intention of

---

[2] Series B, No. 15 (1928), p. 17.

the contracting parties, may be the adoption by the parties of some definite rules creating individual rights and obligations and enforceable by national courts." [3]  It then found that this was in fact the intention of the parties in the case before it, and that, accordingly, the Danzig railway officials had a right of action against the Polish Railway Administration for the recovery of the claims based on the Treaty between Poland and Danzig.

It is difficult to exaggerate the bearing of the Opinion of the Court on the subject under discussion. The acquisition of treaty rights directly by individuals was made a function of the intention of the parties. The view that they can acquire rights only through the instrumentality of the municipal law of States was rejected. The postulated insurmountable barrier between the individual and international law was ignored. The Court denied the exclusiveness of States as beneficiaries of international rights. Had the Court wished to adhere to the traditional view, it would have interpreted the controversial intention of the parties in the light of the traditional doctrine. For it is a legitimate rule of construction that treaties must be interpreted in the light of customary international law. The Court refused, by obvious implication, to recognise that there exists a rule of customary international law to that effect. Moreover, the departure from the traditional view was effected with such ingenious restraint that some were led to believe that the Opinion of the Court amounted to a solemn affirmation of the established doctrine.[4]  Henceforth it was no longer possible to appeal, with any chance of success, to the alleged impossibility of individuals acquiring rights directly under a treaty. The issue must depend on the intention of the parties. What, as the result of that Opinion,[5] remained of the established doctrine was, perhaps, the

---

[3] Series B, No. 15 (1928), p. 17.

[4] See Beckett in *British Year Book of International Law* (1930), p. 4, and the same in *Transactions of the Grotius Society*, vol. XVII (1932), p. 176.

[5] It would have been contrary to the temper of the Court to express an opinion on the more general aspect of the question of subjects of international law. It is not suggested that the Fifteenth Advisory Opinion was intended as a pronouncement of this nature. What is submitted is that the result of the Opinion was to effect a breach in the established doctrine. The pronouncements of the Court emphatically affirming the State control over private claims and the international character of State claims of private origin—Series A, No. 17 (1928) (*Chorzów Factory*. Indemnity; Merits), p. 26; Series A, No. 20 (1929) (*Serbian Loans*), p. 17; Series A/B, No. 61 (1933) (*Peter Pázmány University*), p. 221—are only slightly connected with the question of subjects of international law. See on this question Watrin in *Revue de droit international*, VIII (1931), pp. 185–219. The same applies to the question of nationality of claims.

presumption against direct acquisition of rights; but it was a presumption which could henceforth be rebutted.

54. *The Same. The Case of the* International Status of South-West
    Africa

Thus when, in 1950, the Court was giving the Advisory Opinion on the *International Status of South-West Africa* it assumed, without considering it necessary to labour the point, that as the result of certain resolutions adopted by the Council of the League of Nations in 1923 in the matter of petitions from the inhabitants of mandated territories, these inhabitants acquired a corresponding right—a right under international law—and that that right was subsequently maintained by Article 80 of the Charter of the United Nations.[6] That Article, in the view of the Court, maintained the rights—the international rights—not only of States but also of " peoples " arising out of the provisions of the mandates.[7] In the same Opinion the Court spoke not only of the rights of " States and peoples " but also of those of the inhabitants—rights which, the Court found, although not mentioned in Article 22 of the Covenant of the League of Nations, they acquired by virtue of the rules adopted in 1923 by the Council of the League in the matter of petitions. It was significant of the change which had taken place in the doctrine of international law that the Court should have thus assumed that international rights had been created for individuals by an international act which was not even a treaty. Undoubtedly, some encouragement for that interpretation was found in the terminology of the Charter which spoke of the rights of " peoples." However, the more obvious explanation was that after the unanimous Advisory Opinion given in 1949 concerning the right of the United Nations to bring an international claim in respect of injuries suffered by its agents, the proposition that States only could derive rights and put forward claims under international law was not one upon which the Court could be expected to base its decisions in the future.

55. *The Same. The* Injuries *Case*

That Opinion—often referred to as the *Injuries* case—completed the development inaugurated by the Opinion in the case of the

---

[6] *I.C.J. Reports* 1950, p. 133.          [7] *Ibid.*, and, repeatedly, on pp. 134, 136, 137.

*Jurisdiction of Danzig Courts.* It is the Opinion in the *Injuries* case which, because of the doctrinal boldness and the clarity of its unanimous pronouncement on a fundamental issue of international law, must be regarded as the most important decision of the Court in that sphere and as one of the most significant examples of judicial legislation on its part. In that Opinion the Court held, unanimously, that the United Nations as an Organisation has the capacity to bring an international claim against a State—whether a Member of the United Nations or not—with a view to obtaining reparation in respect of damage caused to the United Nations as the result of an injury suffered by an agent of the United Nations in the performance of his duties. In order to answer that question the Court considered it necessary to examine—and to reply to—the preliminary question of the international personality of the United Nations. For only if the United Nations possessed such personality could it be considered as " an entity capable of availing itself of obligations incumbent upon its Members "—a somewhat circuitous definition, even for the purposes of the particular case, of international personality.

However that may be, the answer of the Court to that question is couched in language so comprehensive as to call for literal quotation. The Court said:

> " The subjects of law in any legal system are not necessarily identical in their nature or in the extent of their rights, and their nature depends upon the needs of the community. Throughout its history, the development of international law has been influenced by the requirements of international life, and the progressive increase in the collective activities of States has already given rise to instances of action upon the international plane by certain entities which are not States. This development culminated in the establishment in June 1945 of an international organization whose purposes and principles are specified in the Charter of the United Nations. But to achieve these ends the attribution of international personality is indispensable." [8]

The Court then proceeded to enumerate the various functions entrusted to the United Nations by its Charter, or in fact exercised in pursuance of it, such as the treaty-making power. It came to the conclusion that such functions could only be explained on the

---

[8] *I.C.J. Reports* 1949, p. 178.

assumption of the international personality of the United Nations. It said:

> "In the opinion of the Court, the Organization was intended to exercise and enjoy, and is in fact exercising and enjoying, functions and rights which can only be explained on the basis of the possession of a large measure of international personality and the capacity to operate upon an international plane. It is at present the supreme type of international organization, and it could not carry out the intentions of its founders if it was devoid of international personality. It must be acknowledged that its Members, by entrusting certain functions to it, with the attendant duties and responsibilities, have clothed it with the competence required to enable those functions to be effectively discharged." [9]

That typical combination of daring and caution explains why, after having held that the United Nations possesses international personality, the Court proceeded to inquire whether such personality implied the right to bring an international claim. It would appear that, apart from physical or similar incapacity, the right to bring a claim is of the essence of juridical personality. It is of the essence of a legal system that an injury inflicted contrary to law gives rise to a claim to reparation; as the Court said in the same Opinion, it is impossible to see how reparation can be obtained if there is no capacity to bring a claim.[10] Nevertheless, the Court still seemed to hesitate: "Whereas a State possesses the totality of international rights and duties recognised by international law, the rights and duties of an entity such as the Organization [of the United Nations] must depend upon its purposes and functions as specified or implied in its constituent documents and developed in practice." However, although the Court thought it proper to inquire whether the international personality of the United Nations implies the right to bring an international claim, it did so, somewhat briefly, in one sentence: "The functions of the Organization are of such a character that they could not be effectively discharged if they involved the concurrent action, on the international plane, of fifty-eight or more Foreign Offices, and the Court concludes that the Members have endowed the Organization with capacity to bring international claims when necessitated by the discharge of its functions." [11]

[9] *I.C.J. Reports* 1949, p. 179.    [10] *Ibid.*, p. 180.
[11] *Ibid.*

The significance of this unanimous Opinion lies not so much in the recognition of the international personality of the United Nations as in the final and formal rejection of the view that States only can be subjects of international law. Its importance has been somewhat obscured by the fact that the Court was divided—the majority was ten against four—on the question whether that right to bring an international claim included also the right to advance a claim in respect of damage caused to persons in the service of the United Nations (as distinguished from damage to the United Nations itself). The Court, disregarding the technicalities of the doctrine of nationality of claims, gave an affirmative answer to that question for cogent reasons discussed elsewhere in this book. In the present context it is the principal aspect of the Opinion to which attention has been drawn, namely, that which bears on the question of the subjects of international law. It is that aspect which would appear to provide a conspicuous example of judicial legislation.

Yet, as in other cases of apparent judicial legislation, it is not altogether certain whether this is the proper characterisation of the Opinion. It would certainly not seem to be warranted by its actual language. For that language is based on an interpretation of the text of the Charter, of the practice of the United Nations and, above all, of the development of customary international law in the matter. From this point of view it may properly be maintained that the Opinion is not of a legislative nature and that it does no more than apply existing law. What adds to the appearance of legislation is the vigour and the clarity with which the Court disregarded a doctrine of international law which for a long time had been almost a truism. Thus the question whether, as to subjects of international law, the Opinion of the Court constituted international legislation, is to a large extent a question of emphasis and degree. As in the case of the Advisory Opinion on the *Jurisdiction of the Courts of Danzig*, the Court did no more than pronounce, on a matter which hitherto had been the object of acute doctrinal controversy, in accordance with changes in the law which had actually taken place. It is the authoritative ascertainment of these changes—against the background of rigid and often uncritical doctrinal preconceptions—which created the appearance, or perhaps more than appearance, of legislative action.

In a less conspicuous fashion a similar trend manifested itself in the Advisory Opinion on *Reservations to the Genocide Convention* where the Court recognised, indirectly, the international personality of the United Nations in admitting its right to ask for an Advisory Opinion involving the interpretation of a Convention to which, it was asserted, it was a stranger. It was maintained that only States which were parties to the Convention were entitled to interpret it or to seek an interpretation of it. The Court rejected that view on the ground, *inter alia*, that the precise determination of the conditions for participation in the Convention constitutes a permanent interest of direct concern to the United Nations (" un intérêt propre et permanent ").[12] That direct and continuing interest of the United Nations, as distinguished from its Members, in a Convention in the acceptance of which it took the initiative, may be regarded, in a distinct sense, as being in itself a manifestation of its separate personality.

56. *International Legislation and the Doctrine of International Status of Territories*

In the *Injuries* case the Opinion of the Court recognising the right of the United Nations to bring an international claim against a Member of the United Nations was based on the interpretation of the Charter and the resulting recognition of the international personality of the United Nations. Judged by traditional standards that interpretation could not prevail against States which are not Members of the United Nations. For these States are not bound by the Charter; neither have they an interest in making it effective or a duty to make it so. The Court disregarded these considerations: " . . . the Court's opinion is that fifty States representing the vast majority of the members of the international community, had the power, in conformity with international law, to bring into being an entity possessing objective international capacity to bring international claims." [13] The Opinion, in thus asserting the binding character of the Charter of the United Nations in relation to non-member States, is of a legislative character. This is not a reason for questioning its soundness. There is no room in a developing international society for a rigid application of the principle according to

---

12 *I.C.J. Reports* 1951, p. 20.
13 *Ibid.*, p. 185.

which the rights and duties of a State can never be determined by a will other than its own.[14]

The Advisory Opinion concerning *Reparation for Injuries Suffered in the Service of the United Nations* is thus of double significance in connection with the process of international legislation. In the first instance, in so far as it expressly affirmed the international personality of the United Nations, it gave expression to a principle of international law which, although grounded in the interpretation of the Charter, was of some novelty when contrasted with the traditional doctrine which limited international personality to sovereign States. What in the Advisory Opinion on the *Jurisdiction of the Courts of Danzig* the Permanent Court did indirectly and with circumspection, its successor did boldly and by way of direct challenge to what was considered the traditional view. Secondly, inasmuch as that Opinion affirmed the right of the Members of the United Nations who adopted the Charter to lay down rules of a general character binding the international community at large, it gave judicial imprimatur—itself of a seemingly legislative character—to international legislation proper.

This was also the case, in a different sphere, in the Advisory Opinion on the *International Status of South-West Africa*. There the Court held—discarding the analogy to private law concepts of mandates,[15] trust or tutelage—that the international rules regulating the Mandate created by Article 22 of the Covenant of the League of Nations " constituted an international status for the Territory recognised by all the Members of the League of Nations "; that the obligations created by the Mandate did not depend upon the existence of the League of Nations; and that " they could not be

---

[14] At the same time the Opinion of the Court tends to focus attention on the slowness and conservatism of international legislative processes. Art. 34 of the Statute still provides that only States can be parties to cases before the Court. If that provision of the Statute, historically grounded in the dogma that States only are subjects of international law, is allowed to remain unaltered, the result will be that although the United Nations is entitled to bring an international claim it is not entitled to do so before its own principal judicial organ even if the State concerned agrees to such a course. There is room for a reconsideration of Art. 34 with the view to drawing the obvious consequences from the Opinion of the Court—at least in relation to the United Nations as such. In this connection the question would arise whether in relation to claims by—and against—the United Nations as such the jurisdiction of the Court should not be compulsory. The system of the Optional Clause of Art. 36 of the Statute cannot properly be applied to the United Nations as a party. It is difficult—and, in a sense, unseemly—to visualise the United Nations as signing the Optional Clause, possibly with reservations.

[15] See below, p. 182.

brought to an end merely because this supervisory organ ceased to exist." [16] The conception of international status overreaching in its legal effects the States parties to the original treaty was elaborated in detail in the Separate Opinion of Judge Sir Arnold McNair. He put it in the form of a general proposition: " From time to time it happens that a group of great Powers, or a large number of States both great and small, assume a power to create by a multilateral treaty some new international régime or status, which soon acquires a degree of acceptance and durability extending beyond the limits of the actual contracting parties and giving it an objective existence." [17] He instanced as an example the report of the Commission of Jurists, appointed in 1920 by the Council of the League of Nations, in the case of the Åaland Islands in which they based their findings on the fact of a " special international status " for the Islands with the result that " every State interested [including Sweden which was not a party] has the right to insist upon compliance " with the obligations created by the treaty in question.

While in the above cited passage of the Separate Opinion of Judge McNair the element of " subsequent acceptance and durability " seems to refer to a requirement additional to the outright legislative effect of the original treaty, even that requirement seems to partake of a legislative quality. For the " degree of acceptance and durability " is not identical with universal acceptance. The result is that there is assumed a method of creating binding obligations which is independent of the will of any particular State held to be bound by them. In the Opinion of the Court that legislative character, independent of subsequent acceptance of the treaty in question, appears even more prominently. Divested of any analogy with its private law prototype, the " Mandates " are clearly given the complexion of a status independent of the continued existence of the parties to the original treaty which gave rise to it. Thus, upon analysis, the doctrine of international status amounts to an affirmation of international legislation. For status implies an area of operation not limited to the original contracting parties or to contracting parties generally. Status operates *erga omnes*.[18]

---

[16] *I.C.J. Reports* 1950, p. 133.

[17] *Ibid.*, p. 153.

[18] It was this aspect of the Judgment which constitutes its main, and significant, contribution to international law, as distinguished from the manner in which it rejected the contention of South Africa that, as the League of Nations had ceased to exist, the Mandate itself had come to an end. In order to establish the view that the obligations

## 57. *Nationality of Claims*

Finally, within a more limited sphere—and once more in connection with the theme of the international personality of the United Nations—the Court went some way in the direction of judicial legislation, by reference to parallel developments in international law, in connection with the seemingly well-established rule of nationality of claims. The traditional rule on the subject, as generally recognised prior to the Opinion of the Court in the *Reparation for Injuries* case, was that diplomatic protection by way of putting forward an international claim could be exercised: (a) only by a State, and (b) only on behalf of a person who was its national both at the time of the alleged injury and at the time when diplomatic protection was being exercised. The problem of the

of the Mandatory continued notwithstanding the demise of the League, the Court found it necessary to state that the " mandate " had " only the name in common with the several notions of mandate in national law " and that it is " not possible to draw any conclusion of analogy from the notions of mandate in national law or from any other legal conception of that law " (*I.C.J. Reports* 1950, p. 132). Yet it is probably true to say that the essential notion of mandate (or trust) in private law was also essential to the system of Mandates, namely, the notion that the powers and rights of the Mandatory were of a delegated character and that the Mandate was intended primarily to serve interests other than those of the Mandatory. This was not inconsistent with the view, propounded by the Court, that the institution of Mandates " exceeded that of contractual relations regulated by national law " (*ibid.*). It was open to the Court, instead—in order to meet the principal contention of South Africa— of questioning what was the essence of the mandate system, to combine it (see the Separate Opinion of Sir Arnold McNair, *ibid.*, pp. 147–162) with the principle, which it adopted, that it created at the same time a " real " right, a status. The " reality " of a right is not inconsistent with its contractual nature; it stems from it. In fact, the Court itself had no difficulty in rejecting the argument of South Africa based on the contention that the League had ceased to exist. It said: " If the Mandate lapsed, as the Union Government contends, the latter's authority would equally have lapsed " (*ibid.*, p. 133).

The rejection of analogy, to private law and otherwise, by dint of attaching decisive importance to the dissimilarities of the situations which are being compared, may on occasions be open to question. It does not constitute a permanent feature of the method pursued by the Court—as may be seen from the relative frequency with which the Court has had recourse to general principles of law (see above, pp. 165 *et seq.*). These, upon analysis, constitute in a distinct sense a recognition of the necessity to develop and to apply international law by way of analogy to municipal law. Analogy is a logical process by which deductions are made and conclusions drawn from a comparison of situations which exhibit similarities in some respects and dissimilarities in others. The dissimilarities are an easy object of attack; they make the comparison appear artificial and often paradoxical; they help to dispose of the problem with a minimum of effort. Yet often it is the similarity which is of the essence of the situation and which is the most instructive and fruitful method of approach. As such, analogy has been the vehicle of progress in every branch of scientific and intellectual endeavour. To this phenomenon law supplies no exception. The historic circumstances which have caused analogy to private law in the sphere of international law to serve a function of particular significance are too well known to require elaboration

applicability of that rule arose in connection with the question, put to the Court, whether the United Nations, as an Organisation, had the capacity to bring an international claim in respect of damage caused to its officials. The Court answered that question in the affirmative. It held that the traditional rule applied only to claims brought by States: " But here we have the different and new case of a claim that would be brought by the Organization." [19] Neither was it willing to concede that even among States that rule applied unconditionally. It said: " Even in inter-State relations, there are important exceptions to the rule, for there are cases in which protection may be exercised by a State on behalf of persons not having its nationality." The Court then proceeded to elaborate the point that the accepted principle of nationality of claims applied to the case before it seeing that one of the considerations on which that principle is based was that only the party to whom an international obligation is due can bring a claim in respect of its breach: " This is precisely what happens when the Organization, in bringing a claim for damage suffered by its agent, does so by invoking the breach of an obligation towards itself." [20] Moreover, after having held that the rule of nationality of claims did not exclude its reasonable adaptation to a novel situation, the Court went on to deny that that rule, apparently identical with the traditional rule of diplomatic protection, applied to the novel situation before it: " It is not possible, by a strained use of the concept of allegiance, to assimilate the legal bond which exists, under Article 100 of the Charter, between the Organization on the one hand, and the Secretary-General and the staff on the other, to the bond of nationality existing between a State and its nationals." [21] It added: " The Court is here faced with a new situation. The questions to which it gives rise can only be solved by realizing that the situation is dominated by the provisions of the Charter considered in the light of the principles of international law." [22] That new situation demanded an interpretation of the Charter in conformity

---

[19] *I.C.J. Reports* 1949, p. 181.

[20] *Ibid.*, p. 182.

[21] *Ibid.*

[22] *Ibid.* The attitude of the Court in the *Injuries* case to the rule of nationality of claims and its reference to the important exceptions to that rule may be contrasted with its Judgment previously rendered in the case of the *Panevezys-Saldutiskis Railway* (Series A/B, No. 76 (1939), p. 16). There the Court fully upheld the rule and elaborated on the subject of its importance and justification in international law. See below, p. 350.

with the principle of effectiveness—a matter which falls more conveniently within the framework of the next chapter of this book.

### 58. *Judicial Legislation as Formulating Previous Changes in the Law*

It is a matter of emphasis and doctrinal interpretation to what extent the Court proceeds by way of judicial legislation in cases in which it lays down rules and principles of some novelty on the ground that they are no more than an expression of changes that have already taken place in the same or cognate spheres. In a system of law—such as international law—in which the machinery of legislation is rudimentary, there is no provision for consequential changes covering and following upon accomplished alterations in the law. The result must often be a series of inconsistencies inimical to the dignity and the authority of the law. That result can be obviated by a parallel change of practice—which is of slow and indeterminate growth and difficult of ascertainment—or by judicial activity. Thus, to mention one example, in traditional international law there existed certain rules and principles which could be logically explained only by reference to the fact that international law permitted war as an instrument of national policy for the purpose both of defending existing legal rights and challenging the undoubted rights of other States. These rules and principles included the disregard of the fact of duress in the conclusion of treaties, the admissibility of conquest as a source of territorial title, and the requirement of absolute impartiality of neutral States regardless of the justice of the war waged by the belligerents. Yet these rules and principles are out of place in a legal system which by way of an express and formal innovation has prohibited recourse to force as an instrument of national policy. It is proper for international courts to draw the unavoidable conclusions following from such developments—except in cases in which the authors of the change have expressly disclaimed, even at the risk of logical inconsistency, any intention of effecting consequential changes. In such cases there is room for the view that judicial legislation does no more than give expression to changes already effected; that it does not therefore constitute legislation in the true sense of the term; and that for international tribunals to adopt any other course would mean to reduce their activity to a mechanical application of the letter of the—no longer existent—law.

# CHAPTER 11

# JUDICIAL LEGISLATION ON ACCOUNT OF ABSENCE OF GENERALLY ACCEPTED LAW

59. *Diversity of Practice.   The Case of the* Reservations to the Genocide Convention

While in the instances discussed so far judicial legislation has taken place by way of application of existing rules or principles of law—whether they be general principles of law or provisions of treaties interpreted in accordance with parallel developments in international law—in some cases the Court has rendered decisions of a general nature and of apparent novelty on the ground, mainly, that there did not in fact exist rules of international law, generally agreed, applicable to the situation with which it was confronted. The Judgment of the Court in the case of the *Norwegian Fisheries* and its Advisory Opinion bearing on the *Reservations to the Genocide Convention* provide significant examples of this aspect of the activity of the Court. In both these cases the Court proceeded on the view that no generally accepted agreed legal rule on the question before it existed and that it was therefore bound and entitled to proceed to an independent examination—and solution—of the problems involved. These two cases provide the two principal instances of judicial legislation in face of an admitted absence of agreed law. It is not necessary to give here a detailed account of minor examples in the same category as illustrated, for instance, by the procedural ruling of the Court in the case of the *Mavrommatis Palestine Concessions*. In that case, when confronted with the absence of provisions, both in its Statute and its Rules, regarding the procedure in cases of objection to jurisdiction *in limine litis*, the Court stated that it was " at liberty to adopt the principle which it considers best calculated to ensure the administration of justice, most suited to procedure before an international tribunal, and most in conformity with the fundamental principles of international law." [1]

With regard to the main aspect of the question involved in the

---

[1] Series A, No. 2 (1924), p. 16.

Opinion on the *Reservations to the Genocide Convention* [2] the view which, prior to the Opinion of the Court, seemed to have been predominant was that a State making a reservation not previously assented to by the other contracting parties was, in effect, rejecting the original instrument and making a proposal for a new treaty; that unless the other contracting parties agreed to the proposal the State making the reservation could not become a party to the treaty; and that, for reasons of logic which appeared obvious, the unanimous consent of the other contracting parties was necessary for the purpose. The generality of the acceptance of that principle was not seriously affected by the circumstance that since 1938 there had come into being, as between some American States, the so-called Pan-American system which made it possible for a reserving State to become a party to the Convention in relation to the States which agreed to the reservation—though not in relation to others. The occasional difficulties and discussions to which the principle of unanimous consent gave rise emphasised rather than detracted from the fact of its general acceptance. This did not necessarily mean that it was a principle which was wholly rational or adapted to the requirements of a growing volume of international regulation by way of multilateral treaties.

It is possible that that lack of belief in the adequacy of the principle of unanimous consent was to some extent responsible for the fact that the Court declined to hold that that principle formed part of international law. It held that the rarity, in the past, of objections to reservations made it impossible to admit that any such rule had in fact arisen; that the clear decision of the Council of the League of Nations upholding the principle of unanimous consent was no more than a recommendation in the field of administrative practice; and that the existence of a different practice among the American States was in itself sufficient to show the absence of any generally accepted rule on the subject.

It is controversial whether the conclusions of the Court can be accepted as an accurate statement of the legal position as then existing. These conclusions were challenged by reference to the impressive authority of practice and doctrine adduced in the Joint Dissenting Opinion of four Judges of the Court. However that may be, the Court, having found that there existed no binding rule

---

[2] *I.C.J. Reports* 1951, pp. 15–30.

on the subject, proceeded to expound—in a necessarily tentative manner—its view on the solution of the difficulties resulting from the denial of the validity of the principle of unanimous consent. It discarded the principle of unanimous consent not only as a rule of existing law, but as a rational rule of law. It held, in effect, that the consent of all the Contracting Parties to a reservation is not necessary in order to enable a reserving State to become a party to the Convention; that it is for every Contracting Party to judge for itself whether a reservation made by another State is such as to preclude the reserving State from becoming a party to the Convention; that such judgement is not one of arbitrary discretion; that it must be determined by the " common duty of the contracting States to be guided in their judgement by the compatibility or incompatibility of the reservation with the object and purpose of the Convention "; [3] and that the question whether that duty has in fact been complied with, is capable of judicial determination, either by special agreement or through the machinery of compulsory settlement of disputes provided by the Convention, in all cases in which a contracting State is of the opinion, which has been contested, that a reservation appended by another is in fact incompatible with the purpose of the Convention. The Court did not consider the question of the application of the rule thus enunciated in cases in which the suitability for judicial determination has not assumed the complexion of a duty to submit the contested issue for compulsory determination by law.

In its Opinion the Court admitted that the disadvantages resulting from the solution which it adopted—*i.e.*, from the fact that some of the Contracting Parties may consider the reserving State to be a party while others may refuse to do so—are real. The Opinion of the Court did not suggest any ready solution of the difficulty. It referred to the " common duty of the contracting States to be guided in their judgment by the compatibility or incompatibility of the reservations with the object and the purpose of the Convention." It added, with some resignation: " It must clearly be assumed that the contracting States are desirous of preserving intact at least what is essential to the object of the Convention; should this desire be absent, it is quite clear that the Convention itself would be impaired both in its principle and in its

---

[3] *I.C.J. Reports* 1951, pp. 27, 28.

application."[4]   It is clear that the Court did not consider that expression of hope to constitute a satisfactory basis of the system formulated by it in preference to the widely accepted principle of unanimous consent.  It envisaged the possibility, in cases in which some parties consider that the assent given by other parties to reservations is incompatible with the purpose of the Convention, of the parties deciding " to adopt a position on the jurisdictional plane in respect of this divergence and to settle the dispute which thus arises either by special agreement " or by the procedure laid down in the Convention.  The case thus referred to by the Court does not touch upon the principal difficulties arising out of the solution foreshadowed by the Court.  These difficulties arise from the disagreement between the State making a reservation and any other contracting State as to the justification of a refusal to agree to a reservation.   They arise, secondly, from the divergent attitudes adopted by the contracting States with regard to the same situation as well as from the resulting phenomenon of a State being a party to a Convention in relation to some contracting States but not to others.

The Opinion of the Court lends itself to somewhat easy criticism conceived in the following terms: The principle of unanimous consent—even if it is admitted that it was, like the requirement of unanimity in general, both rigid and out of keeping with the needs of the international legislative process through multilateral treaties—at least provided a solution capable of general application.  The Opinion given by the Court on the subject, while possibly containing the elements of a more workable solution than that which obtained in the past,[5] left in abeyance this complex aspect of the law of treaties.  To that extent it seemed to have left a gap in that branch of the law of treaties and to have raised the question of the method of judicial legislation which throws doubt upon what was widely believed to be the existing law without substituting in its place a working legal rule.

The criticism, thus expressed, of the Opinion of the Court is less cogent than appears at first sight.  Judicial legislation is not— and ought not to be—like legislative codification by statute.  It cannot attempt to lay down all the details of the application of the

---

[4] *I.C.J. Reports* 1951, p. 27.

[5] See Fitzmaurice in *International and Comparative Law Quarterly*, 11 (i) (1953), pp. 1–27, and Lauterpacht in *Transactions of the Grotius Society*, 39 (1953), pp. 97–118.

principle on which it is based. It lays down the broad principle and applies it to the case before it. Its elaboration must be left, in addition to any doctrinal elucidation of the law by writers, to ordinary legislative processes or to future judicial decisions disposing of problems as they arise. However that may be, the Opinion of the Court is an important instance of a judicial attempt to lay down a new legal régime in the face of what the Court considered to be the absence of a binding customary rule of international law on the subject. To that extent it may properly be regarded as an instance of judicial legislation.

### 60. *Universality or Predominance as a Test of Rules of International Law. The* Anglo-Norwegian Fisheries *Case*

The same problem is illustrated, in very similar terms, in the Judgment of the Court in the *Fisheries* case between the United Kingdom and Norway.[6] There, too, we see the Court declining to give recognition to a rule which, although not universally followed, had secured by far the greatest measure of agreement. Moreover, also in that case it was not so much any inherent excellence of that more widely adopted rule which raises questions concerning the legislative action of the Court as the possibility that no system, fully elaborated, was put in its place.

There was, in that case, no suggestion on the part of the Court that, on the main issue before it, its Judgment was based on rules or principles accepted by the majority of States. But the Court denied that the opposite principle, contended for by the United Kingdom, had secured as wide an acceptance as was asserted. It is not certain, having regard to the generality of the language used by the Court, to what extent it considered that principle as having been predominantly—though not generally or universally—adopted.[7]

It is believed that prior to the Judgment of the Court in the *Fisheries* case the rules on the subject which were regarded as generally, though not universally, accepted, were that the inner

---

[6] See below, pp. 192 *et seq.*, 362 *et seq.*, 368 *et seq.*

[7] See below, p. 369. For the suggestion that it was the system of straight lines which corresponded more closely to the actual practice see Bourquin in *Acta Scandinavica*, 22 (1952), p. 126. However, the general reference to the practice of "nombreux pays" does no more than substantiate the learned writer's submission that there existed on the subject a divergence of practice. The question still remains whether that divergence negatives the claim that the coast line rule constituted the more widely adopted—perhaps the predominant—practice.

limit, *i.e.*, the base-line, of territorial waters was determined by the low-water mark following the sinuosities of the coast and that in case of bays the base-line was, in general, the line drawn across the bay at the point where the bay is ten miles—or approximately so —wide. These rules were not admitted without exception; they were occasionally challenged on historic and other grounds. A relatively small number of States, including Norway, declined to recognise them.[8] The rule that the base-line follows the sinuosities of the coast was qualified in cases of the presence of shoals or groups of islands. The method of its application—in particular, the system of so-called " envelopes of arcs of circles "—was not free of doubt. Similarly, with regard to bays, pretensions on historic grounds as well as occasional claims based on other considerations were at variance with the so-called ten-mile rule—which, in addition to having been somewhat attenuated by the award in the *North Atlantic Fisheries Arbitration*,[9] suffered from the drawback that several lines ten miles wide could be envisaged in relation to the same bay. However, subject to these qualifications, there was, prior to the Judgment of the Court, but slight disposition to question the fact that there had been a wide and preponderant acceptance of the rules in question. The Court declined to regard them in that light.

As in the case of *Reservations to the Genocide Convention*, this particular aspect of the decision of the Court raises a question of considerable practical and doctrinal interest for international law as a whole: If universal acceptance alone is the hall-mark of the existence of a rule of international law, how many rules of international law can there be said to be in effective existence? Any such acceptance of the standard of universality as the test of the existence of a rule of international law may be open to the objection that it puts into question the existence of most rules and principles of international law. For this would appear to be the result of a judicial method which declines to treat a widely adopted practice as

---

[8] For a lucid analysis of the practice of States on the subject see the Dissenting Opinion of Judge McNair, *I.C.J. Reports* 1951, pp. 162 *et seq*.

[9] The *Hague Court Reports* edited by Scott (1916), p. 187, where a Tribunal pointed out that the interpretation of the term " bay " must " take into account all the individual circumstances which for any of the different bays are to be appreciated, the relation of its width to the length of penetration inland, the possibility and the necessity of its being defended by the State in whose territory it is indented; the special value which it has for the industry of the inhabitants of its shores; the distance which it is secluded from the highways of nations on the open sea and other circumstances not possible to enumerate in general." /

constituting accepted international law and which elevates the attitude of a small number of States to the authority of a practice entitled to equal—or greater—respect. In so far as the problem thus put implies a criticism of the Judgment of the Court, it might be thought that the method adopted by it derogated, somewhat unnecessarily, from the stature of an otherwise important contribution of the Court to international law. It will be submitted here that such criticism may, in turn, be open to objection.

### 61. *The Same. Development of Predominant Rules as Alternative to Denial of their Validity*

It is probable that in the *Fisheries* case the refusal of the Court to recognise the validity of the widely accepted rules relating to baselines and, in a lesser degree, to bays sprang from the conviction, articulate or otherwise, of the unsatisfactory nature of these rules in modern conditions, in particular in relation to the geographical and economic circumstances of the situation with which it was confronted and which involved the very livelihood of a fishing population threatened by foreign competition armed with modern and efficient equipment.[10] The Court attached decisive importance to the " realities which must be borne in mind in appraising the validity of the United Kingdom's contention that the limits of the Norwegian fisheries zone laid down in the 1935 Decree are contrary to international law." [11] These realities of the situation were not only the particular—perhaps exceptional—geographical configuration of the Norwegian coast. What mattered was that " along the coast are situated comparatively shallow banks, veritable underwater terraces which constitute fishing grounds where fish are particularly abundant " and that " these grounds were known to Norwegian fishermen and exploited by them from time immemorial." [12] What mattered was that " in these barren regions the inhabitants of the coastal zone derive their livelihood essentially from fishing." [13] These " realities " constituted probably the inarticulate major

---

[10] This aspect of the situation was stressed with all requisite emphasis in the course of the written and oral pleadings. For a recapitulation of these arguments see Bourquin in *Acta Scandinavica*, 22 (1952), p. 102, who points out that " pour la Norvège, il s'agissait incontestablement d'intérêts vitaux," and on p. 104 pointing to " une menace [on the part of British fishing vessels] dont il serait difficile d'exaggérer la gravité."

[11] *I.C.J.]. Reports* 1951, p. 128.

[12] *Ibid.*

[13] *Ibid.*

premise of the decision of the Court reached, but for the dissent of Sir Arnold McNair and Judge Read, with practical unanimity.

Such realities are not, in law, irrelevant. For the full appreciation of these realities constitutes the hallmark of the reasonableness —or the continued reasonableness—of the rule. This is one of the reasons why it is of importance not to exaggerate the element of judicial legislation said to be implied in the recognition by the Court of economic interests as a legitimate element in the delimitation of maritime areas. Moreover, such interests, while not constituting in themselves a source of legal right, may be of relevance as an explanation of a customary rule. It is possible that some such considerations underlay the important passages of the Judgment in which the Court referred to " certain economic interests peculiar to a region, the reality and importance of which are clearly evidenced by long usage," [14] and to " rights, founded on the vital needs of the population and attested by very ancient and peaceful usage." [15] It is of little import that custom and usage are here treated as evidence of a pre-existing right. The Statute of the Court describes, in Article 38, custom as evidence of " a general practice established as law." In that sense evidence of custom is co-extensive with custom itself. Finally, the drawing of straight base-lines in a particular case was authorised by the Court only as part of a general system of straight lines as determined by special circumstances and subject to stringent conditions. [16] Assuming— and this is a wide assumption—that the principles which prior to the Judgment of the Court were regarded as expressive of pre-ponderant practice in the matter of the base-line and bays remained unaffected by the considerations which have been working in the cognate field of the extension of the limit of territorial waters, there would still remain the legitimate question as to the extent to which they are liable to modification, in terms of general principle, to meet situations such as those exemplified in the case of Norway. The Court seems to have fully realised the importance of some such principle able to take the place of the traditional—for that is its

[14] *I.C.J. Reports* 1951, p. 133.　　　　　　　　　　[15] *Ibid.*, p. 142.

[16] These conditions are lucidly summarised, in an authoritative contribution to the subject, by Sir Gerald Fitzmaurice in *B.Y.*, 31 (1954), p. 427, in the sense that they must follow the general direction of the coast; that they are permitted only in respect of waters sufficiently linked with the land and lying *inter fauces terrarum*; and that they must be moderate and reasonable in their substance and method. And see *ibid.*, 30 (1953), pp. 69, 70, for the more general statement, to which the present writer is much indebted, on the subject.

proper description—rule in the matter. The relevant passage, which discloses the legislative aspect of the Court's pronouncement, is of an importance calling for quotation at length.

" It does not at all follow that, in the absence of rules having the technically precise character alleged by the United Kingdom Government, the delimitation undertaken by the Norwegian Government in 1935 is not subject to certain principles which make it possible to judge as to its validity under international law. The delimitation of sea areas has always an international aspect; it cannot be dependent merely upon the will of the coastal State as expressed in its municipal law. Although it is true that the act of delimitation is necessarily a unilateral act, because only the coastal State is competent to undertake it, the validity of the delimitation with regard to other States depends upon international law.

In this connection, certain basic considerations inherent in the nature of the territorial sea, bring to light certain criteria which, though not entirely precise, can provide courts with an adequate basis for their decisions, which can be adapted to the diverse facts in question.

Among these considerations, some reference must be made to the close dependence of the territorial sea upon the land domain. It is the land which confers upon the coastal State a right to the waters off its coasts. It follows that while such a State must be allowed the latitude necessary in order to be able to adapt its delimitation to practical needs and local requirements, the drawing of base-lines must not depart to any appreciable extent from the general direction of the coast.

Another fundamental consideration, of particular importance in this case, is the more or less close relationship existing between certain sea areas and the land formations which divide or surround them. The real question raised in the choice of base-lines is in effect whether certain sea areas lying within these lines are sufficiently closely linked to the land domain to be subject to the régime of internal waters. This idea, which is at the basis of the determination of the rules relating to bays, should be liberally applied in the case of a coast, the geographical configuration of which is as unusual as that of Norway.

Finally, there is one consideration not to be overlooked, the scope of which extends beyond purely geographical factors: that of certain economic interests peculiar to a region, the reality and importance of which are clearly evidenced by a long usage." [17]

[17] *I.C.J. Reports* 1951, pp. 132–133.

While it may be difficult to see any substantial difference between the test of "dependence of the territorial sea upon the land domain" and that of "the more or less close relationship existing between certain areas and the land formations which divide or surround them," they constitute an attempt to provide a rule of a general character. The same applies to the elastic notion of "certain economic interests peculiar to a region." [18] Although these tests make clear the measure of the departure from the traditional rule, they are not necessarily open to criticism on that account. They would have been so open to question if they were the only test, striking in its subjective character, applicable to the situation. However, the Court did not altogether discard the attempt at a more objective and definite test. This it found in the notion of the general direction of the coast. The criteria, referred to above, for the delimitation of the territorial sea are intended to operate within the framework of that test. The result is not free of difficulty. For, piling as it were Ossa on Pelion, the Court combined the above-mentioned subjective criteria with the equally elastic test of the general direction of the coast (what is the general direction of the coast may depend on the scale of the map used)—a test realised through the method of straight base-lines linking points selected by the coastal State.

However, as in the case of the Advisory Opinion on the *Reservations to the Genocide Convention,* the criticism, on account of the element of subjectivity and generality, of the Judgment in the *Fisheries* case must be tempered by the consideration that innovation by way of legislative judicial action cannot properly aim at full elaboration and exhaustiveness. Any such method would tend to formalise the process of judicial legislation which, unavoidable as it may be on occasions, must not assume the complexion of express legislative regulation. There may be substance in the view that it is not reasonable to expect judicial legislation to go the whole length in remedying the law. When faced with a situation in which practice is not uniform and in which the preponderant practice does not yield a rule which, in the case before it, renders possible a solution deemed to be in accordance with justice and

---

[18] It is not certain that the evidence, by a long usage, of the reality and importance of these interests is—or ought to be—a condition of their relevance. For economic interests may arise which, although new, may be fully entitled to recognition. But see Bourquin, *loc. cit.,* p. 116.

economic or geographic reality, the Court may deem itself justified in adopting a solution which, although far from achieving certainty, is deemed to embody the rational principle best suited to provide the basis of the general rule. Some such considerations may mitigate any emphasis of criticism in relation to this aspect of the Judgment of the Court in this and other cases in which the pronouncement of the Court has created, with some, the impression of having substituted one kind of uncertainty for another.[19]

It would have been possible for the Court to combine the general and novel criteria of dependence on the land and the importance of economic interests with the traditional rule of the coast line in the sense that whereas the latter would be the normal rule it would be open to the coastal State to claim, in particular cases, a more extended area of national waters by reference to the more general tests of dependence on land and economic interests—provided that it were ready to submit its claim, if disputed, to impartial determination. The Court did not choose that course on the apparent ground, among others, that the coast-line rule had never secured general recognition. It is possible that the principle of straight base-lines determined by points selected by the coastal State may in certain circumstances provide a formulation consonant with the elasticity of the general tests formulated by the Court and expressly made subject to eventual international determination. The intrinsic merits of these tests as well as the impressive majority of the Court on the subject discourage, apart from the consideration adduced below, any confident criticism of that important venture into the realm of judicial legislation. Similarly, it is desirable to view with understanding the reluctance of the Court to admit any measure of legislation inherent in its Judgment and its preference for describing it not as a derogation from accepted law but as " the application of general international law to a specific case," [20] as " an adaptation [of the general law] rendered necessary by local conditions." [21] The borderline between the two may be somewhat shadowy.

### 62. *The Same. The Limits of Judicial Legislation*

In view of this there may be but limited force in the criticism based on the allegation that the tests laid down by the Court were

---

[19] See above, p. 186, as to the case of the *Reservations to the Genocide Convention* and below, p. 374, as to the *Asylum* case.

[20] *I.C.J. Reports* 1951, p. 131.                                    [21] *Ibid.*, p. 133.

not made applicable to any basic rule or principle on the subject and that it is only by being ancillary to a definite principle that they may be presumed to have a meaning. Apparently, in the Judgment of the Court, they are ancillary to the application of the system of straight lines. This is so although the Judgment does not provide expressly that the system of straight lines, as distinguished from that of the coast line, is the governing principle. Neither does it seem to lay down that the coast-line rule is the governing rule (although in some passages it came near to doing that [22])—subject to exceptions defined by the tests which it formulated and which call for the application of the system of straight lines. Yet the very flexibility of the Judgment in this respect may have been an important contribution to subsequent developments in the law of the sea. Some such solution was subsequently suggested by the International Law Commission.[23] It consisted in the recognition of the coast-line rule as the governing rule subject to its modification, in the case of coasts deeply indented or showing similar geographical peculiarities, by the system of straight lines operating under the conditions and safeguards as determined by the Court. It is a solution which is apt to provide a workable compromise between the somewhat rigid uniformity of the coast-line rule advocated by Great Britain and the mere principle of elasticity as contended for by Norway. It is stated to follow, essentially, the Judgment of the Court. Uniformity is not a virtue in itself—unless as an element of certainty, which element is of the essence of the law. Elasticity and flexibility are desirable but, in order to have a meaning, they must be attached to some definite principle of order—a principle which, notwithstanding the apparent hesitation, is not absent from the Judgment of the Court.

Similar considerations apply to the suggestion that while refusing recognition to the hitherto predominant rule of the base-line determined by the low-water mark of the sinuosities of the coast and

[22] See, *e.g.*, *I.C.J. Reports* 1951, p. 128, where the Court stated that "this method may be applied without difficulty to an ordinary coast, which is not broken." It is not clear whether that method is here envisaged as a legal rule or as a rule of technical convenience.

[23] See Art. 4, entitled Normal Baseline, both of the Draft of 1954 and of the Final Draft of the Commission of 1956 which—subject to exceptions laid down in subsequent Articles—lays down that the breadth of the territorial sea is measured from the low-water line along the coast. Art. 5, entitled Straight Baselines, embodies the exceptions thereto—largely following the wording of the tests as formulated by the Court in the *Anglo-Norwegian Fisheries* case.

while substituting for it a rule based on a combination of elastic tests, the Court could still have made a contribution to the development of international law if it had formulated the new law in a manner enabling it to operate as a working legal rule. Undoubtedly, according to the principle laid down in the Judgment, the limits of the territorial sea of the coastal State may not be known until that State has undertaken the delimitation and until it has notified it to other States. Prior to such delimitation other States may have to remain in a position of ignorance, with all the resulting uncertainty, as to what the coastal State considers to be part of its territorial sea. It might be said that unless international law provides for the obligation of the coastal State to submit to impartial determination, by reference to the tests of its application as formulated by the Court, its disputed claims based on the system of straight lines, the general rule laid down by the Court—being dependent for its operation solely upon the will of the coastal State—does not seem to measure up to an essential requirement of a legal rule.

However, it is not certain that the Judgment of the Court provides no answer to that very difficulty. As shown in the passage cited above, the Court insisted that the delimitation of the sea areas has always an international aspect and that although the act of delimitation is necessarily a unilateral act "the validity of the delimitation with regard to other States depends upon international law." That insistence largely provides an answer to the view that the flexibility of the tests adopted by the Court is so considerable in its cumulative effect and the freedom of initial and subjective appreciation left to the coastal State so comprehensive that unless the principle of the obligatory jurisdiction of international tribunals —conceived as a condition of the validity of any disputed claim purporting to be based on the tests authorised by the Court—is clearly established, the rule laid down by the Court must be deemed to be incomplete in a vital respect. It is probable that the Judgment, in the passages quoted, contains the elements of a principle of that nature inasmuch as it refers to the requirement of international—as distinguished from the municipal—validity of the delimitation decreed by the coastal State. There is room for the view that a more emphatic and more direct affirmation of that principle was indicated if the Judgment of the Court was to be counted as a decisive contribution to international law transcending the issue immediately before the Court. It may also be argued that while judicial legislation on account of actual or asserted absence of rules of law may on occasions stem from compelling considerations of justice and convenience and while as such it may not be open to justifiable criticism, it ought not to result in the substitution of a régime of uncertainty and uncontrolled discretion for what has hitherto been a working, even if unsatisfactory, rule of law.   However, as stated, the Judgment of the Court meets these objections in a substantial manner.  It does not meet them fully.  To have done so would have meant to render its legislative achievement complete almost to the point of perfection.  Yet it is not surprising that a judicial tribunal may shrink from such perfection of the legislative function.  From this point of view the Judgment in the *Fisheries* case is in itself a significant contribution to the theory and practice of judicial legislation.

# Chapter 12

# JUDICIAL LEGISLATION AND THE JURISDICTION OF THE COURT

### 63. *Judicial Legislation and the Flexibility of International Relations*

Judicial discretion has on occasions assumed the complexion of judicial legislation on the part of the Court in those cases in which it has departed from an apparently rigid rule of the existing law because, to use the language of the Court, of the flexibility which ought to characterise international relations. Absence of elasticity is a sign of an undeveloped legal system lacking in legislative agencies able to remedy the existing law. The occasional rigid complexion of the legal situations confronting the Court has been the result either of a customary rule of international law or of the letter of the conventional regulation between the parties.

This aspect of the activity of the Court has been largely confined to questions of procedure and jurisdiction. Thus in the *Mavrommatis Palestine Concessions* case it was contended that the Court had no jurisdiction on the ground that the Greek application was filed at a time when the Lausanne Protocol, upon which the jurisdiction of the Court depended to some extent, had not yet become effective. The Court refused to decline jurisdiction on that ground: "The Court, whose jurisdiction is international, is not bound to attach to matters of form the same degree of importance which they might possess in municipal law. Even, therefore, if the application were premature because the Treaty of Lausanne had not yet been ratified, this circumstance would now be covered by the subsequent deposit of the necessary ratifications."[1] In the same Judgment the Court declined to attach decisive importance to the fact that, contrary to the provision which conferred jurisdiction upon it, there had taken place no formal negotiations between the Greek and British Governments prior to the initiation of proceedings by Greece; there had only taken place negotiations between M. Mavrommatis (the Greek national whose claim was espoused

---

[1] Series A, No. 2 (1924), p. 34.

by Greece) and the British Government. For, the Court said, "when the negotiations between the private person and the authorities have already—as in the present case—defined all the points at issue between the two Governments, it would be incompatible with the flexibility which should characterise international relations to require the two Governments to reopen a discussion which has in fact already taken place and on which they rely." [2]

As stated, it is mainly in the domain of pleas to its jurisdiction that the Court has shown a disposition to brush aside objections which it does not consider to go to the root of the matter. This is an interesting feature of the Court's activity when compared with the meticulous care with which, as we have seen,[3] it is at pains to deduce its powers from the will of States. Once the Court has persuaded itself that the dispute is within the terms of the instrument conferring jurisdiction upon it, it will not allow purely procedural or technical considerations to oust its jurisdiction. In the case concerning *Certain German Interests in Polish Upper Silesia* Poland contended that the Court had no jurisdiction because the existence of a difference of opinion in regard to the application and construction of the Geneva Convention had not been established before the filing of the German application. The Court refused to allow itself to be hampered by a mere defect of form, the removal of which, it said, depended entirely on the party concerned. Even if the existence of a definite dispute was necessary, that condition could at any time be fulfilled by means of unilateral action on the part of Germany. A difference of opinion existed as soon as one of the Governments stated that it disagreed with the attitude adopted by the other.[4] In a subsequent Judgment—the final Judgment in the matter of the *Chorzów Factory*—in the same case the Court accepted jurisdiction on a point, apparently not covered by the original jurisdictional clause, in regard to which neither party raised objections to its jurisdiction.[5]

64. *Assumption of Jurisdiction on the Basis of Pleadings and Acts of Agents*

In the Judgment concerning the *Rights of Minorities in Polish Upper Silesia* the Court went much further. It held that the

---

[2] Series A, No. 2 (1924), p. 15.   [3] See above, pp. 91 *et seq*.
[4] Series A, No. 6 (1925), p. 13.
[5] Series A, No. 17 (1928), p. 37.

submission of arguments on the merits, in the form of submissions in the Counter-case, without making reservations in regard to the question of jurisdiction, must be regarded "as an unequivocal indication of the desire of a State to obtain a decision on the merits of the suit." [6]  The Court pointed out, once more, that its jurisdiction in a particular case is not subordinated to the observance of certain forms such as the conclusion of a special agreement, and that the consent of a State to the submission of a dispute may not only follow upon an express declaration, but may also be inferred from acts conclusively establishing it.  This was a drastic decision which some have regarded as being out of keeping with the Court's solemn insistence on the express will of States as the sole source of its jurisdiction. [7]

That a submission, possibly unguarded, in the Counter-case is interpreted as constituting such a manifestation of express will may appear to some as a *tour de force*.  Such manner of assuming jurisdiction may also appear as an innovation, pregnant with potentialities, in the traditional method of conferring jurisdiction upon international courts.  That method has consisted in concluding formal treaties, subject to ratification, circumscribing elaborately and often with ingenious circumspection the powers of the tribunal, and frequently rendered to a large extent innocuous by reservations. What, it has been asked, is to become of these safeguards, including the constitutional limitations upon the treaty-making power, if the act of an agent, or even a mere omission on his part, is deemed sufficient to confer jurisdiction?  As pointed out elsewhere in this book—where this matter is treated in the chapter entitled " Judicial Caution "—the Court, for the reasons just stated, has been aware of the necessity of restraint on that issue which is, in part, identical with the question of *forum prorogatum*.  On the other hand, there seem to be no cogent reasons why the conduct of agents, duly authorised and able in modern conditions to obtain without undue delay the advice and guidance of their Governments, should not be binding upon a Government within the limits of any constitutional restrictions to which it may be subject.  There is no rule of international law—and none can be found in the Statute of the Court— which requires compliance with definite forms in accepting the

---

[6] Series A, No. 15 (1928), p. 24.
[7] See above, p. 103. See the Dissenting Opinions in this matter of Huber and Nyholm (Judges) and Negulesco (Deputy-Judge)

jurisdiction of the Court or which rules out the conduct of a State or of its representatives as a source of its obligations. Thus there was no strained assumption of implied acceptance of jurisdiction in the Judgment of the Court in the *Corfu Channel* case on the Preliminary Objection of Albania. There the Court, although it invoked the Judgment, referred to above, in the case of the *Rights of Minorities in Polish Upper Silesia*, did no more than draw the consequences from what it considered " a voluntary and indisputable acceptance " of its jurisdiction.[8] In the Judgment given by it as a Chamber of Summary Procedure, in the case of the *Interpretation of the Treaty of Neuilly*,[9] the Court founded its jurisdiction on the fact that the Agent of the Bulgarian Government submitted observations regarding the Greek Government's request for an interpretation, without disputing the Court's jurisdiction to give the interpretation requested, and that " therefore the Court has jurisdiction to do so as the result of the agreement between the Parties."

Similarly, in its Judgment on the Merits in the case of the *Corfu Channel*, while the Court in deciding that its jurisdiction to find on the question of compensation implied also jurisdiction to determine the amount of compensation, invoked also considerations of a general character—*i.e.*, that otherwise its decision would not effectively settle the dispute [10]—it relied to a large extent on the conduct of Albania during the proceedings as signifying her acceptance of its jurisdiction thus conceived. It referred to the declaration of the Albanian Agent pointing to an agreement by the parties covering the " whole procedure." It attached importance to the fact that in its written pleadings the Government of Albania did not contest the jurisdiction of the Court to decide the issue; that, on the contrary, it reserved the right to discuss the amount of the claim of the United Kingdom; and that that statement " must be considered as an implied acceptance of the Court's jurisdiction to decide this question." [11] In the view of the Court this applied also to the Albanian Agent's admission that the Court was entitled to decide on the kind of satisfaction due to Albania. If that was so, the Court concluded, it was difficult to see why it should have no

[8] *I.C.J. Reports* 1947–1948, p. 27.
[9] Series A, No. 4 (1925), p. 6.
[10] See below, p. 247.
[11] *I.C.J. Reports* 1949, p. 25.

jurisdiction to decide on the amount of compensation due to the United Kingdom.   Probably there apply to this reasoning of the Court the considerations adduced above as to the propriety of deriving the jurisdiction of the Court from the implied consent of a party as shown by the conduct of its Agent after the commencement of the proceedings.   Some may think it preferable to regard such conduct as evidence of the original intention revealed in the instrument submitting the dispute to the jurisdiction of the Court rather than as an independent source of the jurisdiction of the Court. From that point of view the manner, though not the substance, of this aspect of the Judgment of the Court seems to give rise to questions.   On that view, the true *ratio decidendi* in this case lies in the considerations adduced in the Judgment concerning *Certain German Interests in Polish Upper Silesia* [12] in which, by reference to the principle of effectiveness, it affirmed its jurisdiction to decide, as implied in the question of responsibility, the amount of compensation due to Germany.

Even more conspicuous, although without reference to the question of jurisdiction, was the importance attached by the Court to the declarations of agents when at the final stage of the *French-Swiss Zones* case the Swiss Agent made on behalf of his Government a declaration to the effect that it would agree, if necessary, to the terms of the exchange of goods between the Free Zones and Switzerland being settled by experts guided by the principles of law laid down in the Judgment.   The French Agent declared the Swiss offer to be unacceptable; he stated that he had in any case no power to entertain the proposal; and he doubted, having regard to Swiss constitutional law, whether the declaration was binding upon Switzerland.   In its Judgment the Court held that, having regard to the circumstances in which this declaration was made, it must be regarded as an offer binding upon Switzerland.[13]   This was a novel way of creating an international obligation in disregard of the delicate question of constitutional limitations upon the treaty-making power.   For it is not clear what was the constitutional authority of the Swiss Agent to undertake that the—possibly far-reaching—decision of the experts would be binding upon his country.   The pedant might have been inclined to ask whether

[12] See below, p. 245.
[13] Series A/B, No. 46 (1932), p. 176.

undertakings of this nature required for their validity registration with the Secretariat of the League of Nations.

On the other hand, where the Court arrives at the conclusion that there was no intention to submit a dispute to its jurisdiction, it will refuse to treat the pleadings or the conduct of the Agents as constituting an independent source of its jurisdiction. In such cases it will decline to act on the rule of so-called *forum prorogatum, i.e.,* conferment of jurisdiction, subsequent to the commencement of proceedings, by the action of a party such as pleading on the merits or the filing of a particular application.[14] It did so in the case of the *Anglo-Iranian Oil Company.*[15]

Although no question of *forum prorogatum* arose in the *Haya de la Torre (Asylum)* case, the Court affirmed there the principle that the conduct of the parties in the proceedings before it may create a sufficient source of jurisdiction. It said: " The Parties have in the present case consented to the jurisdiction of the Court. All the questions submitted to it have been agreed by them on the merits. This conduct of the Parties is sufficient to confer jurisdiction on the Court." [16]

## 65. *Enlargement of the Basis of the Court's Pronouncements*

There are other ways in which the Court has occasionally shown a disposition to act upon the maxim *boni judicis est ampliare jurisdictionem*—so long as that maxim does not conflict with the principle that its jurisdiction is ultimately grounded in the will of the parties. It has affirmed its right, not mentioned expressly in the Statute, to render declaratory judgments giving an abstract interpretation of a treaty. Thus in the case concerning *Certain German Interests in Polish Upper Silesia* it rejected the contention that as the German submission referred to the general—as distinguished from its specific application to a concrete case—effect of the Polish law complained of, the Court could not pronounce upon it. It said: " There is no reason why States should not be able to ask the Court to give an abstract interpretation of a treaty; rather would it appear that this is one of the most important functions which it can fulfil. It has, in fact, already had occasion to do so in Judgment No. 3." [17] The Court relied, for that purpose, on

---

14 See above, p. 105.    15 *I.C.J. Reports* 1952, p. 114. See above, p. 106.
16 *I.C.J. Reports* 1951, p. 78.
17 Series A, No. 7 (1926), pp. 18, 19.

Article 14 of the Covenant of the League of Nations which gave it power to " hear and determine any dispute of an international character which Parties thereto submit to it." It considered that its view on the matter was supported by the very general terms of Article 36 (2a) of the Statute which enumerated interpretation of treaties as one of the possible objects of the compulsory jurisdiction of the Court. Moreover, it was prepared to deduce its right to give declaratory judgments from the language of Article 63 which confers upon States the right to intervene in proceedings in which the construction of a convention to which States other than those concerned in the case are parties is in question, with the result that any State availing itself of that right is bound by the construction given in the judgment. In its interpretative Judgment in the case of the *Factory at Chorzów* [18] the Court reaffirmed once more its power to render declaratory judgments " the intention of which is to ensure recognition of a situation at law, once and for all and with binding force as between the Parties." It explained the apparently contrary provisions of Article 59 which lays down that the decision of the Court has no binding effect except between the parties and in respect of the particular case decided by the Court, by stating that the object of that Article is merely to prevent the principles asserted by the Court in a particular case from being binding also upon other States or in other disputes.

In the Second Order concerning the *Free Zones* it laid down that a " judgment by consent," though not provided for by the Statute, was nevertheless " in accordance with the spirit of that instrument." [19] It has repeatedly expressed the opinion that it had jurisdiction to interpret treaty provisions other than those which the clause conferring jurisdiction authorised it to interpret provided this was necessary for the fulfilment of its task. [20]

## 66. *Remedying Defects of Form in the Submissions of the Parties and Re-formulating Questions Submitted to the Court*

Occasionally, in its desire to prevent frustration of its jurisdiction by reason of mere defects of form, the Court has gone to the

---

[18] Series A, No. 13 (1927): *Interpretation of Judgments Nos. 7 and 8* (the case of the Factory at Chorzów), p. 20. See also Judge Hudson's observation in the case of *Diversion of Waters from the Meuse*: Series A/B, No. 70 (1937), p. 79.

[19] Series A, No. 24 (1930), p. 14.

[20] Series A, No. 2 (1924) (*Mavrommatis Palestine Concessions*), p. 31; Series A, No. 6 (1925), p. 18, and No. 7 (1926), p. 25 (*Certain German Interests in Polish Upper Silesia*).

length of actively remedying defects of this nature by formulating itself the questions put to it by the parties or, in the case of Advisory Opinions, by the Council. When asking for the interpretation, by way of a Judgment, of two previous Judgments of the Court in the *Chorzów Factory* case, Germany put forward a statement of " submissions " instead of an " indication of the . . . points in dispute " as laid down in Article 66 of the Rules of the Court. The Court decided to construe the German submissions as an indication of the points in dispute because " the Court, as it had already had occasion to observe in previous judgments, may within reasonable limits disregard the defects of form of documents placed before it." [21] In the case of the *Société Commerciale de Belgique* the Court, faced with drastic amendments in the submissions of a Party, put on record its view that it could not allow a dispute brought before it by application to be transferred by amendments in the submissions into another dispute which is different in character—one reason being that any such practice might affect the jurisdiction of the Court. However, in view of the special circumstances of the case and the absence of objections on the part of the opposing Government, the Court considered it advisable that " it should take a broad view and not regard the present proceedings as irregular." [22] In the case concerning the *Interpretation of the Statute of the Memel Territory* the Court, while criticising the abstract manner in which the plaintiff States put before it the disputed points and while drawing their attention to the " convenient and appropriate method " [23] in which they ought to have brought before it the difference of opinion, did not refuse to give judgment—a course urged by Judge Anzilotti in his Dissenting Opinion.[24]

In its Judgment No. 11, on the *Interpretation of Judgments Nos. 7 and 8*, the Court laid down the rule that, for the purpose of the interpretation of its own Judgment, it did not consider itself bound to reply by a simple " yes " or " no " to the submissions as formulated by the Parties and that " it cannot be bound by formulae chosen by the Parties concerned but must be able to take an unhampered decision." [25]

[21] Series A, No. 13 (1927), p. 16.
[22] Series A/B, No. 78 (1939), p. 173.
[23] Series A/B, No. 49 (1932), p. 311.
[24] *Ibid.*, p. 349. See also the Advisory Opinion concerning the *Interpretation of the Greco-Turkish Agreement of December 1, 1926*: Series B, No. 16 (1928), pp. 14–17.
[25] Series A, No. 13 (1927), pp. 15, 16.

As pointed out above, the previous jurisprudence of the Court provides authority for the competence of the Court to re-formulate in some such way the request put to it. Apart from Judgment No. 11,[26] relating to the interpretation of the Court's own pronouncements, the Court acted on that principle in some of the Advisory Opinions which it had previously rendered. Thus in the Advisory Opinion on the *Interpretation of the Greco-Turkish Agreement* the Court held that as the request for the Opinion did not state in exact terms the question upon which the Opinion was sought, " it is essential that it should determine what this question is and formulate an exact statement of it." [27] In the *Jaworzina Boundary* case the Court similarly amplified the question put to it. While the request for the Opinion was, in terms, confined to the frontier region of Spisz, the Court decided that it must express a view on the other parts of the frontier in so far as this was necessary having regard to the interdependence of frontiers in the region as a whole.[28]

The Court followed the same method, in a pronounced manner, in the First Order of August 1929 concerning the *Free Zones*. In that case the parties concluded a rather unusual arbitration agreement in which the Court was asked, after the conclusion of its deliberations but before rendering Judgment, to accord to the parties time for the settlement of the dispute. There was at the same time an understanding between the parties that the Court, before giving judgment, should communicate to them unofficially the result of its deliberations. The Court refused, as being contrary to the Statute, to sanction this procedure. But it did not decline to act. It recognised that " the judicial settlement of international disputes, with a view to which the Court has been established, is

---

[26] See above, p. 207.

[27] Series B, No. 16 (1928), p. 14.

[28] Series B, No. 8 (1923), p. 50. See also the Advisory Opinion concerning the *Competence of the International Labour Organisation* where the Court restated and limited the question put to it (Series B, No. 3 (1922), p. 59). A passage in the Advisory Opinion on the *Conditions of Admission of a State to Membership in the United Nations* seems, at first sight, to run counter to this practice of the Court. There the Court said: " It is the duty of the Court to envisage the question submitted to it only in the abstract form which has been given to it; nothing which is said in the present Opinion refers, either directly or indirectly, to concrete cases, or to particular circumstances " (*I.C.J.*) *Reports* 1947–1948, p. 61). This passage must be read in the light of some of the arguments submitted to the Court. The Court, in making the above statement, was concerned with the objection that the question put to it was, in the circumstances of the case, a political one and that, for that reason, it fell outside the jurisdiction of the Court.

simply an alternative to the direct and friendly settlement of such disputes between the parties," and that it was for the Court to facilitate, so far as compatible with its Statute, such " direct and friendly settlement." [29]    Accordingly, it complied in effect with the request of the parties by resorting to the device of issuing an Order formally concerning a small point of evidence but embodying the result of its deliberations on the major aspects of the dispute.

It will thus be seen that, in matters of jurisdiction and of adjective law generally, the activity of the Court occasionally partakes in some limited respects of the nature of judicial legislation on account of the flexibility of relations between States.    In this as in many other matters the Court has endeavoured to steer a middle course between rule and discretion.    The will of the parties is its charter.    It is that will which the Court respects rather than the attempts, based on formal and procedural objections, to render nugatory an undertaking once given.    Although the exercise of judicial discretion is here often confined mainly to matters of form and procedure, these are not by any means of little importance.[30]    Formal and procedural rules represent the element of convenience and certainty in law and in the prosecution of rights.    Thus conceived, they are often regarded as embodying an element of substantive justice.    Witness, for instance, the vigour of the criticism voiced on this ground in Dissenting Opinions and elsewhere against the ruling of the Court in the *Mavrommatis Palestine Concessions*

---

[29] Series A, No. 22 (1929), p. 13. There is an equal absence of rigidity in the Court's practice of allowing amendments of conclusions by the parties in the course of the proceedings. For a survey of the early practice of the Court in this matter see Feller in *American Journal of International Law*, XXV (1931), pp. 490–502. However, in the case of the *Société Commerciale de Belgique* between Belgium and Bulgaria the Court, confronted with some indecision on the part of the Belgian Agent who changed his submissions in the course of the proceedings, indicated that there are limits to its forbearance in the matter. It pointed out that Art. 40 of the Statute and Art. 32 (2) of the Rules of the Court provided that the application must indicate the subject of the dispute. It then uttered the warning that, in principle, it could not allow a dispute brought before it by application to be transformed by amendments in submission into a dispute different in character. Any such practice, the Court said, might prejudice the interests of third States entitled to intervene in accordance with Arts. 62 and 63 of the Statute. Also, the complete change in the submissions might affect the jurisdiction of the Court. However, in view of the circumstances of the case and the absence of objections on the part of Greece, the Court thought it advisable that " it should take a broad view " and not regard the proceedings as irregular (Series A/B, No. 78 (1939), p. 173).

[30] See, for instance, the Order concerning the request for interim measures of protection in the *Polish Agrarian Reform* case (Series A/B, No. 58 (1933)) and the Dissenting Opinion of Judge Anzilotti: " . . . It is only fair that a Government should bear the consequences of the wording of a document for which it is responsible " (*ibid.*, p. 182).

case to dispense with formal negotiations between the two Governments which were, in law, parties to the dispute.[31]

## 67. *Flexibility of International Relations and the Creation of International Obligations*

Although it is largely in regard to the pleas to its jurisdiction that the Court has deemed itself justified in adopting a " flexible " attitude, this is not the only example of this feature of its jurisprudence. We have only to look at the way in which the Court admitted the possibility of creating contractual obligations in forms other than those traditionally recognised in international law. In the *Eastern Greenland* dispute the Court found that an oral declaration made by the Norwegian Minister for Foreign Affairs on behalf of his Government in response to a request by the diplomatic representative of Denmark, on a question within his competence, was binding upon Norway like any other contractual obligation.[32] The Norwegian Minister's declaration was a weighty act of State. It was an undertaking not to raise any difficulties in the settlement of the Greenland question—an undertaking which the Court construed as an obligation to refrain from contesting Danish sovereignty over Greenland as a whole and to abstain from occupying any part of Greenland. Diligent research could doubtless discover other instances of merely verbal agreements such as the agreement referred to by Grotius between Mithridates and Sulla[33] or between Peter the Great and Frederick III, Elector of Brandenburg.[34] It is by reference to these and some other minor instances that writers have occasionally insisted that there is nothing in international law which requires written form as a condition of the validity of treaties.[35] Nevertheless, the pronouncement of the Court constitutes the first instance of an authoritative recognition of the binding force of a verbal undertaking in a matter of considerable importance to a State. It was an innovation which the whole Court (with the exception of the Norwegian national Judge) held

---

[31] Series A, No. 2 (1924), p. 41 (Lord Finlay), p. 61 (Judge Moore), and p. 91 (Judge Pessôa). See also Borchard in *American Journal of International Law*, XIX (1925), pp. 728–738, for a criticism of the enlargement of the compulsory jurisdiction of the Court by judicial construction.

[32] Series A/B, No. 53 (1933), p. 71.

[33] *De jure belli ac pacis*, ii, xvi, xxx.

[34] As quoted by Garner in *American Journal of International Law*, XXVII (1933), p. 494.

[35] See, *e.g.*, McNair, *The Law of Treaties* (1938), p. 47.

to be justified by the circumstances of the case, *i.e.*, the fact that the undertaking was given as a *quid pro quo*, which took full effect, for a similar Danish undertaking in favour of Norway on the Spitzbergen question. It may also be noted that in that case neither the fact nor the contents of the oral declaration were disputed. The declaration appeared to have been recorded simultaneously with its oral transmission. These circumstances explain to some extent this aspect of the Judgment. There is a preponderance of opinion —not to mention the requirement of compliance with constitutional limitations within the State and registration outside it—in support of the view that treaties, to be valid, must be reduced to writing.[36]

However, flexibility is in its nature a matter of degree and it is perhaps for this reason that the drawing of the line may occasionally leave room for controversy. Thus the Court was not inclined to stretch the conception of flexibility to the point of attributing the character of an international undertaking to a concessionary contract between the Iranian Government and the Anglo-Iranian Oil Company—a contract which, in the words of the Court, " removed the cause of a complaint by the United Kingdom against Iran." [37] That contract terminated, for the time being, a prolonged international dispute between the two countries, a dispute which had been brought before the Council of the League of Nations; the concessionary contract itself was formulated and entered into through the good offices of the Council acting through its Rapporteur. It was in consideration of that contract that the United Kingdom withdrew its complaint. On the other hand, in the *Free Zones* case—in the Order of the Court of December 6, 1930—the Court ascribed " the character of a treaty stipulation," binding upon Sardinia, to a manifesto of the King of Sardinia, addressed to Sardinian customs authorities, directing them to withdraw the customs line. This was done in pursuance of a request by the Canton of Valais on the ground that Sardinia was bound to take that step as the result of a treaty obligation. In the view of the Court the manifesto was intended to terminate an international dispute and thus itself acquired an international character. This ruling of the Court was invoked by the United Kingdom in the case of the

[36] For a more detailed discussion of the subject see the comment to Art. 17 of the writer's draft on the *Law of Treaties* (Documents of the International Law Commission, 1953, A/CN.4/63).
[37] *I.C.J. Reports* 1952, p. 113.

*Anglo-Iranian Oil Company* in support of its contention that inasmuch as the concessionary contract between the company and the Iranian Government was concluded in pursuance of a Resolution of the Council terminating an international dispute, it itself acquired an international character. The Court, in declining to treat the contract as a treaty, distinguished the case before it from that of the manifesto of the King of Sardinia in the *Free Zones* case on the ground that in the latter the dispute was " of direct concern to the two countries " while the dispute between the United Kingdom and Iran which gave rise to the complaint before the Council of the League of Nations " arose out of a private concession." [38] It is possible that the distinction thus drawn referred to the form rather than the substance of the matter. On the other hand, the outcome would have been equally startling if the Court had assumed jurisdiction as the result of the assimilation of a contract to a treaty in a situation with regard to which it had otherwise come to the conclusion that there was no intention to confer jurisdiction upon it.

[38] *I.C.J. Reports* 1952, p. 113.

CHAPTER 13

# JUDICIAL LEGISLATION AND ADJUDICATION
## *EX AEQUO ET BONO*

68. *Adjudication* ex aequo et bono *and the Case of the* Free Zones

Adjudication *ex aequo et bono* is a species of legislative activity. It differs clearly from the application of rules of equity in their wider sense. For inasmuch as these are identical with principles of good faith, they form part of international law as, indeed, of any system of law. They do so irrespective of the provisions of the third paragraph of Article 38 which authorises the Court to apply general principles of law recognised by civilised States.[1] On the other hand, adjudication *ex aequo et bono* amounts to an avowed creation of new legal relations between the parties. The importance of that aspect of its activity justifies a somewhat detailed consideration of the *Free Zones* case, seeing that the Court refused to undertake a legislative function with which, in the opinion of one party, it was entrusted in the arbitration agreement. The case is also of interest inasmuch as the majority of the Court expressed doubts whether such legislative function could be undertaken at the wish of both parties in accordance with the last paragraph of Article 38 of the Statute, which gives the Court power " to decide a case *ex aequo et bono*, if the parties agree thereto." [2]

It may therefore be useful to state briefly the facts of this case in so far as they are relevant to the issue. The second paragraph of Article 435 of the Treaty of Versailles provided as follows:

" The High Contracting Parties also agree that the stipulations of the treaties of 1815 and of other supplementary acts concerning the

---

[1] See on this point the instructive observations of Judge Hudson in the case of the *Diversion of Water from the Meuse*, Series A/B, No. 70 (1937), p. 77. He concluded that under " Art. 38 of the Statute, if not independently of that Article, the Court has some freedom to consider principles of equity as part of the international law which it must apply." In that case Judge Hudson sought to apply the principle " equality is equity " in support of the proposition—which, he admitted, international tribunals ought to apply only " very sparingly "—that a State seeking the interpretation of a treaty before an international tribunal must itself have completely fulfilled the obligations of that treaty.

[2] Series A, No. 24 (1930), p. 10.

free zones of Upper Savoy and the Gex district are no longer consistent with present conditions, and that it is for France and Switzerland to come to an agreement together with a view to settling between themselves the status of these territories under such conditions as shall be considered suitable by both countries."

A dispute arose subsequently between Switzerland and France as to the effect of this paragraph and as to the best methods of settling the status of the Free Zones. On October 30, 1924, the parties concluded a special agreement in which the Court was asked: (a) to pronounce on the question whether Article 435 of the Treaty had the effect of abrogating the régime of the Free Zones; and (b) in the event of failure of the parties to reach an agreement on the régime of the Zones in negotiations to be conducted subsequently to the decision of the Court on question (a), to " settle for a period to be fixed by it and having regard to present conditions, all the questions involved in the execution of paragraph (2) of Article 435 of the Treaty of Versailles." On August 19, 1929, the Court gave, in the form of an Order, its decision on question (a) to the effect that the Treaty of Versailles had not abrogated the régime of Free Zones. The Court accorded to the two Governments a period expiring on May 1, 1930, to settle between themselves the new régime in the territories in question.[3] The parties having failed to reach an agreement, the Court was called upon to consider the dispute with a view to giving effect to the second part of the Special Agreement. In its Judgment the Court was sharply divided on the question of its powers under that part of the Special Agreement. Six Judges were of the opinion that in settling the questions involved in the execution of Article 435 of the Treaty of Versailles the Court was bound to proceed on the basis of the existing legal rights as established in its former Order, namely, on the basis of the fact that the Treaty had not abrogated the régime of Free Zones. They also considered that, although the parties themselves were at liberty to dispose of their rights, the Court, failing an express provision to that effect, could not disregard rights clearly established in its former pronouncements. The other six Judges disagreed with the view of the majority.[3a] They appended Opinions to the effect that the Special Agreement conferred upon the Court the same powers,

---

[3] Series A, No. 22 (1929).

[3a] This they did while concurring in the operative part of the Order. The Court was equally divided as to the aspect of the question here discussed—the technical majority including the vote of the President.

including the power to extinguish existing rights, which the parties would have had in direct negotiations, and that it was not prevented from abolishing the special customs line and placing it at the political frontier " if satisfied that this would be the régime most in conformity with the present requirements." [4]

It would not be accurate to deduce from the reasoning of the majority any general conclusion on the attitude of the Court on the subject. Such a conclusion would not be warranted either by the previous practice of the Court as shown in this chapter, or, indeed, by the nature of the case under discussion. The Arbitration Agreement of October 1924 was determined by two conflicting factors. The one was the desire of Switzerland to limit the task of an international tribunal to the ascertainment of the question whether, as maintained by France, the Treaty of Versailles abrogated the régime of Free Zones or not. To such a limitation of the powers of the arbitrator France persistently refused to give her consent. She proposed that he should be empowered, without any restrictions, to lay down the future customs régime of the territory. The history of the prolonged negotiations which led to the conclusion of the Special Agreement explains the unusual and inconclusive nature of its terms as well as the apparently substantial cleavage of opinion between the members of the Court. In the course of the negotiations Switzerland had refused to accept a solution disregarding altogether the existing legal position. She succeeded in securing the agreement of France to a decision by the Court of the question *de lege lata*. She was also successful in obtaining a formulation of the task of the Court in terms which were conspicuous for the absence of a reference to a decision *ex aequo et bono* pure and simple. The Opinion of the majority of the Court, in refusing to disregard the existing legal position and in accepting it as the starting point for its decision on the merits, appears therefore to be in accordance with the intention of the parties. On the other hand, it is probable that the substance of the Opinions of the minority of the six Judges is not entirely incompatible with both the letter and the spirit of the Special Agreement. For it is clear from its terms and from its history that there was no intention to limit rigidly the task of the Court to a simple decision whether the Treaty of Versailles had abolished the Free Zones or not.

[4] Series A, No. 24 (1930), p. 28.

If the view be accepted that the Opinions both of the majority and of the minority of the Court find support in the Special Agreement, then the further conclusion seems to be permissible that the difference between the two Opinions is to a large extent one of emphasis. The majority of the Court was insistent that its respect for the existing legal position did not imply that the final decision of the Court on the future régime of the Free Zones must consist in a simple affirmation of the Swiss right to the maintenance of the Free Zones.[5] On the other hand, it appears from the Opinions of the minority Judges that even a decision starting from the formal abolition of the régime of Free Zones might well be compatible with securing for Switzerland similar advantages to those which she enjoyed under the former régime.[6] As was pointed out by Judge Kellogg in his separate Observations, even assuming that no submission *ex aequo et bono* was contemplated, the Special Agreement conferred upon the Court wide discretionary powers. Upon analysis, it is of little importance whether the régime to be laid down by the Court was to be (as maintained by the minority) in formal disregard of existing Swiss rights, or whether (as maintained by the majority) it was to consist in a modification of these rights and in their adaptation to relevant changes in conditions. Once the principle is admitted that rights, although continuing in their legal validity, are nevertheless subject to some adaptation, the question as to what label is to be attached to the change thus effected becomes of secondary importance. A change made " in modification " may be deeper and more incisive than a change made " in disregard " of a right. The legislative character of the new regulation in relation to the former legal position may well be concealed behind the veil of formal recognition of these rights—as was done in the *Behring Sea Arbitration* and the *North Atlantic Fisheries Arbitration*—but that circumstance does not affect the substance of the change. In fact, the part played by the Court in the history of this protracted dispute shows that without accepting the task of a legislator it contributed in many ways to a satisfactory settlement of the controversy.[7]

The majority of the Court did not associate themselves with the view of Judge Kellogg that Article 38 does not authorise the Court to give decisions *ex aequo et bono* at the request of the parties.

---

[5] Series A, No. 24 (1930), pp. 11, 12.     [6] *Ibid.*, p. 28.
[7] See below, pp. 219, 220.

They merely expressed their doubts on the matter—possibly in deference to the emphatic Opinion of the Judge without whose concurrence it might have been difficult to reach a majority decision. For reasons stated elsewhere,[8] it is difficult to admit that the clear wording of the Statute affords a basis either for the negative view of Judge Kellogg or even for the doubts of the six majority Judges. But there may be substance in the view that the authority to revise the law, being alien to the proper function of the Court, must find clear support in the language of the agreement. This was probably one of the reasons why in the case of the *Société Commerciale de Belgique* the Court declined to undertake the task of altering the terms of an arbitral award rendered between Greece and a Belgian Corporation.[9] Short of that, it did its best to assist the parties in arriving at a settlement in that direction.

### 69. *Recommendations to the Parties*

In some cases the Court, in addition to laying down the existing law, has deemed itself free to formulate solutions *de lege ferenda*. Thus in the *Lotus* case the Court suggested that concurrent jurisdiction of the courts of the country where the offence was committed and of those of the country of which the offender was a national would be the best solution of the problem of jurisdiction in regard to certain crimes committed by aliens abroad.[10] In the case concerning *Rights of Nationals of the United States in Morocco* the Court found that Article 95 of the Act of Algeciras which defined four factors as relevant for valuing merchandise in connection with customs duties " did not afford decisive evidence in support of either of the interpretations contended for by the Parties." [11] After examining both the preparatory work of the Act of Algeciras in relation to the Article in question and the subsequent interpretation of it by the customs authorities, it came to the conclusion that Article 95 " lays down no strict rule on the point in dispute " and that " it requires an interpretation which is more flexible " [12] than either of those contended for the Parties. The Court then proceeded to lay down what were the factors, additional to those enumerated

---

[8] See Lauterpacht, *The Function of Law in the International Community* (1933), pp. 318 *et seq.*

[9] See above, p. 86.

[10] Series A, No. 10 (1927), p. 30.

[11] *I.C.J. Reports* 1952, p. 209.

[12] *Ibid.*, p. 211.

in Article 95, to which the customs authorities in the French Zone must have regard in fixing the valuation of imported goods for customs purposes. The detailed plan for a provisional régime outlined by the Court in its interim Order of protection in the *Anglo-Iranian Oil Company* case [13] provided yet another interesting example of the capacity of the Court to devise, if necessary, solutions of a practical nature.

In this connection reference may be made to the alternative possibility of a conferment upon the Court of powers of recommendation as distinguished from binding decisions which Article 38 (2) authorises it to give, at the request of the parties, *ex aequo et bono*. According to some such alternative system the Court would be at liberty, if so requested by the parties, to make—in addition to, but not in substitution for, a legal decision given by it—recommendations, which are not of a binding character, for a modification of the legal position as established in the Judgment or the Opinion. There are arbitral precedents for a procedure of this nature. [14]   The parties to the dispute or the body requesting the Advisory Opinion may attach importance to knowing what, in the view of the Court which has had the opportunity of a full examination of the question before it, are the desirable modifications of the legal position, as ascertained in the Judgment or the Advisory Opinion, having regard to equitable considerations and to the necessities of friendly neighbourly relations.   The Court is bound, in the first instance, to render a purely legal decision.   But, it may be urged, the parties may be of the opinion that a purely legal decision, while constituting a vital element in the situation, is not necessarily the only element of importance.   The Court itself may find on occasions that the faculty to make recommendations of this nature may do away with a strong inducement to judicial legislation.   For, faced with the necessity of giving a decision which is fully in accordance with the existing law but unsatisfactory from other points of view, the Court may not always find it easy to overcome such inducement unless it is given the opportunity of expressing its opinion, which would not be binding, as to what—from the point of view of equity

---

[13] *I.C.J. Reports* 1951, p. 93.

[14] See, in addition to the *Behring Sea* and *North Atlantic Fisheries* arbitrations, referred to above, the recommendations made by the British-American Claims Arbitral Tribunal under the Convention of August 18, 1910: *The Home Missionary Society* case (*International Arbitral Awards*, VI (1955), p. 41); *Hardman* case, *ibid.*, p. 25; *Cadenhead* case, *ibid.*, p. 40; *Adams* case, *ibid.*, p. 321.

and reasonableness—are the desirable changes in the law which the parties or the organ requesting the Advisory Opinion ought to take into consideration. The recurrent proposals for an International Equity Tribunal making binding pronouncements on a basis other than existing law and thus endowed with formal legislative powers are not likely to prove acceptable to Governments. On the other hand, an authorisation given to the Court to act in accordance with the more limited solution as here outlined would meet an urgent need and would not be inconsistent with the judicial character of the Court. Some such general authorisation might consist in amending Article 38 of the Statute of the Court by the addition of the following paragraph 3: " If the Court finds that its decision, based on the application of the rules of law as enumerated in paragraph 1, results in a situation calling for a modification of the law either in general or in the relations of the parties to the dispute, it shall have the power to make appropriate recommendations. While such recommendations shall not be binding upon the parties, they shall give to them all due consideration." A provision of this nature could also be inserted in Article 68 of the Statute bearing on Advisory Opinions. However, as will be here suggested, it is by no means certain that any such express authorisation is necessary in order to permit the Court to act in that manner.

The Court has stated occasionally that it would not be consistent with its authority to make pronouncements which the parties are at liberty to disregard. In particular, it did so on two occasions in the *Free Zones* case.[15] It said, on the second occasion, that " it would be incompatible with the Statute, and with its position as a Court of Justice, to give a Judgment which would be dependent for its validity on the subsequent approval of the Parties." Possibly considerations of this character might not apply to recommendations which are not binding upon the parties and which the latter specifically requested the Court to put before them. It is arguable that the legal authority of a Judgment or Opinion laying down the existing and binding law is strengthened by an indication, of a non-binding character, of what are its desirable modifications or methods of application as between the parties. In its Judgment of June 13, 1951, in the *de la Torre* case, the Court refrained, on the ground that by acting otherwise " it would depart from its judicial

[15] Series A, No. 24 (1930), p. 14, and Series A/B, No. 46 (1932), p. 161.

function," [16] from giving the parties " any practical advice as to
the various courses which might be followed with a view to terminating the asylum." The resulting situation was that while the
Court held unanimously that the asylum ought to be terminated,
the legal rights and obligations of the parties as to actual solution
of the dispute by reference to which the case was brought before
the Court were left undetermined—primarily because of the
manner in which the parties defined the issue placed before the
Court. [17]

Yet there is room for a clarification of the question whether, in
a case of this nature, if the parties were to request the Court to
indicate for their consideration the course of action which would
appear to it appropriate in the entirety of the circumstances of
the case, such advice would be consistent with the judicial function
of the Court. The same may apply, in a different manner, to
Advisory Opinions. In the past, the Court has, as a rule, refrained
from expressing a view as to the moral or political propriety of the
conduct of Governments as distinguished from their legal obligations. Thus, in its Advisory Opinion on the *Status of South-West
Africa*, the Court, after stating its inability to deduce from the
" general considerations " underlying the instruments before it
" any legal obligation for mandatory States to conclude or
negotiate " trusteeship agreements, stated that " it is not for the
Court to pronounce on the political or moral duties which these
considerations may involve." [18]

## 70. *Expression of Judicial Opinion Short of Recommendation*

However, notwithstanding the above quoted statement by the
Court in the Advisory Opinion on the *Status of South-West Africa*,
there is room for a consideration of the question whether an
express authorisation is essential to enable the Court, while applying
existing law, to make what is in fact a recommendation by way of
expressing an opinion on the wisdom, the convenience, or the
continued justification of the law thus applied or of an insistence by
the successful party on the full application of the law as ascertained
by the Court. Reference has been made above to instances in

[16] *I.C.J. Reports* 1951, p. 83.
[17] See above, p. 148.
[18] *I.C.J. Reports* 1950, p. 140.

which arbitral tribunals, without having received an express authorisation to that effect, have acted in that way. It is a frequent occurrence in the practice of municipal courts that, while feeling bound to apply the law as they find it, they deem it their duty to voice the reluctance with which they apply it and the hope that the legislature may intervene to make it unnecessary in the future to give effect to a legal rule which is or has become lacking in justice or capacity to regulate effectively a problem of social urgency or importance.

However legitimate or unavoidable in some cases, judicial legislation cannot be the normal method of improving the law even when the application of existing law is felt to be unsatisfactory or distasteful as a matter of justice and common sense. Reasons have been given in another part of this chapter why in the international sphere judicial legislation—though often urgently called for on account of the imperfections of international law and the absence of the normal instrument of legislative change—is particularly open to objection and why it must therefore be resorted to only with extreme caution. Such restraint may not be incompatible with an expression of view as to the inadequacy of the law thus applied and the resulting moral duty of the parties—especially the successful party—to agree to, as good members of international society and in a spirit of neighbourliness, or to embark by common effort upon, such modifications of the law as appear necessary. The nature of such desirable changes will, as a rule, appear on the face of the judicial pronouncement. There may be no decisive reason why they should not be referred to with some particularity or, when indicated, why such indication—by a tribunal which had the full opportunity of becoming acquainted with all the intricacies of the problems involved—should detract from the authority of the judicial pronouncement. This the Court did, with some deliberation, in the *Free Zones* case where it said: " The Court does not hesitate to express its opinion that if, by the maintenance in force of the old treaties, Switzerland obtains the economic advantages derived from the free zones, she ought in return to grant compensatory economic advantages to the people of the zones." [19]

Similarly, in the case of the *Serbian Loans* the Court did not consider it inconsistent with its judicial character to express a view

[19] Series A/B, No. 46 (1932), p. 169. And see above, p. 217, for other similar cases.

as to the equities of the case. It refused to admit that the economic dislocations caused by the World War released the debtor State from its obligation—"although," it added, "they may present equities which doubtless will receive appropriate consideration in the negotiations."[20] In the case of the *Société Commerciale de Belgique* the Court put on record the declaration made by Counsel for the Belgian Government on the question of payments with regard to which it was stated that "it would have regard to the legitimate interests of the company, the ability of Greece to pay and the traditional friendship between the two countries." That declaration the Court found to be, in a general way, in accordance with the Greek submission. This, it said, "enables the Court to declare that the two Governments are, in principle, agreed in contemplating the possibility of negotiations with a view to a friendly settlement, in which regard would be had, among other things, to Greece's capacity to pay." The Court added: "Such a settlement is highly desirable."[21] That emphatic expression of opinion is of particular interest seeing that the Court had previously declared that it was "not entitled to oblige the Belgian Government . . . to enter into negotiations" with the view to a friendly arrangement corresponding to the budgetary and monetary capacity of the debtor or still less to "indicate the bases of such an arrangement."[22] These examples are of significance. In the Advisory Opinion on the *Awards of the Administrative Tribunal* the Court, while holding that the General Assembly had no right to refuse to give effect to an award of compensation made by the Administrative Tribunal of the United Nations, intimated that the General Assembly had the power to amend the Statute of the Tribunal and to provide for means of redress by another organ. The Court then proceeded to offer advice in the sense that should the General Assembly make such provision for appeal it could hardly act itself as the judicial organ in question.[23]

These instances suggest that, although the Court cannot change the law, it is not certain that decisive considerations of its judicial function preclude it from indicating, in reliance on the "political or moral duties" of States, that it ought to be changed. An opinion

---

[20] Series A, No. 20 (1929), p. 40.
[21] Series A/B, No. 78 (1939), p. 178.
[22] *Ibid.*, p. 177.
[23] *I.C.J. Reports* 1954, p. 56. And see below, p. 327.

thus expressed by the Court cannot be legally binding upon the parties. Its moral force must to some extent be determined by the persuasiveness of its reasoning. Some such expression of opinion, while disdaining a venture into judicial legislation, may, on occasions, relieve the tension between law and justice or obviate the inducement, to yield to which may be contrary to judicial duty, to seek refuge in a *non liquet* in the form of a refusal to pronounce effectively on the issue before the Court.

*PART FOUR*

*THE EFFECTIVENESS OF THE LAW*

# CHAPTER 14

# THE PRINCIPLE OF EFFECTIVENESS AND THE FUNCTION OF INTERPRETATION

## 71. *The Effectiveness of the Law and the Intention of the Parties*

In the preceding two Parts, on " Judicial Caution " and " Judicial Legislation," respectively, there were surveyed the parallel tendencies to conservatism and empiricism in the work of the Court. It is now proposed to consider what appears to be one of the principal features in the application of the law by the Court, namely, its determination to secure a full degree of effectiveness of international law, in particular of the obligations undertaken by parties to treaties—unless intended absence of effectiveness can be proved by reference to the practice of States or the terms of the treaty in question. Such effectiveness may be menaced by various factors. It may be threatened by the doctrine that obligations imposed upon States ought to be interpreted restrictively.[1] It may be rendered nugatory by artful devices, in the sphere of municipal legislation, of the State burdened with the obligation—for instance, by a combination of literal compliance with the duty to grant equality of treatment and a substantive denial of such equality by way of ingeniously conceived municipal legislation. It may be put in jeopardy by the deliberate inconclusiveness of a treaty embodying a compromise attempted but not actually achieved. In the absence of adequate standards—as distinguished from rules—of interpretation, treaties concluded by Governments may become political instruments safeguarding their freedom of action instead of being a source of legal obligations.

A judicial tribunal, when endowed with requisite jurisdiction, may play a useful part in reducing the incidence of some such danger. The activity of the International Court has shown that alongside the fundamental principle of interpretation, that is to say, that effect is to be given to the intention of the parties, beneficent use can be made of another hardly less important principle, namely, that

---

[1] See below, pp. 300 *et seq*.

the treaty must remain effective rather than ineffective. These two principles seem to express one and the same thing. Yet, in fact, a substantial aspect of the jurisprudence of the Court can be viewed in terms of the effort, which cannot easily be put within the framework of any single rule of interpretation, to strike a balance between these potentially conflicting principles. For they are potentially in conflict for the reason that, deliberately or otherwise, there may have been no intention to render the treaty fully effective. It is in relation to that contingency that the principle *ut res magis valeat quam pereat* assumes a complexion of urgency and importance. This is a major principle, in the light of which the intention of the parties must be interpreted even to the extent of disregarding the letter of the instrument and of reading into it something which, on the face of it, it does not contain—so long as that "something" is not contradicted by available and permissible evidence of the intention of the parties. If any lesson can be derived, in this respect, from the experience of the work of the International Court, it is this: Governments cannot rely on the Court that it will countenance evasion from the *vincula juris* into which they seem to have entered, unless they can show that the legal obligation thus expressed does not correspond to their intention. Subject to the latter consideration, the Court will extract from them every reasonable measure of effectiveness. The will of the parties is the Court's charter. However, they cannot be presumed to have envisaged the treaty as a mere form of words—though, probably, they must be permitted the proof that that exactly was the purport of the instrument. In different words, they must be allowed to attempt to show that what purports to be a treaty is not so in law—though occasionally there may be legal presumptions, by way of estoppel or otherwise, which render such proof inadmissible.[2] These hesitating, and apparently somewhat dialectical, qualifications show the intricacy of the problem involved.

---

[2] Thus, for instance, it has been suggested that, in the absence of evidence to the contrary, an instrument finally accepted by both parties in the customary form of an international undertaking and registered with the United Nations in accordance with Art. 102 of the Charter should be deemed to be an instrument creating legal rights and obligations. See the present writer's *Second Report on the Law of Treaties for the International Law Commission* (Doc.A/CN.4/87, 1954, Ad.1). And see his *First Report* of 1953 (Doc.A/CN.4/63) for a discussion of the nature of instruments not intended to create legal obligations (Comment on Art. 1). See also Fawcett in *British Year Book of International Law*, 30 (1953), pp. 381–400, on "The Legal Character of International Agreements."

## 72. *The Limitations of the Maxim* ut res magis valeat quam pereat

For the principle *ut res magis valeat quam pereat* does not mean that the maximum of effectiveness must be given to an instrument purporting to create an international obligation; it means that the maximum of effectiveness should be given to it consistently with the intention—the common intention—of the parties. However, the proposition, even when thus simplified, is not free of difficulty. For the contingency must be envisaged that in many cases the common intention of the parties is an assumption rather than a reality for some such reasons as that the parties while using identical language as expressed in the treaty did not intend the same thing; or that one party deliberately used language of ambiguity; or that both parties, being unable to reach agreement, resorted to the same device.[3] In such cases the autonomy and the responsibilities of judicial decision are particularly conspicuous. Also, when it is said that the task of interpretation is to give full effect to the scope of the treaty, the question inevitably arises: Is it the scope of the treaty as contemplated by the parties or the scope of the treaty as the judge or arbitrator sees it by reference to what, in his view, are the rational considerations and political circumstances surrounding the conclusion of the treaty or prompted by some general international interest? The two questions are not necessarily identical. Their juxtaposition brings vividly to mind the contingency that, under the guise of the principle of effectiveness, the door may be thrown wide open to a substantial measure of judicial legislation in disregard of the actual intention of the parties.

Moreover, the principle of effectiveness provides no ready-made solution in cases in which a decision must be reached in relation to apparently conflicting provisions of the same treaty as, for instance, in the matter of the principal provision and the exceptions thereto. If a treaty providing for compulsory arbitral or judicial settlement lays down, as a condition of such settlement, the exhaustion of local remedies or previous resort to negotiations, what is the proper object of an interpretation based on the requirement of effectiveness? Is it the general purpose of the treaty which must be rendered effective at all costs or is it the intention of the parties that local remedies must be fully exhausted or all the possibilities

---

[3] For a discussion of these contingencies see Lauterpacht in *British Year Book of International Law*, 26 (1949), pp. 75–80.

of negotiation exhausted? When an extradition treaty provides for exceptions from the general purpose of the treaty—exceptions such as non-extradition of nationals or of political offenders—what is it that must be rendered effective: the general duty of extradition or the determination of the parties, specifically expressed, that there should be no question of extradition in the cases expressly provided for? A choice must thus be made between the effectiveness of the general purpose and the exceptions thereto. There may be no clear definite standard and no rule of thumb to guide the judge in the quest for effectiveness—except, perhaps, that the maxim *ut res magis valeat quam pereat* is a canon of good faith and must as such be acted upon. That the principle of effectiveness is not an automatic guide may be gauged from the circumstance that it may be occasionally controversial what, in relation to a particular situation, constitutes true effectiveness. Thus, in connection with reservations to treaties, the question arises as to what is more conducive to the effectiveness of a treaty: its universality—even if achieved at the expense of substantive derogations, as the result of reservations, from the reality of its provisions—or the unqualified acceptance of the treaty by a limited number of States.[4]

The above questions and considerations suggest that while a substantial part of the jurisprudence of the Court may usefully be surveyed from the point of view of the application of the principle of effectiveness, it is a principle which cannot be counted upon to supply a ready-made solution in all circumstances. This does not mean that it is without significance, or instruction, or authority. Its application—in the practice of the Court—may be conveniently considered under the following heads: (a) Effectiveness and Finality of International Settlement and Adjudication; (b) (as a specific application of the latter) Effectiveness of Provisions Conferring Jurisdiction; (c) Effectiveness of Obligations Relating to Equality of Treatment and Protection of Minorities; (d) Effectiveness of International Institutions and International Organisation.

---

[4] See below, p. 277, as to the Advisory Opinion on *Reservations to the Genocide Convention*.

# Chapter 15

# EFFECTIVENESS AND FINALITY OF INTERNATIONAL SETTLEMENT AND ADJUDICATION

## 73. *Finality of Territorial Settlement*

The Court has, in general, acted upon the view that treaties embodying territorial and cognate settlements, by way of provision for adjudication or otherwise, are intended to settle a difference of legal views—or a conflict of interests—and not to perpetuate them. Thus the affirmation—in a manner approaching judicial legislation [1]—of the principle *nemo judex in re sua* in the Twelfth Advisory Opinion on the *Interpretation of the Treaty of Lausanne* was a means for asserting the effectiveness of a treaty in a case in which, according to one Party, the wording of the treaty merely registered a disagreement and a hope of future settlement. In that case Turkey produced evidence purporting to show that the formula used in the Treaty of Lausanne and empowering the Council of the League of Nations to lay down the frontier of Iraq, was inserted for the reason that, having regard to the rule of unanimity, no decision on the subject would be possible without the concurrence of Turkey who, for that purpose, was a member of the Council. Undoubtedly, the Court arrived at its conclusion by way of more than one avenue of interpretation. In particular, it attached importance to the wording of the crucial Article which spoke of the frontier to be " laid down " and of the territories of which " the final fate will depend " upon the decision of the Council of the League of Nations; it found means of explaining the less peremptory passages of that Article which spoke of reference to—perhaps as distinguished from a decision of—the Council of the League of Nations.[2] What, however, the Court considered to be decisive and what probably influenced the Opinion as a whole was the consideration that the parties intended to " insure a definitive and binding solution of the dispute which might arise between them, namely, the final determination of the frontier ";[3] that " the very

---

[1] See above, p. 158.       [2] See above, p. 160.
[3] Series B, No. 12 (1925), p. 19.

nature of a frontier and of any convention designed to establish frontiers between two countries imports that a frontier must constitute a definite boundary line throughout its length "; and that it is " natural that any article designed to fix a frontier should, if possible, be so interpreted that the result of the application of its provisions in their entirety should be the establishment of a precise, complete and definitive frontier." [4]   It is for that reason that the Court was unwilling to adopt, in reliance upon preparatory work,[5] an interpretation which would have reduced the action of the Council to that of simple mediation—a conclusion " which would eliminate the possibility of a definite decision capable, if necessary, of replacing agreement between the Parties." [6]   This affirmation of finality of adjudication provided an early and interesting example of an outspoken application of the principle of effectiveness as the starting point of a significant piece of judicial legislation modifying, by reference to the general principle *nemo judex in re sua*,[7] the apparently rigid requirement of unanimity of the Council.

In the Advisory Opinion on the *Delimitation of the Polish-Czechoslovak Frontier* the Court insisted on the finality of the decision of the Conference of Ambassadors which it endowed with the character of an arbitral award.[8]   It accepted the right of the Principal Allied and Associated Powers to determine the frontiers of the new States.   It did so although such a right may be questioned on theoretical grounds.[9]   After the cataclysm of a World War there was special cogency in the application of the maxim *interest rei publicae ut sit finis litium*.   For the same reason the Court refused to recognise the right of the arbitrator who had determined the frontier, to interpret or to modify, by revising it, the award given by him.   The Court said: " It is obvious that the opinion of the authors of a document cannot be endowed with a decisive value when that opinion has been formulated after the drafting of that document and conflicts with the opinion which they expressed at that time." [10]   This, the Court pointed out, was particularly so seeing that two years had elapsed since the original decision.   Although the necessarily technical character of the

---

[4] Series B, No. 12 (1925), at p. 20.          [5] See above, p. 120.
[6] At p. 23.
[7] See above, pp. 158 *et seq.*
[8] Series B, No. 8 (1923), p. 29.
[9] See, *e.g.*, Verzijl in *Zeitschrift für Völkerrecht*, XIII (1924–1926), p. 526.
[10] Series B, No. 8 (1927), p. 38.

Judgment in the case concerning the *Diversion of Water from the Meuse* does not easily lend itself to generalisation, it is possible to discern the same temper in that part of the Judgment which refers to the claim of Holland to the effect that the Treaty of 1863 created a position of legal inequality between the Parties by giving her a right of control, with respect to feeding certain canals, which was not enjoyed by Belgium.  Any such interpretation, the Court said, would not be in accordance with an agreement freely concluded by the Parties and intended " to reconcile their practical interests with a view to improving an existing situation rather than to settle a dispute concerning mutually contested rights." [11]

The Advisory Opinion in the matter of the *Jurisdiction of the European Commission of the Danube* offers an even more instructive illustration of the same problem.  In that case Roumania maintained that Articles 5 and 6 of the Definitive Statute of the Danube, which provided that the European Commission shall retain the powers which it possessed before the First World War under the same conditions as previously exercised, were intended to leave unresolved the divergence of views which had existed between Roumania and the signatories of the Treaty of London of 1883. In his Dissenting Opinion Negulesco, Deputy-Judge, relied to a considerable degree on the preparatory work of the Statute in the attempt to show that the Conference which adopted the Definitive Statute of the Danube intended to give the character of a legal rule to a disagreement—namely, to the fact that while Roumania never opposed the exercise of the technical powers of the Danube Commission in the disputed sector, she did not admit its right to exercise jurisdictional powers.[12]  The Court declined to uphold any such construction of the Statute.  It rejected an interpretation which, it said, would result in maintaining over the Danube an uncertain and precarious situation.  The object of the Definitive Statute of the Danube was to convert into a legal right the factual situation existing before the War.  A treaty could not sanction for the future a state of mere toleration, " for toleration implies a negation of right." [13]  The object of the law is order, not perpetuation of

---

[11] Series A/B, No. 70 (1937), p. 20. See also *ibid.*, p. 23.

[12] Series B, No. 14 (1927), pp. 115–121   See also, to the same effect, the Dissenting Opinion of Judge Nyholm, pp. 75–77, who pointed out that the system as it existed prior to the treaty worked quite satisfactorily.

[13] *Ibid.*, p. 37.  The English text of the Opinion is in this case authoritative.  The wording of the French text is: " car tolérance implique absence de droit."

disagreements. For the same reason the Court rejected an interpretation the result of which would have been to leave one sector of the Danube in a position in which neither the European nor the International Commission could exercise legal powers. The Court exhibited the same attitude, bent on rendering possible a working régime, in its Judgment on the *Interpretation of the Statute of the Memel Territory*. It refused to infer either from the words of the relevant Convention or from its silence a solution aiming at recognition of two parallel sovereign agencies in the territory. In particular, it declined to admit an interpretation of the Statute according to which the President of the autonomous territory of Memel, acting with the consent of its Chamber, could disregard the Statute and derogate from the sovereignty of Lithuania. " Both the autonomy," it said, " and the sovereignty were intended to be effective." [14]

The principle of effectiveness, it may be added, was also acted upon in relation to other treaty provisions aiming at securing freedom of navigation on international rivers. In the case relating to the *Territorial Jurisdiction of the International Commission of the River Oder* the Court had to decide whether Article 331 of the Treaty of Versailles extended the jurisdiction of the Commission to those parts of two tributaries of the Oder which were situated in Polish territory. Poland contended that it did not, on the ground, *inter alia*, that the principal object of internationalisation of rivers was to secure the right of passage for upstream States. The Court, finding no assistance in the various arguments put forward by the Parties, decided boldly that it must " go back to the principles governing international fluvial law in general." These principles, which it deduced from the practice of States on the matter, led it to base the Judgment on " the possibility of fulfilling the requirements of justice and considerations of utility " as indicated by the fact of a single waterway traversing or separating the territory of more than one State.[15] These it found in the community of interest in a navigable river, which community of interest " becomes the basis of a common legal right, the essential features of which are the perfect equality of all riparian States in the use of the whole course of the river." The principle of international jurisdiction on certain rivers, as interpreted by the inclusion

[14] See Series A/B, No. 49 (1932), p. 317. See also *ibid.*, pp. 313, 314.
[15] Series A, No. 23 (1929), p. 27.

of non-riparian Powers on the river commission, owed its *raison d'être* not so much to the necessity of protecting the interests of land-locked States as to consideration for the interests of non-riparian States. This being so, the full effectiveness of the principle of internationalisation could be safeguarded only by recognition that the "interest of all States is in liberty of navigation in both directions." [16]

### 74. *Finality of Arbitral and Judicial Adjudication*

In the *Jaworzina* case,[17] as well as in the Advisory Opinions on the *Monastery of Saint Naoum* [18] and the *Polish Postal Service in Danzig*,[19] the Court, acting on the same principle of finality of adjudication, laid down that a person fulfilling arbitral functions is, subsequent to the decision given by him, *functus officio* and that, in the absence of a special agreement, he cannot modify, revoke, or interpret the award once given. In the latter case, by laying down clearly the conditions of *res judicata* in international law the Court made a substantial contribution to the principle of effectiveness of international adjudication. It affirmed the "definitive and obligatory character of arbitral awards" when, in the case of the *Société Commerciale de Belgique* between Belgium and Bulgaria, it refused to admit the right of the latter to subordinate payment of the financial charge imposed upon it by arbitral awards to the conditions of the settlement of the Greek external debt; [20] the Greek Government, it said, was bound to execute the awards as they stood.

When in the Second Phase of the case concerning the *Free Zones of Upper Savoy and the District of Gex*, it agreed to render a

---

[16] Series A, No. 23 (1929), p. 28. In its Judgment on the *Jurisdiction of the Oder Commission*, the Court refused to find that Poland was bound by the relevant provisions of the Barcelona Convention, which she had not ratified but which, according to an agreement of the Signatories of the Treaty of Versailles, were intended to supersede Arts. 332 to 337 of that Treaty in the matter of international rivers. The Court adhered strictly to the ordinary rule of international law according to which treaties, as a rule, are binding only by virtue of their ratification. Series A, No. 23 (1929), p. 20. But see the Observations of Huber, Judge, *ibid.*, p. 33, and Paul de Vineuil in *R.I.*, Series III, vol. XI (1930), pp. 785–792. If the Court had stopped there, its Judgment could have been interpreted as amounting to a nullification of the purpose of the Treaty of Versailles. However, as pointed out, the Court proceeded to affirm the jurisdiction of the Oder Commission over the Polish tributaries by reference to "principles governing international fluvial law in general."
[17] See above, p. 232, and Series B, No. 8 (1923), p. 37.
[18] Series B, No. 9 (1924), p. 21.
[19] Series B, No. 11 (1925), p. 28.
[20] Series A/B, No. 78 (1939), p. 176.

Judgment by consent embodying an agreement previously concluded by the Parties, it put on record its emphatic view that it was incompatible with the character of the Judgments rendered by it and with the binding force attached to them by its Statute to give a Judgment which either of the Parties might render inoperative.[21]  In the final phase of the same case the Court refused to adopt an interpretation of the Special Agreement the result of which would be that " its reply would fail to remove the whole of the divergence which exists between France and Switzerland, and which has led them to have recourse to the Court." [22]

The same case provides an example of the determination of the Court to secure not only the finality of international adjudication but also the effectiveness of the general or special agreements providing for the jurisdiction of the Court.  As is recalled elsewhere in this book,[23] the somewhat unusual Special Agreement between France and Switzerland laid down that after concluding its deliberations but before giving Judgment the Court shall communicate unofficially to the Parties the result of its deliberations with the view to enabling them to reach a settlement on that basis.  For reasons stated above, the Court considered any such procedure to be not in accordance either with the Statute or, more generally, with its judicial function.  Yet it did not refuse to comply, in substance, with the desires of the Parties.  It stated, in an Order, that " judicial settlement of international disputes, with a view to which the Court has been established, is simply an alternative to the direct and friendly settlement of such disputes between the Parties "; that " consequently it is for the Court to facilitate, so far as is compatible with its Statute, such direct and friendly settlement "; and that " in case of doubt, the clauses of a special agreement by which a dispute is referred to the Court must, if it does not involve doing violence to their terms, be construed in a manner enabling the clauses themselves to have appropriate effect." [24]  Confronted with the conflicting considerations of the requirements of the Statute and its desire to facilitate the settlement of the dispute, the Court found an ingenious solution of the difficulty: It could neither give a Judgment which was not binding nor communicate it unofficially to the Parties.  But

---

[21] Series A, No. 24 (1930), p. 14.
[22] Series A/B, No. 46 (1932), p. 137.  The Court had previously intimated, in almost identical words, its attitude to the subject in an Order of substantive import: Series A, No. 22 (1929), p. 16.
[23] See above, pp. 215 *et seq.*                    [24] Series A, No. 22 (1929), p. 13.

it could make an Order which, it stated, unlike a Judgment has no " binding " force in the sense of Article 59 of its Statute nor " final " effect in the meaning of Article 60. In that Order, whose operative part was limited to fixing time limits, it adduced at length considerations and reasons extraneous to the Order but useful to the Parties. Having thus complied with what it considered its duty to secure the effectiveness of the Special Agreement, the Court, by way of guidance for the future, deemed it " important to set forth clearly that special agreements whereby international disputes are submitted to the Court should henceforth be formulated with due regard to the forms in which the Court is to express its opinion according to the precise terms of the constitutional provisions governing its activity, in order that the Court may be able to deal with such disputes in the ordinary course and without resorting, as in the present case, to a construction which must be regarded as strictly exceptional." [25]

In the *Pajzs, Csáky, Esterházy* case the Court declined to interpret and to apply the Paris Agreements of 1930 relating, in particular, to compensation in connection with agrarian reforms, in such a way as to leave the door open to fresh claims on the part of Hungarian nationals and to new demands for expropriation indemnities not covered by those Agreements. If the Court were to do that " it might be said that the appeasement which was aimed at by the Paris Agreement in regard to difficulties raised by the agrarian reforms would not really have been attained." [26] The Preamble to these Agreements referred to the settlement of the questions relating to the agrarian reform; this, the Court said, must refer to a settlement " once and for all." The Court declined to admit that, as urged by two dissenting Judges, the effectiveness of these provisions was somehow impaired by the alleged fact that they constituted a departure from general international law.[27] In the same case the Court refused to accept an interpretation of the arbitration agreement by way of recognising a condition the fulfilment of which would be dependent upon the will of either of the interested Parties.[28]

In the *Ambatielos* case the Court declined to accept an

[25] Series A, No. 22 (1929), p. 13.
[26] Series A/B, No. 68 (1936), p. 60.
[27] See the Dissenting Judgments of Judges Hudson and Hammarskjöld, at pp. 77 and 89 respectively.
[28] *Ibid.*, p. 62.

interpretation, suggested by the United Kingdom, the result of which would have been to leave without a solution claims founded on the Treaty in which the parties submitted to arbitration all disputes based on it. To do so would be contrary " to the continuous will of both Parties to submit all differences to arbitration of one kind or another." [29] It is probable that it was that consideration of effectiveness of the arbitration provisions of the Treaty—as distinguished from the more controversial view that a Declaration somewhat artificially annexed to the Treaty formed an integral part thereof—that underlay the Judgment of the Court. The Treaty had provided for a Commission of Arbitration. It was for the latter to decide whether the claims in question fell within the purview of the Treaty. It is possible that the weakness of the case of the United Kingdom was that, in denial of an established principle of arbitral practice, it seemed to decline to recognise that power as inherent in the Commission.[30]

The subsequent stage of the same case—*The Ambatielos Case: Obligation to Arbitrate*—provides another interesting example of an emphatic affirmation, on the part of the Court, of the effectiveness of international adjudication. In that case the Court was called upon to decide whether, under certain clauses of her Treaty with Greece of 1886, as maintained in being by a Declaration subscribed to by the Parties in 1926, the United Kingdom was bound to submit to arbitration a claim which, in the view of the Greek Government, was " based on " the Treaty of 1886. For reasons which it is not necessary to recount here in detail, the United Kingdom maintained that the claim put forward by the Greek Government on behalf of M. Ambatielos was " not based " on the Treaty of 1886. It appears with some clarity both from the Judgment of the Court and from the Dissenting Opinion of four Judges that the answer to that question might have amounted in substance to a decision on the merits of the Greek case. This the Court, in relation to what was in essence a jurisdictional question, had no power to do. The true issue before the Court was rather whether the " arbitrability " of the dispute (namely, whether it " was based " on the Treaty of 1886) was a matter to be decided unilaterally by the United Kingdom or by the arbitration tribunal provided by the Treaty. The Court, in accordance with what is believed to be a sound principle

[29] Preliminary Objection, *I.C.J. Reports* 1952, p. 45.
[30] See the Dissenting Opinion of Judge Klaestad, *ibid.*, p. 83.

of law,[31] was of the view that " in the absence of any manifestation of a common intention of the Parties to the contrary, the Commission of Arbitration cannot be deprived of part of its competence and no other body can be invested with the authority to determine definitively the validity of the treaty basis of the Ambatielos claim." [32] In fact the Court, by way of conclusion of its reasoning, held that " the United Kingdom is under an obligation to co-operate with Greece in constituting a Commission of Arbitration, in accordance with the Protocol of 1886, as provided in the Declaration of 1926." [33] This could be interpreted as meaning no more than that the United Kingdom was bound to submit for the decision of the Commission of Arbitration the preliminary question whether the claim " was based " on the Treaty of 1886 and whether therefore the Tribunal had jurisdiction to decide on the merits of the dispute. Yet, in the operative part of the Judgment, the Court came to a much wider conclusion. It found that " the United Kingdom is under an obligation to submit to arbitration, in accordance with the Declaration of 1926, the difference as to the validity, under the Treaty of 1886, of the Ambatielos claim." [34] Thus the Court seemed to decide in advance that the Arbitration Commission had jurisdiction on the merits, and that it was not open to the United Kingdom to challenge the jurisdiction of the Commission after it had been constituted with the co-operation of the United Kingdom.

In the Advisory Opinion on the *Effect of Awards of Compensation Made by the United Nations Administrative Tribunal* the formal basis of the Opinion was, in the words of the Court, the " well-established and generally recognised principle of law " according to which a judgment rendered by what must be assumed to be a judicial body " is *res judicata* and has binding force between the parties to the dispute." [35]

The principle of finality and effectiveness of international judicial and arbitral settlement was applied, in a somewhat different sphere, in the Advisory Opinion on the *Interpretation of the Greco-Turkish Agreement* where the Court stated that as a general rule

[31] This was, in effect, a solution clearly foreshadowed in the Dissenting Opinion of Judge Klaestad in the first phase of the *Ambatielos* case (*I.C.J. Reports* 1952, p. 83).
[32] *I.C.J. Reports* 1953, p. 17.
[33] At p. 22.
[34] At p. 23.
[35] *I.C.J. Reports* 1954, p. 53. However, though this was, in a sense, the basis of the Opinion, the pronouncement of the Court sheds light on a more fundamental issue and is treated, more conveniently, elsewhere in this book. See below, pp. 325 *et seq.*

any body possessing jurisdictional powers has a right to determine in the first instance the extent of its jurisdiction.[36] That principle is clearly adopted, so far as the Court itself is concerned, in Article 36 of its Statute. Its authoritative recognition in regard to other arbitral and similar bodies is, in view of the history of this problem in international law,[37] of distinct usefulness. The principle to which the Court thus gave its support in wide terms—it referred to " any body possessing jurisdictional powers "—is of obvious cogency. It has been occasionally denied in the sphere of international arbitration. Its affirmation by the Court is of direct relevance in the sphere of finality of international adjudication in its wider sense. With regard to the finality and the effectiveness of its own Judgments the Court acted on the same principle when in its final decision in the *Corfu Channel (Compensation)* case it interpreted Article 53 of its Statute which provides that, in cases in which it is called upon to give Judgment in default, the Court must satisfy itself that the claim " is well founded in fact and law." The Court declined to give an exacting and literal interpretation of that provision. It refused to admit that in considering the submissions of the Parties the Court was bound to examine their accuracy in all their details: " For this might in certain unopposed cases prove impossible in practice. It is sufficient for the Court to convince itself by such methods as it considers suitable that the submissions are well founded." [38]

## 75. *The Principle of Stability and Effectiveness in Acquisition of Territory*

The bulk of the work of the Court has been devoted to the task of interpreting treaties, and this explains why it is particularly in this sphere that there has revealed itself the emphasis, here discussed, on effectiveness and stability. But, as may be seen from the Judgment of the Court in the *Eastern Greenland* dispute between Denmark and Norway, the practical temper intent upon discouraging uncertainty and instability has shown itself also on other occasions. This was the first time that the Court was occupied with a question

---

[36] Series B, No. 16 (1928), p. 20.

[37] See Lauterpacht, *Private Law Sources and Analogies of International Law* (1927), § 90, and in *British Year Book of International Law*, 9 (1928), p. 117. See also Carlston, *The Process of International Arbitration* (1946), pp. 62–182, and Art. 11 of the Draft Code of Arbitral Procedure formulated in 1953 by the International Law Commission.

[38] *I.C.J. Reports* 1949, p. 248.

which furnished the theme of some of the best known and important arbitrations in the past, *i.e.*, the determination of the degree of actual exercise of sovereignty necessary for the acquisition of territory through occupation. The history of international law in this matter has been a series of attempts to apportion the respective shares of *animus* and *corpus* in the acquisition of territorial title. The answer to the question how much there must have been of actual occupation has varied from time to time. Little of it was required in the sixteenth and seventeenth centuries. Substantially more of it was demanded in the periods which followed. However, while the law clearly requires some manifestation of actual exercise of sovereignty, the degree and extent of such effectiveness must in each case be a matter for determination by the adjudicating tribunal. Its discretion in this matter may legitimately be influenced by a number of factors, including the nature and development of the region in question,[39] the absence of adverse claims for a long period, or the absence of a better claim.

This latter consideration weighed with the Court in the *Eastern Greenland* dispute. The Danish claim to sovereignty in the non-colonised parts of Greenland may have been based on acts no more intensive than legislation concerning navigation in the seas around Greenland, the regulation of fishing or hunting, the issue of permits to visit that area, or the conclusion of commercial agreements referring to the whole of Greenland. But Norway could not even point to that. The alternative before the Court, if it had adhered to the rigid requirement of complete occupation, would have been to declare the territory in question *terra nullius* and open henceforth to a competitive scramble between the two countries— and others—with the ensuing uncertainty and confusion. This the Court refused to do. Any such decision would have been contrary to those principles of finality, stability, and effectiveness of international relations which have characterised the work of the Court. For reasons stated, its Judgment did not constitute a departure from the existing law on the subject.[40]

---

[39] " The intermittence and discontinuity compatible with the maintenance of the right necessarily differ according as inhabited or uninhabited regions are involved, or regions enclosed within territories in which sovereignty is uncontestably displayed, or again regions accessible from, for instance, the high seas." Huber, Arbitrator, in *Island of Palmas* case, *Annual Digest*, 1927–1928, Case No. 68.

[40] " If a territory, by virtue of the fact that it was completely uninhabited, is, from the first moment when the occupying State makes its appearance there, at the absolute and

While in the *Minquiers and Ecrehos* case [41] the Court was in
the position to render its decision by reference to its view of the
historic title to the two islands, apart from the question of effectiveness of possession, it examined also in some detail, as being directly
relevant, the various manifestations of the exercise of State functions
by the two parties. In both cases, having regard to the object of
the dispute—rocky islands of small dimensions—the requisite degree
of intensity of such acts was not exacting. It was sufficient to
prevent an inconclusive finding perpetuating a situation of uncertainty. The same tendency manifested itself, in that case, in the
Court's ruling on the subject of the so-called critical date, *i.e.*, the
date by reference to which a territorial dispute must be deemed to
have crystallised. While the Court admitted that acts of parties
subsequent to that date may be taken into account—an admission
which otherwise might have given rise to a substantial degree of
uncertainty in the matter of territorial disputes—it qualified its
decision by reference to " the special circumstances " of the present
case and by expressly excluding measures " taken with a view to
improving the legal position of the Party concerned." [42]

---

undisputed disposition of that State, from that moment the taking of possession must
be considered as accomplished, and the occupation is thereby completed." Award of
King Victor Emmanuel, January 1931, in the *Clipperton Island* case between Mexico
and France, *American Journal of International Law*, XXVI (1932), p. 394; *Annual
Digest*, 1931–1932, Case No. 50. And see the present writer's discussion of the subject
in *British Year Book of International Law*, 27 (1950), pp. 415–419.

[41] *I.C.J. Reports* 1953, p. 47. And see above, p. 36.

[42] *I.C.J. Reports* 1953, p. 59. For a detailed analysis of the Judgment in this respect see
Fitzmaurice in *B.Y.*, 32 (1955–1956), pp. 20–42.

# CHAPTER 16

# EFFECTIVENESS OF PROVISIONS CONFERRING JURISDICTION

## 76. Scope of the Jurisdiction of the Court. Cumulation of Jurisdictional Instruments

Some aspects of the tendency, pursued by the Court, to secure the effectiveness of clauses conferring jurisdiction upon it have been analysed in the preceding chapter as examples of judicial legislation intent, in reliance on the flexibility of international relations, on disregarding procedural and technical defects.[1] The examples there given might with equal justification form part of the present chapter. They tend to confirm the view that, subject to one major consideration, the Court will apply to conventional clauses conferring jurisdiction upon it the canons of effectiveness which it applies to treaties generally. That major, qualifying, consideration may create the appearance of impairing the principle of effectiveness; it reflects the view, repeatedly expressed by the Court, that its jurisdiction is invariably grounded in the will of the parties and that the Court is not entitled to give an extensive interpretation to treaties conferring jurisdiction upon it.[2]

At first sight—but only at first sight—it may not be easy to reconcile these apparently conflicting attitudes. In fact, such reconciliation is less difficult to achieve once it is realised that the principle of exacting interpretation of jurisdictional clauses applies primarily to the basic original instrument said to confer jurisdiction; once that is established, the Court, in accordance with the requirement of good faith, will strive to make that basic instrument effective and will discourage attempts to defeat it by reference to purely technical considerations or limitations not appearing on the face of the instrument. Thus, in the *Mavrommatis Palestine Concessions* case the Court declined to accept the view that a clause conferring jurisdiction upon it extends only to disputes arising subsequent to the entry into force of the clause in question: " The

---

[1] See above, pp. 206 *et seq.*
[2] See above, pp. 91 *et seq.*, and below, pp. 338 *et seq.*

Court is of the opinion that, in case of doubt, jurisdiction based on an international agreement embraces all disputes referred to it after its establishment." [3]   There was, it said, no such doubt with respect to an Article of the Mandate for Palestine referring to it " any dispute whatsoever . . . which may arise." It declined, by implication, to accept the view that the frequency of the reservation of " past disputes " imparted to it the complexion of a general rule. On the contrary, it considered that that reservation in question seemed to prove the necessity of an explicit limitation of jurisdiction if such limitation was desired by the parties.   We shall return presently to another aspect of the reservation of past disputes.

The case of the *Electricity Company of Sofia and Bulgaria* (*Preliminary Objection*) provides another example, in a different sphere, of the determination of the Court to uphold the effectiveness of treaties conferring jurisdiction upon it.   In that case the Parties, the Court held, were bound by two instruments intended to confer jurisdiction upon the Court: by the Declarations, signed by both Parties, under Article 36 (2) of its Statute (the Optional Clause) in 1921 and 1926 respectively and by a more comprehensive treaty of 1931 providing for conciliation, arbitration and judicial settlement. The Court was called upon to decide whether the latter, being more comprehensive, replaced the former—a question which became relevant for the reason that the condition of exhaustion of local remedies was attached to the Treaty of 1931 but not to the Declarations under the Optional Clause and that the Court held that the Treaty of 1931 did not apply on the ground that the local remedies had not in fact been exhausted.   The Court considered that, in principle, both instruments applied simultaneously and supplemented one another—with the result that although the Treaty of 1931 did not, in the specific case, apply because of the non-exhaustion of local remedies, the Declarations under the Optional Clause still gave the Court jurisdiction.   It held that " the multiplicity of agreements concluded accepting the compulsory jurisdiction is evidence that the contracting Parties intended to open up new ways of access to the Court rather than to close old ways or to allow them to cancel each other out with the ultimate result that no jurisdiction would remain." [4]   It pointed out that there was no justification for holding that in accepting a very comprehensive

---

[3] Series A, No. 2 (1924), p. 35.
[4] Series A/B, No. 77 (1939), p. 76.

system of pacific settlement the Parties intended to weaken the obligations which they had previously entered into with a similar purpose, and especially where such obligations were in some respects more extensive than the otherwise more comprehensive system of pacific settlement. It followed that the Treaty of 1931 could not be adduced to prevent the Declarations under the Optional Clause from exercising their effect.[5]

## 77. Jurisdiction to Award Compensation

An important example of the application of the principle of effectiveness in the matter of jurisdiction has been provided by the cases in which the Court has held that the conferment of jurisdiction to decide upon the question of liability includes also the jurisdiction to assess damages due by the Party held to be responsible. The Court first acted upon that principle in its Judgment in the case concerning *Certain German Interests in Polish Upper Silesia* in which it declared itself competent to decide the question of the indemnity due to Germany by Poland in consequence of her action held to be contrary to her international obligations. Article 23 of the Geneva Convention of May 1922 between Poland and Germany provided that the Court shall have jurisdiction in respect of differences of opinion relating to the interpretation and application of certain Articles of the Convention. In pursuance of that clause the Court gave, in May 1926, judgment to the effect that Poland, by proceeding to certain acts of liquidation and expropriation of German property in Polish Upper Silesia, acted contrary to her international obligations.[6] Subsequent to this Judgment, Germany and Poland engaged in negotiations with a view to giving effect to it. These negotiations were not successful. Thereupon Germany filed an application, based on Article 23 of the Geneva Convention, asking the Court to fix the amount and the mode of payment of the reparation due to Germany in consequence of the violation by Poland of her international obligations. Poland denied that the

[5] In comparison, there was only apparent cogency in the view propounded in Judge Anzilotti's Dissenting Opinion that it was not possible in the same legal system for two rules to exist which attached contradictory consequences to the same fact. It would have been more relevant to say that it was not possible for the same Party to invoke simultaneously the Treaty of 1931 and the Declaration under the Optional Clause. In the event Judge Anzilotti held that the Treaty of 1931 merely suspended the operation of the Declarations and that the Belgian Government was entitled to resubmit in 1938 its application under the Optional Clause after the Treaty of 1931 had expired.

[6] Series A, No. 7 (1926).

Court had jurisdiction. She pleaded that the Article which conferred upon the Court jurisdiction as to differences of opinion resulting from the interpretation and application of certain Articles of the Convention did not contemplate differences in regard to reparation claimed for a disregard of these Articles. The Court rejected this view. It stated that it was a principle of international law that the breach of a treaty involves the duty of reparation; that, accordingly, as reparation was an indispensable complement of a failure to apply a treaty, it was not necessary that this should be expressly laid down in the treaty; and that for this reason differences as to reparation due for a disregard of a treaty were to be regarded as differences relating to its application. The Court pointed out that a decision whether there has been a breach of a treaty is more important than a decision as to the reparation due for a breach of a treaty, and, as it admittedly had jurisdiction in regard to the former, it would be difficult to understand why, " failing an express provision to that effect," it should not have jurisdiction over the latter.[7]

These are impressive reasons, but there may be an answer to them. In particular, so far as the intention of States is concerned, it may not be invariably safe to rely on juridical logic for the purpose of deducing one kind of jurisdiction from another. In conferring jurisdiction upon international tribunals States are not guided by reasons of legal logic. The true *ratio decidendi*—and the one which is of interest for the purpose of the present discussion—will be found in the final reasoning of the Court on this matter: " An interpretation which would confine the Court simply to recording that the Convention had been incorrectly applied . . . , without being able to lay down the conditions for the re-establishment of the treaty rights affected, would be contrary to what would, *prima facie*, be the natural object of the clause; for a jurisdiction of this kind, instead of settling a dispute once and for all, would leave open the possibility of further disputes." [8] This is probably the decisive reason underlying the Judgment: the effectiveness of the undertaking contained in the jurisdictional clause including—as one of its elements—the practical conclusiveness of the decision of the Court as an agency for settling with finality disputes submitted to it.

The same considerations apply to that aspect of the Judgment in

[7] Series A, No. 9 (1927), p. 23.
[8] At p. 25.

the *Corfu Channel* case in which the Court was confronted with an almost identical issue. The latter lay in the following passage of the Judgment: " If . . . the Court should limit itself to saying that there is a duty to pay compensation without deciding what amount of compensation is due, the dispute would not be finally decided." [9] The Court referred to two previous pronouncements of the Permanent Court of International Justice upholding the principle of effective interpretation [10] (although, somewhat strangely, it did not refer to the directly relevant case, discussed above, of *German Interests in Polish Upper Silesia*). The Court pointed out that it would be " incompatible with the generally accepted rules of interpretation " to admit that a provision of a special agreement, which empowers the Court to decide whether there is a duty of compensation, did not at the same time give it the power to decide on the amount of compensation. In comparison there may have been less persuasive force in the reliance, on the part of the Court, on the fact that as the Albanian agent did not deny the jurisdiction of the Court to decide what kind of satisfaction was due to Albania in respect of the violation of her territorial sovereignty, it followed that the Court could decide what was the amount of compensation due to the United Kingdom in respect of the violation, on the part of Albania, of the duty which she owed to the United Kingdom.

However that may be, the Judgments of the Court in the two cases here examined emphasise the length to which the Court— rightly, it is submitted—is prepared to go in upholding the effectiveness of its jurisdiction once it has been conferred upon it. Admittedly, the matter is not free from controversy. It may be argued, though perhaps not very persuasively, that the authority of the Judgment is such that even in the absence of an assessment of compensation the Judgment would not be without efficacy inasmuch as it imposes upon the party held liable the obligation to come to fair and reasonable terms as to the amount of compensation; that, failing such good faith and in the absence of any machinery of enforcement, there is no guarantee that the assessment of compensation will effectively dispose of the dispute; and that there is no good reason why the parties, if they wish the Court to adjudicate upon the amount of compensation due, should not say

[9] *I.C.J. Reports* 1949, p. 26.
[10] Advisory Opinion No. 13, p. 19 (see below, p. 268); and the Order in the *Free Zones* case, Series A, No. 22 (1929), p. 13.

so expressly (especially seeing that they must be deemed to have knowledge of the difficulties to which their silence on the subject is likely to give rise). It is not necessary to examine these arguments. By implication, the Court rejected them. These cases thus provide a further significant illustration of the tendency of the Court to secure the effectiveness, in so far as that lies with it, of clauses conferring jurisdiction upon it.

## 78. *Effectiveness of the Advisory Jurisdiction of the Court*

The same applies generally to the Court's interpretation of its Statute as a source of its advisory jurisdiction. The Court has not been inclined to limit the effectiveness of its Statute in this respect —unless in deference to clearly overriding principles of law. In the case of *Eastern Carelia* [11] it refused to render an Advisory Opinion on the ground that Russia, the State directly involved, was not, and declined to be, a Party to the proceedings, and that answering the question put to it in the request for an Opinion would amount substantially to deciding a dispute between two States. The circumstances of that Opinion—in particular, the fact that at that time the State directly interested was not a member of the League of Nations and that at that time the Court was not as yet fulfilling the functions of the " principal judicial organ " of the Organization— are reviewed elsewhere in this book.[12] However that may be, that case can no longer be regarded as a precedent of authority. For the Court subsequently affirmed its right and duty to give Advisory Opinions, in conformity with its Statute, notwithstanding the absence in the proceedings before it of an interested State or States —at least so long as the Opinion touched only on a question of a preliminary and procedural nature as distinguished from the merits of the dispute. This was the case in the Advisory Opinion on the *Interpretation of Peace Treaties with Bulgaria, Hungary and Romania (First Phase)*, in which it held itself competent to give an Opinion on the question whether there existed a dispute between these States and certain Allied and Associated Powers concerning the interpretation of the Peace Treaties of 1947 in the matter of human rights and freedoms, and whether the former States were bound to comply with the procedure of pacific settlement provided

11 Series B, No. 5 (1923).
12 See above, p. 109.

for in those Treaties.[13]   In the same case the Court affirmed its right and duty to give an Advisory Opinion in a matter involving the interpretation of a treaty on a question alleged to be essentially one within the domestic jurisdiction of the States concerned.[14]   In the case concerning the *Admission of a State to the United Nations (Article 4 of the Charter)* the Court stated that according to Article 96 of the Charter and Article 65 of its Statute it may give an Advisory Opinion on any legal question, abstract or otherwise.[15]

There was less inherent difficulty in rejecting objections to rendering an Advisory Opinion on the ground that the Court is not competent to interpret the provisions of the Charter [16] or that the question which it was asked to answer was of a political nature.[17] In the Advisory Opinion on *Reservations to the Convention on Genocide* the Court, recalling the principles laid down in the above-mentioned Opinion on the *Interpretation of Peace Treaties,* stated in general terms that " a reply to a request for an Opinion should not in principle be refused." [18]   The presumption is in favour of the effectiveness of this aspect of the jurisdiction of the Court.   In particular, the Court declined to admit that the rendering of the Advisory Opinion was not admissible on the ground that the General Assembly was not a Party to the Genocide Convention and that only the Parties had a legal right to the elucidation of its provisions.   On the contrary, the General Assembly, which had taken the initiative in respect of the Convention and had been actively associated with its adoption, had, in the view of the Court, " a prominent interest of direct concern " in the precise determination of the conditions of participation in the Convention.[19]   The care with which the Court answered these and other objections to its advisory jurisdiction in this case shows that the vindication of the effectiveness of its Statute as the principal judicial organ of the United Nations can be combined with a thorough elucidation of the

---

[13] *I.C.J. Reports* 1950, pp. 71, 72.   And see above, p. 107, and below, p. 353.   The question of the effect of that Opinion in relation to the Opinion of the Court in the case of *Eastern Carelia*—a question of some complexity—is discussed in another chapter.

[14] See below, p. 272.

[15] *I.C.J. Reports* 1947–1948, p. 61.   And see above, p. 79.

[16] Advisory Opinion on the *Competence of the General Assembly regarding Admission to the United Nations*: *I.C.J. Reports* 1950, p. 6.

[17] Advisory Opinion on *Reservations to the Genocide Convention, I.C.J. Reports* 1951, p. 19.

[18] *Ibid.*

[19] See above, pp. 108 *et seq.*

various factors which may militate against the exercise of its advisory function in particular cases.

Moreover, in both Opinions—that on the *Interpretation of the Peace Treaties* and that on *Reservations to the Genocide Convention* —the Court affirmed the effectiveness of its advisory jurisdiction by laying down the principle that, notwithstanding the permissive terms of Article 61 of its Statute, the rendering of advisory opinions is in the nature of a duty. As the Court pointed out, " there are certain limits . . . to the Court's duty to reply to a request." [20]    But these limits are of a legal character; they are determined by the fact that the Court is the judicial organ of the United Nations and that in acting in an advisory capacity it must act in accordance with its judicial character, the requirements of its Statute, and the principles of international law. The Court has not considered itself free to decline to render an Advisory Opinion on account of political considerations or for reasons of its own convenience.

## 79. *Declaratory Judgments*

The Court has exhibited a similar tendency in relation to the question of its competence to render declaratory judgments—a matter in a sense connected with Advisory Opinions inasmuch as, unless the rendering of declaratory judgments, *i.e.*, judgments unrelated to a concrete claim for redress in respect of an alleged particular act, is kept within limits, the contentious jurisdiction of the Court might be used as a means for obtaining Advisory Opinions by States (as distinguished from requests by an authorised organ or specialised agency of the United Nations). The Statute wisely makes no provision for requests for Advisory Opinions, which are not binding, by individual States; for while it may be assumed that an organ of the United Nations or a specialised agency would act upon an Advisory Opinion of the Court, there may be no such assurance in the case of individual States. These cannot be permitted, even when the request is made jointly,[21] to use the Court as a source of advice which they are at liberty to disregard.

However, subject to the necessity of preventing declaratory

[20] *Interpretation of the Peace Treaties (First Phase), I.C.J. Reports* 1950, p. 71.
[21] See the case concerning the *Interpretation of the Greco-Bulgarian Agreement*, Series A/B, No. 45 (1932), p. 87. See also the case concerning *Certain German Interests in Polish Upper Silesia*, Series A, No. 6 (1925), p. 21.

judgments from being used by the parties for the purpose of obtaining Advisory Opinions, the Court has declined to sanction a restrictive interpretation of its jurisdiction in this respect.    In particular, it held [22] that it was not prevented from rendering such Judgments as the result of Article 59 of its Statute which lays down that the decisions of the Court are valid only for the parties to the dispute [23]—though it appears clearly from the relevant pronouncements of the Court that it will decline to answer abstract questions and that any declaratory judgment must refer to a controversy relating to the interpretation of a disputed clause of a treaty in cases where the disputed interpretation has resulted or is likely to result in acts alleged to be illegal.    In its Judgment relating to the *Interpretation of the Statute of the Memel Territory* the Court drew attention to the " inconvenience " resulting from the fact that the Parties, in their *compromis*, formulated their questions *in abstracto* without reference to the facts of the dispute.[24]    It observed that " the convenient and appropriate method in which to bring the difference of opinion before the Court would have been by means of submissions directed to the legality of these particular acts, leaving the Court to enunciate in its decision the principles on which that decision was based." [25]    Yet, after having thus discouraged questions of an abstract character—such as in what circumstances there was a right to dismiss the directorate of Memel—the Court assisted in upholding the effectiveness of the *compromis* by basing its Judgment not on the abstract form of the questions of the *compromis* but on the conclusions of the parties as formulated in the course of the pleadings.    It did not follow the radical course proposed in his Dissenting Opinion by Judge Anzilotti who urged that the Court should decline jurisdiction on the ground that the application did

[22] See case concerning *Certain German Interests in Polish Upper Silesia*, Series A, No. 7 (1926), p. 18.    See also to the same effect the Judgment concerning the *Interpretation of Judgments Nos. 7 and 8 (The Chorzów Factory)*, Series A, No. 13 (1927), pp. 20, 21. The Court said : " The Court's Judgment No. 7 is in the nature of a declaratory judgment, the intention of which is to ensure recognition of a situation at law, once and for all and with binding force as between the Parties; so that the legal position thus established cannot again be called in question in so far as the legal effects ensuing therefrom are concerned."

[23] But in the same case the Court declined to decide on a submission which amounted to a question as to what attitude of the Polish Government would have been in conformity with the Geneva Convention—a question which amounted to a request for an Advisory Opinion (p. 34).

[24] Series A/B, No. 49 (1932), p. 311.

[25] At p. 312.    See also above, p. 79, as to the *Anglo-Norwegian Fisheries* case.

not embody " the essential features of a claim for legal redress." [26]
He said: " in its judicial capacity the Court cannot answer
questions; it must pass upon claims " [27]—a somewhat extreme
formulation of the underlying proposition. For it is clear that a
*compromis, i.e.,* a joint application from both parties (as distinguished from a unilateral application) can properly be couched in
the form of questions referring to specific situations.[28]

## 80. *Provisional Measures of Protection*

A similar tendency to extract every legitimate measure of
effectiveness—but no more—from the jurisdictional provisions of its
Statute has manifested itself in the Court's interpretation of
Article 41 of its Statute relating to provisional measures.[29] In the
first instance, it has laid down that it is entitled to indicate provisional measures *proprio moto,*[30] though this clearly must apply
only to cases already brought before the Court. Secondly, it has
clearly rejected the interpretation according to which the indication
of provisional measures must be limited to cases in which the violation of international law cannot be " made good by the payment of
an indemnity or by compensation or restitution in some other
material form." [31]   Although this would have seemed to be
a limitation originally recognised by the Court, it is not certain
that it did in fact act upon it in the very case in which it purported
to apply it, namely, in the case concerning the denunciation by
China of her treaty with Belgium relating to Capitulations.[32] For
in a subsequent case—*Electricity Company of Sofia (Interim
Measures of Protection)*—it " indicated " that " pending the final
judgment of the Court . . . the State of Bulgaria should ensure that
no step of any kind is taken capable of prejudicing the rights
claimed by the Belgian Government or of aggravating or extending
the dispute submitted to the Court." [33]   Thus, contrary to some

---

[26] Series A/B, No. 49 (1932), at p. 349.                    [27] At p. 350.
[28] See on this question the illuminating observations by Beckett in *Hague Recueil*, 50
(1934) (iv), pp. 285 *et seq.*
[29] See above, pp. 110 *et seq.*, for a discussion of this aspect of the jurisdiction of the Court
within the framework of the tendency to judicial caution.
[30] See Order in the case concerning the *Status of South-Eastern Territory of Greenland,*
Series A/B, No. 48 (1932), p. 284.  And see Art. 61 (6) of its Rules.
[31] Order in the case concerning the *Denunciation of the Treaty of 1865 between Belgium
and China,* Series A, No. 8 (1927), p. 7.
[32] See above, n. 31.
[33] Series A/B, No. 79 (1939), p. 199.

views expressed on the subject, the possible irreparability of the damage ceased to be the decisive criterion applied by the Court—an aspect of the question which became of importance in the Order in the *Anglo-Iranian Oil Company* case referred to below.

On the other hand, the Court has safeguarded the usefulness of this provision of its Statute by declining to apply it in cases in which the object of the application for the indication of conservatory measures went beyond a reasonable interpretation of their purpose. Thus it refused to issue a provisional order when it considered that the request for interim protection was in fact " designed to obtain an interim judgment in favour of a part of the claim formulated in the application " [34]; when it was of the view that the application was intended not only to protect the rights involved in the particular dispute, but had a wider object involving " all future cases of the Application of the Polish agrarian reform law to the Polish nationals of German race " [35]; and when, as in the case concerning the *Legal Status of the South-Eastern Territory of Greenland*, the professed object of the application was to prevent " regrettable incidents." In the latter case the Court declined to issue the Order for the further reason that, in the view of the Court, such incidents, or any act of the Parties to the dispute, could not in any case affect the legal rights over the territory in question and that therefore no Party had an interest in causing acts to be performed likely to give rise to incidents.[36]

The combination of the tendency to ensure a full measure of application of this provision of the Statute with a determination to limit its scope in appropriate cases throws, indirectly, some light on the question of the binding force of conservatory measures. While the Statute, in using studiously restrained language on the subject,

---

[34] Case concerning the *Factory at Chorzów (Indemnities)*, Series A, No. 12 (1927), p. 10.
[35] Case concerning the *Polish Agrarian Reform and the German Minority*, Series A/B, No. 58 (1933), p. 177.
[36] Series A/B, No. 48 (1932), p. 287. It is not believed that the refusal, in this case, to consider the possibility of incidents as a reason for granting the Order is inconsistent with the Order in the case of the *Electricity Company of Sofia* (see above, p. 252), where the Court granted the Order with the view to preventing the aggravation and extension of the dispute. It must be a matter of appreciation in every particular case whether there is a danger of aggravation or extension of the dispute. For the reasons given in some detail in the Order in the *South-Eastern Greenland* case the Court did not consider that there was a risk of aggravation of the dispute as the result of the unilateral action of either Party. The Court also attached importance to the fact that the two States were parties to the Geneva General Act of 1928 in which they undertook to abstain from measures likely to aggravate or extend the dispute and that a legal remedy was therefore available in the case of an infringement of that obligation.

seems to negative the notion of a binding effect of conservatory measures as a matter of legal obligation, the caution with which the Court administers this Article of the Statute suggests that outright denial of any binding effect of conservatory measures may be misleading. It cannot be lightly assumed that the Statute of the Court—a legal instrument—contains provisions relating to any merely moral obligations of States and that the Court weighs minutely the circumstances which permit it to issue what is no more than an appeal to the moral sense of the parties. At the same time, the language of Article 41 of the Statute precludes any confident affirmation of the binding force of the measures issued by it under that Article—a circumstance which explains why this subject is treated also in this book as coming within the purview of " judicial caution." [37] Whatever may be the answer—and none is here ventured—to this question, it ought to be clear that a party disregarding an Order indicating provisional measures acts at its peril and that the Order must be regarded at least as a warning estopping a party from denying knowledge of any probable consequences of its action.

## 81. *Jurisdiction and Provisional Measures of Protection*

In this connection, it is not surprising that the Court, in pursuance of an obvious requirement of the effectiveness of its Statute, sanctions the established principle of international jurisprudence [38] to the effect that a mere denial, by one party, of the jurisdiction of the Court on the merits does not prevent the Court from indicating provisional measures so long as there exists an instrument which *prima facie* confers jurisdiction upon it. The contrary principle would make it possible for one party to frustrate the urgent purpose of provisional measures by raising the question of jurisdiction on the merits. The practice of the Court on the subject is surveyed in a preceding Part of this book—the Part

---

[37] See above, p. 110.

[38] See, indirectly, the Order in connection with the case between *China and Belgium Concerning the Denunciation of the Treaty of 1865* (Series A, No. 8 (1927), pp. 8, 10); the Order concerning the *Administration of the Prince von Pless* (Series A/B, No. 54 (1933), p. 153). Numerous decisions of Mixed Arbitral Tribunals are to the same effect. They are discussed in detail by Niemeyer, *Einstweilige Verfügungen des Weltgerichtshofs, ihr Wesen und ihre Grenzen* (1932), and Dumbauld, *Interim Measures of Protection* (1932). And see, again to the same effect, Hudson, *Permanent Court of International Justice* (1943), pp. 425, 426, and Hammarskjöld in *Zeitschrift für ausländisches öffentliches Recht und Völkerrecht*, V (1935), p. 19.

on " Judicial Caution "—as an example not so much of an assertion of caution as of tempering of caution by reference to requirements of convenience and common sense.[39]    When in the case of the *Anglo-Iranian Oil Company* Iran challenged the right of the Court to indicate provisional measures on the ground that its jurisdiction on the merits was at issue, the Court declined to recognise a plea of that character.[40]    The rule which underlies—or which can be deduced from—the Order in this case is that in cases in which its jurisdiction is challenged or doubtful the Court will, without committing itself in any way, make an Order provided that there is an instrument, such as the Optional Clause adhered to by both Parties, which *prima facie* confers jurisdiction upon it and provided that there are no reservations attached to that instrument which clearly exclude the jurisdiction of the Court.[41]    But it is not necessary that the Court should find, as a condition of making an Order for interim protection, that it *probably* has jurisdiction.    Any such finding would, at least to some extent, commit the Court as to its final decision—a result which the Court has repeatedly and expressly disclaimed.[42]

[39] See above, p. 110.

[40] *I.C.J.* Reports 1951, p. 93.

[41] This formulation of the rule seems to approach—though in fact it does not—the construction which the two Dissenting Judges (Winiarski and Badawi) put upon the principle underlying the Order of the Court, namely, that " if *prima facie* the total lack of jurisdiction of the Court is not patent, that is, if there is a possibility, however remote, that the Court may be competent, then it may indicate interim measures of protection ": *I.C.J.* Reports 1951, p. 97.    Possibly, this statement does not fully represent the position taken by the Court.    For in the *Anglo-Iranian Oil Company* case there was not merely " a possibility, however remote."    There was there the Optional Clause adhered to by both Parties, and there was no reservation obviously covering the case and brought to the notice of the Court.    It might seem, therefore, that the Dissenting Judges somewhat understated the actual position in saying that this was a case in which " prima facie the total lack of jurisdiction of the Court is not patent."

[42] The Court would be committing itself to some extent for it would be naturally disinclined to find in the end that its assessment of the probability of its jurisdiction was incorrect.    Moreover, any finding based on the assumption that its jurisdiction on the merits is *probable* presupposes a measure of investigation, in connection with an application for interim measures, which the Court cannot properly undertake at this stage and which it did not in fact undertake in the *Anglo-Iranian* case.    The Court dealt only summarily with two Persian objections which were not of a compelling character.    It did not deal with the third possible objection based on the wording of the Persian acceptance of the Optional Clause.    If the Court were under a duty to satisfy itself as to the probability of its jurisdiction on the merits, then it would not and could not properly have acted on the principle that it can take into consideration such objections only as had been put forward by the Persian Government.    The matter would have been somewhat analogous to the procedure under Art. 53 (judgment by default) where the Court has to satisfy itself that it has jurisdiction.    That function cannot properly be discharged by ignoring, possibly decisive, objections to the

On the other hand, the Court interpreted its right to indicate provisional measures *proprio moto* in the sense that, while the request for such measures proceeds from a party, it is within the province of the Court to indicate the substance of these measures. This the Court did in a constructive fashion which revealed in a significant manner the potentialities of its jurisdiction in this sphere. In addition to indicating that no party shall take action prejudicing the rights of the other party or calculated to extend or aggravate the dispute, it laid down the details of a provisional régime for the oil industry in Iran. This included the appointment by joint action of the parties concerned—or failing that, by the President of the Court—of a Board of Supervision charged with ensuring the continuance of the normal operations of the Anglo-Iranian Oil Company and the payment into a bank of the net revenue from the oil industry pending the final settlement of the dispute.

jurisdiction for the mere reason that the interested party has not put them forward. The Court cannot find that it *probably* has jurisdiction unless it investigates the matter with some care—which in the *Anglo-Iranian* case it did not do and which it did not purport to do. It is for that reason that it may be difficult to accept the view propounded in the Joint Dissenting Opinion in that case. The Dissenting Judges suggested that interim measures cannot be indicated "if there exist serious doubts or weighty arguments against this jurisdiction." It would appear that in order to reach the conclusion that there exist serious doubts, it is essential to investigate the question with some care. But the Dissenting Judges arrived at the "provisional conclusion" that the Court has no jurisdiction on the merits on the basis of "a consideration, entirely summary in character" (*ibid.*). The assumption of the existence of "serious doubts or weighty arguments" cannot be the result of an examination which is "entirely summary in character." These doubts concerning the Dissenting Opinion in that case are also relevant—although not to the same degree—to the view that the Court must find that its jurisdiction is "probable." Probability cannot be predicated on the basis of what is necessarily a summary and cursory investigation. On the other hand, such investigation is sufficient for the purpose of applying the rule as suggested at the commencement of this Note.

# CHAPTER 17

# EFFECTIVENESS OF EQUALITY CLAUSES

**82. *Protection of Minorities. Equality in Fact and Equality in Law***

The tendency to secure the effectiveness of the major purpose of a treaty manifested itself, early in the history of the Court, in the matter of the treaties providing for the protection of minorities. It was not unnatural that the new international system, established in 1919, relating to the protection of minorities should have given rise to attempts at weakening its effectiveness by ingenious practices and procedural objections. A provision of a Minorities Treaty may be violated by a municipal enactment referring directly to the minority in question. The same result can be achieved by a statute which discreetly omits to refer to the minority which is in fact injured by the legislation in question. Thus the Polish Law of 1920 which—as the Court had no difficulty in ascertaining—aimed at dispossessing the German colonists settled in pursuance of the Germanisation policy of Prussia before the First World War did not refer to German settlers *eo nomine.* The Court refused to admit that this device made the provisions of the Minorities Treaty inapplicable; it did not matter that no discrimination appeared in the text of the Law, and that in a few instances it applied also to non-German Polish nationals: " There must be equality in fact as well as ostensible legal equality in the sense of the absence of discrimination in the words of the law." [1] About ten years later Poland had the satisfaction of seeing the Court reaffirm the same principle in her favour in the Advisory Opinion concerning the *Treatment of Polish Nationals in the Danzig Territory.*[2] The Court said on that occasion: " . . . The prohibition against discrimination, in order to be effective, must ensure the absence of discrimination in fact as well as in law. A measure which in terms is of general application, but in fact is directed against Polish nationals and other persons of Polish origin or speech, constitutes a violation of the prohibition." The same principle, in

---

[1] Advisory Opinion concerning *German Settlers in Poland*, Series B, No. 6 (1923), p. 24.
[2] Series A/B, No. 44 (1932), p. 28.

regard to minorities of foreign nationality, was expressed by the Court in the form of the statement that a measure forbidden by a treaty cannot become lawful by reason of the fact that the State applies the measure in question to its own nationals.[3]

In the Advisory Opinion concerning the *Acquisition of Polish Nationality* the Court reaffirmed in explicit terms the view that an interpretation which would deprive the Minorities Treaty of a great part of its value is inadmissible.[4]    Poland contended that the persons who complained on account of Poland's refusal to admit them to Polish nationality and who invoked the Minorities Treaty were not entitled to rely on it, seeing that the protection of this Treaty was limited to Polish nationals.  The Court refused to accept that contention.  Basing itself on the principle, referred to above, of the effectiveness of the Minorities Treaty, it gave a ruling which proved to be of fundamental importance for the protection of minorities, namely, that the conception " minority " includes all inhabitants of Poland of non-Polish origin whether they are Polish nationals or not.[5]   The Court pointed out that if the Polish interpretation of the relevant Article 4 of the Minorities Treaty were accepted, namely, that that Article contemplates exclusively minorities composed of Polish nationals who are inhabitants of Polish territory, " the value and sphere of application of the Treaty would be greatly diminished." [6]   It referred to its view, expressed in the Advisory Opinion on *German Settlers in Poland*, to the effect that an interpretation which would deprive the Minorities Treaty of much of its value is inadmissible.[7]

Reference may be made in this connection to the application of the principle of effectiveness in a cognate sphere, namely, that of exchange of populations.  In the Advisory Opinion concerning the *Exchange of Greek and Turkish Populations* the Court declined to apply a particular date as the crucial date in relation to the Greek inhabitants of Constantinople, for the reason that the proposed date would deprive the relevant Article of the Treaty " of a great deal of its practical value." [8]   The Court referred to this latter pronouncement in its Advisory Opinion on the *Interpretation of the*

---

[3] Series A, No. 7 (1926) (*Certain German Interests in Polish Upper Silesia*), pp. 32, 33: Series A/B, No. 61 (1933) (*Peter Pázmány University*), p. 243.
[4] Series B, No. 7 (1923), p. 17.              [5] Series B, No. 7 (1923), p. 14.
[6] At p. 16.
[7] At p. 17.
[8] Series B, No. 10 (1925), p. 25.

*Greco-Turkish Agreement.* The Court pointed to the duties entrusted to the Mixed Commission as the sole authority for dealing with the exchange of populations. It said: " Special stress should be laid on the fact that these duties have been entrusted to it with the object amongst others of facilitating this exchange. It follows that any interpretation or measure capable of impeding the work of the Commission in this domain must be regarded as contrary to the spirit of the clauses providing for the creation of this body." [9] In similar vein, in its Advisory Opinion concerning the *Greco-Bulgarian Communities* the Court, before answering the main question put to it, considered in detail " the general purpose " which the relevant Convention was designed to fulfil in its measures concerning reciprocal emigration.[10] It was by reference to the effectiveness of these measures that the Court came to the conclusion that churches, schools or foundations having a separate existence must be assimilated to " communities " when persons who are members or beneficiaries of these bodies emigrate.

Perhaps the most important pronouncement of the Court in affirmation of the overriding principle of effectiveness in the interpretation of the Minorities Treaties is its Advisory Opinion on the *Minority Schools in Albania.*[11] In that Opinion the Court rejected the plea of the Albanian Government that, as the abolition of private schools in Albania constituted a general measure applicable to the majority as well as to the minority, it was in conformity with the obligation undertaken by Albania to grant to the minorities the same treatment in law and in fact as that granted to other Albanian nationals. The Court based itself to some extent on the textual interpretation of the Albanian Declaration in support of the view that the equality of rights of the members of minorities meant that in no case would these rights be inferior to those of the majority, but that such equality did not necessarily mean that in no case could the minorities claim a right not enjoyed by the majority. In the view of the Court, they could claim such a right if it was provided for in the Treaty for the purpose of effectively safeguarding their interests as a minority. Thus, with regard to the Albanian legislation—ostensibly applicable to all—abolishing private schools, the Court said: " The abolition of these institutions, which alone

[9] Series B, No. 16 (1928), p. 18.
[10] Series B, No. 17 (1930), pp. 19–23.
[11] Series A/B, No. 64 (1935).

can satisfy the special requirements of the minority groups, and their replacement by government institutions, would destroy this equality of treatment, for its effect would be to deprive the minority of the institutions appropriate to its needs, whereas the majority would continue to have them supplied in the institutions created by the State." [12]   In thus attempting to give effect to equality both in fact and in law the Court acknowledged the difficulty in establishing a clear distinction between these two notions.  " Nevertheless, it may be said that the former notion excludes the idea of a merely formal equality." [13]   The Court recalled what it had previously said on the subject in the case of *German Settlers in Poland*: " There must be equality in fact as well as ostensible legal equality in the sense of the absence of discrimination in the words of the law." [14]

This recognition of the claim of the minorities to rights on the face of it more extensive than those given to the majority of the population the Court explained on grounds which are of importance for the enduring problem of the differentiation between equality in fact and equality in law.  It said: " Equality in law precludes discrimination of any kind; whereas equality in fact may involve the necessity of different treatment in order to obtain a result which establishes an equilibrium between different situations." [15]   To that proposition a minority of three Judges [16] declined to assent.  They declared themselves unable to find in the *wording* of the Declaration anything to show that equality in law may be disregarded and replaced by " a system of different treatments for the minority and the majority so as to establish an equilibrium between them." [17] They held it to be a sound principle of interpretation that " in presence of a clause which is reasonably clear the Court is bound to apply it as it stands without considering whether other provisions might with advantage have been added or substituted for it." [18] For this reason they were of the view that in attaching weight to the question whether the possession of particular institutions may or may not be important for the minority the Court departed from the natural sense of words.  That reasoning of the minority Judges not only brings into relief the differing attitudes to the notion of

[12] Series A/B, No. 64 (1935), p. 20.                    [13] At p. 19.
[14] Series B, No. 6 (1923), p. 24.
[15] Series A/B, No. 64 (1935), p. 19.
[16] Hurst, Rostworowski, Negulesco.
[17] At p. 26.
[18] *Ibid*.

effectiveness of treaty provisions. As the majority of the Court was comprised of nine Judges, it also serves indirectly as a warning against possible exaggerated emphasis, divorced from the purpose of the treaty, on what is " reasonably clear " and corresponding to the " natural meaning " of terms.

Having adopted a steady course in matters of substance in securing the purpose of the Minority Treaties, the Court had no difficulty in rejecting, in its treatment of minority questions, objections of a more technical nature. Thus it refused to admit that it was debarred from interpreting provisions of minority treaties whenever this function necessitated the interpretation of treaties in regard to which it had no jurisdiction.[19] It declined to find that the Council of the League of Nations was not competent to entertain a complaint relating to minorities on the ground that the matter had been brought before it not by one Member but by a Committee of three Members.[20] It rejected the construction according to which the Court had no jurisdiction on the ground that the submission of the question to the Court was a matter for individual Members of the Council, and not for the Council as a whole. To decide differently, the Court said, might mean to render the provisions in question practically ineffective.[21]

The Court was in a position to make these important and progressive contributions to the system of minorities because it proceeded from the assumption that its task was to give effect to what it has called " the value," [22] *i.e.*, the purpose, of the Minorities Treaties. The result would have been different in every case if the starting point had been different. Instead of being bent on the full development of a new institution created in the interest of protection of human rights and international peace, the Court might have interpreted it within the traditional limits of the sovereignty of States. That result appears in its true significance when compared with the parallel—negative—developments in the political sphere. There, the tendency which prevailed in a period of retrogression and international instability was to give a restrictive interpretation to minority treaties and the machinery set up for the purpose. Thus the Council of the League of Nations declined to act on the

---

[19] Series B, No. 6 (1923) (*German Settlers in Poland*), p. 25. See also Series A, No. 6 (1925) (*Certain German Interests in Polish Upper Silesia*), p. 18.
[20] Series B, No. 6 (1923) (*German Settlers in Poland*), p. 22.
[21] *Ibid.*, p. 23.
[22] Series B, No. 7 (1923) (*Acquisition of Polish Nationality*), p. 17.

view that the provisions of these treaties had invested it with a
general guarantee of protection of minorities involving, among other
things, the creation of a permanent minorities commission competent to hear complaints emanating directly from the minorities
concerned.   If the operation of the system of protection of
minorities fell short of the expectations of those who were responsible for having made it part of international law, it was not because
the International Court gave a grudging interpretation to the
instruments which defined its scope and possibilities.

It is also in this sphere that the Court, in its determination to
discourage evasion of international obligations, has affirmed on a
number of occasions the self-evident principle of international law
that a State cannot invoke its municipal law as a reason for the
non-fulfilment of its international obligations.[23]

## 83. *The Standard of Equality in the Treatment of Aliens. The* Oscar Chinn *Case*

The general tendency of the Court to attach importance to actual
rather than formal equality—which is another expression for the
principle of effectiveness in the interpretation of treaties—is illustrated by the important *Oscar Chinn* case [24] in which, though only
by a majority of six to five, it seems to have departed from it.   In
that case it was contended by the United Kingdom that Belgium,
by enjoining a reduction of tariffs on a transport company under its
control in return for a promise of pecuniary compensation, made it
in fact impossible for other fluvial transporters to carry on their
business seeing that, as any compensation was denied to them, they
could no longer compete commercially with the company controlled
by the Government.   That actual discrimination, it was maintained,
was contrary to the treaty obligation assumed by Belgium to maintain commercial freedom and equality, as well as to freedom of
fluvial navigation, in the Congo Basin.

The Court declined to hold that the Belgian action was contrary

---

[23] Series A/B, No. 44 (1932) (*Polish Nationals in Danzig*), p. 24; Series A, No. 24 (1930),
p. 12, and Series A/B, No. 46 (1932), p. 167 (*Free Zones*); Series B, No. 17 (1930) (*Greco-
Bulgarian Communities*), p. 32.   This particular aspect of these cases, while reminiscent
of some of the elements of estoppel in English law, cannot be regarded as an application
of the English doctrine of estoppel.   But see Michel de la Grotte in *Revue de droit
international et de législation comparée*, Series III, vol. X (1929), p. 241, and Paul de
Vineuil, *ibid.*, vol. XI (1930), p. 778.   And see below, pp. 314, 315.
[24] Series A/B, No. 63 (1934).

to the Treaty. Freedom of trade—it said—as established by the Convention, consisted in the right to engage in any commercial activity. It did not mean the abolition of commercial competition; it presupposed the existence of such competition.[25] The Court pointed out that "every undertaking freely carrying on its commercial activities may find itself confronted with obstacles placed in its way by rival concerns which are perhaps its superior in capital and organisation" and that "it may also find itself in competition with concerns in which States participate." The Court denied that the measures taken by the Belgian authorities resulted in creating a *de facto* monopoly; there was no such monopoly in acts calculated to reduce prices or offer other facilities to customers—even if such measures made it more difficult or impossible for other competitors to carry on business. The Court was not prepared to admit that by embarking upon the measures in question the Belgian authorities intended that their action, taken in difficult circumstances for general purposes of the welfare of the country, should result, as it did in fact result, in the concentration of business of this type in the hands of the company under its control. Moreover, in the view of the Court this was not a case of discrimination between Belgian and non-Belgian companies; only such discrimination was prohibited by the Convention.

This apparently somewhat mechanical application of the principle of equality of treatment gave rise to vigorous dissent. Judge Altamira gave expression to a general rule of international law in affirming that a discriminatory rule violative of a treaty did not lose that character by being applied also to some of the nationals of the offending State.[26] Judge Anzilotti attached importance to reducing to its true proportions what was probably the inarticulate major premise of the Judgment, namely, that the measures were not adopted with any intention of discrimination or encouraging monopolistic tendencies but in order to deal with one aspect of the prevailing economic depression. He said: "It is clear that international law would be merely an empty phrase if it sufficed for a State to invoke the public interest in order to evade the fulfilment of its engagements."[27] There was, in his view, no such case of

---

[25] Series A/B, No. 63 (1934), at p. 84.
[26] At pp. 101, 102. Judge Hurst's Dissenting Opinion on this point was to the same effect (p. 128).
[27] At p. 112.

necessity—*i.e.*, "the impossibility of proceeding by any other method than the one contrary to law"—as might have justified the action taken. Sir Cecil Hurst emphasised what was perhaps the main feature of the situation, namely, that this was a case of a measure resulting in inequality in fact whatever may have been the appearance of preservation of equality in law. He pointed out that for the Government to oblige one transport concern by a direct order to reduce its transport charges and to agree to reimburse the resulting losses, and to oblige another transport concern indirectly —the only alternative open to it being to wind up business or to conduct it at a loss—to make similar reductions in order to save its business and to refuse to reimburse it for the resulting losses, cannot be said to amount to maintaining between the two a complete commercial equality.[28] Judge van Eysinga was of the view that the action of the Belgian authorities was contrary to the Treaty in as much as it was calculated to impede "the effective freedom of navigation."[29] He asked: "If all acts of a riparian State which result, in a given case, in putting an end to effective freedom of navigation, are prohibited, why should it be more lawful for a riparian government to take measures which favour one of the two purely shipping enterprises operating on an international river, to such a degree that the other enterprise, not only suffers, but is driven out of business?"[30]

The *Oscar Chinn* case, while not typical of the approach of the Court to the question of effectiveness of treaties providing for equality of treatment, is of particular interest as showing the difficulties of this aspect of the interpretation of treaties. The difficulty cannot be explained away by the mere assertion that the Judgment of the majority of the Court adhered to the letter of the treaties rather than to their spirit. For it is conceivable that a claim to equality of treatment, if pushed to the logical extreme of its apparent meaning, may operate in a way calculated to defeat considerations of justice and the intention of the parties. Moreover, and this circumstance accentuates the inherent complexity of the

---

[28] Series A/B, No. 63 (1934), at p. 127.

[29] At p. 141.

[30] At p. 142. Judge Schücking, while in agreement with the Dissenting Opinion of Judge van Eysinga, limited his Dissenting Opinion to the narrower point of the validity of the Convention of St. Germain of 1919 on which Belgium relied. In his view that Convention was in any case invalid as being inconsistent with the provisions of the Berlin Treaty of 1885.

matter, that literal interpretation of the notion of equality in the *Oscar Chinn* case may have been more apparent than real. It may have been dictated by the desire to meet a situation which had not been foreseen by the authors of the Treaties of 1885 and 1919. For it may be maintained that a conception of equality, such as underlay the Treaties of 1885 and 1919 concluded at a time of relative economic liberalism and *laisser faire*, was no longer appropriate to conditions in which increasing regulation by the State became a dominant feature of national and international economic life. It is arguable that these considerations may apply in particular to situations in which the action of the State, apparently of a discriminatory nature, has been taken with the view to meeting an economic emergency of some gravity.[31]

84. *The Same. The Case of* Rights of Nationals of the United States of America in Morocco

Questions of a somewhat similar nature arose in relation to that aspect of the Judgment of the Court in the case concerning *Rights of Nationals of the United States in Morocco* in which the Court found that certain measures applied by the Moroccan authorities for putting into effect the legislation relating to exchange controls were in violation of the rights to equality of treatment secured by the United States in the Act of Algeciras of 1906.[32] This was so for the reason that these measures discriminated in favour of imports from France. The Court, without elaborating the matter, held that

---

[31] Thus it is possible that, by reference to the considerations outlined above, the Court might have arrived at the same conclusion by a reasoning not open to the reproach of a mechanical application of the notion of equality. In order to do that the Court would have had to consider in some detail the economic aspects of the situation before it. There is probably no foundation in fact for the view (apparently suggested by Kopelmanas in *Journal du Droit International*, 81 (1954), pp. 96–106) that such examination requires an expert knowledge of economics which cannot be expected from the Court. The difficulty in the *Oscar Chinn* case was apparently that the argument of the parties themselves did not go much beyond a textual interpretation of the Treaties in question. As was suggested by Judge Anzilotti (at pp. 111–114), no articulate attempt was made to show either that the economic situation left no remedy other than the measures taken by the Belgian authorities or that these measures could not have been adopted without a degree of actual discrimination. On the other hand, as repeatedly pointed out by Judge Sir Cecil Hurst, in the case presented by the United Kingdom there was absent, somewhat conspicuously, a determination to adduce and examine some of the relevant facts such as whether there was an actual intention of the Belgian authorities to concentrate the river transport in the hands of the Government-controlled company (at p. 116), or that there had been interference with an acquired right belonging to Oscar Chinn (at p. 122).

[32] *I.C.J. Reports* 1952, p. 186.

such discrimination could not be justified by considerations relating to exchange control and that it was therefore unnecessary for it to consider the question of the extent of the control over importation which may be exercised by the Moroccan authorities. The Court did not examine the question to what extent the régime of exchange control, in the form which it assumed before and after the Second World War and in the light of the monetary relations between France and Morocco,[33] was at all present to the minds of the parties to the Treaty of Algeciras. It is possible that any determination of the Court to attach decisive importance to that aspect of the situation would have amounted to judicial legislation which the Court might have felt to be outside its province.

Reference may also be made in this connection to the reasons underlying the rejection by the Court, in the same case, of the argument of the United States in the sense that it retained its capitulatory rights notwithstanding the renunciation by other States of the rights upon which, in virtue of the most-favoured-nation clause, the rights of the United States depended. In the view of the Court any such result " would run contrary to the principle of equality and . . . would perpetuate discrimination." [34] At the same time the Court affirmed the principle of effectiveness in a different sphere. Thus while it held that the rights of the United States, arising out of the operation of the most-favoured-nation clause, lapsed in consequence of the renunciation of these rights by other States, it held that some of them nevertheless continued to exist in so far as it was necessary to render effective those provisions of the Act of Algeciras which depended on the exercise of consular jurisdiction.[35]

---

[33] A point referred to, perhaps somewhat generally, in the French Memoire (see *Mémoires, Plaidoiries et Documents*, vol. I, p. 87), but treated in greater detail in the French *Réplique* (vol. II, pp. 20–26) and in the *Oral Argument* of Professor Gros (*ibid.*, pp. 150–157).

[34] *I.C.J. Reports* 1952, p. 192.

[35] *Ibid.*, p. 199.

# CHAPTER 18

# EFFECTIVENESS OF INTERNATIONAL INSTITUTIONS AND INTERNATIONAL ORGANISATION

### 85. *The Competence of the International Labour Organisation*

The general tendency to secure the effectiveness of treaties has guided the Court in the interpretation of another branch of modern international law, namely, that relating to international institutions and organisation. This applies in particular to its Advisory Opinions bearing upon the International Labour Organisation and the United Nations. Some of the most important questions affecting the competence and the working of the former have been determined by pronouncements of the Court.[1] Almost at the very commencement of its activity the Court was called upon to decide the question whether the International Labour Organisation possesses competence in regard to the international regulation of the conditions of labour of persons employed in agriculture—a question the answer to which was decisive for the character and scope of much of the work of the International Labour Organisation.[2] The Court, in giving an affirmative answer to the question put to it by the Council of the League of Nations, rejected the view that the term " industry " constantly occurring in Part XIII of the Treaty of Versailles referred to industry in the limited meaning of the word to the exclusion of agriculture and navigation. The answer given was largely determined by the consideration that the failure to regulate conditions of work in agriculture by way of international agreement might frustrate the purpose of the Treaty by acting as a check upon the adoption of more humane conditions of labour and by constituting a " handicap against the nations which had adopted

---

[1] An Opinion of the Court on the question of the *Interpretation of the Convention of 1919 concerning the Employment of Women during the Night* (Series A/B, No. 50 (1932) ) was described, in a guarded statement of the International Labour Organisation before the Court, as one likely to affect the whole body of existing international labour legislation (Series C, No. 60, p. 211).

[2] The importance of the matter for the International Labour Organisation may properly be gauged from the impassioned plea made before the Court by the first Director of the Organisation (Series C, No. 1, p. 267).

them, and in favour of those which had not, in the competition of the markets of the world." [3]

When in the Thirteenth Advisory Opinion the Court had to answer the question whether the International Labour Organisation was competent to regulate the personal work of the employer when this was incidental to the regulation of the work of the employees, it adopted a similar method of approach. It based its affirmative answer to the question on the consideration that the Organisation would be prevented from drawing up and proposing measures essential to the accomplishment of its purpose if it were not competent to propose, for the protection of workers, measures " to the efficacious working of which it was found to be essential to include to some extent work done by employers." [4] In discussing the meaning of the International Convention of 1906, on which reliance was put in the course of the argument, concerning the prohibition of white phosphorus in the manufacture of matches, the Court stated once more that in determining the nature and the scope of a measure it " must look to its practical effect rather than to the predominant motive that may be conjectured to have inspired it." [5]

In the Advisory Opinion on the *Interpretation of the Convention of 1919 concerning the Employment of Women during the Night* [6] the Court, relying on the principles enumerated in the Second and Thirteenth Advisory Opinions, referred to above, declined to limit the scope of the Convention on the ground that, as was claimed by some Governments, the Convention was confined to manual workers. The Court gave an affirmative answer to the question whether the Convention applied to women who hold positions of supervision or management and are not ordinarily engaged in manual work. It admitted that the amelioration of the lot of the manual worker was the main preoccupation of those who created the International Labour Organisation. However, the Court was " not disposed to regard the sphere of activity of the International Labour Organisation as circumscribed so closely, in respect of the persons with which it was to concern itself, as to raise any presumption that a Labour convention must be interpreted as being

[3] Series B, No. 2 (1922), p. 25.
[4] Series B, No. 13 (1926), p. 18.
[5] Series B, No. 13 (1926), p. 19.
[6] Series A/B, No. 50 (1932).

restricted in its operation to manual workers, unless a contrary intention appears."⁷  The Opinion here surveyed may be regarded as expressive of the general principle which the Court has followed in respect of international institutions created by treaty, namely, that in the absence of express indications to the contrary the Court will favour an interpretation permitting a wider rather than a more restricted display of activity in order to make effective the general purpose of the Organisation.  It is possible that the last-mentioned Opinion represents a marginal case—a situation expressed by the fact that the Opinion was given by a majority of six to five— inasmuch as there was substantial, though not decisive, support for the contrary Opinion of the minority of the Court in the preparatory work of the Convention and in the history of international protection of labour generally.

86. *The Principle of Effectiveness in the Interpretation of the Covenant of the League of Nations.  Matters of Domestic Jurisdiction*

The Permanent Court of International Justice followed a similar line of interpretation in relation to the Covenant of the League of Nations.  Reference has already been made to the significant piece of judicial legislation in the Advisory Opinion relating to the *Interpretation of the Treaty of Lausanne*, where the effectiveness of the Covenant as an instrument of pacific settlement was upheld by the enunciation and application of the maxim that no one can be judge in his own cause.⁸  It may be added that the Court relied, in a different direction, on the same principle in order to reassert and justify the general rule of qualified unanimity (*i.e.*, of unanimity not including the parties to the dispute): " Only if the decisions of the Council have the support of the unanimous consent of the Powers composing it, will they possess the degree of authority which they must have." ⁹  The Court pointed to the serious consequences of the position which might arise if decisions could be adopted against the will of those Members of the Council who by reason of their political position would have to bear the major responsibility for the decisions taken.  On the face of it, it would appear that by rejecting the submission that the decision of the

---

⁷ Series A/B, No. 50 (1932), p. 374.
⁸ See above, p. 158.
⁹ Series B, No. 12 (1925), p. 29.

Council, acting as an arbitrator, could be rendered by a simple majority vote, the Court adopted a restrictive interpretation of the Covenant. However, the gist of this aspect of the Opinion is that the true effectiveness of the Covenant can be secured only by an interpretation calculated to impart a measure of reality to the decisions of the Council—a result unlikely to be achieved through majority decisions.

The Advisory Opinion, previously given, concerning the *Tunis and Morocco Nationality Decrees* [10] constituted another significant step in the same direction. The Court was asked to give an Opinion on the question whether the matter brought before the Council by Great Britain was one on which the Council was not entitled to make a recommendation under Article 15 on the ground that according to international law it was within the exclusive domestic jurisdiction of France. Thus at an early stage of its existence the Court was called upon to pronounce on the meaning of a clause which if interpreted widely might have seriously impeded the functioning of the League of Nations under a vital Article of the Covenant. The legal effect of the Opinion of the Court was such that henceforth no State could invoke with any hope of success the clause of domestic jurisdiction (as determined by international law), in relation to the Covenant and, perhaps, in other instruments, unless the opposing State openly admitted in advance that its demand was in conflict with existing international law. The Court apparently realised the wide implications of its Opinion. It attempted to limit them by stating that, in order to render the exception of Article 15 (8) inapplicable, it was not enough to invoke international engagements or rules of international law, but that the Council—or, perhaps, the Court—must by a provisional examination satisfy itself that the treaties and rules thus invoked have a bearing on the dispute. [11] However, that limitation, it is submitted, was largely nominal. Either such an examination is sufficiently thorough to touch the merits—and this is a possibility which the Court expressly rejected—or it is merely formal and perfunctory, in which case it does not constitute any check at all. [12] A provisional conclusion in matters of jurisdiction is, assuming

[10] Series B, No. 4.

[11] Series B, No. 4 (1923), p. 26.

[12] See the Observations of Lord Finlay in Series B, No. 7 (1923) (*Acquisition of Polish Nationality*), p. 22, on the intimate connection between preliminary points and a decision on the merits.

that there exists an instrument which *prima facie* is a source of jurisdiction,[13] somewhat in the nature of a juridical euphemism. It can normally result only in an affirmative reply to the question of existence of jurisdiction; it cannot result in a negative finding unless the attempt to invoke jurisdiction is palpably unfounded or clearly abusive. Would the Court have been prepared, on the basis of a provisional conclusion, to give an Opinion which might have had the irreparable effect of ousting the jurisdiction of the Council? In practice, such provisional conclusion could only be in favour of the Council's jurisdiction unless, as stated, the State invoking jurisdiction were to admit that, in a matter normally falling within the domestic jurisdiction of States, it had no case under international law or unless the legal grounds invoked by it were, quite apart from any facts underlying the dispute, so obviously without foundation under international law as to leave no doubt that the subject-matter of the dispute was within the province of domestic jurisdiction.

Moreover, the Court found that it is not only the relevance, from the point of view of international law, of the contentions of the claimant State which is sufficient to take the dispute out of the purview of matters of domestic jurisdiction, but also the nature of the contentions of the State against which the claim is directed. Thus the Court held that as France relied on international law, in order to show that under the rules of international law relating to protectorates she—jointly with the protected State—had exclusive jurisdiction in the matter, the question had to be decided by reference to rules of international law and, accordingly, was no longer one of exclusive domestic jurisdiction. The same, in the view of the Court, applied to the French contention that the relevant treaties creating exterritorial rights had lapsed as the result of the doctrine known in international law as the *clausula rebus sic stantibus*. It is perhaps more in these aspects of the Opinion than in the frequently quoted passage referring to the relativity of the notion of domestic jurisdiction [14] that lies the main contribution of that Opinion to the effectiveness of the Covenant as an instrument of pacific settlement. For the Opinion substantially limited the probability of a State challenging with any considerable chances of

---

[13] See above, p. 110, as to provisional measures.

[14] " The question whether a certain matter is or is not solely within the domestic jurisdiction of a State is an essentially relative question; it depends upon the development of international relations " : Series B, No. 4 (1923), p. 24.

success the competence of the Council—and of the League of Nations at large—by means of the assertion that the subject-matter of the dispute is, according to international law, within its exclusive domestic jurisdiction. An affirmative finding to that effect—which would be tantamount to a decision that the claim is contrary to international law—could properly and legitimately come at the end of the inquiry as part of the final recommendation by the Council. Such finding—and this is the juridically relevant aspect of the Opinion—cannot properly be insisted upon at the beginning of the inquiry with the view to preventing it.

### 87. *Matters of Domestic Jurisdiction in the Charter of the United Nations*

It is possible—although no expression of view on the subject is called for in this connection [15]—that the Opinion of the Court thus interpreted may have a bearing on the construction of the corresponding provision of paragraph 7 of Article 2 of the Charter of the United Nations. With regard to the latter, reference may be made here to the Advisory Opinion of the International Court of Justice on the *Interpretation of Peace Treaties with Belgium, Hungary and Romania*. These States—and several others—challenged the exercise by the Court of its advisory function in this case on the ground that in requesting an Opinion on the matter of observance of human rights the General Assembly was "interfering" or "intervening" in matters essentially within the domestic jurisdiction of States, in disregard of Article 2 (7) of the Charter. They contended that the Court, as an organ of the United Nations bound to observe the provisions of the Charter, was not entitled to give the Opinion.

The Court rejected that submission. It said, in the first instance, that "for the purpose of the present Opinion, it suffices to note that the General Assembly justified the adoption of its Resolution [requesting the Advisory Opinion] by stating that 'the United Nations, pursuant to Article 55 of the Charter, shall promote universal respect for and observance of human rights and fundamental freedoms' . . ." [16] It is not clear from the passage quoted whether in the view of the Court the fact that the General Assembly in adopting a Resolution relies on Article 55 of the Charter in the

---

[15] See below, p. 273.                    [16] *I.C.J. Reports* 1950, p. 70.

matter of human rights and freedoms is sufficient to render inoperative the prohibition in paragraph 7 of Article 2. It is probable that this is no more than a statement of fact drawing attention to the limited scope of the request made to the Court; it does not imply any attitude in relation to the case of the Court being requested to give an Opinion of this nature, *i.e.*, whether certain measures adopted by a State are in conformity with its obligations, if any, under Article 55 or the cognate Articles of the Charter. The Court contented itself with stating that the object of the request put to it was more limited, namely, the obtaining from the Court of " certain clarifications of a legal nature regarding the applicability of the procedure for the settlement of disputes by the Commissions provided for " in the Treaties. The Court continued: " The interpretation of the terms of a treaty for this purpose could not be considered as a question essentially within the domestic jurisdiction of a State. It is a question of international law which, by its very nature, lies within the competence of the Court." [17]

The passage quoted does not make it clear whether the factor which made the question of domestic jurisdiction irrelevant was that the subject was of a procedural nature or that it pertained to the interpretation of a treaty. Apparently the Court attached importance to both considerations. Yet a decision on a procedural issue may be fraught with grave consequences for the parties to the dispute. Also, if any issue which is dependent upon the interpretation of a treaty ceases to be a matter of domestic jurisdiction, then this applies also to the provisions of the Charter in the matter of human rights and fundamental freedoms—as, indeed, to most disputes bearing upon the interpretation of the Charter which may come before the organs of the United Nations, including the Court itself. This being so, the restrained language of the Opinion—a restraint fully justified in view of the fact that the formidable issue of the meaning of paragraph 7 of Article 2 was not directly before the Court—must be regarded nevertheless as following also in this sphere, though in a guarded manner, the general trend towards effectiveness in the interpretation of treaties.

In connection with the interpretation, from this point of view, of the Covenant of the League of Nations, an incidental issue decided in the Advisory Opinion concerning *Railway Traffic*

[17] *I.C.J. Reports* 1950, p. 70.

*between Lithuania and Poland* [18] merits attention. In that Opinion the Court held that the fact that Poland and Lithuania participated in and assented to a Resolution of the Council of the League of Nations recommending them to enter into direct negotiations created a legal obligation to that effect binding upon the two States.[19] This affirmation of the binding force of the Resolution assented to by the parties to the dispute is not only of interest for the law of treaties as an indication of a method of creating a consensual obligation by a way other than the traditional method of a treaty. It is also of interest, in the context of the present Chapter, as a contribution to the effectiveness of the activity of a general international organisation as an agency of pacific settlement. That contribution is, because of its sweeping potentialities, in need of elucidation. Does the ruling of the Court apply only to Resolutions adopted in the course of settling a dispute submitted to a body such as the Council of the League of Nations—or, for that matter, of the Security Council of the United Nations? Or does it have a wider import in the sense that, as a matter of good faith, the assent to any kind of recommendation is binding upon States who have voted for it ? It is not necessary to pursue these wider potential implications [20] of the Opinion of the Court; possibly they are too wide. It is clear that, in general, no full binding force attaches to recommendations.[21] On the other hand, the Opinion of the Court, even when rigidly limited to the case of recommendations adopted in the course of a settlement of a dispute and assented to by the parties thereto, adds significantly to the effectiveness of international organisation as an agency of pacific settlement.[22]

## 88. *The Principle of Effectiveness in the Interpretation of the Charter. The Implied Powers of the United Nations*

In general, in relation to the interpretation of the Charter of the United Nations the Court has repeatedly and on a large scale

---

[18] Series A/B, No. 42.  [19] At p. 116.

[20] For an illuminating discussion of the question of the binding force of recommendations of the General Assembly see Sloan in *British Year Book of International Law*, 25 (1948), pp. 1–33.  [21] See above, p. 47.

[22] The problem involved is of more general importance than that raised by the Advisory Opinion regarding the *Delimitation of the Polish-Czechoslovak Frontier (Question of Jaworzina)* where the Court held that a formal declaration, signed by duly authorised representatives of Poland and Czechoslovakia, accepting the provisions of a decision of the Conference of Ambassadors gave that decision " the force of a contractual obligation entered into by the Parties " : Series B, No. 8 (1923), p. 30.

acted upon the principle of effectiveness—on a scale so large as to bring its pronouncements on the subject within the category of judicial legislation. This applies in particular to the Advisory Opinion on *Reparation for Injuries Suffered in the Service of the United Nations*—an Opinion examined in some detail in Part 3 of this book as a conspicuous example of the activity of the Court approaching judicial legislation. While, as a matter of substantive law, that Opinion is of outstanding importance on the question of the juridical personality of the United Nations and of the subjects of international law in general, the true basis—which reveals itself as the constant theme of the reasoning of the Court—of that Opinion is the consideration that certain powers must be implied in the Charter as being essential to the effectiveness of the Organisation. That " supreme type of international organisation," the Court said, " could not carry out the intentions of its founders if it was devoid of international personality." [23]  For that reason " it must be acknowledged that its Members, by entrusting certain functions to it, with the attendant duties and responsibilities, have clothed it with the competence required to enable those functions to be effectively discharged . . ." [24]  " The functions of the Organisation are of such a character that they could not be effectively discharged if they involved the concurrent action, on the international plane, of fifty-eight or more Foreign Offices, and the Court concludes that the Members have endowed the Organisation with capacity to bring international claims when necessitated by the discharge of its functions." [25]

It is of interest to note that the Court was unanimous in applying the principle of effectiveness for the purpose of affirmation of the international personality of the United Nations to enable it to bring an international claim in respect of the damage *done to itself*. Three Judges did not follow the substantial majority of the Court in extending the rule of effectiveness so as to enable the Organisation to bring an international claim in respect of injuries suffered *by its agents*. The Opinion of the majority of the Court on that aspect of the case is nevertheless—or, perhaps, for that very reason—of significance. The Court, in invoking the principle applied in the Thirteenth Advisory Opinion in relation to the *Competence of the*

[23] *I.C.J. Reports* 1949, p. 179.
[24] *Ibid*.
[25] *Ibid*., p. 180.

*International Labour Organisation*, held that "under international law, the Organisation must be deemed to have those powers which, though not expressly provided in the Charter, are conferred upon it by necessary implication as being essential to the performance of its duties." [26]   It held that in order to ensure the efficient and independent performance by its agents entrusted by it with important missions, the Organisation as such must provide them with adequate protection and not suffer them to rely exclusively on the protection of the States of which they may be nationals.   (The Court could perhaps have added force to its reasoning by pointing to the possibility that some of the agents of the United Nations might be stateless with the result that there would be no State able to protect them.)   It was thus "clear that the capacity of the Organisation to exercise a measure of functional protection of its agents arises by necessary intendment out of the Charter." [27]

Identical language was used by the Court in its Advisory Opinion on the *Effect of Awards of Compensation made by the United Nations Administrative Tribunal* when it held that the United Nations had the power to establish a tribunal to decide disputes between the Organisation and members of its staff.   The Court quoted the crucial passage from its Opinion in the *Reparation for Injuries* case in which it stated that "under international law, the Organisation must be deemed to have those powers which, though not expressly provided in the Charter, are conferred upon it by necessary implication as being essential to the performance of its duties."   It held, accordingly, that as the establishment of the tribunal in question "was essential to ensure the efficient working of the Secretariat, and to give effect to the paramount consideration of securing the highest standards of efficiency, competence and integrity . . . capacity to do this [*i.e.*, to set up the tribunal] arises by necessary intendment out of the Charter." [28]   Neither was the Court prepared to give a restrictive interpretation to the implied powers thus attributed to the General Assembly.   In particular, it rejected the view that that implied power did not enable the General Assembly to establish a tribunal clothed with the authority to make decisions binding on the General Assembly itself—a view based on the contention that an implied power can only be exercised to the

[26] *I.C.J. Reports* 1949, p. 182.
[27] *Ibid.*, p. 184.
[28] *I.C.J. Reports* 1954, p. 57.

extent which is absolutely essential. The governing consideration was that the General Assembly, after mature deliberation, had decided to set up a tribunal empowered to render judgments which were to be final and without appeal. For the same reason the Court refused to admit that the implied power in question must stop short of imposing legal limitations upon the competence expressly granted to the General Assembly by virtue of the Charter. However, this aspect of the Opinion, which has reference to the more fundamental question of the limitation of the sovereignty of the General Assembly itself, falls within the purview of the next Part of this book, which analyses the attitude of the Court to State sovereignty in general.[29]

In so far as general international conventions concluded within the framework of the United Nations are relevant in this connection, reference may be made to the reasoning of the Court in relation to the main feature of its Advisory Opinion on the *Reservations to the Genocide Convention*, namely, the formulation of the test of the compatibility of a reservation with the object and purpose of the Convention. Any other view, the Court said, would lead either to the acceptance of reservations destructive of the purposes which the General Assembly and the contracting parties had in mind, or to recognition that the parties to the Convention have the power of excluding from participation in it any State making a reservation of a minor character and fully compatible with the objects of the Convention.[30] The ultimate effectiveness of the Convention is thus made the governing consideration for the test adopted by the Court.

## 89. *The Effectiveness of the System of Mandates*

The same method of reasoning was followed by the Court, in a different sphere, in relation to the interpretation of the instruments bearing upon the system of mandates in connection with the Advisory Opinion on the *International Status of South-West Africa*. The central theme of that Opinion—namely, that the provisions creating the system of mandates established a *status* in the nature of a real right, as distinguished from a purely personal obligation— was in itself an addition to the apparent effect of the instruments in

---

[29] See below, pp. 325 *et seq.*
[30] *I.C.J. Reports* 1951, p. 24.

question. For that interpretation of the obligations of the mandatory State as binding not only in relation to the original contracting Parties—whether these be the Members of the League of Nations or the Council of the League of Nations—but also in relation to the international community at large, independently of the existence of the League, was not a self-evident proposition. At least, it was contested by South Africa who contended that these obligations ceased to exist with the demise of the League. That contention the Court unanimously rejected. It held that South-West Africa " is " —*i.e.*, that it continued to be—a territory under the international mandate assumed by South Africa; that the Union of South Africa acting alone had not therefore the competence to modify the international status of the Territory of South-West Africa, such competence resting with the Union only when acting with the consent of the United Nations; and that the provisions of the Charter on the subject of the Trusteeship System were applicable to the Territory of South-West Africa in the sense that they provided a means by which the territory could be brought under the Trusteeship System.[31]

From the view that the territory remained subject to the system of mandates there followed, as a corollary, the conclusion that the central aspect of that system, namely, the system of international supervision as established by it, continued in existence notwithstanding the fact that the League of Nations as the specific agency charged with such supervision ceased to exist. This the Court in fact held by a large majority.[32] To hold otherwise would have meant to deprive of effect most—though perhaps not all[33]—of

---

[31] *I.C.J. Reports* 1950, pp. 143–144.

[32] Of twelve votes to two—Judges McNair and Read dissenting.

[33] *Some* effectiveness would have remained associated with it by virtue of the—again unanimous—ruling of the Court that the *judicial* supervision by the International Court of Justice continued having regard to the fact that, in accordance with Art. 37 of its Statute, the obligatory jurisdiction of the Permanent Court of International Justice was replaced by that of the International Court of Justice. It would have been open to the Court to base its recognition of the continuation of the judicial supervision on grounds wider than the provision of Art. 37 of the Statute of the Court in a manner analogous to the continuation of the supervisory jurisdiction of the United Nations. However, the particular ground chosen was sufficient for the purpose. Also, the Opinion of the Court would not have been purely nominal even if (as did the two Dissenting Judges) it had denied the obligation to submit to continued international supervision inasmuch as it lays down that one of the consequences of the system of mandates conceived as a status is that it cannot be altered by the Mandatory acting alone—a finding whose practical import, however, would have been limited by the denial of international supervision. For what, it might have been urged, would have been the value of the theoretical continuation of an unmodified status without its crucial aspect, namely,

the meaning naturally attaching both to the main pronouncement of the Court and to the system of mandates conceived as a status. For while the principle that the powers of the administering authority are exercised in the interest of the population of the territory concerned constitutes an affirmation of a moral and political principle to which general recognition was given even prior to the establishment of the system of mandates and trusteeship, its essential novelty lay in the machinery of international supervision intended to secure the effectiveness of the system. To hold that the system continued but that its international supervision ceased to operate would have been, to a large extent, to reduce to a form of words the main aspect of the decision. Seldom was there a more compelling occasion for applying—as the Court did in fact—the *cy-près* doctrine which common law courts apply in order to render effective a general charitable intention in face of the impossibility of applying it according to the literal language of its author. In the case of the *Status of South-West Africa* the Court applied the essence, though not the terminology, of that doctrine—with full propriety, it is believed—to something less than the substance of the relevant provision; it applied it merely to the procedure of its execution. If, as the Court held unanimously, the institution of mandates constituted a status, then it was proper to apply to the matter before it the principle of succession in international organisation—a principle which the present writer has stated in the following terms with reference to the Opinion of the Court in the case concerning the *Status of South-West Africa*: " While as a rule the devolution of rights and competencies is governed either by the constituent instruments of the organisations in question or by special agreements or decisions of their organs, the requirement of continuity of international life demands that succession should be assumed to

---

effective international supervision? There was perhaps from this point of view an element of dialectics in the submission of Judge Read, in his Dissenting Opinion, that the cessation of international supervision although it might weaken the mandate would not bring it to an end and that " as a matter of fact, the record shows that the paralysis of these agencies during six war years had no detrimental effect upon the maintenance of the well-being and development of the peoples " (at p. 165). The same applies to the statement, by reference to the continued force of judicial supervision by virtue of Art. 37 of the Statute of the Court, that " the very existence of a judicial tribunal, clothed with compulsory jurisdiction, is enough to ensure respect for legal obligations " (at p. 169). It will be noted that, subsequent to the Opinion of the Court, South Africa did in fact purport to modify the international status of the mandated territory without, at the time of writing, the obligatory clause in question having been invoked by any State entitled to invoke it.

operate in all cases where that is consistent with or indicated by the reasonably assumed intention of the parties as interpreted in the light of the purpose of the organisations in question." [34] It is submitted that such importation, on the part of the Court, of the rules of succession in relation to international organisations is no more than an example of legitimate application of the principle of effectiveness to basic international instruments. [35]

It is probably this application of the principle of effectiveness which constitutes the main feature of the Opinion of the Court in this case. This is so although it relied also in this respect on the somewhat general wording of Article 80 (1) of the Charter, which lays down that nothing in it shall be construed to alter in any manner the rights of any States or any peoples or the terms of existing international instruments to which Members of the United Nations may be parties. The Court said, with a repeated emphasis on the effectiveness of this provision of the Charter: " The purpose must have been to provide a real protection for those rights; but no such rights of the peoples could be effectively safeguarded without international supervision and a duty to render reports to a supervisory organ." [36]

At the same time—and this is a timely reminder of the limitations of the principle of effectiveness—while the Court unanimously held that the provisions of the Charter in the matter of trust territories are applicable to the Territory of South-West Africa in the sense that they provide a means by which the Territory may be brought under the Trusteeship System, it held that the provisions of the Charter did not impose upon the Union of South Africa a legal obligation to place the Territory under the Trusteeship System. [37] The Court arrived at this conclusion by means of a logical interpretation of the Charter—the most prominent ground being that if the parties to the Charter had intended to create an obligation of this kind " such intention would necessarily have been expressed in positive terms." [38] It is possible that an exacting examination of the issue by reference to the proceedings of the San

---

[34] In Oppenheim's *International Law*, vol. I (8th ed., 1955), p. 168.
[35] But see the Dissenting Opinion of Judge McNair describing as " pure inference " the automatic succession by the United Nations to the rights and obligations of the League of Nations (*I.C.J. Reports* 1950, at p. 159).
[36] At p. 137.
[37] See above, p. 278.
[38] *I.C.J. Reports* 1950, p. 140.

Francisco Conference and other attendant circumstances would have led the Court to the same result, namely, to an absence of agreement between the parties concerned to create a clear legal obligation on the part of the mandatory to conclude a trusteeship agreement. That absence of agreement could not properly be supplemented by an inference aiming at securing for the instrument in question a higher degree of effectiveness than was warranted by the intentions of the parties. From the point of view of the more general efficacy of this part of the Charter and of the purpose of the system of mandates that particular limitation of the Opinion of the Court was, it would appear, without decisive importance. For once the Court had affirmed the principle of continuing international supervision—as well as of the international status of the territory, unmodified and unmodifiable except in accordance with the Charter—the problem of the formal conclusion of trusteeship agreements acquired a symbolic rather than practical significance. In fact, a closer analysis of the dissenting views of the minority of the Judges who asserted the existence of a legal obligation to conclude a trusteeship agreement suggests that the distance separating them from the Opinion of the majority of the Court was more apparent than real.[39]

[39] The minority Judges were content, in this respect, to associate themselves with the views expressed in the Dissenting Opinion of Judge de Visscher who urged upon the Court the "acknowledged rule of interpretation that treaty clauses must not only be considered as a whole but must also be interpreted so as to avoid as much as possible depriving one of them of practical effect for the benefit of others" (at p. 187). However, notwithstanding that emphasis upon effectiveness, the learned Judge did not go further than to suggest that the "mandatory Power, while remaining free to reject the particular terms of a proposed agreement, has the legal obligation to be ready to take part in negotiations and to conduct them in good faith with a view to concluding an agreement" (at p. 188). He then proceeded to refer to the Advisory Opinion of the Court in the case of the *Railway Traffic between Lithuania and Poland* (October 15, 1931; Series A/B, No. 42 (1931), p. 116) to the effect that an obligation to enter into negotiations implies also the duty "to pursue them as far as possible with the view to concluding agreements." Yet he also cited verbatim the accompanying passage from that Opinion in which the Court said: "But an obligation to negotiate does not imply an obligation to reach an agreement." It was that latter proposition which determined the issue in the case of the *Railway Traffic between Lithuania and Poland.* For that reason the only difference between the Opinion of the Court and that of Judge de Visscher was whether there existed an obligation to enter into negotiations with the view to concluding an agreement. But the latter agreed that the Charter does not impose a legal obligation to conclude a Trusteeship Agreement in the sense that South Africa was free to accept or to refuse the particular terms of a draft agreement. Yet this was exactly what the Court held in the operative part of its Opinion, namely, that "the provisions of Chapter XII of the Charter do not impose upon the Union of South Africa a legal obligation to place the Territory under the Trusteeship System."

# CHAPTER 19

# THE LIMITS OF THE PRINCIPLE OF EFFECTIVENESS

## 90. *Rule and Tendency in the Practice of the Court*

The various instances, surveyed in this Part, of the application of the principle of effectiveness in the interpretation of treaties and otherwise show the Court as a tribunal applying the law in a constructive spirit with its eyes on the practical necessities of international life and the efficacy of the *vincula juris* by which Governments profess to have bound themselves. This manner of interpretation of the law has resulted not only in a clarification of the law relating to international institutions but also in what may be described as its progressive development. That principle of effectiveness of obligations, conceived as a vehicle of interpretation, is an instrument of considerable potency. It may be as comprehensive as all the rules of interpretation taken together. In a great number of cases, in regard to treaty interpretation and otherwise, it renders unnecessary any recourse to subsidiary sources of law. This is one of the reasons why the Court has so far seldom resorted, *expressis verbis*, to " general principles of law recognised by civilised nations " as laid down in Article 38 of its Statute [1]—unless it can be said that in applying the principle of effectiveness it has acted, in an inarticulate way, upon the oldest and paramount general principle of law in the matter of interpretation, namely, the canon of good faith.

It would betray a certain degree of complacency if we were to regard this aspect of the Court's activity as somewhat obvious. A court operating under less favourable conditions of continuity might have approached these questions in a different temper and arrived at correspondingly different results. This may seem surprising to some, for is not the result of interpretation determined primarily by the intention of the parties, and not by the attitude of the court? Undoubtedly this is so. However, much depends on the principles by reference to which a court interprets

---

[1] See above, p. 167.

the intention of the parties.  Is the determining factor the bare language of the treaty or is it the ever-present assumption that treaties are meant to constitute a source of obligations and not diplomatic devices for avoiding obligations?  Is it the principle of the full development of the institutions of international value or is it the rule that the State's freedom of action must not be unduly limited?  Although confined to the administration of the existing law, an international tribunal, no less than a municipal court, is—within these limits—to a certain degree a free agent acting with due regard to the needs of the community.

That particular quality of the judicial temper in which the Court approaches its task has now by reason of continuity and tradition become part and parcel of the Court as an institution independent to a large degree of the Judges who compose it.  The Court as an institution is nothing else than the spirit of its pronouncements from its very inception.  It is not in the long run a permanent court so far as its composition is concerned—though by a statesmanlike innovation, introduced on the occasion of the setting up of the International Court of Justice in 1945, the unavoidable changes in the membership of the Court have been combined, by a procedure securing the election of five judges every three years, with a substantial continuity of its membership as a whole.[2]  However, the true permanence of the Court is that of a tendency and a method of approach transcending the continuity of its membership.  There is probably no exaggeration in the submission that that spirit is not divorced from the progress of international life and that it has been an agency of its integration and development.

At the same time it must be borne in mind that the principle of effectiveness is only one of the standards of interpretation; that its function as an instrument designed to assist, in accordance with good faith, in giving effect to the intention of the parties must not be permitted to displace such intention; and that it ought not properly to be allowed to degenerate into a rule of thumb as distinguished from a flexible, critical and discriminating guide to interpretation.  These considerations may have been obscured by the survey, undertaken in this Part, of the instances of the application of the principle of effectiveness on the part of the Court.  The main and primary purpose of this Part has been to give an

[2] See above, p. 11.

account of and to analyse such examples. But that purpose would be imperfectly achieved if the variety and the abundance of these instances were to create the impression of any uniformity or exclusiveness in the application of the principle of effectiveness on the part of the Court. Its practice shows that the rule of effectiveness is not an automatic principle of interpretation. There are numerous pronouncements of the Court—discussed in this and the other chapters—in which the Court declined to give a full, or any, measure of effectiveness to the provisions of a treaty. This it did on account of considerations overriding those of effectiveness.[3]

To put it differently, while effectiveness as dictated by the requirement of good faith and the natural purpose of treaties conceived as *vincula juris* is the general rule and the starting point of the task of interpretation, proof is admissible—direct or indirect —that something less than full effectiveness was intended. It is in that sense that an answer must be sought to the question whether the Court interprets the intention of the parties by reference to the principle of effectiveness or whether, conversely, it modifies the maxim *ut res magis valeat quam pereat* by reference to the intention of the parties. It is only by reference to the rule of effectiveness thus qualified that it is possible, for instance, to follow the apparent inconsistencies of the Court such as exhibited by its tendency, on the one hand, to give full effect to clauses conferring jurisdiction upon it and, on the other hand, its outspoken determination to make the intention of the parties the exclusive source of its jurisdiction.

91. *Apparent Denial of the Principle of Effectiveness. The Advisory Opinion on* Interpretation of Peace Treaties with Bulgaria, Hungary and Romania (Second Phase)

That qualified conception of effectiveness explains the occasional refusal of the Court to endow a treaty with an efficacy which, in the view of the Court, the parties intended to deny to it. The Advisory Opinion of the Court on the *Interpretation of Peace Treaties with Bulgaria, Hungary and Romania (Second Phase),* provided an instructive example of the issue involved.[4] In that Opinion the Court was concerned with the powers of the Secretary-General of the United Nations upon whom the Peace Treaties had conferred the power to appoint the third member of a Commission

---

[3] See above, pp. 262–265, and below, pp. 284–292.		[4] *I.C.J. Reports* 1950, p. 221.

entrusted with the task of settling disputes concerning the interpretation or execution of the Treaties, in case the parties should fail to agree on his appointment. The Court held that the Secretary-General had no power to appoint a third commissioner if one of the parties had previously refused to appoint its own commissioner on the ground that, in its view, there was no dispute to be submitted to the Commission. In a previous Opinion the Court had held that there existed a dispute in the meaning of the Treaty and that the parties in question were bound to appoint commissioners.[5]

It will be noted that the issue before the Court was not whether the Secretary-General was entitled to appoint the commissioner for the party refusing to make such appointment—a matter not provided for expressly by the Treaty. The issue was the question of the appointment by the Secretary-General of a third commissioner although, so far, only one commissioner had been appointed by one party, the other party declining to appoint its commissioner for the reason that, in its view, there was no dispute between the parties. The language of the Treaties was sufficiently elastic to render possible divergent interpretations. The Treaties with Bulgaria, Hungary and Romania provided [6] that disputes concerning their interpretation or execution shall be referred to the three Heads of Missions. The relevant Article laid down as follows:

> " . . . Any such dispute not resolved by them within a period of two months shall, unless the parties to the dispute mutually agree upon another means of settlement, be referred at the request of either party to the dispute to a Commission composed of one representative of each party and a third member selected by mutual agreement of the two parties from nationals of a third country. Should the two parties fail to agree within a period of one month upon the appointment of the third member, the Secretary-General of the United Nations may be requested by either party to make the appointment."

Was it essential, before the Secretary-General could legitimately appoint a third member, that the parties should have previously appointed the two members? Or did that power come into operation as soon as, for any reason (including the refusal of one party to appoint its own commissioner), the parties have failed to appoint the third commissioner?

---

[5] *Interpretation of Peace Treaties with Bulgaria, Hungary and Romania*: *I.C.J. Reports* 1950, p. 65. See above, p. 248.
[6] In Arts. 36, 40 and 38 respectively.

As stated, the Court held that no such power rested with the Secretary-General.  It was of the opinion that the powers of the Secretary-General derived from the consent of the parties and that " by its very nature such a clause must be strictly construed and can be applied only in the case expressly provided for therein." [7]   It pointed out that, in the circumstances before it, the appointment of a third member by the Secretary-General would result in the constitution of a two-member Commission only; that that was not the kind of commission contemplated by the treaty; that the opposition of a member appointed by the only party represented could prevent a Commission so constituted from reaching any decision whatsoever; that such a Commission could only decide by unanimity whereas the treaties provided that the decision of the majority of the members of the Commission shall be the decision of the Commission; that the Commission thus constituted would not have the same authority as a three-member Commission; and that " in every respect, the result would be contrary to the letter as well as the spirit of the Treaties." [8]

As will be suggested presently, the Opinion of the Court cannot accurately be regarded as being in the nature of a departure from the general recognition, on its part, of the value of the principle of effectiveness.  At the same time, the Opinion represents what is probably a marginal case in relation to a problem which has been a constant theme of its activity.  This being so, it may be useful to examine in some detail the alternative solution—a solution which the Court rejected.  In particular it is necessary to consider—without necessarily subscribing to it—the view according to which the clause in question, far from calling " by its nature " for a restrictive interpretation and designed as it was to secure the effectiveness of the Treaty against any obstructive designs of the parties, ought to be given a liberal construction.  That view may be summarised as follows:

The Court held that " according to the natural and ordinary meaning of the terms it was intended that the appointment of both national Commissioners should precede that of the third member." [9] It may be maintained, perhaps not less plausibly, that the natural and ordinary meaning of terms applies only to natural and

---

[7] *I.C.J. Reports* 1950, at p. 227.
[8] At p. 228.
[9] At p. 227.

ordinary situations—namely, in this case, to a situation in which the parties, consistently with the meaning of the Treaty, fulfilled their obligation to appoint their respective commissioners—and that it might have been contrary to the intention of the parties to apply that natural and ordinary meaning of terms to an extraordinary situation in which one of the parties, in violation, as the Court held, of its obligations, asserted that no dispute existed and that it was therefore not called upon to appoint a commissioner. According to that line of reasoning, to attribute to the Treaties in question a meaning safeguarding the effectiveness of the machinery therein provided would not have been contrary to their letter and spirit. It would have been so if there had been conclusive evidence that the Treaties intended to leave room for the frustration, by the unilateral will of one of the parties, of the purpose of the machinery of pacific settlement as therein provided. (The Court considered that there was such intrinsic evidence in the very terms of the Treaties and that it would be revising the Treaties—and not interpreting them [10]—if it had declined to apply their terms to a situation brought about by a breach of the Treaty.)

On that line of reasoning, it might be thought that a solution aiming at securing the effectiveness of the Treaty, as against the action of a party whose conduct in preventing the constitution of a three-member Commission was held by the Court to be a violation of its undertakings, could not be contrary to the spirit of the Treaty; that, as the Treaty set up the Secretary-General as the guardian of the effectiveness of the provision in question in relation to the only device of obstruction which is of normal occurrence and which alone was present to the minds of the parties, the appointment of the third member in a chronological order possibly not contemplated by the Treaties was not legally improper; and that the moral authority of a Commission thus constituted would not be less than that of a Commission reduced to two members after the withdrawal of one member—a contingency which the Court envisaged but which it regarded as irrelevant on the ground that in the latter case there would have been no doubt as to the initial validity of the constitution of the Commission. For it may be said that in that case the

---

[10] This particular statement—namely, that it is the duty of the Court to interpret treaties, not to revise them—is of frequent occurrence both in the pronouncements of the Court and in Dissenting Opinions. However, the question, which is often controversial, is, which of the opposing views interprets the treaty and which revises it?

Commission thus reduced in numbers would also be in the position of having to render unanimous decisions—a method described by the Court as contrary to the Treaties which spoke only of "the decision of the majority" as being binding (though, clearly, the Treaties could not possibly have intended to exclude unanimous decisions by all three members of the Commission).[11]

## 92. *The Same. Deliberate Absence of Effectiveness*

The Opinion of the Court in the case of the *Interpretation of the Peace Treaties* can nevertheless, it is believed, be accommodated within the framework of legal principle on the assumption that the Court had come to the conclusion that the possible failure, as the result of deliberate action of one of the parties denying the very existence of a dispute, of the machinery provided in the treaties was a contingency foreseen—or at least not deliberately discarded—by the parties and that it was given expression in the flexible terms of the relevant Article.

It is possible that by means of a meticulous examination of the history of the Peace Conference of 1946—of the "preparatory work"—the Court could have found persuasive support for its reasoning culminating in a conclusion of this nature. But the Court had before it an analysis of the preparatory work as submitted by one of the parties only [12] and this may provide an explanation why it did not deem itself free to undertake that task through its own

[11] The Court referred to the possible mischief likely to arise, as the result of its decision, in relation to similar provisions in numerous arbitration treaties. It answered that objection as follows: "The ineffectiveness in the present case of the clauses dealing with the settlement of disputes does not permit such a generalisation" (at p. 229). From the fact that only few treaties contain provisions to cover the situation resulting from the refusal of a party to appoint a commissioner the Court drew the conclusion that the parties to those treaties "felt the impossibility of remedying this situation simply by way of interpretation." A contrary conclusion could have been reached—especially if such treaties, as did the Peace Treaties before the Court, had provided machinery for the cognate case of non-appointment of a third member as the result of the disagreement of the parties. The Court concluded this aspect of its reasoning by the statement—possibly somewhat remote from the precise situation with which it was confronted—that "in fact, the risk of such a possibility of a refusal is a small one, because normally each party has a direct interest in the appointment of its commissioner and must in any case be presumed to observe its treaty obligations" (*ibid.*). For a detailed criticism of the Opinion of the Court—as well as a comprehensive statement of an alternative solution by referring to the principles of effectiveness, of good faith and of the necessity of avoiding an interpretation which leads to an absurdity—see the Dissenting Opinion of Judge Read (at pp. 231–247).

[12] See the Section on "The history of the peace treaties while under negotiation" in the *Written Statement of the United States of America* (*Pleadings, Oral Arguments, Documents,* pp. 221–226).

researches. An examination of the preparatory work might have shown that the loophole in the treaties was intended—at least by one group of the parties; that the refusal, at the Peace Conference, of some Governments to agree to the compulsory jurisdiction of the International Court of Justice may have been prompted by the desire, acquiesced in—grudgingly or otherwise—by other Governments, to limit the effectiveness of the obligation of pacific settlement by some such devices as those which gave rise to the case before the Court; and that such evidence of the intention of the parties—an intention to accept no more than a flexible and pusillanimous formulation of the relevant provisions—displaced the otherwise imperative principle of interpretation in accordance with the requirement of effectiveness. However, the absence of specific reference, in the body of the Opinion, to preparatory work does not mean that the Court did not in fact examine it and that it was not acquainted with the circumstances surrounding the unusual, vague, and—to a large extent—non-committal provisions of the Treaties in the matter of settlement of disputes. The decisive question—here as elsewhere—is: What was the intention of the parties? On the face of it, that intention was to prevent the possibility of the operation of the machinery provided in the Treaties being frustrated by the obstructive conduct of one of the parties. Such possible obstructive conduct they visualised in its typical manifestation, namely, in the inability to agree on the appointment of a third commissioner. For that contingency they provided in the Treaties. They did not provide for the contingency which actually arose, namely, the refusal of one of the parties to appoint its own commissioner. Did they deliberately leave that particular gap for the reason that there was no disposition, at least on one side, to make the Treaties effective in this respect? Or did they leave the gap for the more simple reason that that particular contingency did not occur to them and that, in view of the scarcity, admitted by the Court, of treaty provisions on that aspect of possible obstruction by the parties, it could not reasonably be held to have occurred to them? The task of interpretation legitimately comprises that of an answer to concrete situations which were not, in the form in which they arose subsequently, in the minds of the parties when they concluded the compact. In fact, this seems to be the main—and the most difficult—object of interpretation of both contracts and treaties. As a rule, there is no substantial difficulty in applying the provisions of an instrument to a case foreseen by its authors. The difficulty arises in relation to cases which they did not foresee.

In the absence of proof to the contrary, there may be no justification for any emphatic dissent from the view which underlies the Opinion of the Court in that case. That view was: (a) that the parties did not envisage the contingency of the Secretary-General having to make the appointment of the third member before the two other members had been appointed, in case one of the parties failed to appoint its commissioner and (b) that in so far as the parties had envisaged that contingency, there was no agreement between them to provide for it. However that may be, the Advisory Opinion of the Court on the *Interpretation of the Peace Treaties (Second Phase)* affords an instructive example of a much needed warning of the limitations of the principle of effectiveness. The circumstance that the Opinion was rendered with practical unanimity must inspire hesitation in respect of any confident assertion that the Opinion constitutes a departure from the established canons of effectiveness.[13]

At the same time there is probably no need to generalise the import of that Opinion in the sense that, when confronted with a breach of an international obligation by one of the parties, the Court is not entitled to substitute a different remedy or different process for that which has been frustrated by the party in question.[14] This may be so if, as in the case of the Opinion here discussed, it is apparent that the parties did not intend a full measure of effectiveness of the Treaty. In other cases there may be room for the view that if a legal instrument cannot be applied in accordance with its terms owing to a breach of its provisions by one of the parties a court of law has the power to apply it, in the matter of its execution,

---

[13] There is room for noting, in this connection, a possible aberration of the principle of effectiveness inasmuch as a judicial tribunal may on occasions be moved to consider as relevant the question of effectiveness not of the provisions which it is called upon to interpret but of the possible or probable effectiveness of its own decision. No such considerations weigh as a rule with a municipal court; the powerful arm of the State makes any such preoccupation unnecessary. On the other hand, it is conceivable that an international tribunal may, in an inarticulate fashion, be guided by the desire to avoid solutions which may have no prospect of being acted upon in practice and which may add to the political difficulties of the situation. Any such leaning, which is alien to the true purposes of the judicial function, has been absent from the practice of the Court.

[14] See, *e.g.*, Fitzmaurice in *B.Y.*, 27 (1950), p. 7, and, with regard to the Advisory Opinion on the *International Status of South-West Africa*, *ibid*., 28 (1951), pp. 23, 24. And see above, p. 279, and below, p. 292.

in a way approximating most closely to its primary object. Such judicial change of the instrumentalities of operation of a treaty may approximate to judicial legislation—but, then, the difference between the latter and the application of the principle of effectiveness is one of degree.

Similar considerations apply to the Advisory Opinion on the *International Status of South-West Africa*. In that case, which is discussed elsewhere in this Part,[15] the Court, after having come to the conclusion that South-West Africa continued to be a territory under the international Mandate assumed by South Africa, was confronted with two further questions. As already stated, the first was whether the continuation of that status, one of the principal features of which was supervision by the League of Nations of the administration of the mandated territory, implied—after the demise of the League of Nations—continued supervision by the United Nations. This question the Court answered in the affirmative. It held that the continued status of South-West Africa as a mandated territory required the continuation of international supervision and of the duty to render reports to an international organ. In their absence the " rights of the peoples " under that system " would not be effectively safeguarded." In view of this the Court considered as irrelevant the circumstance that the supervisory functions of the League of Nations with regard to those mandated territories which were not placed under the Trusteeship system were not expressly transferred to or assumed by the United Nations. It held that as the United Nations had another, though not identical, international organ fulfilling the functions of supervision, these functions devolved upon it. It said: " The obligation incumbent upon a mandatory State to accept international supervision and to submit reports is an important part of the Mandate System. When the authors of the Covenant created this system, they considered that the effective performance of the sacred trust of civilisation by the mandatory Powers required that the administration of mandated territories should be subject to international supervision. The authors of the Charter had in mind the same necessity when they organized an International Trusteeship System. The necessity of supervision continues to exist despite the disappearance of the supervisory organ under the Mandates System." [16]

15 See above, pp. 277 *et seq.*
16 *I.C.J. Reports* 1950, p. 136.

Thus the Court, in order to render effective the instruments before it, read into them an agency of supervision different from that originally contemplated. However, though by a considerably smaller majority, it declined to go beyond that. In replying to a further question put by the General Assembly, it refused to read into the relevant provisions of the Charter a degree of effectiveness to the point of holding that South Africa was under an obligation to conclude a Trusteeship Agreement in respect of the mandated territory of South-West Africa. The Opinion shows that the circumstance that the Court has gone a long way towards safeguarding the effectiveness of the texts before it does not mean that it will go all the way in that direction. Effectiveness, being—in general—a principle of good faith, is a matter of circumstances and degree. Like some other tendencies in the jurisprudence of the Court, it does not lend itself to formulation as a rigid maxim which can be used as a basis for confident prediction.

### 93. *The Limits of Effectiveness and the Requirement of Good Faith*

The cases of the *Interpretation of the Peace Treaties* and the *International Status of South-West Africa* have been reviewed here in some detail for the reason that the first seems to constitute a departure from the general trend of the practice of the Court in the matter of applying the canons of effectiveness and the second because it illustrates in an instructive manner the limits of the operation of that principle. In a different sphere, in the matter of equality of treatment,[17] the case of *Oscar Chinn* provides a warning against any facile assumption that that principle is a rule of invariable application. As stated, in essence it is no more than a requirement of good faith. But good faith requires no more than that effect be given, in a fair and reasonable manner, to the intention of the parties. This means that on occasions, if such was the intention of the parties, good faith may require that the effectiveness of the instrument should fall short of its apparent and desirable scope. The principle of effectiveness cannot transform a mere declaration of lofty purpose—such as the Universal Declaration of Human Rights—into a source of legal rights and obligations. It cannot endow the non-committal statement that certain categories

---

[17] See above, pp. 262–265.

of disputes are a proper object of compulsory arbitral settlement [18] with the effect of creating a duty to submit them to arbitration. It cannot impart legal vitality and efficacy to a formula which, in the view of some, amounts in fact to a denial of legal obligation— such as those declarations of acceptance of the Optional Clause of the Statute of the Court which reserve for the State accepting the compulsory jurisdiction of the Court the right to determine the extent of the jurisdiction thus accepted.

Equally, although a recommendation, which is not binding, by an organ of the League of Nations or the United Nations is of less potency than a binding decision, this does not mean that it is open to a judicial tribunal to endow with a binding character an expression, however politically or morally weighty, of collective opinion. In the *Corfu Channel* case, although the matter was outside the actual decision of the Court, seven Judges deemed it necessary, in a Separate Opinion, to dissociate themselves from the suggestion, advanced by the United Kingdom, that in the circumstances of the case a recommendation of the Security Council was binding upon the parties.[19] At the same time, as shown in the case of the *Railway Traffic between Lithuania and Poland*,[20] it may be inaccurate to lay down an invariable rule in the sense that a recommendation can never be binding. Here, once more, we are confronted with the disadvantages of any attempt to study the work of the Court with the view to extracting from it rigid rules as distinguished from tendencies which, while predominant and useful as a guide in assessing the future action of the Court, are no more than trends in the quest for both justice and continuity—which latter is in itself an element of legal justice. The same applies to the subject of the final Part of this book, in which an attempt will be made to survey the jurisprudence of the Court as a tribunal in turn curbing and yielding to claims of sovereignty.

---

[18] See, *e.g.*, Arts. 16 and 38, respectively, of the Hague Conventions of 1899 and 1907 for the Pacific Settlement of International Disputes which laid down that " in questions of a legal nature, and especially in the interpretation or application of international conventions, arbitration is recognised by the signatory Powers as the most effective, and at the same time the most equitable, means of settling disputes which diplomacy has failed to settle." From a similar point of view reference may be made to the useful distinction made by Professor Stone between " ' effectiveness ' of international law in terms of observance of its *actual* provisions and its ' effectiveness ' in terms of some *desired* objectives as yet not embodied " in it: *Proceedings of the American Society of International Law*, 1956, p. 201.

[19] *I.C.J. Reports* 1947–1948, p. 31. See above, p. 47.

[20] See above, p. 274.

PART FIVE

THE COURT AND STATE SOVEREIGNTY

## Section A

## Restraints Upon Claims of Sovereignty

CHAPTER 20

## IN GENERAL

### 94. *International Law and Freedom of Action*

It has been suggested in the preceding chapters that in a considerable number of cases the Court, in interpreting international law, has been in fact confronted with a choice between the principle of the minimum of restrictions upon the sovereignty of States and the attribution of full effect to what appears to be the purpose of the obligations binding upon or undertaken by them. We have seen that the result of that choice has been such that the jurisprudence of the Court in this sphere can to a large extent be conceived in terms of a restrictive interpretation of claims of State sovereignty. It is sufficient to recall the rejection of the rule of absolute unanimity in the interpretation of the Covenant of the League of Nations; the cases of affirmation of the competence of the Court through a bold interpretation of jurisdictional clauses, the assumption of an implied submission by the parties and the disregard of requirements of form; the interpretation of Minorities Treaties in favour not of States but of the system of protection of minorities, and, generally, the construction of clauses providing for equality of treatment in a manner calculated to secure their observance not only in law, but also in fact; the wide interpretation of the scope of the competence of the International Labour Organisation and of other international organs such as the International River Commissions; the recognition of the prohibition of abuse of rights; the pronouncements confining within its proper scope the exception of domestic jurisdiction both under Article 15 of the Covenant of the League of Nations and elsewhere; and the emphasis upon the superiority of international obligations over municipal law.

In fact, the two preceding Parts expounding the manner in which the Court has applied the principle of effectiveness and in which it has acted by way of judicial legislation provide in themselves illustrations of an attitude restrictive of the sovereignty of States.    Interpretation resulting in effectiveness, as distinguished from ineffectiveness or limited effectiveness, of treaty obligations implies a limitation of sovereignty—although such limitation may be the consequence of an obligation freely undertaken.  Similarly, it is clear that judicial creation or extension of international law derogates from the sovereignty of States in so far as they are considered to be bound only by such rules of international law as are the product of their express will.  The same applies to pronouncements of the Court affirming the legislative character of instruments, such as Mandates, creating a status,[1] or, as in the case of the Charter of the United Nations, establishing procedural rights of action against non-member States.[2]  This is also, in a distinct sense, the effect of the Opinions recognising the possibility of direct conferment of treaty rights upon individuals—for is not the exclusiveness of States as subjects of international law yet another aspect of the traditional doctrine of State sovereignty?—and, generally, laying down that States are not the only subjects of international law and that other entities, including the United Nations, may bring an international claim.[3]

The object of the present Part is to examine the pronouncements of the Court bearing more directly upon the question of the sovereignty of States and not covered by the preceding Parts on Judicial Legislation and Effectiveness of the Law.  In one sense, the results of the activity of the Court may appear to be to a large extent co-extensive with—or expressive of—limitations upon the sovereignty of States.  This is so not in the sense of the inaccurate proposition that the Court will, in case of doubt, find for the plaintiff State rather than for the defendant, or that, in its non-contentious jurisdiction, it will lean to a solution which impairs the sovereignty of the State affected by the proceedings.  What it amounts to is that in so far as the Court declares the law and in

---

[1] See above, p. 182.

[2] See below, p. 311.

[3] It may also be said that in this category there can be included the instances in which the Court has declined to let its decisions be determined by the formulation of their claims by the parties.  For its function, the Court says, is to declare the law without being confined to choosing one of the two views propounded by the parties; both sovereign States may be wrong: Series A/B, No. 46 (1932) (*Free Zones* case), p. 138. See also Series A, No. 2 (1924) (*Mavrommatis Palestine Concessions*), p. 24.  And see above, pp. 206 *et seq.*

so far as that law implies restraint upon freedom of action, its decisions are liable to be interpreted as being in the nature of a restraint upon sovereignty. This is perhaps no more than a transposition into the international sphere of what is a general phenomenon in the administration of the law—for law, although its ultimate end and effect in a society are the realisation of freedom, normally operates in the first instance by way of restricting the freedom of action of one of the parties. However, the ascertained tendency of the Court goes beyond that unchallenged operation of the law. The Court has, as a rule, taken a critical and independent view of some of the notions which have been traditionally associated with the conception of sovereignty in the international sphere and which are inimical to the basic ideas of a society under the rule of law. While, however, this is probably an accurate description of the general attitude of the Court, it ought not to be allowed to obscure the fact that in cases where such manifestations of the international sovereignty of States have clearly become part of international law the Court will, for the simple reason that it administers the existing law, give effect to them. This applies, for instance, to the rule that, unlike within the State, in the international sphere the jurisdiction of tribunals, including that of the International Court of Justice itself, is essentially based on consent and that strict proof is required of voluntary submission to such jurisdiction. For this reason, while the present Section of this Part of the book is devoted to an analysis of the cases in which the Court has curbed the claims of sovereignty, the Section which follows will give the other side of the picture.

# CHAPTER 21

# THE PROVINCE OF TREATIES

### 95. *The Doctrine of Restrictive Interpretation of Treaties*

The appeal to the principle of restrictive interpretation of obligations is a constant feature of the written and oral proceedings before the Court. It was confronted with it when it gave its first Judgment and its first important Advisory Opinion. It has been confronted with it ever since. Thus, in the case of *The Wimbledon*, Germany contended that Article 380 of the Treaty of Versailles relating to free passage through the Kiel Canal would, unless interpreted restrictively, " imply the abandonment by Germany of a personal and imprescriptive right, which forms an essential part of her sovereignty." The Court refused to accept this line of reasoning. It conflicted, it said, " with general considerations of the highest order. . . ."

> " The Court declines to see in the conclusion of any Treaty by which a State undertakes to perform or refrain from performing a particular act an abandonment of its sovereignty. No doubt any convention creating an obligation of this kind places a restriction upon the exercise of the sovereign rights of the State, in the sense that it requires them to be exercised in a certain way. But the right of entering into international engagements is an attribute of State sovereignty." [1]

While admitting that in case of doubt limitations upon the exercise of sovereign rights ought to be interpreted restrictively, it said: " The Court feels obliged to stop at the point where the so-called restrictive interpretation would be contrary to the plain terms of the article and would destroy what has been clearly granted." [2]

The Court was merely elaborating in more general language what it had already said in the Advisory Opinion given on the question whether the competence of the International Labour Organisation extends to international regulation of conditions of work of persons employed in agriculture. In that case it was urged

---

[1] Series A, No. 1 (1923), p. 25. And see Series C, No. 3 (1923), pp. 43, 44, 66–73.
[2] Series A, No. 1 (1923), p. 24.

in argument before the Court that the establishment of the International Labour Organisation involved an abandonment of rights of national sovereignty and that the competence of the Organisation should not therefore be extended by interpretation. It is of interest to note some details of this argument as put forward by the French Government, which, together with some other Governments, opposed what it believed would be an extension of the competence of the Organisation. The contention was that the provisions of the Treaty of Versailles relating to the International Labour Organisation constituted a limitation of the sovereignty of States. It was admitted that the obligations of the Treaty in this respect had been undertaken with studied circumspection, and that the resolutions of the Conferences of the International Labour Organisation were in law and in fact merely in the nature of recommendations. However, it was pointed out that, according to the Constitution of the Organisation, there was an obligation to submit these recommendations to the national legislatures, and that this was therefore a case of the exercise of an international as opposed to a purely national initiative. This, it was argued, implied a restriction of national sovereignty with the resulting duty to interpret these provisions strictly and in the narrowest sense. In private law, it was said, freedom cannot be restricted in case of doubt; this is particularly so in international law, which, it was urged, includes not only freedom but sovereignty.[3] The Court admitted that there might be some force in the argument, but proceeded to state that " the question in every case must be resolved into what the terms of the treaty actually mean." [4]

The argument as put forward by France in this case shows to what use the plea of restrictive interpretation can be put even in regard to somewhat nominal limitations of State sovereignty. Naturally that plea has also been propounded in cases where more substantial obligations were at issue. It was advanced by Roumania when opposing the jurisdiction of the European Danube Commission between Galatz and Braila,[5] and by Poland in opposition to that of the International Oder Commission over the Polish tributaries of the river Oder.[6] Turkey invoked it in the matter of the

[3] Series C, No. 1, p. 174.
[4] Series B, No. 2 (1922), p. 23.
[5] Series B, No. 16 (1928), p. 36.
[6] Series A, No. 23 (1929), p. 26.

*Exchange of Greek and Turkish Populations*[7] and in the *Mosul Boundary* case.[8] Danzig appealed to it in opposition to the Polish claim to set up Polish post-office boxes in the territory of the City.[9] The much overworked tool was used, once more, in connection with the Thirteenth Advisory Opinion concerning the incidental regulation of the work of employers,[10] where the argument was advanced that while a law within the State, being an instrument of social life, may be developed by way of extensive interpretation, this cannot be the case in regard to a treaty which is the result of the voluntary consent of sovereign States and the scope of which is unalterably limited by the consensus of the contracting parties. In all these cases the Court, in referring to what it had already said on this matter in the case of *The Wimbledon* and elsewhere, rejected the argument of restrictive interpretation of limitations of State sovereignty. The doctrine of restrictive interpretation is in fact one of the matters on which the Court has developed what may be called a constant " jurisprudence." For a time its constancy proved but a small deterrent to those responsible for the written or the oral pleadings of Governments before the Court—until, as it did in the Advisory Opinion concerning the *Albanian Minority Schools*, the Court no longer considered it necessary to answer that particular argument.[11] It is possible that, as a result, parties to proceedings before the Court may come to regard that kind of argument as a source of embarrassment rather than of strength inasmuch as it may suggest the absence of more convincing argument.

In a sense the Court has not discouraged the plea of restrictive interpretation as clearly as it could have done. For its refusal to concede claims based on the sovereignty of States has been occasionally accompanied by a courteous obeisance to the tradition of respect for State sovereignty. On such occasions the Court has prefaced its finding on the substance by a concession to form. It has begun by admitting that there may be some force in the plea of restrictive interpretation, but—it has added—the question must resolve itself into finding what the terms of the treaty actually mean. Thus in *The Wimbledon* while, as shown above, it rejected in

---

[7] Series B, No. 10 (1925), p. 21.
[8] Series B, No. 12 (1925), p. 25.
[9] Series B, No. 11 (1925), pp. 37, 39.
[10] Series C, No. 12, p. 63.
[11] See Series A/B, No. 64 (1935), p. 15, for a reference to this argument on the part of Albania. The Court does not appear to have answered it.

principle the argument of restrictive interpretation, it conceded that the circumstance that a provision implies a limitation of sovereignty " constitutes a sufficient reason for the restrictive interpretation, in case of doubt, of the clause which produces such a limitation." It then proceeded to qualify in the following terms the principle of restrictive interpretation by refusing to apply it where the result would be contrary to the plain terms of the Treaty and would run counter to the clear intention of the parties.[12] Or, while agreeing that the argument of restrictive interpretation is " sound in itself," the Court has insisted that it must be employed with the greatest caution: " To rely upon it [the principle of the least restriction on the freedom of States], it is not sufficient that the purely grammatical analysis of a text should not lead to definite results; . . . it will be only when, in spite of all pertinent considerations, the intention of the Parties still remains doubtful, that that interpretation should be adopted which is most favourable to the freedom of States." [13] Yet it is difficult to imagine the Court exhausting all the available rules of interpretation without being able to discover the intention of the parties and having therefore to fall back upon the rule of restrictive interpretation.[14]

Similarly, it is not often that a situation will arise in which the " ordinary methods of interpretation have failed " to the extent of resulting in an interpretation leading to " something unreasonable or absurd " [15] and which can be avoided only with the assistance of the plea of restrictive interpretation. Thus in the Advisory Opinion on the *Treatment of Polish Nationals in the Danzig Territory* the Court, which was called upon to interpret an Article relating to the protection of minorities—a substantial limitation of the sovereignty of a State—admitted that the Treaty was not " absolutely clear." [16] This circumstance did not lead the Court to interpret the treaty restrictively in favour of the sovereignty of Danzig. Instead it proceeded, in order to elucidate the disputed meaning of the Treaty,

---

12 Series A, No. 1 (1923), p. 24.
13 Series A, No. 23 (1929) (*International Commission of the Oder*), p. 26.
14 Jessel M.R. in *Taylor* v. *St. Helens Corporation*, 6 Ch.D. 264, 280, commenting on the maxim that the words of an instrument shall be taken most strongly against the party employing them, says: " The rule is to find out the meaning of the instrument according to the ordinary and proper rules of construction. If we can thus find its meaning, we do not want the maxim. If, on the other hand, we cannot find out its meaning, then the instrument is void for uncertainty. . . ."
15 Series B, No. 11 (1925) (*Polish Postal Service in Danzig*), p. 39.
16 Series A/B, No. 44 (1932), p. 33.

to examine in detail the various drafts preceding its adoption. " The duty of the Court is to interpret the text as it stands, taking into consideration all the materials at the Court's disposal." [17]  For these reasons the Court has on occasions qualified the admissibility of the plea of restrictive interpretation by excluding cases in which the obligations of the contracting parties are equal and reciprocal.[18] While it may not be easy to follow the meaning of the reference to the equality of obligations—a requirement which does not easily lend itself to computation—reciprocity of obligations is the typical phenomenon in international treaties.

This being so, it may be conducive to clarity if, in the pleadings of the parties, restraint is exercised in giving currency to language which is liable to be misunderstood and to which, it has been shown, the Court attaches in practice little importance.  Thus, the parties may find it less useful than appears at first sight to invoke the maxim enunciated by the Court in the final Judgment in the *Free Zones* case to the effect that " in case of doubt a limitation of sovereignty must be construed restrictively." [19]  If the case calls for restrictive interpretation, it may not be difficult to find in support of it a principle of law of greater generality and persuasiveness.[20]  For instance, when a State claims special rights and privileges in the territory of another, it must point to some juridical basis for the claim.  When Poland claimed for her war vessels the right of access to the port of Danzig, the Court declared that such a right, being in derogation of the rights of the Free City, must be established on a clear basis.[21]  High municipal tribunals have not adhered to the

---

[17] Series A/B, No. 44 (1932), p. 40.

[18] Series B, No. 11 (1925) (*Polish Postal Service in Danzig*), p. 39.  In the Advisory Opinion on the *Exchange of Greek and Turkish Populations* the Court added the following significant observations : " In the present case, moreover, the obligations of the contracting States are absolutely equal and reciprocal.  It is therefore impossible to admit that a convention which creates obligations of this kind, construed according to its natural meaning, infringes the sovereign rights of the High Contracting Parties." (Series B, No. 10 (1925), p. 21.)

[19] Series A/B, No. 46 (1932), p. 167.  And see Series A, No. 24, p. 12.

[20] As counsel for the Free City of Danzig put it in the case concerning the *Access of Polish Men-of-War to the Port of Danzig* : " The argument of restrictive interpretation can be based on a general principle which obtains not merely in international law, but which is a general principle of human intercourse : if you want to check or hamper any State, company or person in dealing with something which is its own, the onus is upon you to show that you possess something in the nature of an overriding right or privilege which checks or hampers the normal right which everyone has over the use and disposition of his own property " : Statement by Sir John Fischer Williams, Series C, No. 55, p. 219.

[21] Series A/B, No. 43 (1931), p. 142.

view that in case of doubt treaty provisions have to be interpreted restrictively. The Supreme Court of the United States has repeatedly affirmed the principle that when a " treaty fairly admits of two constructions, one restricting the rights that may be claimed under it and the other enlarging them, the more liberal construction is to be preferred." [22] International tribunals have frequently followed the same rule.[23] It is a rule of old standing, going back to Grotius.[24] The preponderant practice of the Court itself has, as we have seen, been based on principles of interpretation which render the treaty effective rather than ineffective.[25] These principles are not easily reconcilable with restrictive interpretation conceived as the governing rule of construction. While in some cases the principle that a contractual provision must be interpreted in favour of the party which contracted the obligation may lead to results consistent with justice, it may not do so in other cases.

Accordingly, there is reason to believe that the appeals to restrictive interpretation of limitations of State sovereignty will disappear from the pleadings of the parties and that it will be found practicable to dispense with the soothing concession of restrictive interpretation in " doubtful cases." As already stated, reliance upon that particular argument has been disappearing in fact; that process may be regarded as well-nigh completed. This is one of the main lessons which can be derived from the activity of the Court. For the reasons stated, this development must be regarded as beneficial. Apart from the practice of the Court, it receives a weighty accession of authority from the fact that restrictive interpretation of contractual obligations does not constitute a general principle of law.[26] It does not follow—it is often opposed

---

[22] *Jordan* v. *Tashiro*, 278 U.S. 123; *Nielsen* v. *Johnson*, 279 U.S. 47; *Asakura* v. *Seattle*, 265 U.S. 332.

[23] See, for instance, the *Aspinwall* and *Kummerow* cases: Moore, *Arbitrations*, p. 3624, and Ralston, *Venezuelan Arbitrations*, p. 557, respectively. In the Advisory Opinion on the *Delimitation of the Polish-Czechoslovak Frontier* the Court declined to give a restrictive interpretation to the provisions of an Article providing that the Delimitation Commission shall be empowered to propose to the Conference of Ambassadors any modifications of the frontier considered justified in the interest of individuals or communities by reason of the special local circumstances: " Since the object of this clause is one of equity, it must not be interpreted in too rigid a manner " (Series B, No. 8 (1923), p. 40).

[24] *De jure belli ac pacis*, ii, xvi, xii.

[25] See above, pp. 282–284.

[26] For an elaboration of this submission see the present writer's article on " Restrictive Interpretation and the Principle of Effectiveness in the Interpretation of Treaties " in *British Year Book of International Law*, 26 (1949), pp. 56–57.

to—the paramount principle of interpretation in good faith which requires that both parties to the contract should be treated on an equal footing and that the party upon which the treaty has conferred benefits in return for valuable consideration should not have its rights whittled away as the result of restrictive interpretation of the obligations of the party which obtained the consideration. A restrictive interpretation of the obligations of one party implies a restrictive interpretation of the rights of the other party. Undue regard for the sovereignty of one State implies undue disregard of the sovereignty of another. It is of some interest to note that a Chief Justice of the Supreme Court of the United States—formerly one of the Judges of the International Court—relied on the passage, quoted above, in *The Wimbledon* as well as on writers on international law when in a case involving the obligations of the United States in respect of a gold clause in government bonds he said: " But the power to make binding obligations is a competence attaching to sovereignty." [27] There could be only one reasonable explanation, if it were an accurate explanation, of the principle of restrictive interpretation of treaty obligations, namely, that, unlike in the relations of individuals, the party undertaking the obligation somehow—notwithstanding the position of formal equality with the other contracting party—acted under compulsion. This would not normally be an accurate explanation.

## 96. *Conferment of Treaty Rights upon Third States*

The attitude of the Court in regard to the claims of State sovereignty and of a restrictive interpretation of the obligations undertaken by States has revealed itself in a significant way in relation to the question of the conferment of international rights by treaty upon States which are not parties to it. To that question the Court gave an affirmative answer in the *Free Zones* case between Switzerland and France. It arrived at its decision not without some hesitation.[28] Even after it had reached it, it still insisted that " it cannot be lightly presumed that stipulations favourable to a third State have been adopted with the object of creating an actual right in its favour." In fact, however, it conceded the doctrine of *stipulations pour autrui* by making the acquisition of rights by third States

---

[27] Chief Justice Hughes in *Perry* v. *United States* (1935) 294 U.S. at p. 353.
[28] Series A/B, No. 46 (1932), p. 147. It will be noted that in the first Order in this case (Series A, No. 22, p. 20) the Court declined to commit itself on this question.

dependent upon the will of the contracting parties. After the qualifying summons to caution as quoted above, the Court proceeded as
follows: " There is, however, nothing to prevent the will of sovereign States from having this object and this effect. The question
of the existence of a right acquired under an instrument drawn
between other States is therefore one to be decided in each particular
case; it must be ascertained whether the States which have stipulated
in favour of a third State meant to create for that State an actual
right *which the latter has accepted as such.*" [29]

Possibly the passage as italicised introduces an element of
uncertainty with regard to the ruling as a whole. It creates the
impression that the Court made the acquisition of a right by a third
State dependent upon its prior express acceptance by that State.
This was actually the position in the case before the Court. For it
found that Switzerland had, by an express act of accession by her
Diet, formally accepted the provision of an instrument forming
part of a Declaration made by the Parties to the Treaty of Vienna
of 1815 in pursuance of that Treaty and laying down the principle
of a free customs line in the Gex Zone bordering on Geneva.

However, a closer analysis of the Judgment suggests that the
Court affirmed the possibility of the creation of rights in favour of
third States irrespective of their prior formal acceptance of the
clauses in question. The Court found, in the first instance, that
Switzerland acquired the rights under the Declaration by virtue of
express acceptance. In view of this the Court observed that it was
not necessary for it to " consider the legal nature of the Gex Zone
from the point of view of whether it constitutes a stipulation in
favour of a third Party." Nevertheless it proceeded, in the passage
quoted above, to express its considered view on the admissibility,
even without express acceptance, of the acquisition of a right under
a treaty to which a State is not a party. The authority of that part
of the Judgment is not substantially weakened by the fact that it
was, strictly speaking, *obiter*; for the Court had already decided
that Switzerland did in fact become a party to the Declaration by
way of adhesion. On the contrary, the fact that it expressed a view
on a general and controversial issue, although it was not necessary
for it to do so, adds weight to its pronouncement. This being so,
the qualifying passage cannot be regarded as weakening the general

---

[29] *Ibid*. Italics are the writer's.

import of the rule laid down by the Court. Possibly it does no more than reproduce Article 1121 of the French Civil Code which in permitting *stipulations pour autrui* adds the following qualification: "He who had made the stipulation cannot revoke it if the other party has declared that he desires to take advantage of it." It may be noted in this connection that the Court used guarded language when, in the case concerning *Certain German Interests in Polish Upper Silesia*, it held that as Poland was not a party to the Armistice Convention of 1919 or to the subsequent Spa Protocol she could not acquire rights thereunder. The Court said: "A treaty only creates law as between the States which are parties to it; *in case of doubt* [the italics are the writer's] no rights can be deduced from it in favour of third States." [30]

It would seem at first sight that the connection between State sovereignty and *pacta in favorem tertii* is somewhat remote. But it was a connection which not only the parties in the case of the *Free Zones* sought to establish. In his Dissenting Opinion in the *Free Zones* case Judge Nyholm held that stipulations *in favorem tertii* are not admissible in inter-State relations, on the ground that they are in opposition to the principle of sovereignty. [31] The French Judge *ad hoc* was able to invoke in his Dissenting Opinion the authority of a treatise written by Judge Anzilotti to the effect that such stipulations, if understood as conferring directly a right upon the third party, are contrary to the very structure of the international legal system. [32] While it is difficult to see what is the basis of that view—privity of contract is not a general principle of law [33]—their alleged connection with the sovereignty of States may be surmised. Thus it is asserted that treaties between sovereign States should not be construed as imposing upon them obligations in excess of the duties explicitly undertaken, *i.e.*, in regard to parties specifically referred to in the Treaty.

Conceived in these terms, the objection to *pacta in favorem tertii* is merely another expression of the view, rejected by the Court, that limitations of State sovereignty must be interpreted restrictively.

---

[30] Series A, No. 7 (1926), p. 29.

[31] Series A, No. 22 (1929), p. 26.

[32] *Op. cit.*, p. 44. Judge Anzilotti did not regard himself as bound by his treatise, and apparently voted with the majority of the Court.

[33] The judicial practice of many States provides instructive examples of gradual emancipation from the rigidity of principles affirming privity of contract. See, *e.g.*, Buckland and McNair, *Roman Law and Common Law* (1936), pp. 164–167. And see Cardozo, *The Nature of Judicial Process* (1928), pp. 99, 100.

However, it goes beyond that. It is primarily a manifestation of the opposition to the distinct measure of international legislation implied in the recognition of *pacta in favorem tertii*. Herein lies probably the explanation of the suggestion that such rejection of the principle of privity of contract in the sphere of treaties is contrary to the international legal system—apparently on the assumption that the latter must be regarded as inconsistent with international legislation. Recognition of rights of third parties in such circumstances paves the way for what have been called international settlements whose essence is to make possible the creation of legal rights with an effect transcending the scope of the original parties to the treaty. International settlements are incipient international legislation.[34] It is also for this reason that the doctrine of the international status of certain territories was treated, in one of the preceding chapters, as an example of judicial legislation.[35] When the Commission of Jurists which in 1920 considered the Åaland Islands controversy expressed the view that the Treaty of Paris created a special international status for these islands with the result that " every State interested has the right to insist upon compliance " with it, it affirmed the legal possibility of treaties creating rights in favour of third States.[36] In the case at issue, Sweden—who was not a party to the Treaty of Paris—was considered to be a legal beneficiary of its provisions relating to the demilitarisation of the Aaland Islands. This was also the true meaning of the statement by the Court in the case of *The Wimbledon*[37] in which the Court observed that the Kiel Canal " has become an international waterway intended to provide under treaty guarantee easier access to the Baltic for the benefit *of all nations*[38] of the world." [39] In fact this recognition of the right of all nations, as distinguished from its limitation to the contracting parties, is a frequent feature of treaties relating to international waterways.[40] In the absence of a normally functioning international

---

[34] In this connection reference ought to be made to the Court's readiness to interpret, when necessary, treaties other than those in regard to which States have conferred jurisdiction upon it. See above, p. 261.

[35] See above, pp. 180 *et seq*.

[36] Commented upon in some detail in the Separate Opinion of Sir Arnold McNair in the case concerning the *International Status of South-West Africa (I.C.J. Reports* 1950, p. 154). [37] Series A, No. 1 (1923), p. 22.

[38] Italics are the writer's. [39] Series A, No. 1 (1923), p. 22.

[40] See, *e.g.*, the Preamble to the Convention of Lausanne of July 24, 1923, relating to the Dardanelles and the Treaties of 1901 and 1903 between the United States of America and Great Britain relating to Panama. In Art. 3 of the Barcelona Statute of 1921 the reference is to the " Contracting Parties."

legislature, the admission of the right of third States to benefit from the provisions of a Treaty in accordance with the intention of the parties thereto must be regarded as beneficial from the point of view of the international interest and the development of international law.[41] The threat, implicit in any such development, to the sovereignty of States is more apparent than real; it is directed not against State sovereignty but against its exaggerations.

Reference may be made also in this connection to the Advisory Opinion on *Reservations to the Genocide Convention* in which the Court rejected the argument that the request, on the part of the General Assembly, for an Advisory Opinion was inadmissible as it constituted an interference by the General Assembly in the interpretation of the Convention and that only States which were parties to it were entitled to interpret it or to seek its interpretation. The Court pointed out that as the General Assembly had taken the initiative in drawing up the Convention and as, by virtue of its provisions, it had been associated with it in various ways " there can be no doubt that the precise determination of the conditions for participation in the Convention constitutes a permanent interest of direct concern to the United Nations which has not disappeared with the entry into force of the Convention." [42] It is also arguable that in so far as the Advisory Opinion in the *Injuries* case [43] gave, by reference to the Charter, an international right of action to the United Nations, it conferred to that extent a right upon a " third party "—for the United Nations was not a party to the Charter.

### 97. *State Sovereignty and Imposition of Treaty Obligations upon Third States*

While the conferment of legal benefits of treaties upon States which are not parties thereto raises indirectly the problem of State sovereignty—on account both of the corresponding imposition of burdens upon the actual parties and of the implied phenomenon of international legislation—the creation of obligations binding upon third States raises the issue of sovereignty directly and drastically. Obviously, this is a process which is of the essence of international

---

[41] But see, for a different point of view, Rousseau, *Principes généraux du droit international public*, vol. 1 (1944), pp. 452–457. The learned writer does not claim that his views on the admissibility of *pacta in favorem tertii* are, *de lege lata*, in full accordance with international practice.

[42] *I.C.J. Reports* 1951, p. 20.

[43] See above, p. 179, and below, p. 311.

legislation; it is synonymous with it. To that extent, in so far as some pronouncements of the Court amount to recognition of international legislation [44] they have a direct bearing upon the assessment of the attitude of the Court to the sovereignty of States inasmuch as they can be interpreted as imposing duties upon States which are not parties to the instruments in question. The Advisory Opinion of the Court on *Reparation for Injuries Suffered in the Service of the United Nations* provides an interesting example, within a limited sphere, of the recognition of international legislation imposing, in legal effect, obligations upon States which are not parties to the treaty in question. In that Opinion the Court held, *inter alia*, that the Charter conferred upon the United Nations an international right of action also in relation to non-member States. It is convenient to reproduce here the relevant passage, bearing upon a subject discussed elsewhere in this book,[45] of the Opinion of the Court: " On this point, the Court's opinion is that fifty States, representing the vast majority of the members of the international community, had the power, in conformity with international law, to bring into being an entity possessing objective international personality, and not merely personality recognised by them alone, together with capacity to bring international claims." [46] The meaning of this passage is that the Charter has imposed upon non-member States the legal obligation to recognise the international personality, and the consequences following therefrom, of the United Nations. The power to impose that obligation was " in conformity with international law." The Court answered in the negative the question whether " the defendant State, not being a member, is justified in raising the objection that the Organisation lacks the capacity to bring an international claim." [47]

It cannot be the object of this chapter to inquire into the bearing of the Opinion of the Court upon the question raised by Article 2 (6) of the Charter of the United Nations which lays down that " the Organisation shall [48] ensure that States which are not Members of the United Nations act in accordance with these Principles so far as may be necessary for the maintenance of

[44] See above, pp. 180 *et seq.*
[45] See above, pp. 176 *et seq.*
[46] *I.C.J. Reports* 1949, p. 185.
[47] *Ibid.*
[48] The text of the Dumbarton Oaks Proposals was less peremptory. It used the expression " *should* ensure."

international peace and security "—a provision which seems to confer upon the United Nations a right of intervention in relation to non-member States. What is relevant is that, in the view of the Court, non-member States are not legally entitled to challenge, on the sole ground that the United Nations has no international *locus standi*, the jurisdiction of an international tribunal—other than the Court itself—in respect of a claim by the United Nations.[49] They are obliged to entertain the claim on its merits, though—like the Members of the United Nations—they are not, in the absence of previous commitment to the contrary, bound in this respect by any specific duty of obligatory arbitral or judicial settlement. Nevertheless, however attenuated may be the practical effect of the pronouncement of the Court on the subject, having regard to the general absence of compulsory jurisdiction and the Statute of the Court itself, its general effect is to impose a measure of legal obligation upon States which are not members of the United Nations. This is the reason why, although it may be possible to adduce some, probably controversial, international precedents reminiscent of a similar result,[50] the Opinion of the Court in the *Reparation for Injuries* case—drastically affecting, as it does, the traditional right of the sovereign State to freedom from regulation and obligation except with its consent—has been discussed as an instance of judicial legislation.[51]

On the other hand—the subject may be mentioned for the sake of completeness—there was no element, in the sense here considered, of imposition of obligations upon third parties in the Advisory Opinions in which the Court was concerned with the limitations upon the sovereignty of Danzig in virtue of the Treaty

---

[49] The wording of Art. 36 of the Statute of the Court does not envisage the United Nations as a party to contentious proceedings before the Court.

[50] These might include cases, such as the Opinion of Jurists in the case of the *Aaland Islands* (see above, p. 182), in which, however, the obligation of the third State follows normally from the principles of State succession rather than from the legislative character of the instrument construed as international settlement. This may also be the case, though not to the same extent, with regard to obligations relating to freedom of communications. See, *e.g.*, the view expressed in 1850 by the King's Advocate to the effect that the Governments of Rome and Modena, although not parties to the Treaty of Vienna, were bound to permit navigation on the River Po: Smith, *Great Britain and the Law of Nations*, vol. II (1935), pp. 356–358.

[51] See above, p. 176. The Dissenting Opinion of Judge Krylov put that aspect of the matter with all requisite clarity. He said: " It is true that non-member States cannot fail to recognise the existence of the United Nations as an objective fact. But, in order that they may be bound by a legal obligation to the Organisation, it is necessary that the latter should conclude a special agreement with these States " (at p. 219).

of Versailles, to which Danzig was not a party. In the Advisory Opinion on the *Free City of Danzig and the International Labour Organisation* [52] the Court held that the true source of the rights of Poland as the Protecting Power—and the corresponding obligations of Danzig—lay not so much in the special Treaty of 1920 concluded between the two States as in the Treaty of Versailles. The Court held that in so far as the rights of Poland involved a limitation upon the independence of Danzig "they constitute organic limitations which are an essential feature of its political structure." [53] Probably when the very existence of a new State is due to an international instrument, that State in accepting the rights ensuing therefrom must be deemed to have consented to any limitations of sovereignty provided therein. This would also appear to be the burden of the relevant portions of the Advisory Opinion on the *Treatment of Polish Nationals in Danzig.* [54]

### 98. *Sovereignty and Reservations to Treaties*

In giving its Advisory Opinion on the *Reservations to the Genocide Convention* the Court was confronted with the assertion that, by virtue of its sovereignty, a State is entitled to become a party to a convention regardless of any reservations it may wish to append. The Court had no difficulty in rejecting that view. It said: "It is obvious that so extreme an application of the idea of State sovereignty could lead to a complete disregard of the object and purpose of the Convention." [55] It could have added that any such application of the notion of sovereignty would run counter to the sovereignty of the other contracting parties compelled to enter into a treaty relationship with States whose participation in the treaty they may consider wholly deceptive and amounting to an abuse of the treaty-making power. [56]

[52] Series B, No. 18 (1930).  [53] At p. 11.

[54] Series A/B, No. 44 (1932), p. 31—where the Court, while holding that Danzig had "in a sense" accepted Art. 104 of the Treaty of Versailles by having accepted the Convention which the Allied and Associated Powers had concluded in pursuance thereof, held also that the provisions in question were binding upon Danzig by virtue of a specific Treaty between her and Poland. At the same time the Court considered that the Treaty of Versailles could be resorted to for the purpose of elucidating the meaning of the Treaty between Danzig and Poland (at p. 32). A substantial majority of the Judges held that the Treaty of Versailles was directly applicable.

[55] *I.C.J. Reports* 1951, p. 24.

[56] See the writer's observations on the subject in *Transactions of the Grotius Society*, 39 (1953), pp. 103–108, and in his Report on the Law of Treaties (Documents of the International Law Commission, A/CN.4/63 (1953), pp. 107–127).

# Chapter 22

# STATE RESPONSIBILITY AND THE CLAIMS OF SOVEREIGNTY

## 99. *The Plea of Non-Discrimination*

In the sphere of State responsibility the jurisprudence of the Court has assisted—indirectly, but emphatically—in discouraging a view closely connected with an extreme assertion of sovereignty, namely, that a State incurs no international responsibility if, with regard to measures adopted by it, it treats aliens and nationals alike. The Court has repeatedly laid down that the so-called plea of non-discrimination is not a valid defence against a charge of violation of international law. This the Court has done in the numerous cases, referred to elsewhere in this book,[1] in which it affirmed the principle that equality of treatment must be an equality of both fact and law, and that a State cannot avoid its obligations by the device of framing its law in general terms equally applicable to all. However, the jurisprudence of the Court goes further than that. A measure, even if genuinely applicable both to nationals and to aliens, does not, for that reason, become lawful if it is otherwise prohibited by treaty. After finding, in the case of *Certain German Interests in Polish Upper Silesia*, that expropriation without indemnity was contrary to the Convention between Poland and Germany, the Court held expressly that " a measure prohibited by the Convention cannot become lawful under this instrument by reason of the fact that the State applies it to its own nationals."[2]  It invoked that principle once more in its Judgment in the *Peter Pázmány University* case.[3]  Previously, in the Advisory Opinion on *German Settlers in Poland*, the Court considered as irrelevant the fact that in a few instances the Polish law in question applied also to non-German Polish nationals who took as purchasers from original holders of German race.[4]

It is legitimate to assume that these principles apply not only to international obligations established by treaty but also to customary

---

[1] See above, pp. 257 *et seq*.
[3] Series A/B, No. 61 (1933), p. 243.
[2] Series A, No. 7 (1926), p. 33.
[4] Series B, No. 6 (1923), p. 24.

international law. The plea of non-discrimination as a defence against a charge of violation of international law amounts, upon analysis, to a claim of the sovereign State to disregard international law and to erect its own law as the sole standard of the legitimacy of its action so long as such action is of general application. That claim the Court has declined to countenance. The attitude of the Court on the subject is fully in accordance with its repeated affirmation, as a matter of course, of the priority of the obligations of international law over municipal law.[5] It did so in particular by refusing to permit the parties to plead their municipal law as a justification for non-compliance with an international obligation; that, in the words of the Court, " would amount to relying upon the non-fulfilment of an obligation imposed . . . by an international agreement." [6]

### 100. *Measure of Damages*

In connection with State responsibility it is of interest to note the attitude of the Court to the question of the measure of damages due as compensation for a breach of an international obligation. In the international sphere the principle established in general jurisprudence to the effect that damages must, as a rule, include full restitution *in integrum* did not at first secure ready acceptance by writers. It was asserted that the responsibility of States must be limited to damages arising directly out of the injurious event, to the exclusion of all indirect and consequential damages. This was, to some extent, in accordance with certain tendencies in national law —now in process of disappearing in countries under the rule of law—to limit both the amenability of the State to suit and the consequences of its liability. While discouraging the award of purely speculative and remotely consequential damages, international jurisprudence has not, in general, accepted these assertions.[7]

---

[5] See the Advisory Opinion in the case of the *Greco-Bulgarian Communities*, Series B, No. 17 (1930), p. 32; in the *Free Zones* case, Series A/B, No. 46 (1932), p. 167; in the Advisory Opinion on the *Treatment of Polish Nationals in Danzig*, Series A/B, No. 44 (1932), p. 24; in *The Wimbledon* case, Series A, No. 1 (1923), p. 29; in the case concerning *Certain German Interests in Polish Upper Silesia*, Series A, No. 7 (1926), p. 19; and in the *Chorzów Factory (Merits)* case, Series A, No. 17 (1928), pp. 33, 34.

[6] Advisory Opinion on the *Jurisdiction of the Courts of Danzig*, Series B, No. 15 (1928), p. 27.

[7] For a survey of the literature and practice see Lauterpacht, *Private Law Sources and Analogies of International Law* (1927), pp. 219–221, 270–273; Reitzer, *La réparation comme conséquence de l'acte illicite en droit international* (1938), pp. 158–197.

The suggestion of a general limitation of the responsibility of States in this matter was rejected by the Court in the Judgment in the case concerning the *Chorzów Factory*. The Court declined to agree that the compensation due to the German Government was limited to the value of the undertaking at the moment of dispossession, plus interest to the day of payment. The Court distinguished between expropriation which was lawful but for the fact of the State having failed to pay the just price of the property taken—in which case the compensation might properly be limited to the value of the undertaking at the time of the dispossession—and expropriation which had been resorted to in violation of an international undertaking. In the latter case, the Court said, the reparation " must, so far as possible, wipe out all the consequences of the illegal act and re-establish the situation which would, in all probability, have existed if that act had not been committed." [8] The Court laid down in detail the principles governing compensation in these cases: " Restitution in kind, or, if this is not possible, payment of a sum corresponding to the value which a restitution in kind would bear; the award, if need be, of damages for loss sustained which cannot be covered by restitution in kind or payment in place of it." The Court then proceeded to assess compensation for losses in a manner which might have caused a less authoritative tribunal some apprehension lest it be charged with awarding damages for speculative profits. [9]

## 101. *State Responsibility in Relation to Action in Self-Preservation and Intervention*

The right of the sovereign State when acting, or pretending to act, in self-preservation has been variously described either as a fundamental right of States or, inasmuch as it implies the uncontrolled claim of a State to attack the sovereign rights of another State, as a grave challenge to the authority of international law. In the *Corfu Channel* case, in a part of the Judgment which was unanimous, the Court rejected the claim of the United Kingdom that in entering the Corfu Channel, against the express wish of the

---

[8] Series A, No. 17 (1928), p. 47.

[9] See on this matter the Dissenting Opinion of Lord Finlay, *ibid.*, p. 73. In the *Corfu Channel* case the Court, in addition to awarding compensation for the loss of and damage to the British destroyers, also awarded a sum representing the cost of pensions and other grants made by the Government of the United Kingdom to the victims of the explosions and their dependants: *I.C.J. Reports* 1949, p. 249.

Albanian Government, for the purpose of effecting a mine-sweeping operation, she acted legitimately in the exercise of the right of self-preservation or self-help. Although it found that there existed extenuating circumstances for the action of the United Kingdom, such as the failure of Albania to carry out her duties after the explosions in the Channel, it formally declared that the action of the British Navy constituted a violation of Albanian sovereignty.[10] It said: "Between independent States, respect for territorial sovereignty is an essential foundation of international relations." [11]

In this connection, in so far as the United Kingdom described her action in entering the Channel as an act of intervention for the purpose of securing evidence in Albanian territory, the Court seems to have rejected the right of intervention in general and emphatic terms which, unqualified as they were, may have created the impression of an innovation. The Court said: "The Court can only regard the alleged right of intervention as the manifestation of a policy of force, such as has, in the past, given rise to most serious abuses and such as cannot, whatever be the present defects in international organisation, find a place in international law. Intervention is perhaps still less admissible in the particular form it would take here; for, from the nature of things, it would be reserved for the most powerful States, and might easily lead to perverting the administration of international justice itself." [12] It is probable that these observations, so comprehensive in scope, were limited to the particular circumstances of the case before the Court. There is in general international law no absolute prohibition of intervention; traditional international law permits intervention in a number of cases. It is possible—and perhaps probable—that inasmuch as intervention takes the form of physical force it is, by virtue of Article 2 (4) of the Charter of the United Nations, no longer open to its Members. However that may be, the Judgment of the Court amounts to an outspoken restriction of the sovereignty of States as traditionally interpreted and as implying the right of intervention. Obviously, it indirectly affirms at the same time the right of sovereign States to immunity from intervention on the part of other States. To that extent it protects sovereignty. However, the right thus protected is the right of independence rather than that of

---

[10] *I.C.J. Reports* 1949, p. 35.
[11] *Ibid.*
[12] *Ibid.*

sovereignty which in traditional, and largely obsolete, international law implied the right of intervention.

It may be noted in this context that in the *Asylum* case the disapproval, on the part of the Court, of the right of intervention went to the length of the proposition that the grant of asylum in an embassy constitutes, inasmuch as it withdraws the offender from the jurisdiction of the territorial State, " an intervention in matters which are exclusively within the competence of that State " and that " such a derogation from territorial sovereignty cannot be recognised unless its legal basis is established in each particular case." [13]　In so far as sovereignty is invoked in support of the right of self-preservation it is of interest to note the manner in which the Court rejected the plea of *force majeure* put forward by Brazil and Yugoslavia, respectively, in the two *Gold Clause* cases concerning the payment of loans contracted in France.[14]　The Court refused to admit that the World War and its grave economic consequences affected the legal obligations between the debtor States and the bondholders.　Although the Court envisaged that consideration might be given, at a subsequent stage and before appropriate arbitral organs, to the equities of the case, it held that the economic disturbances caused by the war did not release the debtor States from their obligations.　It is of interest, in this connection, that in the *Oscar Chinn* case the Court preferred to base its decision on the interpretation of the relevant treaties rather than on any right of Belgium to depart from their provisions on account of the exceptional conditions of the economic depression which caused the Belgian authorities to grant, in effect, privileged treatment to the navigation company under its control.[15]　This aspect of the question was referred to in outspoken terms by Judge Anzilotti in his Dissenting Opinion, in which he denied the absolute right of the State to invoke public interest in a manner amounting to an evasion of its international obligations.[16]

---

[13] *I.C.J. Reports* 1950, p. 275.
[14] Series A, Nos. 20 and 21 (1929), pp. 39 and 120, respectively.
[15] See above, p. 263.
[16] Series A/B, No. 63 (1934), p. 112.

# Chapter 23

# WIDER ASPECTS OF SOVEREIGNTY

## 102. *State Succession*

It is not necessarily in the direct answers given by the Court to reliance upon the rights of State sovereignty that we have to look for expressions of the Court's attitude on the matter. That attitude often reveals itself in an indirect fashion. Of this, the contribution of the Court to the law of State succession supplies a significant example. The relation between State sovereignty and the doctrine of State succession appears, on the face of it, to be remote. However, this is so only as a matter of appearance. One of the manifestations of absolute State sovereignty in traditional international law was the right of one State to destroy another as the consequence of a successful war or, alternatively, to annex parts of its territory or to obtain the same result by a formally voluntary act of cession. The right of conquest was thus recognised. But was it recognised absolutely, or subject to compliance with certain obligations, in particular the obligation to respect acquired rights of private persons? To put the question in a more general form: Are the questions arising out of changes of territorial sovereignty decided exclusively by the unfettered will of the State acquiring the territory, or are they regulated by international law? For the question of State succession is not limited to acquisition or transfer of territory as the result of conquest. It applies also to cases of voluntary cession of territory.

The problem is essentially the same in all cases of change of sovereignty: Is the new sovereign entitled to extinguish private rights, or are these protected by international law? The principle that private property must be respected has been frequently recognised. In *United States* v. *Percheman* Chief Justice Marshall gave eloquent expression to that principle: " The modern usage of nations, which has become law, would be violated; that sense of justice and of right which is acknowledged and felt by the whole civilised world would be outraged, if private property should be generally confiscated, and private rights annulled." [1]   However, that recognition of the principle of respect for private rights was, although emphatic, somewhat vague and, with regard to various aspects of private rights, frequently contested.   At the time when the Permanent Court of International Justice was called upon to pronounce upon questions of State succession there was no generally admitted rule of international law on the subject.   There was, in particular, no general recognition of the rule that private rights arising out of a contract with the predecessor State, concessions granted by it, and its public debt, must be respected.   Even among the adherents of the view asserting positive obligations on the part of the new sovereign, there was a tendency to assume that there can be no question of recognition of private rights when such recognition might conflict with requirements of public policy and reason of State of the successor.

In view of this, the Sixth Advisory Opinion in the case of *German Settlers in Poland* not only provided a contribution to the law of State succession but also, indirectly, a pronouncement closely affecting a cherished aspect of State sovereignty.   For the rights which were at issue in that Opinion were not ordinary property rights; they were property rights of a highly political origin.   They were contracts concluded in pursuance of the policy followed by the Prussian Government before the First World War and aiming at eradicating the Polish element in ancient Polish provinces.   These contracts—some of which were transformed after the Armistice, in apparent anticipation of impending cession of territory, into full property rights or contracts approaching property rights—the Polish Government was called upon to recognise.   Before the Court, Counsel for Poland, in explaining the inability of the Polish Government to recognise the contracts in question, put the matter with considerable, almost excessive, restraint.   He said: " The former possessors of Polish provinces had not always during more than a century governed and administered these provinces in a spirit that could be called favourable to the natural development of the populations concerned." [2]   If ever there was a case for treating as relevant the political origin of private rights, this was one.   The Court refused to do so.   It admitted that the Polish measures " may be comprehensible," but it regarded them as contrary to the rules of

---

[1] *7 Peters' Reports*, 51, 86, 88.
[2] Series C, No. 3, vol. I, p. 488.

international law in the matter of State succession. " Private rights acquired under existing law do not cease on a change of sovereignty." [3] The contrary contention, said the Court, would conflict with an almost universal opinion and practice. " Even those who contest the existence in international law of a general principle of State succession do not go so far as to maintain that private rights including those acquired from the State as the owner of the property are invalid as against a successor in sovereignty." [4] But was not the origin of these contracts, intended to deal a mortal blow to the Polish element in these provinces, such as to call for a departure from the general principle of State succession? The Court was not of this opinion. " The fact that there was a political purpose behind the colonisation scheme cannot affect the private rights acquired under the law." [5] Seldom had national sentiment and " reason of State " been subjected in such uncompromising manner to a principle of international law—on a subject, it may be added, in which that rule itself was and still is controversial. [6]

The Court has affirmed that general principle also in other cases. In the Judgment concerning *Certain German Interests in Polish Upper Silesia* it repeatedly gave expression to the duty of respect for private rights as forming part of generally accepted international law. [7] In the *Mavrommatis Palestine Concessions* case it assumed, as a matter of course, that Great Britain was bound to recognise the Jaffa concessions by virtue of " a general principle of international law, *i.e.*, the general principle of subrogation." [8] The Court said: " The Administration of Palestine would be bound to recognise the Jaffa concessions, not in consequence of an obligation undertaken by the Mandatory, but in virtue of a general principle of international law to the application of which the obligations entered

[3] Series B, No. 6 (1923), p. 36.
[4] *Ibid.*, p. 36.
[5] *Ibid.*, p. 33. And see to the same effect p. 39.
[6] The importance of that aspect of the Opinion, in relation to private rights of political origin, is not seriously affected by the circumstance that it was treated by the Court with some brevity. The political origin of the contracts in question constituted the crucial and distinctive feature of the case. The question of respect for private rights of political origin, in particular with respect to odious debts " hostile to the interests of the territory " (see Hyde, *International Law* (2nd ed., 1945), vol. I, p. 404), had been previously the subject of much controversy in international practice and in the literature of international law.
[7] Series A, No. 7 (1926), pp. 22, 23, 41, 42.
[8] Series A, No. 2 (1924), p. 28.

into by the Mandatory created no exception." [9] The existence of that general principle of subrogation in the matter of concessions has frequently been denied by English courts. [10] In fact, it appears that after the First World War British authorities in Palestine declined to act upon it in relation to British subjects [11]—although it would be of some interest to speculate as to the extent to which English courts, which apply international law as part of the law of the land, would be disposed to give effect to the principles affirmed by the International Court in relation to British subjects enjoying no diplomatic protection on the part of foreign States. While it is clear that acquired private rights must be subject to the general legislation of the successor State, the jurisprudence of the Court in the matter has contributed substantially to a restriction of the otherwise unlimited sovereignty of the successor State in respect of interference with private rights on account of the sole fact of a change of territorial sovereignty.

## 103. *Divisibility of Sovereignty*

A number of cases decided by the Court are instructive not so much as pointing to a restrictive interpretation of rights of sovereignty as, in affirming its divisibility and capacity for modification, in denying to it any rigid quality of absoluteness. Thus the Advisory Opinion on the *International Status of South-West Africa* is not only of interest as an affirmation of the doctrine of international status and international settlement—a species of judicial legislation which has an indirect bearing on the matter of sovereignty. [12] It is directly germane to the issue here discussed in as much as it lays down in emphatic language that " the creation of this new international institution did not involve any cession of territory or transfer of sovereignty to the Union of South Africa." [13] The power of the Union Government was no more than " to

[9] Series A, No. 2 (1924), p. 28.
[10] See *West Rand Central Gold Mining Co., Ltd.* v. *The King* [1905] 2 K.B. 391; *Vereeniging Municipality* v. *Vereeniging Estates, Ltd., Annual Digest,* 1919–1922, Case No. 33; *Shingler* v. *Union Government, ibid.,* 1925–1926, Case No. 50. And see O'Connell in *British Year Book of International Law,* 27 (1951), pp. 92–124, for a survey and criticism of British practice on the subject. Two years after the Sixth Advisory Opinion was given, the arbitrator in the *Ottoman Debt Arbitration (Sentence Arbitrale,* p. 62) declared that notwithstanding the existing precedents there was no rule of international law according to which a State acquiring territory by cession is bound to take over the corresponding part of the public debt.
[11] See O'Connell, *op. cit.,* p. 113.
[12] See above, p. 181.
[13] *I.C.J* Reports 1950, p. 132.

exercise an international function of administration on behalf of the League, with the object of promoting the well-being and development of the inhabitants." The Opinion is of importance not only so far as it denies the sovereignty of the Mandatory. It is significant in as much as it separates from formal sovereignty the otherwise complete authority of the Mandatory. The result—in accordance with what is the essence of the system of mandates and trusteeship—is to stress the functional divisibility of sovereignty and, thus, the absence from it, notwithstanding doctrinal logic, of any rigid element of absoluteness.

This is also, in a different sphere, the incidental result of the Judgment of the Court in the case of the *Lighthouses in Crete and Samos*.[14] The true issue in that case was whether the very wide measure of autonomy granted by the Sultan of Turkey to those islands produced the consequence of " detaching " them, in law, from Turkish sovereignty, with the result that concessions granted by the Sultan of Turkey in respect of the islands were not properly granted. To put it differently, the issue was, once more, that of the divisibility of sovereignty, of the severability of its contents, of its capacity to modification to the point, as in the case of mandated territories, of separation of the exercise of sovereignty from the formal possession thereof. The Court answered that question in the affirmative: " Even though the Sultan had been obliged to accept important restrictions on the exercise of his rights of sovereignty in Crete, that sovereignty had not ceased to belong to him, however it might be qualified from a juridical point of view." [15] In thus attaching importance to what, in all appearance, may have been no more than a nominal sovereignty of Turkey, the Court was not adopting a purely formal method of approach—although this seems to have been the view of Judge Hudson, who, in a Dissenting Opinion, subjected to trenchant criticism this aspect of the Judgment. He said: " If it can be said that a theoretical sovereignty remained in the Sultan after 1899, it was a sovereignty shorn of the last vestige of power. He could neither terminate nor modify the autonomy with which Crete had been endowed against his will. . . . A juristic conception must not be stretched to the breaking-point, and a ghost of hollow sovereignty cannot be permitted to obscure the realities of this situation." [16]

[14] Series A/B, No. 71 (1937).    [15] At p. 103.
[16] At p. 127.

However, it is believed that the recognition by the Court of such situations, involving as they do the separation of some functions and attributes of sovereignty from others, is bound, apart from affirming the relative nature of sovereignty, to be beneficial for the development of international law and the peaceful adjustment of territorial and political problems. Unless autonomy and delegated exercise of sovereignty are made distinguishable both in fact and in law from outright cession of territory, it may be difficult to secure for them the place to which they are entitled as an international institution rendering possible territorial arrangements and adjustments short of cession. The convenience of a rigid dichotomy of full sovereignty and the entire absence thereof is probably deceptive.

The Judgment of the Court in the case of the *Interpretation of the Statute of the Memel Territory* follows, from a different angle, the same line of thought. There, too, the Court was confronted with a situation following upon the separation of the Lithuanian sovereignty over the Memel Territory from the exercise of that sovereignty by the Directorate and Chamber of Representatives of the Territory in pursuance of the Convention of Paris of 1924 which conferred a very wide degree of autonomy upon the Territory. The Court held that the Lithuanian Governor was entitled to dismiss the President of the Directorate, even if supported by the Chamber, in case of acts of a serious character which violated the Convention of Paris and which were calculated to prejudice the sovereignty of Lithuania.[17] It adopted the view that while Lithuania was to enjoy full sovereignty over the Territory, subject to limitations imposed on its exercise, the autonomy of the Memel Territory was to operate only within the limits fixed and expressly specified in the Statute and the Convention: " Both the autonomy as defined and the sovereignty were intended to be effective." [18]  The similarity between the essential aspects of the *Memel Territory* and *Lighthouses* cases is striking. On the face of it these decisions seem to belong to the category not of a restrictive but of an extensive interpretation of sovereign rights. Both uphold the reality of what a superficially realistic interpretation might consider as the purely residuary and nominal rights of sovereignty. Actually the true import of both decisions is that sovereignty is not in the nature of an absolute and rigid category, but that, being no more than a

[17] Series A/B, No. 49 (1932), pp. 313, 317.
[18] At p. 317. See above, p. 234.

bundle of rights, it is capable of division and separation in a manner permitting a real measure of competence on the part both of the residuary sovereign and of the authority charged with its total or partial exercise.

## 104. *The Sovereignty of the General Assembly of the United Nations*

The Advisory Opinion of the Court on the *Effect of Awards of Compensation made by the United Nations Administrative Tribunal* is of considerable interest—although the connection is not immediately apparent—on the question of its attitude to some of the wider aspects of sovereignty. In that Opinion the Court held that the General Assembly " has not the right on any grounds to refuse to give effect to an award of compensation made by the Administrative Tribunal of the United Nations in favour of a staff member of the United Nations whose contract of service has been terminated without his assent." [19] On the face of it there may seem to be no clear connection between the Opinion, thus phrased, and the more general question of claims of sovereignty as surveyed in this chapter. For the Opinion was based largely on more specific considerations such as that the Administrative Tribunal of the United Nations was a judicial tribunal; that according to general principles of law a judgment rendered by a judicial body is *res judicata* and has binding force between the parties to the dispute; that, as the preparatory work showed, the omission, in the Statute of the Administrative Tribunal, of the remedy of appeal was deliberate; and that the General Assembly had the power to establish a Tribunal competent to render decisions, binding upon the General Assembly itself, without any accompanying right of appeal. However, the Court did not attempt to avoid an answer to the wider question whether there was any legal limit to the alleged absolute power of the General Assembly to approve or disapprove the expenditure of the Organisation as proposed to it. It denied that that power was of an absolute nature: " For some part of that expenditure arises out of obligations already incurred by the Organisation, and to this extent the General Assembly has no alternative but to honour these engagements." [20] These obligations, in the view of the Court,

[19] *I.C.J. Reports* 1954, at p. 62.
[20] At p. 59.

comprised awards of compensation made by the Administrative Tribunal in favour of staff members—awards which were *res judicata* and which the Court considered legally binding upon the General Assembly.

It is clear—although perhaps more precise language to that effect could have been used—that in stating that " the General Assembly has no alternative but to honour these obligations," the Court was referring to a compulsion which is of a legal and not of a moral or political nature. In fact the Court proceeded to hold expressly that the assignment of the budgeting function to the General Assembly could not be regarded as conferring upon it the right to refuse to give effect to an obligation arising out of an award of the Administrative Tribunal. The implications of the Opinion of the Court, thus formulated, in relation to the subject here discussed are far-reaching. While, obviously, the General Assembly is neither the sovereign nor the legislative organ of the international community, it is the common and probably the highest organ of the sovereign States organised in the United Nations. It is, in a distinct sense, the repository of such ultimate authority as there exists in organised international society. The Opinion of the Court affirms that that ultimate authority is itself bound by law—in the particular case by the law as laid down by a judicial tribunal created by it; such sovereignty as that ultimate authority possesses is limited by law. Possibly there was an element of simplification in the observation of the Court that " it is common practice in national legislatures to create courts with the capacity to render decisions legally binding on the legislatures which brought them into being." [21] For, normally, there is no limit to the power of the sovereign legislature to alter existing legal rights—whether established by statute or judicial decision—although in some countries such power may be limited by virtue of the provisions of the Constitution safeguarded by the power of courts to declare unconstitutional legislation inconsistent with the Constitution.[22]

The Court apparently realised the potentially far-reaching

---

[21] *I.C.J. Reports* 1954, p. 61.

[22] But see the Statement of the Netherlands Government in *Pleadings, Oral Arguments, Documents*, p. 106. The Statement quotes an observation of the New Zealand representative to the effect that it would be " a most grave decision for Parliament " to use its powers of retroactive legislation to deprive individuals of the benefits of judgments given in their favour. That observation does not in fact deny the legal power of Parliament to act in that way.

consequences of a ruling denying the General Assembly the power to refuse *on any grounds* to comply with the awards of the Administrative Tribunal. In a somewhat hesitating part of the Opinion it set out to intimate that the words " on any grounds " could not have had reference, in the intention of the General Assembly, to awards vitiated by absence of jurisdiction or other defects having the same effect.[23] However, it appears that in the view of the Court the General Assembly had no remedy with regard to awards already made and that the only remedy available to it was in relation to future cases—a remedy consisting in amending the Statute of the Administrative Tribunal so as to provide for redress in cases of this nature. In giving the Opinion the Court was clearly aware of the more general significance of the issue involved—namely, the question whether the General Assembly of the sovereign States comprising the United Nations is rigidly bound by the law as ascertained by a judicial tribunal established by it. This question the Court answered in a clear affirmative. It was not prepared to grant to the sovereignty of States when acting jointly a degree of latitude which, as shown in this Part, it was not disposed, on many occasions, to concede to sovereign States acting in their own interest. These wider aspects of the issue before the Court loomed large in the written and oral proceedings —although the Court preferred not to examine all of them in detail.[24]

It is of some interest to speculate to what extent the effect of the Opinion, thus interpreted, would have been impaired if at the end of its operative part as quoted above the Court would have added: " unless, if so held in an Advisory Opinion of the Court specially requested for that purpose, the award is vitiated by excess of jurisdiction or other ground of nullity." [25] For there may be room for the view that nullity, when properly ascertained by a judicial tribunal, as distinguished from a party to the dispute, cannot be

---

[23] *I.C.J. Reports* 1954, at p. 55. The Court pointed out that if the General Assembly had intended the expression " on any grounds " to cover awards made in excess of jurisdiction or vitiated by other faults, then " there would arise a problem which calls for some general observations " (p. 55). The Opinion does not in fact contain such general observations—except one stating that these contingencies can properly be covered only by an amendment of the Statute of the Tribunal providing for appropriate remedies.

[24] See above, p. 276.

[25] See, to a similar effect, the Statute of the Administrative Tribunal of the International Labour Organisation as commented upon in the Statement of the Organisation before the Court: *Pleadings, Oral Arguments, Documents*, p. 73.

disregarded except at the risk of grave injury to the authority of the law; that some such view must be considered as implied in every instrument creating an arbitral tribunal; and that the clear intention to dispense with the remedy of appeal does not necessarily cover the setting aside of an award on account of nullity, when judicially ascertained.[26]

From this point of view it was open to the Court, if it had been minded to render its Opinion more complete, to hold that while the awards thus given were binding upon the General Assembly in the meaning that that organ could not set them aside, it was entitled to challenge their validity by way of a decision other than its own, in particular by way of a decision of its highest judicial organ, that is to say, of the International Court of Justice itself.  A pronouncement thus formulated would probably not have been outside the question put to the Court by the General Assembly, which question was whether the General Assembly has the right on any grounds to refuse to give effect to an award of compensation made by the Administrative Tribunal in favour of a staff member of the United Nations.  It is in accordance with sound jurisprudential considerations as well as with the pronouncements of the Court itself that in framing the answer to the question put before it it is not hidebound by the formulation adopted by the parties.[27]  On the other hand, it is possible that any such extension, on the part of the Court, of the scope of its pronouncement might have blurred the significance of its decision on the major issue.  As was pointed out by some dissenting Judges, an award rendered in circumstances which do not provide for the remedy of appeal or revision may be tainted with nullity for a number of reasons, such as excess of jurisdiction or other defect of a fundamental nature.[28]  It is one thing to hold that an award thus given is binding upon the General Assembly in the sense that the latter cannot set it aside.  It is another matter to hold that an award of that nature is absolutely binding, even in face of an obvious ground of nullity, for no other reason than that the instrument under which it was rendered did not provide,

---

[26] But see the Individual Opinion of Judge Winiarski to the effect that the right to refuse to give effect to an award on the ground of nullity is independent of the existence of a procedure for the ascertainment of the alleged nullity (at p. 65). Any such view if accepted would render the legal effect of the Opinion of the Court somewhat theoretical.

[27] See, for instance, Judgment No. 11 (*Interpretation of Judgments Nos. 7 and 8 Concerning the Case of the Factory at Chorzów*), Series A, No. 13 (1927), pp. 15 and 16. And see above, pp. 206 *et seq.*, and 298, n. 3.

[28] See, in particular, the Dissenting Opinion of Judge Hackworth, at pp. 89–91.

accidentally or by design, for a remedy on account of nullity. The existence of the highest judicial organ of the organised international community makes it possible to find a solution to some otherwise insoluble aspects of nullity of arbitral awards, *e.g.*, on account of excess of jurisdiction. Thus it is axiomatic that a tribunal is inherently competent to determine the extent of its jurisdiction; it is equally axiomatic that an award rendered in excess of the jurisdiction conferred upon the tribunal is null and void. In the absence of an appropriate judicial organ to make a finding on an allegation, made by one party, of excess of jurisdiction, the problem thus arising is insoluble. On the other hand, the existence of an organ of that nature probably renders illegal a refusal to comply with an award on account of alleged excess of jurisdiction if the party making the allegation is unwilling to agree to a judicial determination of the issue. To that extent it is accurate to hold that there is no nullity unless judicially determined.

However, the incompleteness, if any, of the Opinion in this respect is, it is believed, compensated by the emphatic affirmation of a binding legal award as against every possible attempt at legislative justice by way of action by the General Assembly setting aside awards binding upon it [29]—legislative action with all its dangers of partisanship, political prejudice, and uncertainty. Thus conceived, the Opinion is an affirmation of the principle of legality rising sovereign over the sovereign States assembled in the General Assembly.

[29] As to which see the interesting observations of Dean Pound, *Justice According to Law* (1951), pp. 65–70.

# CHAPTER 24

## CONCLUSIONS

*105. The Basis of Judicial Restraint upon Claims of Sovereignty*

The present Section is devoted to an attempt to survey the attitude of the Court to some of the traditional claims and emanations of sovereignty. In this respect the Court has exhibited an instructive and, from one point of view, uniform tendency. It has done so indirectly in the course of its activity described in Parts 3 and 4 of this book as Judicial Legislation and the Principle of Effectiveness. It has done so, more directly, in the various ways surveyed in this Section, by discouraging undue reliance on restrictive interpretation of treaties; by stressing the obligations of sovereign States in the matter of State succession; by admitting the possibility of treaty rights extending to non-parties; by recognising the propriety of extending the obligations of general treaties to States which are not parties thereto; by rejecting the plea that the application of national legislation to aliens and nationals alike constitutes a sufficient justification for the avoidance of international obligations; by framing the law relating to damages in accordance with general principles and not with the claims of the sovereign State to a more restrictive assessment of the duty of compensation; by denying or confining within narrow limits the traditional claims of the State to full freedom of action in cases of self-preservation, necessity and intervention as well as with regard to reservations to treaties; by treating sovereignty not as an absolute but as functionally and otherwise divisible and separable; and, finally, by subjecting to the rule of law such collective sovereignty of States as is embodied in the General Assembly of the United Nations.

The principal reasons which have shaped this attitude of the Court have been explained at the beginning of this Part. They stem, in the main, from the overriding fact that while the law, in its ultimate result and purpose, protects the freedom—in the international sphere, the sovereignty and independence—of those subject to its sway, it does so at the same time by subjecting them to its restraints and obligations. It is on that account that a survey of the attitude of the Court towards claims of State sovereignty may well be regarded as a fit subject for the concluding Part of this book. It is a theme which runs throughout the entire activity of the Court. We saw it when following the Court in its caution, in its legislative courage, in its practical temper in insisting on the effectiveness of international obligations, and in its treatment of questions directly affecting the traditional claims of sovereignty. It is not surprising that what from one—though only one—point of view appears to be the net result of this encounter between the Court and the claims of sovereign States should have been a check upon some of the assertions put forward in the name of State sovereignty. For the first time in history there has functioned an international judicial institution of acknowledged continuity, able and determined to assess the legal value of some of the traditional pretentions of sovereignty. In the atmosphere of diplomatic negotiations and conferences these claims are high-sounding, uncompromising, clad in the garb of the dignity of States, and occasionally supported by a passage conveniently extracted for the purpose of an *ex parte* argument from the work of an author or even from a judicial decision. On the plane of extra-judicial controversy an assertion by one sovereign State, provided that it is advanced in the plausible form of a legal phrase, is as good as that of another. When in the Advisory Opinion concerning the *Interpretation of Peace Treaties with Bulgaria, Hungary and Romania (First Phase)* the Court stated— a statement which formed an essential part of the Opinion—that " whether there exists an international dispute is a matter for objective determination " and that " the mere denial of the existence of a dispute does not prove its non-existence," [1] it was giving expression to what, but for the fact that the issue was raised by three sovereign States, would have been a platitude. But the fact that it was necessary for the Court to make a trite—and essential—observation of that kind, shows the nature of unilateral assertions advanced in the atmosphere of diplomacy unaided by a system of authoritative judicial determination.[2] Prior to the establishment of the Court there was no agency of comparable status able to reduce to their proper proportions assertions of that nature and

[1] *I.C.J. Reports* 1950, p. 74.
[2] See the Dissenting Opinion of Judge Winiarski for a suggestion of a unilateral right of States to determine, in some cases, the extent of their obligations: at pp. 90, 94, 96.

to show in proper cases by clear and final decisions that they were one-sided and—in essence—contrary to law. The firmness with which the Court applied the " generally accepted principle of international law " [3] according to which the provisions of the municipal law of a State, including its Constitution, cannot prevail over its obligations under conventional or customary international law has been a frequent feature of its activity.

It has been, in a distinct sense, unavoidable that the Court should have acted in that way—unavoidable in the sense that no Court acting in the fulfilment of its judicial duty could have proceeded otherwise. The frequent instances of a critical attitude of the Court towards claims of State sovereignty are not the result of judicial idealism in deference to which the judges allow their view as to what is desirable to prevail at the expense of the existing law. The explanation of this otherwise startling spectacle of claims of State sovereignty being weighed in the balance of the law conceived in its entirety is that once a State has accepted the jurisdiction of the Court, in a given case or generally, the mystical majesty of sovereignty has largely departed from it. It has become a plain party governed by the Statute and the rules of the Court and, above all, by impartially administered rules of international law—a party who may put forward any argument to which he attaches importance, but who can derive no hope from the mere fact that the argument has been advanced by a sovereign State. This may be a new experience, but there is no escape from it once a State has submitted to the jurisdiction of the Court. Such submission means subjection to law with all its generality, comprehensiveness, and impatience of inconsistencies and evasion. From this point of view it has been inevitable that the contrast between unlimited discretion and subjection to law should have been marked so pointedly.

For these reasons there is no room for justifiable apprehension on account of the realisation of the cumulative effect, as here outlined, of the decisions of the Court on matters affecting the sovereignty of States. Undoubtedly, in submitting to the obligatory jurisdiction of the Court a State relinquishes that important part of its sovereignty, as traditionally understood, which gives it the right to remain its own judge in disputes with other States. Undoubtedly,

---

[3] Case of the *Greco-Bulgarian Communities*, Series B, No. 17 (1930), p. 32; *Jurisdiction of the Courts of Danzig*, Series B, No. 15 (1928), pp. 26, 27; *Treatment of Polish Nationals in Danzig*, Series A/B, No. 44 (1932), p. 24. And see above, p. 315, n. 5.

whether such limitation of sovereignty is the result of an undertaking of compulsory judicial settlement or of a voluntary submission in respect of a single case, the State concerned assumes the risks inherent in the uncertainties of judicial decision and judicial discretion within the law. But in so doing it opens the door wide to a corresponding accession to its sovereignty. It acquires the right to a decision of its contested rights on the basis of law as distinguished from a clear and outright denial of a legal remedy or, what is the same, a denial clad in the transparent garb of a legal argument conclusively asserted by the interested State. Moreover, as will be shown in the Section which follows, the curbing of claims of State sovereignty constitutes only one of the two aspects of the attitude of the Court to claims asserted by reference to the sovereignty of States.

## Section B

## Recognition of Claims of Sovereignty

CHAPTER 25

## IN GENERAL

106. *Sovereignty as Part of International Law. Form and Substance. Dignity of Sovereign States*

However significant may be the occasional tendency of the Court, as described in the preceding Section, to keep in check certain claims of State sovereignty, it would be misleading to assert that an account of that tendency gives a complete picture of the jurisprudence of the Court on the subject of sovereignty. For some of the consequences of the sovereignty of States in the international sphere are part of international law. While they are expressive of its weakness as a system of law, they nevertheless form part of it. And while there may be no reason to add to their vitality, it is not open to a judicial tribunal to ignore them or to fail to give them their proper effect. Of these consequences of sovereignty, the principal is—as will be seen—the rule that, unlike within the State, in their mutual relations States are under no obligation to submit their disputes to judicial determination unless they have previously agreed to do so either generally or in relation to a particular case. There are other principles of a similar—though more controversial— nature.[1] Obviously, the fact that sovereignty is in many respects part of international law does not always provide an automatic solution of the difficulty; for specific derogations from sovereignty may also be part of international law. Thus the right of intervention, which is prima facie contrary to the independence and sovereignty of States, has been regarded—within certain limits—as being part of international law. So has, to some extent, the institution of asylum in foreign embassies. It is for this reason that special significance attaches to the pronouncements of the

[1] See above, p. 156.

Court in which it relegated in general terms the right of intervention to the category of violations of international law [2] and in which
it assimilated the granting of asylum in legations to an exercise of
the right of intervention [3] involving a derogation from the sovereignty of the territorial State—a derogation which "cannot be
recognised unless its legal basis is established in each particular
case." These cases show that the Court has occasionally tended to
give a restrictive interpretation to those rules of international law
which in turn constitute a limitation upon the sovereignty of States.

On the other hand, on occasions the respect shown by the Court
for the sovereignty and the dignity of States has been concerned
with form rather than with substance. We have noted the frequent
cases in which the Court, while departing from the orthodox path
congenial to the sovereignty of States and its emanations, has
substantially modified the impact of its decisions by reducing the
application of the traditional view to cases of doubt or by making it
dependent upon the clearly expressed intention of the parties.[4] The
inclination to treat sovereign States with due consideration for their
dignity has also evidenced itself in matters of minor importance.
Thus, in the cases of *The Wimbledon* and the *Chorzów Factory* the
Court refused to award interim interest at a higher rate in the event
of the Judgment not being acted upon within the period fixed by the
Court: "The Court neither can nor should contemplate such a
contingency." [5]

For the same reason the Court has occasionally shown restraint
in imputing responsibility to States or in awarding damages to
them. In the case of *The Lotus* it held that the responsibility of the
State is not involved if its judicial authorities in assuming jurisdiction relied on a statutory provision which is contrary to
international law although in taking the same action they could
have based themselves on a rule of their statutory law which *is* in
accordance with international law.[6] In the *Corfu Channel* case it
declined to attribute responsibility to a State merely on account of the
fact that it was on its territory that a foreign State had suffered an

[2] See above, pp. 87 *et seq.*
[3] *I.C.J. Reports* 1950, p. 275, and see above, p. 318.
[4] See above, p. 303. This method as well as random passages in Dissenting Opinions
have led some commentators to the view that the Court is a "partisan of State
sovereignty." See, *e.g.*, Genet, *Précis de Jurisprudence de la Cour permanente de
Justice Internationale* (1933), pp. 95 *et seq.*
[5] Series A, No. 1 (1923), p. 32; Series A, No. 17 (1928), p. 63.
[6] Series A, No. 10 (1927), p. 24.

injury.[7]  Moreover, in that case, apparently owing to the fact that the defendant party was a sovereign State, the Court attached importance to observing exacting standards in the weighing of evidence: " A charge of such exceptional gravity against a State would require a degree of certainty that has not been reached here." [8]  In the case of the *Mavrommatis Jerusalem Concessions* the Court, while finding that the action of the Palestine authorities was contrary to international law, refused to award damages on the ground that no loss to M. Mavrommatis had been proved as the result of the existence, for a certain period of time, of a right on the part of a third person to require the annulment of the concessions.[9]  Again in the *Corfu Channel* case, after declaring that the United Kingdom had violated the sovereignty of Albania, it held [10] that such declaration made in accordance with the request of the Albanian agent provided in itself appropriate satisfaction.  It is of interest to note in this connection Judge Anzilotti's observation, in his Dissenting Opinion in the case of *Diversion of Water from the Meuse* concerning the Dutch request that the Court " condemn " Belgium to discontinue certain action.  He said: " In my opinion the word *condemn* (" *condammer* ") is not entirely appropriate in international proceedings; in any case it is employed in a sense which is only remotely connected with that of *condemnation* in national law." [11]  Possibly the same line of reasoning underlies the same Judge's disinclination, in the case of *Eastern Greenland*, to describe the Norwegian declaration of sovereignty over that territory as being " null and void " (as distinguished from being merely " invalid " or " unlawful ").[12]  Such description, he held, was not accurate " in the case of the occupation of a *terra nullius* by a sovereign State in conformity with international law, merely [*sic*] because the occupying State had undertaken not to occupy it." [13]  Similarly, in the case concerning the *Interpretation of the Statute of Memel*, the Court, after finding that the action of the Lithuanian Governor in dissolving the Chamber of the Memel Territory was contrary to the Treaty, held that nevertheless it was not void and

---

[7] See above, pp. 87 *et seq.*          [8] *I.C.J. Reports* 1949, p. 17.

[9] Series A, No. 5 (1925), p. 51.

[10] *I.C.J. Reports* 1949, p. 35.

[11] Series A/B, No. 70 (1937), p. 49.

[12] Series A/B, No. 53 (1933), p. 95.

[13] *Ibid.*  He was, however, prepared to hold that the occupation by a State of territory belonging to another State would be null and void inasmuch as that territory must be *res nullius* in order to constitute a fit object of acquisition.

produced effects in the sphere of municipal law; that the dissolved Chamber continued to exist; and that the new Chamber since elected had a legal existence.[14]

In this category may also be included the disinclination of the Court to award costs against the unsuccessful party. Article 64 of the Statute provides that " unless otherwise decided by the Court, each party shall bear its own costs." In no case has the Court found it necessary to depart from the general rule laid down in this Article, although on occasions a party has asked the Court to award costs against its opponent.[15] Would such award be contrary to the sovereignty and dignity of a State?[16] To award costs against a sovereign State may imply that, without its conduct necessarily amounting to an abuse of the process of the Court,[17] that State somewhat lightly invoked or resisted the jurisdiction of the Court. On the other hand, the award of costs may be—and normally is— devoid of any element of penalty or disapproval of the conduct of the party concerned. It is no more than a measure of justice and common sense that the successful party should not be made to pay for doing no more than seeking to vindicate what the Court has found to be its due. There may be, in the international sphere, particular reasons[18] explaining the adoption of a rule such as that adopted in the Statute of the International Court of Justice. There still remains the question whether it is desirable to follow an invariable practice suggesting that the permissive provision of Article 64 is devoid of all value inasmuch as its application might be deemed offensive to the dignity or sovereignty of States.

---

[14] Series A/B, No. 49 (1932), p. 376.

[15] See, *e.g.*, the case of *Eastern Greenland*, Series A/B, No. 53 (1933), p. 74; *Pajzs* case, Series A/B, No. 68 (1936), p. 65.

[16] For a time the view prevailed in English courts that it is contrary to the dignity of a sovereign to award costs even *in his favour*. In *Monaco* v. *Monaco* the Court held that it would not be contrary to the dignity of a foreign sovereign to award to him costs, at his request, in an action in which he has been successful: (1937) 157 T.L.R. 231; *Annual Digest*, 1935–1937, Case No. 10.

[17] In the *Ambatielos (Merits)* case it was submitted by the United Kingdom, though not in connection with the question of costs, that there was on the part of Greece undue delay and abuse of process of the Court in that Greece did not refer the matter to the Court until 1951, although reference to the compulsory jurisdiction of the Court was possible from 1926. The Court did not consider the Greek action to have been improper: *I.C.J. Reports* 1952, p. 23.

[18] Thus it may be said that a rule different from that adopted in the Statute might discourage Governments from accepting the jurisdiction of the Court. On the other hand, it is arguable that Governments may be reluctant to undertake the commitments of obligatory settlement if the prospect of having to pay the costs of the successful party does not discourage potential opponents from bringing unwarranted applications.

# CHAPTER 26

# PROBLEMS OF JURISDICTION

## 107. *State Sovereignty and the Jurisdiction of the Court*

There are few rules of modern international law which are more widely acknowledged than the rule that the jurisdiction of international tribunals is derived from the will of the parties and that to that extent the principle—which is generally recognised in civilised States—that no one is entitled to be judge in his own case does not obtain in international law. Upon that rule the Court has acted consistently—though it has avoided the exaggerations which have often followed in its wake. These exaggerations have found expression in the assertion that a treaty or other instrument, such as a Declaration under the so-called Optional Clause of Article 36 of the Statute of the Court, in which a State accepts in advance the obligations of judicial settlement, must be interpreted restrictively. The same, it has been maintained, applies to the interpretation of an instrument conferring upon the Court competence in a specific case, for instance, to the question whether jurisdiction in the matter of liability implies also jurisdiction in respect to compensation. The line of reasoning underlying that trend of thought is not only that the stringency of the proof required in this matter follows from the principle of restrictive interpretation of all treaty obligations as implying limitations of sovereignty, but also that the voluntary character of international jurisdiction is a factor of so decisive a nature as to make restrictive interpretation doubly imperative.

It is difficult to acknowledge the validity of either of these two reasons. As stated elsewhere in this book, notwithstanding some appearance to the contrary, the notion of a restrictive interpretation of treaty obligations finds no support in the practice of the Court and is indefensible on grounds of principle.[1] Moreover, as already suggested, there is a distinct measure of exaggeration in the view that the undertaking of commitments of obligatory judicial settlement implies a one-sided abandonment of sovereign rights.[2] What

[1] See above, pp. 300 *et seq*.
[2] See above, pp. 305, 306, 333.

is true is that that undertaking must be the result of the intention—express or implied—of the parties and that such intention must, and can, be proved in the same way as any other obligation undertaken in a treaty or an instrument equivalent thereto. The practice of the Court supplies, on the whole, uniform authority for that proposition—though none going beyond it. The notion that the instruments in question are subject to specially exacting and restrictive interpretation is, in general, confined to the pleadings of the parties and, occasionally, to individual Opinions of Judges.[3]

## 108. *Restrictive Interpretation of Jurisdictional Clauses*

It is only in two cases that the Court, by way of what must be regarded as an *obiter* observation, seems to have given countenance to the idea that the Declaration under the Optional Clause of Article 36 (2) of its Statute must be interpreted restrictively. In the case of the *Free Zones*, the Court did not " dispute the rule invoked by the French Government, that every Special Agreement, like every clause conferring jurisdiction upon the Court, must be interpreted strictly." [4] However, it pointed out that that rule could not be applied in such a way as to give the Special Agreement, " under the guise of strict interpretation, a construction according to which it would not only fail entirely to enunciate [5] the question really in dispute, but would, by its very terms, have prejudged the answer to that question." [6] Moreover, the apparent approval of the principle of strict interpretation of jurisdictional instruments was *obiter* not only in the sense that it was not acted upon, but, primarily, because no question of jurisdiction seems to have been involved at all. The Special Agreement between Switzerland and France laid down that the Court shall decide whether Article 435 of the Treaty of Versailles " has abrogated or is intended to lead to the abrogation " of certain provisions of former treaties relating to

---

[3] See, *e.g.*, for an emphatic formulation of that view the Dissenting Opinion of Judge Badawi in the *Corfu Channel* case: " And if there still were any doubt, the exceptional nature of the Court's jurisdiction, founded on the consent of the parties and, as a corollary, on the restrictive interpretation of the Special Agreement, should in any case exclude such jurisdiction " (*I.C.J. Reports* 1949, p. 67). Significantly, this line of reasoning is absent from the Dissenting Opinion of Judges McNair, Basdevant, Klaestad and Read in the *Ambatielos* case in which the Court affirmed the jurisdiction of an arbitral tribunal: *I.C.J. Reports* 1953, pp. 25–32.

[4] Series A/B, No. 46 (1932), p. 139.

[5] " *Poser* " in the French text.

[6] *Ibid*.

customs zones. France, relying on the letter of the Article, maintained that the function of the Court was limited to finding either that the treaty was abrogated or that it must lead to the abrogation of the customs zones—whereas Switzerland asked the Court to find that neither of these alternatives was intended by the treaty. The Court declined to consider itself bound by the formulation put forward by either party.[7]

There was a similar suggestion of restrictive interpretation of jurisdictional provisions in the case of the *Phosphates in Morocco* which is referred to in some detail elsewhere in this book [8] and in which the crucial question before the Court was the meaning of the reservation of " past disputes." There the Court declined to sanction a restrictive interpretation—a refusal which referred to a restrictive interpretation of a *restriction*, namely, of the reservation of past disputes. The Court pointed out that the terms of the French reservation limiting the jurisdiction of the Court *ratione temporis* were " perfectly clear ": " The only situation or facts falling under the compulsory jurisdiction are those which are subsequent to the ratification and with regard to which the dispute arose, that is to say, those which must be considered as being the source of the dispute." [9] " In these circumstances," the Court added, " there is no occasion to resort to a restrictive interpretation that, in case of doubt, might be advisable in regard to a clause which must on no account be interpreted in such a way as to exceed the intention of the States that subscribed to it."

On the other hand, in the case of the *Electricity Company of Sofia* [10] the important contribution of the Court to the doctrine and practice of the reservation of " past disputes "—a potentially most comprehensive limitation of its jurisdiction—shows that it will not permit its decisions to follow the short-cuts of a ready-made rule of restrictive interpretation, but that it will endeavour to give effect to the actual intention of the parties. Its occasional explanation of the reasons underlying a particular reservation need not necessarily be taken as constituting approval of these reasons.

It has been shown that while the Court will not assume jurisdiction without having satisfied itself that the parties intended

---

[7] Series A/B, No. 46 (1932), at p. 138.
[8] See above, p. 96.
[9] Series A/B, No. 46 (1932), at p. 138.
[10] See above, p. 97.

to confer jurisdiction upon it, and while it gives full effect to the traditional attitude of international law on the subject, it will not assist in nullifying the intention of the parties by reference to technicalities or a purely literal interpretation of words.[11] On the contrary, it has invoked the " flexibility " of international relations and it has applied boldly the view that effect must be given to the ostensible purpose of jurisdictional clauses.[12] It is for that reason that, on the one hand, in this book the question of the jurisdiction of the Court is treated in the present Section as an example of the recognition of claims of sovereignty and, as an instance of the same line of approach, in the chapter on Judicial Caution. On the other hand, the problem of jurisdiction also occupies, as showing an altogether different side of the picture, a prominent place in the Parts on Judicial Legislation and on the Principle of Effectiveness. As in other matters, no rule of thumb—by way of restrictive interpretation or otherwise—can be usefully applied to the question of the jurisdiction of the Court. In fact, it is significant that notwithstanding the frequency of pleas to the jurisdiction—probably the majority of the Judgments given by the Court has been concerned with them in one way or another—there are, as has been shown, only two *obiter* observations of the Court which appear to give countenance to the argument of restrictive interpretation of jurisdictional clauses. As a rule, the Court limits itself to the statement that consent of the parties is the essential requisite of its jurisdiction and proceeds to inquire whether such consent has been given.[13] It recalls the necessity of consent even in cases in which it finds that it has jurisdiction by virtue not of express but of implied agreement of the parties [14]—such implied consent extending to questions not falling ostensibly within the category of those in respect of which compulsory jurisdiction has been accepted.[15]

---

11 See above, pp. 91 *et seq.*
12 See above, pp. 200 *et seq.* And see the Dissenting Opinion, which provides much instruction, of Judge Read in the case of the *Anglo-Iranian Oil Co.*: *I.C.J. Reports* 1952, pp. 142–144.
13 See, *e.g.*, the *Ambatielos* case: *I.C.J. Reports* 1953, p. 19 (a case of jurisdiction of a tribunal other than the Court itself); and the case of the *Anglo-Iranian Oil Company*, *I.C.J. Reports* 1952, p. 103.
14 See above, pp. 201 *et seq.* And see the case of the *Mavrommatis Palestine Concessions*, Series A, No. 2 (1924), p. 16, and the case of *Factory at Chorzów* (*Indemnity*, *Merits*), Series A, No. 17 (1928), p. 37.
15 *Rights of Minorities in Upper Silesia* (*Minority Schools*), Series A, No. 15 (1928), pp. 22–24.

109. *The Consistency of the Application of the Principle of Consent to Jurisdiction.   The Case of* Monetary Gold Removed from Rome

The fact that the Court has reduced to its true proportions the reliance on restrictive interpretation of jurisdictional clauses ought not to be allowed to obscure its insistence, in conformity with a clear rule of international law, on the principle that consent of a State is an essential to the exercise by the Court of jurisdiction over it. The case of the *Monetary Gold Removed from Rome* [16] supplies an instructive example of the emphatic application of the principle involved.   There the Court, in pursuance of an Italian application following upon the Declaration made in 1951 by the United States of America, the United Kingdom and France concerning certain gold removed from Rome in 1943 by the German authorities and belonging at that time to Albania, was called upon to decide whether it had jurisdiction: (a) to determine whether the gold belonged to Italy or Albania; and (b) in the event of its finding that the gold belonged to Italy, to decide whether the claim of the United Kingdom to the gold, in respect of the unsatisfied Judgment of the Court previously given against Albania in the *Corfu Channel* case, was nevertheless entitled to priority over the Italian rights. Italy, although she had brought the matter before the Court, subsequently raised the issue of the jurisdiction of the Court on the ground, mainly, that Albania was not a party to the proceedings. [17]   The Court upheld the Preliminary Objection raised by Italy.   It found that the matter upon which it was asked to adjudicate was in fact concerned with a claim of Italy against Albania for redress of an international wrong said to have been committed by the latter—a claim for the decision of which it was necessary to determine whether the Albanian nationalisation law was contrary to international law.   It said: " The Court cannot decide such a dispute without the consent of Albania.   But it is not contended by any Party that Albania has given her consent in this case either expressly or by implication.   To adjudicate upon the international responsibility of Albania without her consent would run counter to a well-established principle of international law

[16] *I.C.J. Reports* 1954, p. 19.
[17] The explanation of this, otherwise puzzling, spectacle of a State challenging the jurisdiction of the Court in a case in which it appears as plaintiff is not relevant for the purpose of the issue here discussed.

embodied in the Court's Statute, namely, that the Court can only exercise jurisdiction over a State with its consent." [18] Accordingly, the Court held that it had no jurisdiction to adjudicate upon the original claim of Italy against the United States of America, the United Kingdom and France that these States should deliver to Italy such of the monetary gold as might otherwise be due to Albania; it had no jurisdiction although both Italy and the three States in question had conferred it upon the Court.

The case of the *Monetary Gold* is remarkable not only because of the clear application of the principle that consent of the State directly involved [19] is essential for the exercise of the jurisdiction of the Court, but also because of the virtual unanimity [20] of the decision of the Court in circumstances in which a Tribunal less wedded to the principle of consent might well have arrived at a different conclusion. For it will be noted that the three Great Powers not only submitted to the jurisdiction of the Court; they had invited it in their original Declaration of Washington. Were these Powers unacquainted with the principle so consistently acted upon by the Court? It cannot be assumed that they expected Albania to submit to the jurisdiction of the Court, to whose Judgment in a previous case she refused to give effect.[21] Or is it probable that in conferring upon the Court jurisdiction in a matter directly involving Albania they considered, on legal grounds, that her consent was in fact irrelevant inasmuch as she could gain nothing by appearing before the Court for the reason that even if the Court adjudged the gold to belong to her, they—the three Powers—were at liberty to hand it over to the United Kingdom; that they were, in law, entitled to do so either by way of execution

---

[18] *I.C.J. Reports* 1954, at p. 32.

[19] The Court distinguished the case before it from the situation contemplated in Art. 62 of its Statute under which a State, not directly interested but having an interest of a legal nature in the matter, may intervene in the dispute. The case before it, the Court said, was not merely one in which the legal interests of Albania would be affected by the decision; the Albanian interest "would form the very subject-matter of the decision."

[20] The Dissenting Opinion of Judge Read was limited to the expression of the view that the original Application of Italy was legally ineffective inasmuch as it failed to name Albania as a party to the proceedings (at pp. 37, 38). Judge McNair's Declaration was to a similar effect (p. 35). Judge Levi Carneiro's Dissenting Opinion was confined to the question whether the Court had jurisdiction to determine the priority of the respective claims of Italy and the United Kingdom.

[21] There arises here the interesting question, which was not considered by the Court, to what extent a State which has failed to comply with a previous Judgment of the Court can appear before it by consent.

of a valid Judgment of the Court given in the *Corfu Channel* case
or, in the case of the United Kingdom, by way of self-help in a
form not prohibited by the Charter of the United Nations and
aiming at giving effect to a previous Judgment of the Court; that
the provisions of Article 94 of the Charter relating to the execution
of the Judgments of the Court were not exhaustive but permitted
other means not inconsistent with the Charter; that, as the interests
of Albania were thus in fact not involved, the principle that
jurisdiction must be grounded in consent ought not to be interpreted in an exacting manner; and that in so far as the proceedings
aimed in the last resort at securing the effectiveness of the Judgment
in the *Corfu Channel* case, in which the Court exercised jurisdiction
by virtue of the consent of Albania, the consent of Albania must be
implied in the same way in which the Court implied her consent
to its exercising jurisdiction in the matter of determining the
compensation due to the United Kingdom? [22]   It is not considered
here necessary to examine the soundness of any such chain of
argument.   But it is indicative of the firmness with which the Court
applies the principle of consent to its jurisdiction that that argument
finds no place either in the Judgment of the Court, or in the
Dissenting Opinions, or—it would appear—in the pleadings of the
Parties.

### 110. *Restrictive Interpretation of Unilateral Declarations Accepting the Jurisdiction of the Court. The Case of the* Anglo-Iranian Oil Company

The case of the *Anglo-Iranian Oil Company* seems, at first sight,
to give support to the view that the Court may favour a restrictive
interpretation of instruments purporting to confer jurisdiction upon
it by declining to interpret them in the same way as ordinary treaties
and by attaching decisive importance to the meaning given to a
unilateral declaration of acceptance by the party making it as distinguished from its legal effect as determined by ordinary methods of
interpretation.   In that case the Court held, with regard to a
particular principle of interpretation invoked by the United Kingdom,[23] that although that principle was in general applicable to the
interpretation of the text of a treaty, the text before the Court—the

---

[22] See above, p. 247.
[23] The principle that a legal text must be interpreted in such a way that a reason and
meaning must be attributed to every word in the text (at p. 105).

Iranian Declaration of Acceptance of the jurisdiction of the Court —was not a treaty resulting from negotiations between two or more States, but the result of unilateral drafting by the Government of Iran and that therefore there was no room for applying the principle in question; this was so, in particular, as the words to which, in the submission of the United Kingdom, effect was to be given, were inserted by Iran merely *ex abundanti cautela*.

The issue raised by this ruling of the Court is of wider importance in relation to the subject here discussed. On the face of it it is not clear from the wording of the Judgment whether in the view of the Court the unilateral declaration of acceptance is not a treaty *tout court* or whether it " is not a treaty text resulting from negotiations between two or more States." [24] The latter is probably the case. There ought to be no difficulty in considering the text of Article 36 (2) of the Statute of the Court—the so-called Optional Clause—as the text of a treaty to which the declaring State gives its adherence. As the Court said in the case concerning the *Austro-German Customs Union*: " From the point of the obligatory character of international engagements, it is well known that such engagements may be taken in the form of treaties, conventions, declarations, agreements, protocols, or exchanges of notes." [25] The question is whether the reservations, unilaterally framed, deprive the declaration of the character of accession to the established text of a treaty. Serious consequences might follow from the assumption that a declaration thus qualified by reservations and, as the result, not partaking of the nature of a treaty ought to be given a meaning attributed to it by the State making it as distinguished from the meaning as given by an interpretation aiming at eliciting the common intention of the parties—a common intention which is the result of the intention both of the State making the declaration and of the manner in which the States to which it is addressed must be held to have understood it in accordance with generally accepted principles of interpretation. Undoubtedly, the declarations under Article 36 (2) of the Statute, made as they are at different times and by different States, are not in all respects exactly like a treaty. But they are essentially a treaty. By their very terms they connote a reciprocity of rights and obligations although—as the result of practice rather than of the language of Article 36 (2)—it is

[24] *I.C.J. Reports* 1952, p. 105.
[25] Series A/B, No. 41 (1931), p. 47.

for every declaring State to determine, through reservations, in a manner consistent with the Statute of the Court, what shall be the content of these reciprocal rights and obligations. Admittedly, it may not be easy to determine when and by means of what analytical construction there takes place, in such circumstances, the " meeting of minds " required for the creation of a treaty obligation. However, the situation is not essentially dissimilar from that represented by accession to a treaty.

This being so, there may be some difficulty in accepting without qualification a view—which is not the view of the Court—that declines to apply to a unilateral declaration of acceptance of the undertaking of compulsory judicial settlement the general principles of interpretation of treaties and which attributes decisive significance to the meaning attached to it by the individual declaring State. The Optional Clause of Article 36 (2) of the Statute is actually and potentially the most important source of the jurisdiction of the Court and caution would seem to be indicated lest it be reduced to a purely unilateral undertaking which is subject to a restrictive interpretation divorced from the generally accepted canons of construction. The Judgment in the *Anglo-Iranian Oil Company* case revealed the implications of some such view.

There are two other factors which tend to give to that Judgment the appearance of restrictive interpretation. In the first instance, while declining to attribute in every respect to the declaration under the Optional Clause the character of a treaty concluded as the result of negotiations and to apply to it all the rules of interpretation of treaties, the Court attached importance to the Iranian understanding of the declaration—an understanding elaborated in an Iranian Law published in the official collection of Laws of Iran.[26] Secondly, the Court was not inclined to give full and formal effect, in the nature of things not easily envisaged by Iran, to the operation of treaties which, it was contended, as the result of the operation of the most-favoured-nation clause contained therein brought within the jurisdiction of the Court acts and situations otherwise not subject to its jurisdiction. While the Court based its rejection of the appeal to the most-favoured-nation clause on an interpretation of its purpose and effect, Judge McNair—who agreed with the result

---

[26] An instrument of which Judge McNair in his Separate Opinion said that " its admissibility in evidence is open to question, and its evidentiary value slight " (*I.C.J. Reports* 1952, at p. 121).

reached by the Court—referred, with some cogency, to the "artificial and much strained" character of the interpretation advanced by the United Kingdom on the subject.[27]  However, it is arguable that it is of the essence of the most-favoured-nation clause that it involves an element of artificiality inherent in its automatic operation.[28]  It would appear that although, on the face of it the case of the *Anglo-Iranian Oil Company* suggests that in the event of doubt the scales will be weighted against the assumption of jurisdiction, it is not a case which easily lends itself to generalisation.[29]

111. *Indirect Manifestations of Restraint in the Exercise of Jurisdiction*

The preceding chapters suggest the conclusion that although there is probably no warrant for the view that, having regard to the sovereignty of States, the Court will as a rule give a restrictive interpretation to instruments purporting to confer jurisdiction upon it, its practice has shown that it exercises restraint in the matter and that it has not been disposed to assume jurisdiction without clear proof of the intention of the parties to confer jurisdiction upon it. That leaning towards restraint shows itself in many ways:

(a) *Examination of Questions of Jurisdiction* proprio motu.  In the first instance, regardless of the question of consent, the Court has examined the question of its jurisdiction *ex officio, proprio motu*.  Thus in the case concerning the *Administration of the Prince von Pless* [30] the Court raised of its own accord the question—which, in the event, it was not called upon to answer—whether a State acting in its capacity as a member of the Council of the League of Nations may claim the award of an indemnity to a national of the respondent State when that person is a member of a minority

---

[27] *I.C.J. Reports* 1952, at p. 123.

[28] The Dissenting Opinions of Judges Hackworth and Read relied almost exclusively on the argument based on the most-favoured-nation clause.

[29] Iran had previously declined to act upon the Order of the Court decreeing conservatory measures (see above, p. 111).  However, she was not bound by a clear legal obligation to comply with that Order.  Nevertheless she denounced, on July 10, 1951, her Declaration of Acceptance on the ground of the alleged absence of impartiality on the part of the Court in issuing the Order.  Her agent in his submissions invoked this fact as one of the reasons why the Court should declare itself incompetent: *Pleadings, Oral Arguments, Documents*, p. 443.  That particular objection to the jurisdiction of the Court was not in fact proceeded with and the Court did not refer to it in its Judgment.

[30] Series A/B, No. 52 (1933), p. 15.

protected by the Treaty. In the case of the *Société Commerciale de Belgique* the Court referred *proprio motu* to the question whether it had jurisdiction to adjudicate upon the Belgian submission, which had undergone a change in the course of the proceedings. The Court found, apparently with the agreement of the parties, that it could exercise jurisdiction seeing that the Greek Government had raised no objections and that it submitted arguments on the merits and asked for a decision on them.[31] In the case of the *Treatment in Hungary of Aircraft and Crew of the United States of America* the Court, by an—apparently unanimous—Order and without resorting to contentious procedure by way of written or oral argument, simply ordered the removal from the list of the case submitted against Hungary by the United States of America. The latter admitted in its application that Hungary was not bound by any prior commitment to accept the jurisdiction of the Court. In a communication to the Court the Hungarian Government expressed its inability to submit the dispute to the Court.[32] It will also be noted that Article 53 of the Statute, relating to judgment by default, enjoins upon the Court the duty to satisfy itself, both with regard to the jurisdiction and the merits, that the claim is well founded.

(b) *Exhaustive Treatment of Unsubstantial Pleas to the Jurisdiction.* Secondly, the Court has signified its sense of the importance of this aspect of its activity by examining in some detail objections to jurisdiction which on the face of it have appeared somewhat lacking in substance—a fact evidenced by the unanimous rejection of the plea to its jurisdiction in such cases. It did so when in the *Corfu Channel* case [33] Albania, after having addressed to the Court a letter voluntarily accepting the jurisdiction of the Court, challenged its jurisdiction on the ground that the application in which the United Kingdom instituted proceedings was not in accordance with the Statute. In particular, the Court rejected the contention that, except in cases of compulsory jurisdiction, proceedings can be instituted only by special agreement.[34]

---

[31] Series A/B, No. 78 (1939), p. 174.

[32] *I.C.J. Reports* 1954, p. 100.

[33] *I.C.J. Reports* 1947, p. 15 (Preliminary Objection). See above, p. 104.

[34] The Court pointed out that there was nothing in the Statute to prevent the parties from accepting the jurisdiction of the Court by two separate and successive acts instead of jointly and by special agreement. It recalled the passage from the Judgment of the Permanent Court of International Justice in the case of the *Rights of Minorities in Upper Silesia (Minority Schools)*, Series A, No. 15 (1928), p. 23, where the Court

Similarly, in the *Nottebohm* case between Liechtenstein and Guatemala the Court in a unanimous Judgment considered it desirable to answer in some detail the two objections, raising somewhat elementary points of law, which Guatemala advanced against its jurisdiction. Thus, in the first instance, Guatemala contended that the Court could not, in reliance on the original Guatemalan acceptance of its compulsory jurisdiction, decide by reference to Article 36 (2) of the Statute of the Court whether it had jurisdiction. This was so, it was maintained, for the reason that the categories of disputes enumerated in that Article did not cover the question whether the expiry of the time limit of the Guatemalan declaration of acceptance of the compulsory jurisdiction of the Court put an end to the jurisdiction of the Court to adjudicate on the claim brought by Liechtenstein prior to the expiry of the time limit. The Court went into some detail in showing that the power of a tribunal to decide upon its jurisdiction was a rule " consistently accepted by general international law in the matter of international arbitration," [35] that it applied with special force to the principal judicial organ of the United Nations, that it formed part of the jurisprudence of the Court, and that it was fully covered by the terms of Article 36 (2) of the Statute. The Court considered in even greater detail the interpretation put forward by Guatemala upon her declaration of acceptance to the effect that the jurisdiction of the Court in relation to a case already pending before it ceased on the date on which the declaration expired. That interpretation the Court described as novel in the sense that it had never been previously advanced although similar situations had arisen before the Permanent Court of International Justice. However, the Court considered that the attitude of States which had omitted to invoke the interpretation now put forward by Guatemala did not absolve it from the duty to examine the issue thus raised. It proceeded accordingly to devote some exhaustive passages to substantiating the proposition that while the seising of the Court must take place within the period of validity of the declaration of acceptance of its jurisdiction, once it has been regularly seised within that period it must continue to exercise jurisdiction in all its aspects. There is

said: " The acceptance by a State of the Court's jurisdiction in a particular case is not, under the Statute, subordinated to the observance of certain forms, such as, for instance, the previous conclusion of a special agreement."

[35] *I.C.J. Reports* 1953, p. 119.

significance in the disinclination of the Court to dismiss in a summary manner seemingly unsubstantial objections to its jurisdiction and in its determination to answer with meticulous care the issues involved in the plea thus raised. Such care cannot properly be regarded as misplaced. In the international sphere the questions of jurisdiction call no less than questions of substance for a full combination of administration of justice with the preservation of all requisite appearance that justice has been done.

(c) *Exhaustion of Legal Remedies.* Thirdly, inasmuch as the rule as to exhaustion of legal remedies is directly related to the question of jurisdiction, the Court has shown no disposition to set aside that particular restraint upon its competence. In the principal case in which it has been confronted with that question—the case, which is discussed in more detail elsewhere,[36] of the *Railway Line Panevezys-Saldutiskis* between Estonia and Lithuania—it acted affirmatively, with some emphasis, upon the objection of Lithuania, which it treated as a preliminary objection, regarding the non-exhaustion of the remedies available under her law. It held that the claim could not therefore be entertained.[37] While the rule as to exhaustion of legal remedies is primarily a rule of substantive international law in the field of State responsibility, it has an important —though indirect—bearing upon the jurisdiction of the Court. It is a rule which, if applied with a requisite degree of flexibility, is expressive of considerations of convenience and common sense which preclude the imputation of responsibility to the State so long as the State has not acted with finality. At the same time it constitutes, by reference to the sovereignty of States, a limitation of more than a procedural nature upon the jurisdiction of international tribunals. To that extent the manner of the application by the Court of the rule of exhaustion of legal remedies is of interest.

(d) *Nationality of Claims.* Similar considerations apply to the so-called rule of nationality of claims according to which a State may put forward a claim on behalf of a person only if that person was a national of that State both at the time of the injury and at the time of the presentation of the claim. This is so although in the case of the *Railway Line Panevezys-Saldutiskis* the Court declined to

[36] See above, p. 100.
[37] Series A/B, No. 76 (1939), p. 22.

treat as a preliminary objection the plea based on the rule of nationality of claims and considered it as part of the case on the merits. At the same time, subject to one important qualification, it fully affirmed the rule of nationality of claims. It said:

> "This right [of diplomatic protection] is necessarily limited to intervention on behalf of its own nationals because, *in the absence of a special agreement*,[38] it is the bond of nationality between the State and the individual which alone confers upon the State the right of diplomatic protection. . . . Where the injury was done to the national of some other State, no claim to which such injury may give rise falls within the scope of diplomatic protection which a State is entitled to afford nor can it give rise to a claim which that State is entitled to espouse." [39]

The Court denied that the precedents which Estonia adduced as derogating from the rule of nationality of claims actually had that effect: ". . . When these precedents are examined it will be seen that they are cases where the governments concerned had agreed to waive the strict application of the rule, cases where the two governments had agreed to establish an international tribunal with jurisdiction to adjudicate on claims even if this condition as to nationality were not fulfilled." [40]

It is not clear from the passage quoted whether such waiver must be express or whether the mere fact of the establishment of an adjudicating agency whose jurisdiction is not expressly circumscribed by reference to the rule of nationality of claims may be construed as amounting to waiver. When, in instruments such as the Convention on the Prevention and Punishment of Genocide or the Convention on the Legal Status of Refugees, provision is made for the compulsory jurisdiction of the International Court of Justice in disputes concerning the interpretation or application of these Conventions, does the conferment of that jurisdiction by itself imply the setting aside of the traditional rule of nationality of claims? This, it is believed, is probably the case—especially when the object of the treaty is to protect persons who may not possess any nationality at all. It would thus appear that notwithstanding the emphatic affirmation of the principle of the rule of nationality of claims the Court envisaged exceptions to that rule. Probably it

[38] Italics are the writer's.
[39] At p. 16.
[40] *Ibid.*

was not incumbent upon it to elaborate the nature of these exceptions.[41] It did not consider it necessary to do so when in the
*Reparation for Injuries* case it denied the applicability of the rule of
nationality of claims in the case before it and merely stated, broadly,
that there existed important exceptions to the rule.[42] There
is thus no warrant for the assumption that the Court will invariably
respect the claim of a sovereign State not to be made accountable
for the infliction of an injury upon an individual, in a manner
contrary to international law, except at the instance of the State of
which that individual is a national at the time of the occurrence of
the injury and of the institution of the proceedings before the Court
(and, possibly, at the time of rendering of the Judgment).

As with regard to the principle of exhaustion of legal remedies,
so also in the matter of the rule of nationality of claims, the border-
line between a jurisdictional objection and appeal to a substantive
rule of international law is a matter of emphasis. Both rules
interpose an obstacle in the way of the jurisdiction of an international tribunal on the merits of the complaint. To that extent
they imply a corresponding limitation, even if only in the procedural
sphere, of the responsibility of the State and an addition to its
sovereign freedom of action. To that extent, too, they are related
to the problem surveyed in the present Section.

## 112. *The Principle of Consent in Relation to Advisory Jurisdiction*

The importance which the Court attaches to the principle that it
will not assume jurisdiction over the substance of a dispute unless
the parties have previously conferred jurisdiction upon it may be
gauged from the fact that, at least at the outset of its activity, it
applied that principle to its advisory jurisdiction. It is for that
reason that it refused, in the case of *Eastern Carelia*, to give an
Advisory Opinion requested by the Council of the League of
Nations. The Court declined to do so on the ground that Soviet
Russia, who was in fact a party to the dispute, had not accepted the
jurisdiction of the Court or of the Council of the League of

---

[41] See the Dissenting Opinions of Judges van Eysinga and Hudson. See, in particular, the
observation of Judge van Eysinga on the doubtful reasonableness of a rule " which
would entail that, when a change of sovereignty takes place, the new State or the State
which has increased its territory would not be able to espouse any claim of any of its
new nationals in regard to injury suffered before the change of nationality " (at p. 35).

[42] See above, pp. 177 *et seq*.

Nations.[43] The Opinion which the Court was to give was intended to provide an answer to the very question which was in dispute between Finland and Russia, namely, whether a certain Declaration attached to the Treaty of Dorpat concluded between these two States had the same binding force as the Treaty itself. This question the Court declined to answer. It relied on a " fundamental principle of international law, namely, the principle of the independence of States "—a principle " well established in international law " by virtue of which " no State can, without its consent, be compelled to submit its disputes with other States either to mediation or to arbitration, or to any kind of pacific settlement." [44] The Court also pointed to the fact that, apart from that fundamental difficulty, it was unable, having regard to the refusal of Soviet Russia to appear before it, to investigate adequately the facts underlying the dispute.

It is not clear to what extent the principle thus acted upon by the Permanent Court of International Justice in the case of *Eastern Carelia* was followed by the International Court of Justice in the first phase of the *Interpretation of the Peace Treaties with Bulgaria Hungary and Romania* [45]—a case in which it answered in the affirmative the question whether there existed a dispute, within the meaning of the Peace Treaties of 1947, between these three States and certain Allied and Associated Powers and whether the former States were under an obligation to carry out the provisions of those Treaties relating to the settlement of disputes. In giving its Opinion the Court attached importance to distinguishing it from its Opinion in the case of *Eastern Carelia* on the ground that the circumstances of the two cases were " profoundly different." In the latter case, it said, the question asked of it touched directly the main point of the dispute; the present Opinion related to questions of procedure and had been requested for the purpose of enlightening the General Assembly on a question of that kind.[46] It is not clear to what extent that explanation " distinguished " the case before the Court from the Opinion in the case of *Eastern Carelia*. An answer—if acted upon—to a question of procedure may in substantial respects affect the outcome of the dispute. In fact, as the Court pointed out

[43] Series B, No. 5 (1923).
[44] At p. 27.
[45] *I.C.J. Reports* 1950, p. 65.
[46] See above, p. 108.

in the subsequent Opinion relating to the second phase of the issue, in its Opinion in the first phase it found that the three Governments were bound to pursue a certain line of conduct by appointing representatives to the Commission provided for in the Peace Treaty. In the second Opinion it declared—although this was not the issue directly before it—that the refusal to fulfil that obligation involved international responsibility and that in fact a breach of treaty obligations, in this respect, on the part of the three Governments concerned had taken place.[47]  An Opinion which involves a finding that a State has become guilty of a breach of a treaty probably goes beyond mere enlightenment on a question of procedure.  From this point of view it may be difficult to deny some persuasive force to the three Dissenting Opinions in the first of these cases in so far as they are based on the principle enunciated in the case of *Eastern Carelia* and in so far as that latter case continues to be expressive of existing law.  However, it is not certain that that basis of the ruling in the case of *Eastern Carelia* continues to express a valid legal proposition.[48]

For, probably, the more convincing explanation of the Opinion in the first phase of the case of the *Peace Treaties* lay in those observations of the Court in which, in effect though without actually disavowing the principle laid down in the case of *Eastern Carelia*, it refused to admit that Advisory Opinions are rigidly governed by the rule that no judicial proceedings relating to a legal question between States can take place without their consent.  The objection to its jurisdiction based on any such rule " reveals a confusion between the principles governing contentious procedure and those which are applicable to Advisory Opinions."  It is convenient to quote in full the passage of the Opinion in which the Court affirmed the fundamental difference, in this respect, between its advisory and its contentious jurisdiction :

> " The consent of States, parties to the dispute, is the basis of the Court's jurisdiction in contentious cases.  The situation is different in regard to advisory proceedings even where the Request for an Opinion relates to a legal question actually pending between States.  The Court's reply is only of an advisory character : as such it has no binding force.  It follows that no State, whether a member of the

---

[47] *I.C.J. Reports* 1950, pp. 227, 228.
[48] Opinions of Judges Winiarski, Zoričić and Krylov : *ibid.*, pp. 89, 98 and 105, respectively.

United Nations or not, can prevent the giving of an Advisory Opinion which the United Nations considers to be desirable in order to obtain enlightenment as to the course of action it should take. The Court's Opinion is given not to the States, but to the organ which is entitled to request it; the reply of the Court, itself an ' organ of the United Nations,' represents its participation in the activities of the Organisation, and, in principle, should not be refused." [49]

The apparent meaning of these observations is that there exists a basic difference, with regard to the matter at issue, between Judgments and Advisory Opinions. That difference lies, in the first instance, in the fact that the latter are not binding and, secondly, that it is the duty of the Court, as the organ of the United Nations, to assist it in obtaining enlightenment as to the course of action to be taken. However, after having thus stated the broad principle involved, the Court proceeded to qualify it to some extent. It pointed to the limits of its duty to render Advisory Opinions inasmuch as it is not merely an organ of the United Nations, but is also its principal judicial organ. It then proceeded, in distinguishing the case before it from that of *Eastern Carelia*, to stress that the Opinion which it had been requested to give related to a point of procedure and not of substance. It may not be easy to follow, in all its implications, the distinction thus expressed. If taken literally it would amount to stating that the fundamental difference, just elaborated, between Advisory Opinions and Judgments is relevant only in respect of matters of procedure—a result of limited compass in relation to the wide comprehensiveness of the reasoning which preceded it and the cogency of which it is difficult to resist. There also arises the question of the force of the proposition that the issue decided by the Court in fact related merely to a matter of procedure. Possibly the distinguishing element, in relation to the case of *Eastern Carelia*, lay in a different sphere, namely, in that the Treaty of Dorpat conferred no functions at all upon the League of Nations while the Treaties of Peace of 1947 did so by express reference to the Secretary-General of the United Nations and otherwise.

However, that possible distinction between the situations underlying the two Opinions hardly goes to the root of the matter. It is arguable that the reasoning of the Court in the case of the *Peace Treaties* goes some way in the direction of an abandonment of the

[49] *I.C.J. Reports* 1950, at p. 71.

principle impliedly laid down in the case of *Eastern Carelia*—
the principle that the participation of States whose legal interests
are involved either directly or indirectly is a condition of the valid
exercise of the advisory function of the Court. If that is so then
there may perhaps be no occasion to deplore the substantial qualification, in the case of the *Peace Treaties*, of the precedent established
in the case of *Eastern Carelia*. This is so for the reason that, largely
on the grounds stated in the Advisory Opinion in the case of the
*Peace Treaties*, the Opinion in the case of *Eastern Carelia* can no
longer be accepted as expressing fully a valid legal proposition—at
least, for reasons to be stated presently, in relation to Members of
the United Nations. It is not easy to accept the view that there is
direct interference with the sovereignty of a State as the result of
the Court expressing an opinion which is not legally binding either
upon the State thus indirectly interested or upon the organ receiving
the Opinion.[50] Moreover, there must be taken into account the
place of Advisory Opinions in the scheme not only of the Statute
of the Court but also of the Charter of the United Nations.

The General Assembly, the Security Council or any other organ
or specialised agency of the United Nations authorised for the purpose are entitled to ask for an Advisory Opinion—which the Court
is bound to render within the limits of its judicial function[51]—on
any legal question which may involve a member of the United
Nations in connection with any dispute brought before these organs.
The fact that the Member concerned may refuse to take part in the
proceedings connected with the Advisory Opinion or otherwise
assist the Court is not decisive. Neither is the circumstance that
the Advisory Opinion asked of the Court is substantially identical
with the legal issue of a dispute under consideration by the United
Nations. In view of this there would seem to be no room for the
argument, by reference to the case of *Eastern Carelia*, that the Court

---

[50] It is possible that the negative Opinion of the Court in the case of *Eastern Carelia* was
influenced by the view that the assumption of jurisdiction by the Council of the League
of Nations in a dispute between a member of the League of Nations and a State which
was not a member was contrary to international law. It is not necessary to express here
an opinion on the conformity of Art. 17 of the Covenant of the League of Nations with
international law. That Article, it will be noted, imposed no legal obligation upon non-
members either to participate in the procedure of pacific settlement initiated by the
League or to accept the finding following upon such procedure—though sanctions were
provided in the case of the non-member State resorting to war in disregard of the
finding thus arrived at.

[51] See above, p. 109.

must not, without the consent of a State, pronounce upon legal rights involving that State.[52] Members of the United Nations, in giving the Court the general power of rendering Advisory Opinions, thereby consented to its advisory jurisdiction on any legal question, whether it involves such disputed interests or not. Thus, in the course of the proceedings connected with the Advisory Opinion on the *International Status of South-West Africa*, the Government of the Union of South Africa submitted a statement on the merits of the question put before the Court. It did not raise the issue of the jurisdiction of the Court to render the Opinion. However, if it had done so, if it had refused to take any part in the proceedings, and if it had protested against the rendering of the Advisory Opinion, any such attitude would not, it is submitted, have prevented the Court from exercising its advisory function. In the Advisory Opinion on the *Reservations to the Genocide Convention* the Court interpreted widely the provision of Article 96 of the Charter which, in general terms, gives the General Assembly and the Security Council the right to request of the Court an Advisory Opinion " on any legal question." It held that the right to ask for an interpretation of a treaty by way of an Advisory Opinion was not affected by the circumstance that the Treaty included provisions for the contentious jurisdiction of the Court with regard to the interpretation or application of the Treaty.[53]

It would thus appear that, at least in relation to the Members of the United Nations, the Charter has created a species of quasi-compulsory jurisdiction of the Court by way of Advisory Opinions the request for which may be made, by a requisite majority, in disregard of the adverse vote of the State or States affected. This means that notwithstanding the general absence of compulsory jurisdiction of the Court under the scheme of the Charter, it is open to the General Assembly and the Security Council—as well as to

---

[52] In connection with the Advisory Opinion in that case some States, in particular Poland, denied the competence of the Court to give the Opinion. See Written Statement of Poland: *Pleadings, Oral Arguments, Documents*, pp. 283–285. And see above, p. 109. This was not a typical case of States objecting to an Advisory Opinion on the ground that the request referred to a legal question forming the subject-matter of a dispute between the objecting State and another State. For Poland became a party to the Genocide Convention without reservations. On the other hand, some of the States whose legal right to become a party to the Convention was at issue on account of the reservations appended by them, did not challenge the right of the Court to give the Advisory Opinion.

[53] *I.C.J. Reports* 1951, p. 20.

other duly authorised organs of the United Nations and specialised agencies—to ,obtain, through the instrumentality of an Advisory Opinion, a finding of the Court on the legal merits of a dispute between States. That pronouncement is not legally binding— though in the case of *Eastern Carelia* the Court considered that that circumstance did not exclude the operation of the principle requiring consent to the jurisdiction of the Court however exercised. To that extent the latter case can no longer be regarded as fully expressing the law in force. It was not followed, in fact, in the Advisory Opinion on the *Interpretation of Peace Treaties*. This was so notwithstanding the differences, as elaborated by the Court, between the two cases. There seems to be no decisive reason why the sovereignty of States should be protected from a procedure, to which they have consented in advance as Members of the United Nations, of ascertaining the law through a pronouncement which, notwithstanding its authority, is not binding upon them. At the same time, the circumspection with which the Court expressed the departure from the precedent in the case of *Eastern Carelia*, bears testimony to its attitude of restraint in subjecting, however indirectly, sovereign States to its jurisdiction.

# CHAPTER 27

# SOVEREIGN FREEDOM OF ACTION

### 113. *Presumptive Freedom of Action of Sovereign States. The Case of* The Lotus

One of the main tests of the attitude of the Court to claims of State sovereignty is the manner in which it has approached the doctrine that, as the will of sovereign States is the only source of international law, any derogation from their freedom of action must be deduced from an express manifestation of their will. A survey of the work of the Court as undertaken in this book shows that— subject to exceptions, of which some call for consideration—no support can be found in the decisions of the Court for the doctrine thus expressed. It is sufficient to recall the various examples of judicial legislation such as the application of general principles of law resulting in a limitation of the State's freedom of action [1]; the refusal of the Court to apply the rule of restrictive interpretation to the construction of treaties [2]; the numerous instances of reliance on the principle of effectiveness in the interpretation of treaty obligations [3]; and the cases of assumption of jurisdiction in consequence of the implied consent of the parties.[4]

To this general trend, the reasons for which have been explained above,[5] there are exceptions, both real and apparent, which form the subject of this Section and preclude any suggestion of an obvious and unqualified uniformity. It is not surprising that this should be so with regard to what is perhaps the central aspect of international law—perhaps of all law. Some of these exceptions reveal themselves upon analysis to be more apparent than real. This applies in particular to the frequently quoted affirmation, in the case of *The Lotus*, of presumptive freedom of action in the sphere of international custom. In that case the Court, in refusing to admit that

---

[1] See above, pp. 158 *et seq.*
[2] See above, pp. 300 *et seq.*
[3] See above, pp. 227 *et seq.*
[4] See above, pp. 201 *et seq.*
[5] See pp. 330 *et seq.*

customary international law denied to States the right to prosecute aliens for offences committed abroad, said in a much-quoted passage: " International law governs relations between independent States. The rules of law binding upon States therefore emanate from their own free will as expressed in conventions or by usages generally accepted as expressing principles of law. . . . Restrictions upon the independence of States cannot therefore be presumed." [6] Some may have found it startling that the six Judges composing the majority of the Court committed themselves to the view that the rules of international law emanate—exclusively, it would seem— from the free will of States. Viewed in that light, the Court's statement, which seemed to amount to a full acceptance of the rigid positivist doctrine, gave the impression of being obsolete and contrary to the very terms of Article 38 of the Statute.[7] On closer investigation, however, the principle enunciated by the Court is less dogmatic and more flexible than a first reading makes it appear. In fact, in the very passage cited above, the Court qualified considerably the observation that rules of international law emanate from the free will of States. For it referred to their free will as expressed not only by conventions but also implicitly by " usages generally accepted." A " usage generally accepted " is one accepted by the generality of States, not necessarily by every single State.[8]

The second part of the principle as enunciated by the Court, namely, that restrictions upon the independence of States cannot be presumed, was, on the face of it, more open to question. Actually, it has laid itself open to criticism not because it means too much but because its apparent comprehensiveness proves upon analysis to be somewhat deceptive. The passage quoted means, in effect, that when the Court, with the help of all the sources of law which Article 38 of the Statute places at its disposal, has found no reason for limiting a State's freedom of action, it will not presume the existence of any such limitation. However, the range of sources of law contemplated by Article 38 is wide and comprehensive; it is

[6] Series A, No. 10 (1927), p. 18.
[7] See above, p. 165.
[8] See *West Rand Central Gold Mining Co., Ltd.* v. *The King* [1905] 2 K.B. 391, on the requirement of proof that " the particular proposition put forward has been recognised and acted upon by our country, or that it is of such a nature, and has been so widely and generally accepted, that it can hardly be supposed that any civilised State would repudiate it."

not limited to express manifestations of the will of States. Thus conceived, the passage in question is reminiscent of the frequent statements, referred to above, that only when the terms of a treaty are not clear and only when all other rules of interpretation have failed will recourse be permitted to preparatory work or to restrictive interpretation of treaty obligations.[9] Interpreted in that way, the principle of presumptive freedom of action appears to be almost a tautology.

Moreover, in a sense, the passage referred to was no more than an *obiter dictum*; it could have been omitted without affecting the Judgment of the Court. In the first instance, the Court's finding that Turkey did not disregard a rule of international law by assuming jurisdiction over an alien for an offence committed on the high seas was based not on an abstract rule but on an examination of the practice of States and of relevant municipal decisions showing the almost entire absence of protest against the assumption of such jurisdiction. Secondly, the main alternative ground of the Judgment of the Court was that, according to the widely accepted view which attaches decisive importance to the locality not of causation but of the effect of the action, the offence in the case of *The Lotus* took place not on the high seas but on a Turkish ship, *i.e.*, on Turkish territory. The reason why the Court may have felt impelled to engage in abstract considerations of the independence of States and the resulting presumptive freedom of action was probably the fact that the argument based on sovereignty was, as may be seen from the Dissenting Opinions and the written and oral pleadings, invoked with equal vigour by both parties.[10]

---

[9] See above, pp. 138 *et seq.* and pp. 300 *et seq.*

[10] It is also relevant to note—although that consideration is of limited importance—that the action with regard to which the Court applied the principle of presumptive freedom from restriction, namely, the act of assuming jurisdiction, related, though not wholly, to events which occurred in the territory of the defendant State as distinguished, for instance, from its conduct on the high seas or in the territory of another State. *Prima facie*—but only *prima facie*—a State has freedom of action, presumptively unencumbered by restrictions, within its territory in the sphere of what is usually described as matters falling within its exclusive domestic jurisdiction. Alleged restrictions in that sphere are subject to proof more stringent than in other cases. Such stringency of proof is not tantamount to a rigid application of the positivist view in the sense that every restriction must be traced to the consent, expressly given, of the territorial State. On the contrary, in so far as restrictions are grounded in customary international law and in general principles of law, no such particular consent is required in every case. This is of importance if it is borne in mind that the bulk of the rules of international law have reference to matters which take place within the territory of the States concerned.

114. *The Test of Prohibition (as distinguished from Permission) as the Standard of International Obligations. The Burden of Proof. The* Anglo-Norwegian Fisheries *Case*

The case of *The Lotus* calls for reflection, in the matter of the attitude of the Court to the sovereignty of States, also from another point of view. In that case—following upon the wording of the special agreement of the two Parties—the Court held in the operative part of the Judgment that in assuming jurisdiction over a French subject in respect of a collision which occurred on the high seas, Turkey " has not acted in conflict with the principles of international law." [11] Similarly, in the *Fisheries* case between the United Kingdom and Norway, in the operative part of its Judgment the Court held that " the method employed for the delimitation of the fisheries zone by the Royal Norwegian Decree of July 12, 1935, is not contrary to international law " and that " the base-lines fixed by the said Decree in application of this method are not contrary to international law." [12] The negative formulation of the Judgment followed that expressed in the Norwegian submissions which asked the Court to adjudge and declare that the Norwegian decree " is not contrary to international law." [13]

Does the form of these Judgments warrant the opinion that the Court has committed itself, in a manner fraught with far-reaching consequences, to the view that States are entitled to act as they please provided there is no express rule of international law prohibiting such action—provided, that is to say, their action is " not contrary to international law "—as distinguished from the view that, as sovereignty is a competence conferred and limited by international law, a State whose action is challenged must adduce positive proof that its action is permitted by international law? It has been suggested by a writer of authority [14] that if the first view is accepted—the view that a State's freedom of action is absolute unless specifically limited—then it might be sufficient for a State to " manoeuvre itself into the position of defendant " in order to benefit from the presumption of legality and freedom of action, a presumption which could be displaced only by proof that the action of the defendant State was contrary to international law. Such

[11] Series A, No. 10 (1928), p. 32.
[12] *I.C.J. Reports* 1951, p. 143.
[13] At p. 124.
[14] See Fitzmaurice in *B.Y.*, 30 (1953), p. 12.

proof, it has been pointed out, would be difficult to adduce while, by comparison, the burden of the proof—assuming that it rests upon the defendant—that the action was not contrary to international law, would be relatively easy in view of the unsettled and controversial character of many of the rules of international law.[15] A similar point of view was expressed in lucid terms by Judge Read in his Dissenting Opinion in the *Fisheries* case. He said:

> "The true legal character of the problem has been obscured. It has been treated as if the issue concerned the existence or non-existence of a rule of customary international law restricting the exercise of sovereign power by coastal States. It has been assumed that the United Kingdom must establish the existence of such a restrictive rule in order to challenge the validity of the 1935 Decree. It has been suggested that the British case must fail, unless it can be proved that such a restrictive rule is founded on customary international law."[16]

However, it may be asked whether this aspect of the matter in fact played any significant part—or any part at all—in the Judgment of the Court. That question must be answered in the negative notwithstanding the importance which the parties, amidst a conspicuous mixture of ingenuity and indecision, attached to it.[17] There is no

---

[15] *Loc. cit.*
[16] *I.C.J. Reports* 1951, p. 189.
[17] Norway contended generally that the burden of proof rested upon the United Kingdom for the reasons: (a) that, by contesting the validity of the Norwegian Decree of 1935, the United Kingdom was the plaintiff and that therefore the burden of proof rested upon her; (b) that, legally and historically, the rules of international law relating to the extent of the maritime domain of States emerged as restrictions of the sovereignty of States and not as its foundation. See, in particular, the *Counter-Memorial* of Norway, *Pleadings, etc.*, vol. I, p. 417, and the *Duplique, ibid.*, vol. III, pp. 282–286. In addition, with regard to the latter argument, Norway emphasised the primary competence—which, she maintained, was universally acknowledged—of the littoral State to delimit the coast. She contended that when an act performed by a State in the normal exercise of its competence is challenged by another State, it is for that State to prove the illegality of the action complained of and that, "in principle, a State need not justify a measure which it takes in the normal exercise of its competence" (*Duplique*, para. 333). Both parties agreed that, in general, the question of the burden of proof was irrelevant for the purpose of evidence of customary international law of a general character. They were also in agreement that exceptions from the general law must be proved by the party alleging them. But the agreement was qualified by reservations. Thus while Norway admitted that the Court was supposed to know the law and to gather itself the available evidence, she insisted that if such independent search did not substantiate the claim and if the plaintiff State failed to supply the evidence, the Court was bound to reject the claim (*Duplique*, para. 335). In the event, much of the forensic effort of both parties was directed towards showing that the other party was the complaining party and that the burden of proof therefore rested upon it. The explanation of the British apprehension in the matter of the burden of proof was given

reference to it in the Judgment of the Court and there is no reason to believe that in some inarticulate fashion the Court gave preference to one of the rival theories propounded by the parties on the subject. The decisive question was that of substantive law: Was there, or was there not, a customary rule of international law requiring that the territorial waters should be measured from a base-line parallel to the sinuosities of the coast? Was there, or was there not, a rule of international law that bays which are not more than ten miles wide should be assimilated to the national waters of the territorial State? It might be objected that the very answer to these questions was to a large extent dependent upon the theory which was adopted as to the burden of proof, inasmuch as the party upon which the burden of proof rested was in fact deemed to be under the duty to prove its assertion up to the hilt; that international practice on the subject, although generally concordant and warranting the assumption of the existence of a rule of international law, was not universally adopted; and that therefore the State upon which the *onus probandi* rested was, because of the tactical position in which it had been placed, unable to procure the proof thus required.

frequent expression in the course of the pleadings: " If it were the case that there were a burden of proof on the applicant State to prove the general rules of international law and if, owing to the conflicting practice of States, there might be said to be doubt as to what the relevant rules of international law were, then it would follow that because of the burden of proof the Court should reject the applicant's demand because the applicant State had not proved the existence of its rules beyond doubt and had thus not discharged the burden of proof." (Statement by Sir Eric Beckett, *Pleadings*, vol. IV, p. 33.)

It is somewhat difficult to see why the controversial duty to discharge the burden of proof should be combined with the equally controversial obligation—resulting from alleged presumptions against restrictions of sovereignty—of discharging it beyond doubt and thus making proof practically impossible. In the opening statement by the Attorney-General of the United Kingdom the question of the burden of proof was described as the second vital aspect of the case. The Court was informed at the outset that the point which the United Kingdom intended to stress was that the real issue before the Court was whether the United Kingdom was under an international obligation to accept Norway's claim rather than whether Norway was debarred by international law from making it (*Pleadings, etc.*, vol. IV, p. 25). The issue, as stated later, was not whether the Norwegian Decree must be held to be binding upon the United Kingdom unless shown by it to be positively forbidden by a specific rule of international law. It was contended by the United Kingdom that the rules of international law concerning the delimitation of coastal waters do not take the form of prohibitions restricting coastal States from making claims, but that they express themselves through laying down limits which the non-coastal State is bound to treat as enforceable against it (*Reply* by Professor Waldock, *Pleadings, etc.*, p. 395). Thus stated, the issue amounted to a complaint by Norway that the United Kingdom refused to recognise the Norwegian Decree as enforceable; that therefore Norway was the complaining State; and that therefore the burden of proving that the delimitation was in accordance with international law lay upon her.

It is probable that the doubts thus formulated simplify the situation. They attribute to the Court an inclination to decide issues of this nature by reference to technical rules or to doctrinal considerations as to the nature of sovereign rights conferred by or enjoyed by virtue of international law. The more substantial problem raised by this and similar cases, and discussed in another part of this Section,[18] was the attitude of the Court, by reference to express or implied claims of State sovereignty, to the question of the recognition of the existence of a customary rule of international law in cases in which the practice of States, while generally uniform, falls short of universal acceptance. It is this aspect of the problem which raises more substantially the question of the attitude of the Court to State sovereignty than the problem of the burden of proof as resulting from opposing views of the nature of the rights of the State under international law.

Even if the Court had gone to the unusual length of expressly subscribing to the view that sovereignty is a quality conferred by international law and that the same applied to specific rights of sovereignty, this would not necessarily have meant that Norway, whose conduct was impugned, would have been held bound to adduce positive and exacting proof that its action was permitted by international law. Such proof may in the nature of things be impossible except by showing that the action at issue is not contrary to international law. From this point of view it is probably not of decisive importance whether a State is called upon to prove that its action is permitted by international law—which proof is often conveniently discharged by evidence of its not being contrary to international law—or whether it has to show that its action is not prohibited by international law, which latter proof may legitimately be discharged by showing that the action in question is permitted by international law. The material question is in each case what is the substantive rule of international law applicable to the dispute. The actual distribution of the *onus probandi* may occasionally confer a tactical advantage upon one of the parties, but it is not easy to concede that that advantage can, in the long run, be decisive. Thus in the *Fisheries* case between the United Kingdom and Norway the question before the Court was, essentially, whether the method

---

[18] See below, pp. 368 *et seq*.

adopted by Norway for the delimitation of her territorial sea—for this was the primary fact with which the Court was confronted—was contrary to international law. Whatever may be the technical rules as to the distribution of the burden of proof, both parties in fact were at pains to adduce evidence of both a negative and a positive character. Norway pleaded that her action was permitted by international law and was not contrary to it; the United Kingdom argued that the Norwegian action was not permitted by international law and that it was contrary to it.

It would therefore appear that while the *Fisheries* case is of interest for the general issue here discussed, the lesson which can be derived from it in this respect is somewhat negative. Whatever may be the significance of the controversy as to whether the rights of sovereignty are derived from international law or whether they exist independently of it unless specifically restricted, the importance of that controversy for the settlement of disputes before the Court is distinctly limited. It is limited because its probable consequences in the field of evidence—the burden of proof—are somewhat narrowly circumscribed in the international sphere in which flexibility is the guiding principle. This is so not because there is no place for the refinements of the law of evidence in what Hall called the "rough jurisprudence of nations." [19]   It is so because the importance of the interests at stake precludes excessive or decisive reliance upon formal and technical rules. Moreover, even if the issue of the burden of proof were more relevant than it is in fact, it would be of decisive importance only if there were more undisputed validity in the principle of the presumptive freedom of action of States. No such principle can justifiably be deduced from the practice of the Court.[20] As pointed out in various parts of this book, there is room for doubt as to some of the aspects of the Judgment in the *Fisheries* case.[21] But it is submitted that less than justice is done to that important pronouncement of the Court by the

---

[19] *International Law* (8th ed., 1924, by Pearce Higgins), p. 395, n. 2.

[20] It will be noted that the Norwegian contention as to the restrictive character of rules of international law was not couched in general terms. It had reference only to the matter directly before the Court, namely, in respect of the rival claims of the freedom of the sea and the rights of littoral States. There is no suggestion in the Judgment of the Court that it was disposed, even in the field thus limited, to reduce the issue to the somewhat technical complexion of the predominance of one of the two rival principles —of the freedom of the seas or of State sovereignty over the adjacent sea.

[21] See above, pp. 196 *et seq.*, and below, pp. 368 *et seq.*

assumption that it was based, in a significant manner, on a technical rule of evidence in the shape of a rigid apportionment of the burden of proof or on a questionable doctrine of the paramountcy of sovereign rights in all cases where they are not specifically restricted by rules of international law.[22]

---

[22] But see the suggestion of Sir Gerald Fitzmaurice that "it is not too much to say that in the last analysis the *Fisheries* case was lost and won on this issue": *B.Y.*, 30 (1953), p. 9, n. 1. However, see p. 11 of the article where Sir Gerald—rightly, it is believed—points out that in fact the Court refused to act upon that doctrine and held, ultimately, that the validity of the delimitation of coastal waters depends upon international law.

# Chapter 28

# STATE SOVEREIGNTY AND CUSTOMARY INTERNATIONAL LAW

115. *Judicial Discretion and Ascertainment of Customary International Law. Universality and Generality of Practice. The* Anglo-Norwegian Fisheries *Case*

The issue which bore more directly upon the final decision of the Court in the *Fisheries* case than technical considerations of the burden of proof or doctrinal arguments as to the permissive or prohibitive nature of the rules of international law was the attitude of the Court to the creation of binding rules of customary international law. That issue, as will be suggested here, is not confined to the *Fisheries* case. There is a clear relation between claims of sovereignty and the creation and judicial recognition of binding customary international law. In few matters do judicial discretion and freedom of judicial appreciation manifest themselves more conspicuously than in determining the existence of international custom. The number and the importance of the States whose participation is necessary for the creation of custom; the presence of the conviction that the conduct in question is followed as a matter of legal obligation; the degree of relevance, in a particular situation, both of protest and of absence thereof; the determination whether the express adoption in treaties or otherwise of particular rules is expressive of existing or growing custom or whether the fact that the explicit adoption of such rules was deemed necessary points to the absence of custom—with regard to all these questions there are no clear limits to the comprehensiveness of judicial freedom of appreciation. Many an act of judicial legislation may in fact be accomplished under the guise of the ascertainment of customary international law. In all these cases there is a corresponding potential impairment of the freedom of the sovereign State conceived as the arbiter of its rights. This applies, in particular, to questions such as these: What is, in the language of Article 38 of the Statute, the degree of the requirement of generality of the " practice accepted as law "?  To what extent is it accurate to maintain that sovereign States can be held bound by implied consent only under the irresistible impact of universal and not merely general acceptance of what are considered to be rules of law?  Do departures from general practice, or claims inconsistent therewith, deprive such practice of its quality as binding custom not only in relation to the State or States departing from or objecting to that general practice, but absolutely?  To what extent does it lie with one sovereign State—or a small number of them—to decline to be bound by general custom for the reason that it, or they, have refused assent to it?

It would be misleading to suggest that in respect of all these points of contact between State sovereignty and the finding of rules of customary international law the jurisprudence of the Court exhibits a complexion of uniformity.  In a series of cases the Court has created the impression of having adopted a restrictive method of ascertaining the existence of customary international law in a manner which, unless carefully examined, may suggest a leaning towards the recognition of the claim of States not to be bound by rules of law unless clearly and unequivocally accepted.  This is so although the true explanation of that attitude may be different in individual cases.  Moreover, it is necessary to view these cases by constant reference to the fact that the Court has frequently applied customary international law as a matter of course even where practice did not exhibit any conspicuous complexion of uniformity.

In the *Anglo-Norwegian Fisheries* case the Court declined to admit that there existed a general rule of international law prescribing that the base-line of territorial waters must follow the sinuosities of the coast.[1]  Similarly, it refused to concede the existence of a general rule of international law laying down a ten-mile limit for the base-line of territorial waters in the case of bays.  With regard to both principles there had crystallised, prior to the Judgment of the Court in the *Fisheries* case, a preponderant,

---

[1] It is probable that on that issue the size of the majority was smaller than that which is indicated in the operative part of the Judgment and which was ten to two.  Judge Hsu Mo, of the majority of the Court, expressed the view that there existed a general rule of international law that " apart from cases of bays and islands, the belt of territorial sea should be measured, in principle, from the line of the coast at low tide " (at p. 154).  Possibly this may also have been the view of Judge Hackworth whose concurrence in the Judgment was limited to a statement expressing recognition of prescriptive rights of Norway.

though not a uniform or universal, practice. The Court declined to treat that practice as expressive of a binding rule of international law. In the case of the coast line it based its denial of the existence of a binding general rule on the numerous exceptions in the application of the rule and on the diversity of the methods employed. In the case of bays the Court stated that " although the ten-mile rule has been adopted by certain States both in their national law and in their treaties and conventions, and although certain arbitral decisions have applied it as between these States, other States have adopted a different limit " and that " consequently the ten-mile rule has not acquired the authority of a general rule of international law." [2]

The fact that the Court found itself unable to give to a practice which was preponderant, though not universal, the status of a binding rule of customary international law raises, in this sphere, an issue of a fundamental nature. If universality is to be made the condition of the application of customary rules, it may become doubtful whether many rules would qualify for that purpose. For while in most fields of international law there is agreement as to broad principle, there is almost invariably a pronounced degree of divergence with regard to the application of specific rules.[3] To say, therefore, that with regard to any particular matter no rule of international law exists unless practice is unanimous or approaching unanimity may result in giving judicial imprimatur to the existence of wide gaps in international law unless at the same time the Court lays down, by reference to existing practice and principle, what is the alternative binding and effective rule on the subject. This the Court attempted to do in the Judgment in the *Fisheries* case with regard to the base-line of territorial waters generally, when it indicated " certain basic considerations inherent in the nature of the territorial sea " which " bring to light certain criteria which, though not entirely precise, can provide courts with an adequate basis for their decisions, which can be adapted to the diverse facts in question." [4] Reasons have been given elsewhere why in cases such as these it may not be useful to attempt a more pronounced degree of elaboration.

---

[2] *I.C.J. Reports* 1951, at p. 131.

[3] See for an elaboration of the issues involved, in connection with the codification and development of international law, the present writer's article in *American Journal of International Law*, 49 (1955), pp. 16–43.

[4] At p. 133. These criteria are reproduced at length above at p. 194.

116. *The Same. Denial of Custom and the Completeness of the Law*

The Court seems to have added weight to the general principles which it laid down in the matter of the delimitation of territorial waters by affirming that they make it possible to judge the validity of the action undertaken by a State in the sense that such delimitation is subject to these principles. The Court said: "The delimitation of sea areas has always an international aspect; it cannot be dependent merely upon the will of the coastal State as expressed in its municipal law. Although it is true that the act of delimitation is necessarily a unilateral act, because only the coastal State is competent to undertake it, the validity of the delimitation with regard to other States depends upon international law." [5] The passage quoted goes a long way towards remedying the consequences of the denial of the validity of the base-line rule hitherto generally regarded as binding. This is so although it was not felt feasible to lay down in detail the law or the procedure of such international determination. The alternative solution would have been for the Court to lay down as a binding rule that any State which denies the validity of the hitherto predominant principle and appeals to those laid down by the Court in general terms must, if the validity of the determination undertaken by it is challenged, submit the dispute to adjudication by an international tribunal. No such binding rule can be deduced from the passage quoted unless it is interpreted as meaning that as "the validity of the delimitation with regard to other States depends upon international law" those other States may legitimately refuse to assent to its application against themselves except when its validity, when challenged, is upheld by an international tribunal applying the principles laid down by the Court.

No expression of view is here intended on the question whether these principles were of a novel character. The Court stated expressly that the drawing of straight lines by Norway constituted no more than "the application of general international law to a specific case." [6] Reasons have been given elsewhere in this book [7] which explain the refusal of the Court to face in detail all the implications of its apparently legislative approach to a situation in

[5] *I.C.J. Reports* 1951, at p. 132.
[6] At p. 131.
[7] See above, pp. 195, 196.

which previous practice, though general, was not uniform and in which equitable considerations underlying a Judgment given by an overwhelming majority of the Court called for the application of new methods. It is probably in that situation—the "realities" of which the Court resolved to meet in accordance with what it considered to be the requirements of justice [8]—that lies the explanation of this aspect of the Judgment of the Court as distinguished from the exaggerations of emphasis on the operation of the burden of proof [9] or on the ascertainment of customary international law by reference to State sovereignty presumed to be free from obligations unless their binding force is evidenced by unanimous consent.

### 117. *The Same.    The Case of the* Reservations to the Genocide Convention

Similar issues were raised in the Advisory Opinion of the Court on the question of *Reservations to the Genocide Convention.* To a degree even more pronounced than in the *Fisheries* case there appeared to exist a general rule of international law on the matter before the Court, namely, the rule requiring the unanimous consent of all signatories of a treaty to a reservation appended by a State desirous of becoming a party thereto. The Court denied the existence of a customary rule on the subject for the reasons that "examples of objections made by reservations appear to be too rare in international practice to have given rise to such a rule"; that the express resolution of the Council of the League of Nations, arrived at after a detailed examination of the practice of Governments, constituted "at best . . . the point of departure of an administrative practice" [10]; that there existed among the American States a different practice; and that the debates on the subject in the relevant Committee of the United Nations revealed a profound divergence of views.

It may be doubted whether the method adopted by the Court was indicative of any deliberate tendency to insist, in deference to State sovereignty or for similar reasons, on exacting proof of a universal or quasi-universal adherence to a given rule as a condition of its recognition as a binding rule of customary international law. The more convincing explanation is that the generally recognised

---

[8] See above, p. 192.          [9] See above, p. 363.
[10] *I.C.J. Reports* 1951, at p. 25.

rule in the matter of consent to reservations, based as it was on the principle of unanimity with all the concomitant disadvantages and anomalies inherent in its rigid application, was unsatisfactory and ripe for revision in the light of changed circumstances. The Court itself enumerated various factors as " manifestations of a new need for flexibility in the operation of multilateral conventions." [11] These factors included " more general resort to reservations, very great allowance made for tacit assent to reservations, the existence of practices which go so far as to admit that the author of reservations which have been rejected by certain contracting parties is nevertheless to be regarded as a party to the convention in relation to those contracting parties that have accepted the reservations." [12] Moreover, the Court referred to various circumstances connected with the Genocide Convention calculated to lead to " a more flexible" application of the principles underlying the rule of unanimous consent to reservations. In particular, it pointed to the universal character of the United Nations under whose auspices the Genocide Convention was concluded and to the very wide degree of participation in it as envisaged in the Convention.

This being so, the question arises whether it would not have been feasible for the Court to reach the conclusions at which it actually arrived without going to the length of denying the existence of a customary rule of international law on the subject. In the administration of international law, when the opportunities for the creation of obligatory rules are in any case rare and exposed to the vicissitudes of controversy, there may be disadvantages in denying the character of law to practices generally followed *opinione necessitatis juris*. That circumstance explains why, notwithstanding appearances to the contrary, the Opinion of the Court in this case, far from being based exclusively—or mainly—on the denial of what hitherto had been thought to constitute the customary rule on the subject, was in fact based on wider and more persuasive considerations. In the interests of justice and the necessities of international intercourse it is legitimate to attach decisive importance to the peculiarities of a given situation—as already noted, such peculiarities did exist in the case of the Genocide Convention—and, in reliance upon more general principles forming part of the existing law, to distinguish that situation from that subject to the normal application of the accepted rule and to adjudicate accordingly. It is in some

[11] *I.C.J. Reports* 1951, at p. 22.  [12] At pp. 21, 22.

such way that it may be feasible for the Court, in certain cases, to have recourse to an unavoidable measure of judicial legislation without raising doubts to which judicial legislation is naturally open. To put it in different words, it may be possible for judicial legislation to proceed not by way of attaching conditions of some rigidity to the existence of customary law but by the less conspicuous process of coping with particular situations by reference to general legal considerations of recognised validity as distinguished from a specific rule of law directly applicable. There were indications, in the previous practice of the Court, of the possibility of some such approach. Thus in the Advisory Opinion on the *Interpretation of the Treaty of Lausanne* the Court, while adhering in principle to the traditional requirement of unanimity, modified it in effect by holding that as no State could be judge in its own case only qualified unanimity was necessary.[12a] In the Opinion on the *Reservations to the Genocide Convention* the traditional rule of unanimous consent, to any particular reservation, of the parties to the Convention lent itself to a similar, though more drastic, modification—by reference, possibly, to the same, though more reasonably interpreted, principle of sovereignty which gave birth to the original rule of unanimous consent. Admittedly, the sovereignty of the contracting parties requires that they should not be compelled to enter into a treaty relation with a State attaching a reservation varying the terms of the Treaty as agreed. But there is also force in the view, which seems to underlie the Opinion of the Court, that the sovereignty of the contracting parties demands that they should not be deprived of the participation of a State making a reservation—however reasonable—by the refusal, however unreasonable and however unrepresentative, of other States to consent to such reservation. Thus viewed, the Opinion of the Court in the case of the *Reservations to the Genocide Convention* must, notwithstanding some of the arguments contained therein, be regarded not as a denial but as a development, through the technique of apparent judicial legislation, of the customary law on the subject.

118. *The Conditions of International Custom. The* Asylum *Case*

This case provides another example of an apparently exacting interpretation of conditions of international custom. The Court, by

---

12a See above, p. 160.

a substantial majority of fourteen votes to two, held that, contrary to the contention of Colombia, there existed no customary rule of international law among Latin-American States which gave to a State granting asylum the right to determine, by a unilateral and definitive decision, whether circumstances and the nature of the offence justified the grant of asylum. In referring to Article 38 of its Statute, the Court pointed out that " the Party which relies on a custom of this kind must prove that this custom is established in such a manner that it has become binding on the other Party " and that " the Colombian Government must prove that the rule invoked is in accordance with a constant and uniform usage practised by the States in question, and that this usage is the expression of a right appertaining to the State granting asylum and a duty incumbent on the territorial State." [13] After thus formulating the conditions determining the existence of a customary rule, the Court proceeded to apply them in an exacting manner. It held that the Montevideo Convention of 1933 which, *inter alia*, recognised the right of unilateral qualification, on the part of the State granting asylum, of the offence with which the refugee seeking asylum was charged, could not be invoked as having merely codified the existing law for the reason, among others, that it was ratified only by a limited number of States and that, as stated in its preamble, it modified the Havana Convention (which did not expressly incorporate the principle of unilateral qualification).

It is not necessary to scrutinise here in detail these considerations adduced by the Court. In some cases the absence of wide ratification of a signed treaty may be due to reasons other than opposition to a particular provision of that treaty. The Judgment did not elaborate either this aspect of the situation or the question of the weight which was to be attached to that part of the Colombian argument in which explanations were adduced of the absence of ratification of the Montevideo Convention by Peru and in which alleged instances were enumerated of Peru having acted upon the contested provisions of that Convention.[14] This does not necessarily mean that these elements of the problem were not considered by the Court.

The Court was equally exacting with regard to the reliance of Colombia on the frequent cases in which diplomatic asylum had

[13] *I.C.J. Reports* 1950, p. 276.
[14] See *Pleadings, Oral Arguments, Documents*, vol. II, pp. 95–97 (*Plaidoirie* of M. Yepes).

actually been granted and respected. It considered that Colombia had not shown that the right of unilateral and definitive qualification was "exercised by the States granting asylum as a right appertaining to them and respected by the territorial States as a duty incumbent on them and not merely for reasons of political expediency." [15] For these reasons the Court declared itself unable to find that Colombia had proved the existence of a custom as contended by her. Moreover, the Court held that even if such practice existed between a limited number of Latin-American States, it could not be invoked against Peru; the latter, in the view of the Court, was to be deemed to have repudiated it by refraining from ratifying the Montevideo Convention which was the first to include a rule concerning the qualification of the offence in the matter of diplomatic asylum. As stated, the Court did not entertain the possibility that the failure to ratify that Convention may have been due to reasons other than disagreement with the provisions on the subject of qualification of the offence. Probably—assuming that the right of qualification of the offence constituted in some respects a rule of Latin-American customary law—this feature of the Judgment illustrates the danger, often alluded to, that treaties which attempt to codify existing law may result in a set-back to established or incipient international custom wherever, for one reason or another, there is a failure to ratify.

What, however, is of more general interest, for the purpose of the attitude of the Court in that case, to the problem of customary international law is the manner in which, in the *Asylum* case, it assessed the probative value of the facts presented to it as having provided a basis for the creation of a rule of customary law. It said:

> "The facts brought to the knowledge of the Court disclose so much uncertainty and contradiction, so much fluctuation and discrepancy in the exercise of diplomatic asylum and in the official views expressed on various occasions, there has been so much inconsistency in the rapid succession of conventions on asylum, ratified by some States and rejected by others, and the practice has been so much influenced by considerations of political expediency in the various cases, that it is not possible to discern in all this any constant and uniform usage, accepted as law, with regard to the alleged rule of unilateral and definitive qualification of the offence." [16]

[15] At p. 277.      [16] *Ibid*.

The above general reference to the "uncertainty and contradiction," the "fluctuation and discrepancy," the inconsistencies in the rapid succession of treaties, and the considerations of political expediency in various cases, embodies the result of what must have been a thorough examination by the Court of the relevant issues of fact showing wherein lay the absence both of the requisite constancy of practice and of the conviction of the legally binding force of such practice as was followed. Constancy of practice is a recognised condition of custom. But constancy is a relative—not an absolute— term. The same applies to consistency and its counterpart, namely, political expediency, to which the Court alluded as vitiating the assumption of a legal conviction. Legal rules are often the result of an attitude—pursued for a long time—of reasonableness, of accommodation, of neighbourliness. The definite rise of custom, conceived as a binding rule, from the stage of revocable usage and courtesy, is a matter of degree. The transition does not easily lend itself to exact definition and precise determination. Its ascertainment may, in the last resort, be one of impression. It is a, necessarily controversial, problem of judicial technique whether it is conducive to the authority and the clarity of the decision that the exacting task of weighing and assessing the often conflicting relevant factors should appear on the face of the decision or whether its performance should be assumed.

### 119. *Treaties as an Element of Customary International Law*

From this point of view it is useful to draw attention to the view according to which the incorporation in a treaty of certain rules and principles suggests that these rules and principles have not hitherto formed part of the law. The Court relied on that reasoning in the *Asylum* case when it stated that "the fact that it was considered necessary to incorporate in that [the Montevideo] Convention an article accepting the right of unilateral qualification, seems to indicate that this solution was regarded as a new rule not recognised by the Havana Convention." [16a] It did the same in the case of the *Mavrommatis Palestine Concessions* where it held that, in case of doubt, jurisdiction based on an international agreement embraces all disputes referred to it after its establishment, and that "the reservation made in many arbitration treaties regarding disputes arising out of events previous to the conclusion of the

[16a] At p. 276.

treaty seems to prove the necessity for an explicit limitation of jurisdiction and, consequently, the correctness of the rule of interpretation referred to above." [17] It is possible to hold—and the Court has held so on occasions—that the frequency and identity of treaty provisions on a given subject, far from proving that they constitute an exception from the customary rule, result in the creation of international custom.[18]

That aspect of the situation was given expression, from a different point of view, in the *Lotus* case where the Court examined the French argument based on the existence of certain treaties which expressly reserve to the State of the flag jurisdiction over offences committed on the high seas. The Court pointed out that it was "not absolutely certain that this stipulation is to be regarded as expressing a general principle of law rather than as corresponding to the extraordinary jurisdiction which these conventions confer on the state-owned ships [19] of a particular country in respect of ships of another country on the high seas." [20]

This ambivalence of conclusions illustrates the wide range of judicial discretion in determining the existence of customary international law. Thus no simple rule can solve the difficulty inherent in the question whether uniform treaties recognising obligations on the part of the successor State merely give more specific expression to the general customary principle of State succession or, on the contrary, whether they are constitutive of obligations which but for their express conventional regulation would not exist at all; or whether the frequent, almost uniform, provisions of treaties of pacific settlement laying down the obligation of previous negotiations create, are

---

[17] Series A, No. 2 (1924), p. 35.

[18] However, while in some cases the Court relied in that way on treaties, it was rather the practice interpreting these treaties which it considered as evidence of international custom. Thus in the case of *The Wimbledon*, where it rejected the German contention that being a neutral State she was authorised to prohibit the passage of munitions through the internationalised Kiel Canal, the Court in discarding that contention as being contrary to "consistent international practice" relied both on the Suez and Panama Canal Conventions and on the actual interpretation of these treaties by the States concerned: Series A, No. 1 (1923), pp. 26–28. Its Judgment in the case of the *International Commission of the River Oder* (Series A, No. 23 (1929), p. 27) was based on the assumption of a customary "international river law" as laid down by the Congress of Vienna and "applied or developed by subsequent conventions." See also on this point Kopelmanas in *B.Y.*, 18 (1937), p. 136; Sørensen, *Les sources du droit international* (1946), p. 98; and Kosters, *Les fondements du droit des gens* (*Bibliotheca Visseriana*, IV (1925), p. 98).

[19] A somewhat unsatisfactory translation of "navires d'Etat" in the French text of the Judgment.                [20] Series A, No. 10 (1927), p. 27.

evidence of, or—by implication—deny the existence of a customary rule on the subject.   Only an analysis of the relevant practice in all its available manifestations can provide an answer to these and other aspects of customary international law.   An exacting effort applied to the task of examining in detail the actual situations underlying an appeal to custom may assist in coping with the mystery of custom oscillating inconclusively between being a law-creating source of legal rules and mere evidence of pre-existing law.[21]

### 120. *The Same.   The Conditions of* opinio necessitatis juris

It is only through some such approach that we may hope to overcome the undoubted difficulties of the so-called psychological conception of international custom—a somewhat pretentious notion which is no more than a description of the requirement of *opinio necessitatis juris, i.e.,* of the consciousness that the conduct, frequently or constantly pursued, is due to the existence of a sense of legal obligation or at least of the will to undertake a legal obligation.   It is not easy—although, as will be suggested, by no means impossible—with regard to any particular line of conduct to adduce positive proof that it was accompanied by this or any particular state of mind.   This is probably the reason for the occasional suggestion that while the ascertainment of the constancy of practice creates no problem, the utmost that can be hoped for with regard to the more intractable aspect of the matter, namely, the determination of *opinio necessitatis juris,* is to rely on the power of the judge to find whether in any given case there existed a conviction that the rule in question was followed as a matter of legal obligation.   In a sense, the solution suggested merely postpones

[21] For an instructive contribution to the perennial effort to elucidate the rise of custom from amongst the obscure recesses of mere conduct see the observations of Basdevant in " Règles générales du droit de la Paix " (*Hague Recueil*, 58 (1936) (iv), pp. 508–514). According to that analysis, practice—whether of Governments or of courts—is no more than a series of precedents which recognise, or accept, as binding an already existing rule.   However, it is not clear from the exposition of the learned writer whether that pre-existing rule is a rule of law or a mere notional expression of international social necessity, a rule of " raison pure " which by virtue of a precedent or of a series of precedents acquires the complexion of a legal rule.   In fact, it appears that even that is not sufficient and that the precedent does not as such result in a binding rule unless its authority is enhanced by becoming " the object of a favourable reaction on the part of those who count sufficiently in international law."   This includes not only Governments and courts, but also " la doctrine."   The value of that searching exposition lies in the reminder of the difficulty of giving a satisfactory analytical account of a phenomenon which, in the language of Art. 38 of the Statute of the Court—and of most definitions—is both a source and the evidence of binding rules.

the difficulty. Yet it is a solution which is preferable to the view that having regard to the difficulties of proof the requirement of *opinio necessitatis juris* ought to be dispensed with altogether.[22] Any such view which denies an essential element of custom both generally and in the international sphere, seems contrary to practice. Its explanation—though certainly not its justification—lies in the summary manner in which tribunals have occasionally applied that requirement.

Unless judicial activity is to result in reducing the legal significance of the most potent source of rules of international law, namely, the conduct of States, it would appear that the accurate principle on the subject consists in regarding all uniform conduct of Governments (or, in appropriate cases, abstention therefrom) as evidencing the *opinio necessitatis juris* except when it is shown that the conduct in question was not accompanied by any such intention.[23] The Judgment in the *Asylum* case is not inconsistent with some such approach. The solution may not be altogether satisfactory, but it is probably more acceptable than the alternative method of exacting rigid proof of the existence of international customary law in a manner which may reduce to a bare minimum its part as a source of law. Of this, the decision in the *Lotus* case, discussed below, provides an interesting example.[24] While it is impracticable to demand positive proof of the existence of legal conviction in relation to a particular line of conduct, it is feasible and desirable to permit proof that in fact the *opinio necessitatis juris* was absent.

There is no warrant for the assumption that the requirement of proof of the absence of a sense of legal obligation is impracticable or necessarily so exacting as to be unfair—even though it may be true that the state of mind of a Government may not be more easy to ascertain than the state of mind of an individual. For, on occasions, a statement accompanying an act—or abstention from action—on the part of a governmental or judicial authority makes it feasible to ascertain the conviction, on the part of the authority in question, that its conduct was dictated by a legally binding rule.

---

22 See Guggenheim in *La technique et les principes du droit public* (collection of essays in honour of Georges Scelle), vol. I (1950), pp. 275–284, for a valuable exposition of the subject.

23 For a lucid and penetrating examination of the problem from this point of view see Sørensen, *Les sources du droit international* (1946), pp. 88–111.

24 See below, pp. 386 *et seq.*

Thus diplomatic correspondence and the practice of national authorities provide sufficient proof that certain aspects of diplomatic privilege and immunities—as, for instance, with regard to freedom from customs examination—rest on revocable considerations of courtesy alone. The same applies, in countries such as the United States or Great Britain, to the practice of abstention from exercise of jurisdiction, in many respects, over foreign vessels in national waters.[25] From this point of view, the Judgment in the *Asylum* case is not—on account of its insistence on proof of an unspecified nature and degree—open to question as denying the existence of custom by reference to any exaggerated leaning towards the recognition of claims of sovereignty.

Moreover, it is probable that in the *Asylum* case the size of the majority of the Court which denied the existence, as a customary rule of law, of the right of unilateral qualification of the faculty of asylum, was due to the somewhat uncompromising manner in which the right of unilateral qualification of the offence was expressed both in the pleadings [26] and in the terms of the Convention of Montevideo which provided, *tout court*, that " the qualification of political offences belongs to the country which grants asylum." The appearance of rigidity of that claim was not altogether removed by the insistence of Colombia that she recognised an identical right of other States as against herself and that there was therefore no question of intervention or absence of equality.[27] On the other hand, it is of interest to note that in denying the legality of the action of Colombia in granting asylum in a case which she considered to be of an urgent nature, the Court was more sharply divided—the majority being one of ten to six.

## 121. *Restrictive Interpretation of Custom and Regional International Law*

It is perhaps in that aspect of the Judgment in the *Asylum* case that there lay, more than in anything else, a refusal to act upon one

[25] See, *e.g.*, the reply of Great Britain on the question of jurisdiction over foreign vessels in British territorial waters: Hague Codification Conference, 1930, *Bases of Discussion*, vol. II, Territorial Waters, p. 82.

[26] *I.C.J. Reports* 1950, p. 274.

[27] *Pleadings, Oral Arguments, Documents*, vol. II, p. 72 (*Plaidoirie* of M. Vasquez). See, on the other hand, *ibid.*, pp. 129, 140, for Professor Scelle's elaboration of the subject which seems to have impressed the Court. He said: " La solution de la qualification irréfragable est une solution d'inégalité flagrante, c'est une solution qui donne tous les droits à l'une des parties et qui les refuse tous à l'autre " (at p. 129).

of the distinguishing features of so-called American customary international law presumed to favour political asylum in foreign embassies and legations. In that sphere the Judgment provides an example of a restrictive interpretation of an alleged particular, or regional, custom by reference to what the Court considered to be general principles of international law. As pointed out above, the Judgment of the Court based as it was to a substantial extent on the prohibition of intervention—a prohibition held in particular esteem by Latin-American States—acknowledged to that extent both a claim of sovereignty [28] and a doctrine of much authority within the orbit of so-called American international law. That doctrine was, it appeared, in conflict with another institution of so-called American international law as embodied in the practice of political asylum. The Court, in an understandable quest for logical consistency, resolved the difficulty by giving decisive weight to one of these considerations. It decided in favour of the claim of sovereignty as embodied in the prohibition of intervention. On the other hand, the right to full recognition of a traditional practice adopted, by reference to their particular needs, by Latin-American States may in turn be claimed as deriving from their sovereignty. It is not certain that the exacting application of logic is invariably, or naturally, congenial to the genius of institutions of customary law in the relations of Latin-American States. It may not be easy to reconcile two potentially contradictory tenets of the regional law in question—the disapproval of intervention and the approval of the right to grant asylum which, in the view of the Court, is a species of intervention. Yet there may have been, perhaps unavoidably, an element of simplification in treating the grant of asylum as a kind of intervention particularly obnoxious to traditions of American international law. For both principles—that of emphatic rejection of intervention and that of political asylum in extraterritorial premises—have grown up together in that part of the world as appropriate to its needs, traditions and legal conceptions.

It was, perhaps, inevitable that the Judgment should acknowledge the decisive prominence of one set of these principles at the expense of another. This is so although the result thus reached was liable to be interpreted as doing a measure of violence to what the large majority of Latin-American States had come to

---

[28] See above, pp. 374 *et seq.*

regard as a set of ideas peculiar to their political and legal tradition from the very inception of their independent statehood—namely, that rebellion is not a crime and that prosecution, even if conducted in accordance with ordinary and orderly legal processes, for participation in rebellion is in the nature of persecution.[29]  There may or may not be justification for the view that revolutions, conceived as a regular method of political change, ought not to be encouraged through the institution of asylum or otherwise, and that some revolutions aim at or result not in the vindication of human freedom but in its suppression.  There may or may not be substance in the view that asylum secures immunity and impunity to professional politicians while leaving the masses pressed into the rebellion to the revengeful fury of the victorious party.  Such considerations, although they may have underlain in some measure the Judgment of the Court, were not germane to the issue actually confronting it. For they had not in fact prevented the rise of the Latin-American institution of asylum which had grown in competition, if not in conflict, with other notions equally dear to Latin-American communities.  The burden of the decision of the Court, which stands out in a startling manner in the maze of controversy, was that the attempted prosecution, by what the Court assumed to be normal judicial processes, of a leader of an unsuccessful rebellion did not constitute an " urgent case " warranting the grant of asylum.  To that extent, whatever may be the merits of the institution of asylum in general, the Judgment of the Court, in applying the yardstick of general international law to a particular regional custom, was calculated to create the impression of diminishing—in reliance, to a large extent, upon the claims of sovereignty of the territorial State— the area of customary law.[30]

On the other hand, the practical—as distinguished from the doctrinal—effect of the ruling of the Court was confined within narrow limits as the result of its refusal to hold that the offending

---

[29] From this point of view there was probably but scant appreciation of the spirit of the Latin-American institution of political asylum in the suggestion of Professor Scelle, acting as Counsel for Peru, with regard to both common and political crimes: " L'asile n'as pas pour but d'assurer l'impunité; tout criminel doit être condamné " (at p. 141), or of M. Alvarez, Counsel for Peru, that all the formalities required by Peruvian law had been fulfilled with regard to the prosecution of M. de la Torre (p. 72).

[30] For the suggestion that for that reason the Judgment may have the effect of discouraging resort to the Court on the part of Latin-American States, see Green in *International Law Quarterly*, 4 (1951), pp. 232 *et seq.*  But see the more restrained observations of Miss Morgenstern in *The Law Quarterly Review*, 67 (1951), p. 382.

State was bound to restore the legal position in conformity with the principal finding of the Court and its determination to leave the actual settlement of the dispute to some of those features of regional relations, history and psychology, which characterise the Latin-American institution of asylum.[31]  These peculiarities the Court deemed itself unable to take decisively into account for the purposes of the main aspect of its Judgment, namely, the basis and the limits of the Latin-American institution of political asylum in embassies and legations.  To that—perhaps negative—extent the Judgment of the Court in the *Asylum* case must be regarded as having made a contribution to the elucidation of some of the intractable aspects, both practical and jurisprudential, of the function of custom as a source of international law.

### 122. *Abstention as a Factor in the Creation of Custom.   The Case of the* Lotus

The insistence, in the *Asylum* case, on the " psychological element " in customary law was not in the nature of a new departure in the practice of the Court.  The Permanent Court of International Justice had acted upon it, in a conspicuous fashion, in the *Lotus* case in answer to the French contention that criminal prosecutions in the matter of collisions with respect to persons belonging to a ship had as a rule taken place only before the courts of the State whose flag the ship flew and that that circumstance showed that the other States whose ships or nationals were involved had recognised, by abstaining from prosecution, that as a matter of positive international law they were bound so to abstain. The Court, in a frequently quoted passage, considered that conclusion not to be warranted.   It said:

> " Even if the rarity of the judicial decisions to be found among the reported cases were sufficient to prove in point of fact the circumstance alleged by the Agent for the French Government, it would merely show that States have often, in practice, abstained from instituting criminal proceedings, and not that they recognised themselves as being obliged to do so; for only if such abstention were based on their being conscious of having a duty to abstain would it be possible to speak of an international custom.  The alleged fact does not allow one to infer that States have been conscious of having

[31] See above, p. 382.

such a duty; on the other hand, as will presently be seen, there are other circumstances calculated to show that the contrary is true." [32]

What were these circumstances? The Court pointed, in the first instance, to the differences in the practice of municipal courts on the subject. It recalled two decisions favouring the exclusive jurisdiction of the country of the flag and two based on the opposite principle; and it referred to the written proceedings in which the Parties expressed conflicting views on the importance of these decisions. By reference to these decisions the Court regarded it as sufficient to observe that " as municipal jurisprudence is thus divided, it is hardly possible to see in it an indication of the existence of the restrictive rule of international law which alone could serve as a basis for the contention of the French Government." [33] The Court then proceeded to note the fact that in the two cases to which it referred no protest had been made by the two Governments concerned against the exercise of jurisdiction and that that fact was " directly opposed to the existence of a tacit consent on the part of States to the exclusive jurisdiction of the State whose flag is flown."

This reasoning of the Court calls for comment. It is possible to contend—a somewhat strained contention—that as in one case to which the Court referred the French Government failed to protest against the assumption of jurisdiction by a foreign court, France was precluded from arguing that such jurisdiction was contrary to international law. The difficulty arises from the fact that by reference to two cases, counterbalanced by two opposing decisions, the Court arrived at a finding as to the state of international practice on the matter and that it did so in disregard of practically continuous abstention from the exercise of criminal jurisdiction on the part of States, other than the State of the flag, affected by the collision. That difficulty the Court countered by the statement, referred to above, that no proof had been adduced that the abstention was due to the consciousness of a legal duty to abstain. Yet it is not clear what proof of such consciousness could feasibly be adduced. It is possible that prolonged search—and a certain amount of good fortune—might have enabled counsel for France to adduce instances of cases in which such assumption of criminal

---

[32] Series A, No. 10 (1927), p. 28.
[33] *Ibid.*, p. 29.

jurisdiction was contemplated or demanded by the parties affected
but in which the courts and other authorities of the country concerned, after mature deliberation duly recorded, abstained from
exercising such jurisdiction because of a rule of international law
which prohibits it.    It may seem exacting to demand such proof
in face of a continuous practice of abstention.    Such abstention is
particularly impressive when it is considered that the inducements
to assumption of criminal jurisdiction, in matters of collision and
otherwise, are often of particular potency in the realm of sentiment
and national interest and security.    Here, more than elsewhere,
there was room for acting on the view that continuous conduct
within legally relevant spheres of action must be deemed *prima
facie* to be expressive of a consciousness of a legal duty and that
proof was required to negative that assumption.    This applies both
to positive conduct and to mere abstention; it applies in particular to
the latter seeing that it is by nature inarticulate and not likely to be
accompanied by explanations for the benefit of scholarly research
or future litigation.    The Judgment of the Court in the *Lotus* case
does not specify the reasons for which continuous abstention in the
matter of exercise of jurisdiction should not be regarded as expressive of a legal duty.    Indeed, the passage quoted ends with the
words: "On the other hand, as will presently be seen, there are
other circumstances calculated to show that the contrary is true."
However, these circumstances are not apparent from the Judgment
of the Court.    The fact—and that is the only fact which appears
from the Judgment of the Court—that on two occasions jurisdiction
was exercised and that its exercise met with no protest on the part
of the State concerned, would have been relevant for the purpose of
finding that there was no uninterrupted practice; it had no relevance
to the question whether such practice as existed took place under the
aegis of *opinio necessitatis juris*.

### 123. *The Same. The Degree of Proof of Custom and the Sove-reignty of States*

As in the other cases bearing on customary international law
and reviewed above, so also the method thus adopted in the *Lotus*
case calls for reflection.    Undoubtedly, in the field of custom the
ascertainment of the requisite frequency of conduct or of the *opinio
necessitatis juris* is a matter of degree and to that extent a matter of

discretion. However, that discretionary element in the determination of custom gains in persuasiveness by a detailed indication of the manner by which it has been applied. This is so specially in relation to what is the primary source of international law. In the municipal sphere custom is not, in the modern State, a primary source of law. This is so although occasional legislative attempts, as in the case of the history of the German Civil Code,[34] to abolish it altogether as a formal source of law have remained unsuccessful. In the modern State, in particular under the systems of the civil law, custom is a secondary source of law. In the international sphere, where legislation in the true sense of the word is non-existent, custom is still the primary source; it supplies the framework, the background and the principal instrument of interpretation of treaties. Accordingly, a judicial technique which leads to narrowing down the scope of application of custom may be open to some objection as weakening one of the main foundations of the law.

To call attention to the disadvantages of any such method does not imply that tribunals are free—or called upon—to give the imprimatur of custom to any kind of conduct, however sporadic and however devoid of a sense of legal obligation. What it does imply is that it is incumbent upon courts to examine all available evidence in a manner revealing the factual links of judicial reasoning resulting in the acceptance or rejection of practices as constituting binding custom. There is no reason why such scrutiny should be conducive to a relaxation of the essential conditions of custom. This applies in particular to the requirement of the conviction of legal obligation. To deny the necessity of such conviction is to adopt for the creation of international custom a standard different from that obtaining within the State; to ignore the practice of international tribunals; and to disregard the distinction, which is a matter of daily experience in international practice, between custom which implies a legal obligation and mere usage which is no more than a generalisation of revocable acts of courtesy and accommodation. But there is a difference between admitting that and putting the requirement of conviction of legal necessity so high as, in the words of a scholar of authority, to " erect a barrier " in the way of creation and recognition of customary international law.[35] In the

---

[34] For an instructive account see Gény, *Méthode d'interprétation et sources en droit privé positif*, vol. I (1919), pp. 432–439.

[35] Basdevant, *loc. cit.*, p. 517. And see generally MacGibbon in *B.Y.*, 31 (1954), pp. 146–151.

case of the *Lotus* the Court created with many the impression of having done so—a fact which led some, as a counsel of despair, to deny altogether the requirement of *opinio necessitatis juris*.

Neither, and here we turn once more to the central theme of the present discussion, must we lose sight, in this connection, of the relation between the judicial treatment of custom and the doctrines of sovereignty—a reminder particularly apposite in the *Lotus* case in which the Court seemed to affirm the presumptive freedom of action of sovereign States as one of the guiding principles on the subject. It is in the name of the sovereignty of the legislature that the modern State has tended to limit the sphere of binding operation of custom. It is by reference to State sovereignty that writers of the positivist school have occasionally assimilated custom to a treaty in the sense that it requires not only the conviction of the existence of a legal obligation on the part of the acting or abstaining States, but also its acceptance as such by other States. They have also contended that the creation of international custom is limited to those organs of the State which represent it in the international sphere.[36] It is of importance that international tribunals should not infuse a further element of vitality into the real or spurious emanations of sovereignty by exacting conditions of hampering stringency upon the limitations of that sovereignty through conduct which in fact and in law may properly be held to amount to binding custom.

### 124. *The Same.* *The Case concerning* Rights of Nationals of the United States of America in Morocco

The considerations adduced in the preceding paragraphs and relating to the method and degree of elaboration in ascertaining customary rules of international law apply also, to a limited extent, to some of the principal issues in the case of the *Rights of Nationals of the United States in Morocco*. One of these issues, which was whether the consular jurisdiction and other capitulatory rights of the United States in Morocco were founded upon " custom and usage," presented itself to the Court in two ways: in the first instance, the Court was confronted with the question whether in the period between 1787 and 1937—this being the period in which

---

[36] See, for instance, Anzilotti, *Cours de droit international* (French ed., 1929), p. 73; Cavaglieri, *Corso di diritto internazionale* (3rd ed., 1934), p. 56. And see for comment thereon Kopelmanas in *B.Y.*, 18 (1937), p. 131.

there were in force treaties concluded by Great Britain and, by virtue of the most-favoured-nation clause, forming the basis of the rights of the United States—the rights of the United States were also based on " custom and usage " (with the result that they continued subsequent to the cessation of the British treaties). The Court rejected that assertion. It alluded to the contention adduced by the United States that at the Conferences at Madrid and Algeciras there were represented Powers which had concluded no treaties with Morocco but whose rights were apparently recognised as based on custom and treaty by the very fact of their participation in the Conferences. It also referred to the argument that after the establishment of the Protectorate in Morocco the rights of a large number of States similarly situated were indirectly recognised by the fact that France had obtained from them declarations of renunciation. The Court held, in a brief statement, that " this is not enough to establish that the States exercising consular jurisdiction in pursuance of treaty rights enjoyed in addition an independent title thereto based on custom or usage." [37]

The apparent basis of that finding raises issues of some interest. Is it that a State whose right is grounded in a treaty is, as a result, no longer in the position to assert these rights by virtue of custom? It may be interesting to speculate on the consequences of some such rule and on the resulting willingness of States to conclude treaties confirming or defining their customary rights. One of these results might be that if a State possessing customary rights becomes a party to a most-favoured-nation treaty and if, in consequence, it acquires rights by virtue of a treaty subsequently concluded by a third State, then it may be deprived of all its rights—customary and other—as soon as the treaty concluded by that third State lapses. However, it is not certain that the brief passage quoted above was intended to convey the view of the Court as to the final merger of customary and treaty rights. It is possible—perhaps probable—that in using the expression " this is not enough " the Court merely intended to hold that the two circumstances adduced above [38] were not sufficient to establish a customary right.

The Court did not examine the circumstances which an impressive Dissenting Opinion of four Judges held to be sufficient, such as

[37] *I.C.J. Reports* 1952, p. 200.
[38] Namely, the participation of non-treaty Powers in the Madrid and Algeciras Conferences and the declaration of renunciation on the part of States similarly situated.

that, in fact, at the period in question both treaty and usage, as conceived in particular in British legislative instruments as a source of jurisdiction, were at work; that there was an admission by France to the effect that the treaty of 1856 incorporated existing usages in this respect; that a treaty between Spain and Morocco of 1861 referred to existing usages on the subject; and that in the legislation of the United States constant reference was made, during that period, to established usages on the subject.[39]  It is beyond the scope of the present discussion to examine the relevance and justification of these arguments adduced by the Dissenting Judges.  The Court did not refer to them in detail.  This being so, only limited importance can be attached to the textual reference—the citation in full —in the Judgment of the Court to the passage from the Judgment in the *Asylum* case in which the Court defined the conditions of admissibility of custom.[40]  The Court, after citing the passage in question, merely reiterated its view that " in the present case there has not been sufficient evidence to enable the Court to reach a conclusion that a right to exercise consular jurisdiction founded upon custom and usage has been established in such a manner that it has become binding upon Morocco." [41]  This aspect of the case tends, it is submitted, to lend support to the view that the complexities—indeed the mysteries—of the rise of binding customary law from amidst the amorphous and, when taken in isolation, inconclusive manifestations of conduct cannot be solved by mere reliance on a definition of customary law.  They can be solved only by an examination of concrete situations and by an attempt at evaluating, by reference to general standards, the bearing of these manifestations upon the requirement of constancy of conduct and conviction of legal necessity.

In comparison, no literal importance need be attached to the aspect of the Judgment, connected with that discussed above, in which the Court—again by a majority of six to five—rejected the view that subsequent to 1937 the conduct of the French and Moroccan authorities in fact amounted to a recognition of the claim of the United States as based on custom and usage.  The Court held that such acquiescence in the continued exercise of consular

---

[39] *I.C.J. Reports* 1952, at pp. 219–221 (Dissenting Opinion of Judges Hackworth, Badawi, Levi Carneiro and Sir Benegal Rau).
[40] See above, p. 380.
[41] At p. 200.

jurisdiction and other capitulatory rights was merely provisional pending the contemplated settlement by negotiation. This aspect of the question, which is more properly germane to the question of admission and acquiescence, is related to the problem of custom only in so far as, in the view of the Court, the conduct of France was in the nature of an act of courtesy not amounting to a recognition of legal obligation. The Court declined to attach importance to the fact that the accommodating conduct of France followed upon the legal assertion, on the part of the United States, of a legal right.[42] It treated such formal assertions as being isolated expressions, " considered without regard to their context," [43] in the course of diplomatic correspondence. It might have been open to the Court to hold that the very fact that negotiations were continuing, in face of a formal initial assertion of a right by one of the parties, may properly be construed as a disinclination of the other party to acknowledge the existence of that right although, as a matter of

---

[42] See the emphatic statement, as quoted in the Dissenting Opinion (at p. 221), in a Note of the Government of the United States of October 19, 1937: " In order that there may be no misunderstanding, I think it is pertinent to point out that American capitulatory rights in Morocco are derived not only from the American-Moroccan Treaty of 1836, but also from other treaties, conventions, or agreements and confirmed by long-established custom and usage." The Court, by way of an alternative to a general treatment of the subject, was free to examine the French Note of August 26, 1937 (*Pleadings, etc.*, vol. I, p. 729) which, it was alleged in the French *Réplique* (*Pleadings, etc.*, vol. II, p. 55), contained a formal intimation that France was entitled to terminate the régime of extraterritoriality but that she wished to negotiate on the question of the termination of the régime. It would appear that the Note does not necessarily bear out the interpretation put upon it in the French *Réplique*. An expression of the view of the Court on the subject would have been of direct interest for the issue involved as well as of general bearing on the question of the limits of acquiescence. The same applies to the contention put forward by France that, contrary to the view of the United States as well as of that eventually expressed by the Dissenting Judges (see above, p. 390), the participation by certain States, which claimed no rights by virtue of treaties, in the Conference of Algeciras did not imply that they possessed rights based on custom seeing that that Conference was concerned with the problem of protection of nationals by reference to general international law (*Réplique*, p. 56). Similarly, it would have been of interest to have the answer of the Court to the contention of the United States, supported by the Dissenting Judges, that the express renunciation of capitulatory rights by non-treaty States was consistent only with the existence of customary rights independent of treaty (*Réplique*, p. 57; see also the Oral Argument of Mr. Fisher, *ibid.*, p. 285). As the Court found in favour of the French contention on this aspect of the question, it was not probably necessary for it to express an opinion on the French submission based on the doctrine of so-called inter-temporal law to the effect that even if the United States had succeeded in establishing the existence of a customary right of capitulations in Morocco, the collective conviction of the obligatory force of that custom had long ceased to exist as the result of the general tendency to substitute for that régime a new system based on the principle of equality of States (*ibid.*, p. 69).

[43] At p. 200.

courtesy and accommodation, it permits the continued operation, pending the negotiations, of the right thus contested.

Thus both aspects of the question bearing on customary law in this case emphasise, indirectly, what is the proper function of international tribunals in this matter. That function is to ascertain the existence or otherwise of customary international law by reference to the complex facts underlying its emergence into the realm of binding rules of conduct.

### 125. *Normal Application of Customary International Law*

There is a danger that emphasis upon one particular aspect of a problem may tend to distort the perspective in which the problem as a whole ought properly to be viewed. Thus the preceding observations on the occasional unwillingness of the Court to recognise the existence of customary international law on account of what it considers to be insufficient proof of the requisite degree of uniformity or conviction of *necessitas juris* may, if considered in isolation, create the impression that the Court has but seldom applied customary international law. Any such impression finds no true confirmation in the activity of the Court. It relies on customary international law constantly and as a matter of course—a fact which explains the inconspicuous character of the process. Thus it is only seldom that the Court in applying a rule of customary international law does so *eo nomine* as, for instance, in the case of the *Corfu Channel* where it stated that " it is . . . generally recognised and in accordance with international custom that States in time of peace have a right to send their warships through straits used for international navigation between two parts of the high seas without the previous authorisation of a coastal State, provided that the passage is *innocent*." [44]  In the same case the Court conceded that " as international practice shows . . . a State on whose territory or in whose waters an act contrary to international law has occurred, may be called upon to give an explanation." [45]  It then proceeded to elaborate, without any direct reference to international custom, the range and implications of this aspect of State responsibility.

Actually, whenever the Court applies international law it has

[44] *I.C.J. Reports* 1949, p. 28.
[45] *Ibid.*, p. 18.

recourse to international custom—unless expressly or by implication it is a treaty which provides the source of the decision. It is this fact which is decisive—and not the occasional restrictive tendency in the matter of recognition of custom or the use of language expressly referring to international custom as a source of law. The latter is infrequent and occasionally lacking in precision—as in the case of the *Lotus* where the Court referred to " usages generally accepted as expressing principles of law " [46] or in the case of the *Serbian Loans* where it spoke of the creation of rules of private international law by international conventions or customs, which rules in " the latter case may possess the character of true international law governing the relations between States." [47] It is also clear that the Court in fact relies on international custom when it uses such expressions as " consistent international practice " in relation to the passage of ships through international canals,[48] an " almost universal opinion and practice " in the matter of respect for private rights by the successor State,[49] " generally accepted international law " with regard to the expropriation of property of aliens,[50] " the unvarying tradition of all diplomatic meetings or conferences " [51] in the matter of the rule of unanimity, and the like. It is not necessary to elaborate by further examples what, as already stated, is the obvious and constant phenomenon of the application of customary international law on the part of the Court.

---

[46] See above, p. 360.
[47] Series A, No. 20 (1929), p. 41.
[48] *The Wimbledon*, Series A, No. 1 (1923), p. 25.
[49] *German Settlers in Poland*, Series B, No. 6 (1923), p. 36.
[50] *German Interests in Polish Upper Silesia*, Series A, No. 7 (1926), p. 22. And see *ibid.*, p. 42, for the reference to " the principle of respect for vested rights, a principle which, as the Court has already had occasion to observe, forms part of generally accepted international law."
[51] *Interpretation of the Treaty of Lausanne*, Series B, No. 12 (1925), p. 30.

# CHAPTER 29

CONCLUSIONS

*126. The Rule of Law, Judicial Discretion and State Sovereignty*

The normal application, as surveyed in the preceding Section, of customary international law on the part of the Court brings into prominence one of the crucial aspects of the problem of sovereignty in relation to the Court—the problem of the measure of surrender of sovereignty implied in the submission to its jurisdiction. Both expressions—" surrender " and " sovereignty "—are here used in a provisional sense; they are concerned with a *prima facie* impression. For there is no question of sovereignty, conceived as independence in relation to other States, being affected as the result of such submission. Neither, having regard to the ordinary meaning of words, can there be any question of impairment of sovereignty. The true relation between the exercise of jurisdiction by the Court and the sovereignty of States is expressed by the fact that as the result of such jurisdiction the rights of States are determined not by a unilateral assertion of their adversaries but by the arbitrament of the law.[1]

However, in so far as sovereignty is, inaccurately, identified with the traditional legal right of States to be judges in their cause, submission to the jurisdiction of the Court does imply a surrender of sovereignty. The measure of that surrender is to some extent proportionate to the degree of discretion open to the Court when deciding cases submitted to it. When the law is clear and non-controversial, judicial discretion is correspondingly circumscribed within narrow limits. Even then it is far from being wholly eliminated. For it may, and must, express itself substantially, albeit inconspicuously, by the manner in which it ascertains the facts relied upon by the parties and in which it applies to them the existing law. But when, as in the field of international custom, the law is rarely clear and undisputed, judicial freedom of determination gains in significance. There are only few branches of customary international law in which the concrete regulation of details—as

---

[1] See above, pp. 338 *et seq.*

distinguished from the acknowledgment of general principle—shows any ascertainable degree of agreement and uniformity.[2] The problem is necessarily rendered more acute in proportion to the tendency—which has been noted above—to attach exacting conditions to the ascertainment of custom both in the matter of the requisite generality of conduct and the conviction of the existence of a legal obligation.

The position thus viewed with regard to customary international law affects also the measure of judicial discretion in the matter of interpretation of treaties. For although the primary object of the judicial function in this sphere is to ascertain the intention of the parties, that intention can often be ascertained only against the background of customary international law.[3] Moreover, even when a treaty can be interpreted without reference to customary international law, and even when the latter is clear and undisputed, the international judicial function does not on that account become purely automatic. For the ascertainment of the intention of the parties is by no means a mechanical operation. Often, particularly in relation to multilateral treaties, to discover the intention of the parties is no easier than to ascertain the intention of the legislature. Of this aspect of the question the preceding chapters of this book provide instructive illustrations.[4] The " plain " or " ordinary " or " natural " meaning of terms may provide no help; to assume it may amount to avoiding rather than to accomplishing the true object of interpretation. There are, in the first instance, occasions in which the parties did not at all contemplate the cases or types of cases which present themselves to the Court. There are instances in which, largely for that very reason, although the language which the parties have used is clear, its automatic and literal application may lead to an absurdity or a travesty of what must reasonably be assumed to have been the intention of the parties. Finally, even in the absence of difficulties of that character, the Judge is often confronted with a choice between conflicting and equally legitimate principles of interpretation. It is his duty to give effect to the intention of the parties. But he is bound to interpret that intention in accordance with the paramount principle of good faith which demands that, again within the limits determined by circumstances,

---

[2] For an elaboration of this point in relation to the codification of international law see the present writer's article in *A.J.*, 49 (1955), pp. 17–23.

[3] See above, pp. 26 *et seq.*  [4] See above, pp. 134 *et seq.*

the maximum of effect must be given to the instrument in which the parties have purported to create legal obligations. At the same time he must take into account the fact that, especially in the international sphere, their intention may have been to create only a limited or even a nominal obligation. To what extent is that intention decisive? To what extent is it subject to the apparently overriding principle that the object of treaties is to create legal obligations?

Of this constant necessity of making a choice, not easily predictable in advance, between varying and conflicting principles of acknowledged validity, the jurisprudence of the Court in the matter of its own jurisdiction offers an instructive example. According to one set of principles, acted upon by the Court, the parties, in subscribing to a treaty which purports to confer jurisdiction upon the Court, have entrusted it with the power to make that obligation effective. According to another principle, similarly recognised by the Court, its jurisdiction, which is grounded in the will of States, cannot be lightly presumed and must be proved up to the hilt. Which set of considerations is to prevail? The opposing parties will appeal exclusively to one or the other. They will find impressive authority in the jurisprudence of the Court in support of both of these opposing contentions.

In this and most other cases, the choice which the Court may eventually make between conflicting principles does not lend itself to easy prediction. That choice can be made only after conscientious and exhaustive scrutiny; even then the decision, when made, is not invariably accompanied by any feeling of inevitability. The only sentiment that can be registered with confidence is that the decision is accompanied by a consciousness of duty performed. The salient factor in most situations is that the legal merits of a case are seldom so obvious as to permit the elimination of the necessity to balance the conflicting or competing legal considerations—all of which are relevant to the case and all of which, though in different degrees, are worthy of consideration. This is so, unavoidably, for the reason that, like every other tribunal, in the cases which confront it the International Court of Justice is not, as a rule, faced with situations which, upon examination, reveal a clear and obvious preponderance of the legal merits of the claim of one party as against that of the other. Both parties advance contentions which deserve recognition. As before any other court, it is seldom a question of a clear and undisputed right against the entire absence of a right. It is, as a rule, a question of giving effect to a better right against a right of less compelling legal merit. For this reason, the survey of the practice of the Court undertaken in this book is not intended to provide a ready solution to problems which may confront the Court. It is, more accurately, an analysis of the considerations and problems which, in the light of experience, have proved relevant to forming the Judgments and Opinions of the Court. There are no uniform rules or even principles which can be spelt out from the available practice. The instances of judicial caution are counterbalanced by the examples of judicial valour. The application of the principle of effectiveness is tempered by regard for the sovereignty of States and the intention of the parties interpreted in the light of their presumptive freedom of action. Conversely, experience has shown that considerations of sovereignty are not uniformly or preponderantly decisive. They are, in turn, put in the requisite perspective by the imperative demands of good faith and the requirement of effectiveness of the obligations voluntarily entered into by the parties.

In all these spheres judicial responsibility, in its quest for justice,[5] has full scope. That quest can derive no decisive assistance from exclusive reliance upon one single doctrine, or tendency, or formula. Unavoidably, in the zeal of forensic effort which it is their business to display, parties will rely upon some such exclusive consideration —just as they will often appeal to what may be no more than an argumentative stratagem. Thus they will assert that it is the business of the Court to interpret treaties and not to rewrite them, or that its task is to apply the law and not to change it. That brand of argument, which depicts the judicial function as obvious and automatic, may be no more than a piece of dialectics which begs the question. For the point is what the treaty, properly interpreted, means; the question is what the law is. That question is not answered by the assertion that the interpretation contended for by the other party would amount to rewriting the treaty or changing the law.

---

[5] It is of interest to note Chancellor Kent's revelations of his own judicial processes in reaching a decision after having made himself " master of the facts ": " I saw where justice lay, and the moral sense decided the Court half the time; I then sat down to search the authorities. . . . I might once in a while be embarrassed by a technical rule, but I almost always found principles suited to my view of the case " (as quoted by Frank, *Law and the Modern Mind* (1930), p. 104).

It is that necessity of making a decision not between claims which are fully justified and claims which have no foundation at all but between claims which have varying degrees of legal merit—it is that necessity which, in common with the activity of legal tribunals generally, characterises the work of the International Court. For reasons stated, that factor is particularly conspicuous in the international sphere. It is also for these reasons that many a case decided by the Court would not necessarily have given the impression of a manifestly wrong application of the law if the decision had gone the other way. It would provide an exercise of some interest and instruction to survey the work of the Court from that point of view. Undoubtedly, it is proper and imperative to consider the decision of the majority of the Court as representing the better law—*the* law. For it is the law which expresses definitely the rights and obligations of the parties. However, while it is the decision thus given which is henceforth the authoritative law, it ought not to be treated as a preordained decree arrived at with an ease stemming from a consciousness of or a claim to infallibility. It is the result of travail and searching which in themselves evidence the ever-present element of judicial responsibility.

The degree of precariousness of the line dividing the content of a decision from its opposite is not invariably indicated by the size of the majority by which it has been reached or even by the fact that it may have been arrived at by a vote amounting to or approaching unanimity. For such unanimity may indicate not that the opposing view was entirely devoid of legal merit but that, however strong and compelling it may have been, it was not found to be as strong and compelling as the view which the Court has found to represent the better law. With only a slight preponderance of merit in the opposite direction the unanimous vote might have gone the other way. This means that although frequently the unanimous Judgment or Opinion is an indication of the overwhelming strength of the view upheld by the decision of the Court, on occasions unanimity may not be incompatible with the fact that the scales between the opposing views were almost evenly balanced and that the decision reached was by no means a matter of course. Again, an examination of that aspect of the work of the Court might yield results which would not be devoid of instruction as showing the nature of the responsibility discharged by the Court.

Neither is the necessity of judicial choice eliminated by the fact

that a matter is covered by apparently uniform precedent—a phenomenon which in the work of the Court has not proved to be as
invariable an occurrence as is occasionally assumed.[6] Just as judicial
legislation cannot be eliminated by considerations of rigid respect
for existing customary law, so judicial freedom cannot be ruled
out on account of subservience to the Court's own precedents. The
Court, while rightly conscious of the need for continuity, has not
treated them in that way.[7]

Moreover, the explicit authority—though essentially of a declaratory nature—which the Statute has conferred upon the Court to
apply general principles of law has emphasised and must tend to
stimulate the element of judicial decision, within the limits of the
recognition of such principles, in fulfilling its function.

While all these considerations bring into relief the element of
judicial discretion, they must not be allowed to obscure the fact—
which is ultimately of overriding importance—that such discretion
is circumscribed by the duty to apply the existing law and that it
moves within the orbit of the tendencies, enshrined in precedent,
whose operation forms the principal theme of this book. None of
these tendencies, when viewed in isolation, provides an accurate
answer or solution to any particular problem confronting the Court
or the parties. When examined in their interaction, they give a
picture—which, it is hoped, may not be without usefulness—of
judicial discretion as governed by law. Subject to that overriding
primacy of the existing law, they bring to mind the fact that the
necessity of a choice between conflicting legal claims is of the very
essence of the judicial function, whether within the State or in the
international sphere; that so also is the occasional necessity of
supplementing and developing the law in a manner approaching, or
creating the impression of, judicial legislation; that although in the
international sphere the inducements to such action are on occasions
more compelling than within the State, the restraints upon it are
more immediate and more tangible having regard to the voluntary
character of international jurisdiction; that in its voluntary character
—as evidenced in particular by its liability to termination—there is
an effective answer to the question *quis custodiet ipsos custodes*;
and that the realisation of its responsibility has generally caused the

---

[6] See above, p. 19.
[7] See above, pp. 108 *et seq.*, 353 *et seq.*

Court to make its pronouncements reflect, in ample measure, the processes by which it arrives at its conclusions.

The method thus pursued by the Court has, as a rule, increasingly aimed at taking fully into account the contentions of the parties, both those which are upheld and those which are found unacceptable. It has induced the Court to wrestle with the intricacies of the law not only in the secrecy of its private deliberations but also in the revealed reasoning of its pronouncements. Such a method is bound to bring into full prominence the fact that although, as already stated, no single trend or principle of judicial process as analysed in the successive chapters of this book can be accurately relied upon as determining automatically the content of any future decision of the Court, its activity is nevertheless determined by these trends and principles. The deliberate process of revealing fully the manner of their operation is the only concession which an international tribunal may properly make to the susceptibilities and claims of sovereignty. It is also a concession which is consistent with the character of the principal judicial organ of the international community in relation to its indirect but significant contribution towards the development of the law of nations.

# INDEX

[This Index does not refer to cases decided by the International Court of Justice, which will be found in the *Table of Cases* at the beginning of this volume.]